Women Entrepreneurs in the Middle East

Context, Ecosystems, and Future Perspectives for the Region

ASIA-PACIFIC BUSINESS SERIES **(ISSN: 1793-3137)**

Series Editor
Léo-Paul Dana
Professor
ICD Business School, Paris, France & Dalhousie University, Canada

---

Published

Vol. 14 *Women Entrepreneurs in the Middle East: Context, Ecosystems, and Future Perspectives for the Region*
edited by Dina Modestus Nziku, Léo-Paul Dana, Helene Balslev Clausen & Aidin Salamzadeh

Vol. 13 *Indian SMEs and Start-Ups: Growth through Innovation and Leadership*
edited by Léo-Paul Dana, Omvir Gautam, Ashish Gupta & Naman Sharma

Vol. 12 *Cooperatives as a Catalyst for Sustainability: Lessons Learned from Asian Models*
edited by Léo-Paul Dana, Naman Sharma, Sneha Kumari, K K Tripathy, B P Pillai & R Jayalakshmi

Vol. 11 *Organising Entrepreneurship and MSMEs Across India*
edited by Léo-Paul Dana, Naman Sharma & Satya Ranjan Acharya

Vol. 10 *Guanxi and Business (Third Edition)*
by Yadong Luo

Vol. 9 *Asian Models of Entrepreneurship: From the Indian Union and Nepal to the Japanese Archipelago: Context, Policy and Practice (Second Edition)*
by Léo-Paul Dana

Vol. 8 *Catalyst for Change: Chinese Business in Asia*
edited by Thomas Menkhoff, Hans-Dieter Evers, Chay Yue Wah & Hoon Chang Yau

Vol. 7 *From Adam Smith to Michael Porter: Evolution of Competitiveness Theory (Extended Edition)*
by Dong-Sung Cho & Hwy-Chang Moon

Vol. 6 *Islamic Banking and Finance in South-East Asia: Its Development and Future (Third Edition)*
by Angelo M. Venardos

Vol. 5 *Guanxi and Business (Second Edition)*
by Yadong Luo

The complete list of the published volumes in the series can also be found at
http://www.worldscientific.com/series/apbs

Asia-Pacific Business Series – Vol. 14

Women Entrepreneurs in the Middle East

Context, Ecosystems, and Future Perspectives for the Region

Edited by

Dina Modestus Nziku
University of the West of Scotland, UK

Léo-Paul Dana
ICD Business School, Paris, France & Dalhousie University, Canada

Helene Balslev Clausen
Aalborg University, Denmark

Aidin Salamzadeh
University of Tehran, Iran

World Scientific

NEW JERSEY • LONDON • SINGAPORE • BEIJING • SHANGHAI • HONG KONG • TAIPEI • CHENNAI • TOKYO

Published by

World Scientific Publishing Co. Pte. Ltd.

5 Toh Tuck Link, Singapore 596224

USA office: 27 Warren Street, Suite 401-402, Hackensack, NJ 07601

UK office: 57 Shelton Street, Covent Garden, London WC2H 9HE

Library of Congress Cataloging-in-Publication Data

Names: Nziku, Dina M., editor. | Dana, Leo Paul, editor. | Clausen, Helene Balslev, editor. | Salamzadeh, Aidin, editor.

Title: Women entrepreneurs in the Middle East : context, ecosystems, and future perspectives for the region / edited by Dina Modestus Nziku, University of the West of Scotland, UK, Léo-Paul Dana, ICD Business School, Paris, France & Dalhousie University, Canada, Helene Balslev Clausen, Aalborg University, Denmark, Aidin Salamzadeh, University of Tehran, Iran.

Description: New Jersey : World Scientific, 2024. | Series: Asia-Pacific Business Series, 1793-3137 ; volume 14 | Includes bibliographical references and index.

Identifiers: LCCN 2023046443 | ISBN 9789811283482 (hardcover) | ISBN 9789811283499 (ebook) | ISBN 9789811283505 (ebook other)

Subjects: LCSH: Entrepreneurship--Middle East. | Businesswomen--Middle East. | Economic development--Middle East.

Classification: LCC HB615 .W648 2024 | DDC 658.4/210956--dc23/eng/20231117

LC record available at https://lccn.loc.gov/2023046443Classification: LCC HB615 .W648 2024 | DDC 658.4/210956--dc23/eng/20231117

LC record available at https://lccn.loc.gov/2023046443

British Library Cataloguing-in-Publication Data

A catalogue record for this book is available from the British Library.

For any available supplementary material, please visit
https://www.worldscientific.com/worldscibooks/10.1142/13599#t=suppl

Desk Editors: Balasubramanian Shanmugam/Lai Ann

Typeset by Stallion Press
Email: enquiries@stallionpress.com

To Mlando, an entrepreneur who embraced Ora et Labora. Devoted his career to helping others succeed. Our hearts go to all women entrepreneurs in the conflict zones.

– Dina Modestus Nziku (PhD)

https://doi.org/10.1142/9789811283499_fmatter

Foreword

Entrepreneurship has become an increasingly popular and promising career choice for women in recent years, and this is particularly true in the Arab world. Despite the unique cultural, social, and economic challenges women in the region face, there has been a noticeable rise in female entrepreneurs starting and growing their businesses. This trend should be celebrated and encouraged, as it supports economic growth and development and empowers women to achieve greater financial independence and agency.

The stories of the women entrepreneurs in this book are inspiring and illuminating. Through their experiences, we see how they have overcome obstacles, navigated cultural norms, and challenged gender stereotypes to pursue their dreams and build successful businesses. In addition, we learn about the industries and sectors in which they operate, the strategies and tactics they use to scale their businesses, and their impact on their communities and societies.

But this book is not just about the individual achievements of these women entrepreneurs, it is also about the future of entrepreneurship in the Arab world. As the region continues to undergo a rapid economic and social transformation, there is a growing recognition of the importance of entrepreneurship as a driver of innovation, job creation, and economic diversification. And as more and more women enter the workforce and become entrepreneurs, there is an opportunity to harness their talents, skills, and creativity to shape the region's future.

However, achieving this vision will require a concerted effort from all stakeholders — governments, civil society, the private sector, and international organizations. We need policies and programs supporting women entrepreneurs, including access to finance, training, mentorship, and networks and partnerships. We must challenge the cultural and social norms limiting women's economic and entrepreneurship participation. And we need to foster a culture of innovation and risk-taking that encourages women to pursue their entrepreneurial ambitions.

This book, titled *Women Entrepreneurs in the Middle East: Context, Ecosystems, and Future Perspectives for the Region*, is a timely and vital contribution to the growing body of knowledge on women entrepreneurs in the Arab world. It provides valuable insights and perspectives to inform and inspire policymakers, investors, and aspiring entrepreneurs. But more importantly, it is a testament to the courage, resilience, and ingenuity of the women shaping the region's future.

I congratulate Dr. Léo-Paul Dana on this book and look forward to its impact on the lives of women entrepreneurs and their communities.

Ayman El Tarabishy
President & CEO, International Council for Small Business
Deputy Chair, Department of Management
GW School of Business

https://doi.org/10.1142/9789811283499_fmatter

Acknowledgment

Dina Modestus Nziku, Léo-Paul Dana, Aidin Salamzadeh, and Helene Balslev Clausen, would like to thank all members of the editorial board and the project manager at World Scientific Publishing Company Limited as well as all the blind reviewers who reviewed the chapters and provided valuable feedback to all our chapter contributors on the manuscript. Appreciation to Ayman El Tarabishy for providing the foreword of our edition.

Chanel Bikorimana	Glasgow Caledonia University (GCU), United Kingdom
Flair J. Karaki	Al-Quds Open University, Palestine
Gözde Inal	World Peace University, Cyprus
Hiroko Kawamorita	Hachinohe Gakuin University, Japan
Mehdi Tajpour	University of Tehran, Iran
Meisam Modarresi	Semnan University, Iran
Mirjana Radovic-Markovic	Institute of Economic Sciences, Serbia
Sawsan Malik	Arab Open University-Kuwait Branch, Kuwait
Shahamak Rezaei	Roskilde University, Denmark

https://doi.org/10.1142/9789811283499_fmatter

Disclaimer: Author's Responsibility

The views and opinions expressed in this work are solely those of the author(s) and do not necessarily reflect the official policy or position of the editors, publishers, or any other entity associated with the publication. The author(s) take full responsibility for the contents, including any statements or declarations made within this work. The editors and publisher disclaim any liability or responsibility for errors, omissions, or damage arising from the use of the information contained in this work.

https://doi.org/10.1142/9789811283499_fmatter

About the Editors

Aidin Salamzadeh is an Assistant Professor at the University of Tehran. His interests are startups, new venture creation, and entrepreneurship. Aidin serves as an associate editor for the *Humanities and Social Sciences Communications* (Nature.com); *Journal of Enterprising Communities; Revista de Gestão; Innovation Management Review* (Emerald), *Entrepreneurial Business and Economics Review, Journal of Women's Entrepreneurship and Education* as well as *The Bottom Line* (Emerald). Besides, he is a reviewer in numerous distinguished international journals. Aidin is a member of the European SPES Forum (Belgium), the Asian Academy of Management (Malaysia), Ondokuz Mayis University (Turkey), and the Institute of Economic Sciences (Serbia). He co-founded the Innovation and Entrepreneurship Research Lab (London).

Dina M. Nziku is a Senior Lecturer and Researcher at the University of the West of Scotland, UK. She is in the executive team at the Global Women Entrepreneurship Policy (GWEP) network and the Lead of GWEP in Sub- Saharan Africa (GWEP-SSA); Dina is also an Entrepreneurship Thought Leader at Women Economic Imperative (WEI). Her research focuses on women's entrepreneurship, government policies, and strategies for pro¬moting entrepreneurship in developing countries. She has published in academic journals, books, and book chapters, as well as edited scientific research books and professional reports. She has also presented her research work on women entrepreneurship in Sub-Saharan Africa (SSA) at the United Nations (UN) as well as other national and international conferences.

Helene Balslev Clausen founded the Creative Learning Lab in which students collaborate with a broad range of different stakeholders from startups to international businesses, governments, and NGOs to practice, learn, and co-create sustainability solutions to local, societal, or systemic challenges. Creative Learning Lab has been implemented in a range of different contexts all over the world. The model generates teaching-based research as well as research-based teaching.

Léo-Paul Dana is Professor at ICD Business School, Paris, and at Dalhousie University and is also associated with the Chaire ETI at Sorbonne Business School. A graduate of McGill University and HEC-Montreal, he has served as a Marie Curie Fellow at Princeton University and Visiting Professor at INSEAD. He has published extensively in a variety of journals including *Entrepreneurship: Theory & Practice, International Business Review, International Small Business Journal, Journal of Business Research, Journal of Small Business Management, Journal of World Business, Small Business Economics,* and *Technological Forecasting & Social Change*.

https://doi.org/10.1142/9789811283499_fmatter

About the Authors

Osnat Akirav earned her Ph.D. from The Hebrew University of Jerusalem. She is a researcher and faculty member at Western Galilee College. Osnat has always been involved in a wide range of public and volunteer activities; among them, she is a member of the Women Power Association and Chair of the Education Committee of the Kfar V'radim Local Council. Osnat was an ISEF Scholar from her first degree through her post-doctorate studies. Born in Beer Sheva, Osnat is married and has four children.

Mohammad Alarifi is a Trainer in Technical and Vocational Training Corporation, Alula, Saudi Arabia. He teaches and trains students in business courses. He has a Master of Business Administration (MBA) from Imam Mohammad Ibn Saud Islamic University, Riyadh, Saudi Arabia. He also received his Bachelor's degree in Business Administration from Imam Mohammad Ibn Saud Islamic University, Riyadh, Saudi Arabia. He has work experience in both the private and public sectors. He is interested in entrepreneurship, human resources, and supply chain.

Haya Al-Dajani (PhD) is a Professor of Entrepreneurship at the Mohammed Bin Salman College for Business and Entrepreneurship (MBSC) in the Kingdom of Saudi Arabia. Haya's award-winning research focuses on the intersectionality of gender, entrepreneurship, and empowerment, and their collective impact on sustainable development. She co-chairs the Middle East and North Africa Gender and Enterprise Network, and the international Gender and Enterprise Network. She is a member of several Editorial Boards of leading entrepreneurship journals and is an advisor to a number of entrepreneurship education, research, and policy centers around the world.

Wassim J. Aloulou is an Associate Professor at the College of Economics and Administrative Sciences at Imam Mohammad Ibn Saudi Islamic University, Riyadh, KSA. He received his PhD in Management Sciences from the University of Pierre Mendes France, Grenoble 2, France, and from the Faculté des Sciences Economiques et de Gestion de Sfax, Tunisia, in 2008. His research interests focus on digital entrepreneurship, entrepreneurial intentions, and orientations of individuals and organizations. He has authored and co-authored multiple articles in international journals with impact factor, books with IGI Global, and book chapters on incubation, social entrepreneurship, and women's economic empowerment in the Saudi context.

Abdullah Alshammaa is a Research Assistant and student in the Faculty of Management at the Canadian University Dubai. He has successfully undertaken courses in entrepreneurship and innovation. Mr. Shammaa is actively engaged in business development with various industries in the United Arab Emirates.

Doaa Althalathini is a Senior Lecturer in Business and Enterprise at Oxford Brookes University, UK. She holds a PhD in Business and Management from the University of Plymouth, UK. Her research focuses on resilience, entrepreneurship, and gender in the contexts of violent conflict and refugee entrepreneurship. She has extensive work experience with local and international NGOs in programs aimed at reducing poverty, empowering women, and enhancing economic development through entrepreneurship in Palestine.

A. Allan Degen is an Emeritus Professor at Ben-Gurion University of the Negev, where he was the Head of the Desert Animal Adaptations and Husbandry Unit (1985–2015) and the Chairman of the Wyler Department of Dryland Agriculture (2001–2004 and 2013–2015). Allan held the Bennie Slome Chair for Desert Livestock Production (2004–2015) and served as the Co-Editor-in-Chief of the *Israel Journal of Zoology* (1999–2007). He is studying the livelihood of ethnic groups and, in Israel, is doing research on Negev Bedouin. Allan has authored or co-authored 25 books or chapters and over 340 publications in peer-reviewed journals.

Slimane Ed-Dafali is an Assistant Professor at the National School of Commerce and Management (ENCG), Chouaib Doukkali University, Morocco, where he conducts teaching and research activities. His current research is focused on venture capital investments, entrepreneurship, SME financing, and corporate governance. Also, he contributed to different research projects with various scholars and universities.

Bella L. Galperin is a Dana Professor of Management and the Senior Associate Director of the TECO Energy Center for Leadership at the Sykes College of Business at the University of Tampa. Her interests include cross-cultural management, leadership, ethics, and workplace deviance, both destructive and constructive. She has published in the *Journal of Business Ethics*, *International Journal of Human Resource Management*, *Leadership Quarterly*, *International Business Review*, and other journals. She co-authored a book entitled *LEAD: Leadership Effectiveness in Africa and the African Diaspora*. She is an Associate Editor of the *Journal of Managerial Psychology*.

Roula Gergess is a PhD candidate in entrepreneurship at Cnam, Paris, France. Her dissertation focuses on women entrepreneurship, feminism, sorority, and entrepreneurial support. She is a lecturer in entrepreneurship and innovation at several business schools in Paris.

Gergess is having promising academic contributions, including publications with international authors. She was awarded the best research contribution prize for the Global South at the "9èmes Journées Georges Doriot", Montréal, Canada, in July 2023. Gergess is recognized for her innovative approach and contributions to the field of entrepreneurship and organization studies. Beyond the academia, Gergess is an active member of the entrepreneurial community, offering coaching and mentoring to startups and participating in various industry events.

As a strong human resources professional, Roula worked for large organizations. She has a track record of proven success in all areas of Human Resources. Her industry expertise includes manufacturing, telecommunications, and insurance.

Sayed Abdul Majid Gilani is currently an Assistant Professor (Lecturer) at De Montfort University (Dubai campus). Dr. Sayed completed his PhD research at Glasgow Caledonian University in Rural Entrepreneurship in Scotland. In his current role, he is leading courses at the undergraduate and postgraduate levels. Sayed is a Fellow of the Higher Education Academy UK and has published in various international journals and books on entrepreneurship education.

Suaad Jassem is an Assistant Professor of Accounting at the College of Banking and Financial Studies, Muscat, Sultanate of Oman. She has a Ph.D. in accounting from the University of Malaya in Malaysia. She has over 16 years of teaching experience and has organized and presented papers at international conferences. Her articles have been published in *Scopus* and *WoS* indexed journals. Her expertise is in management accounting, sustainability management practices, and environmental sustainability.

Meron Medzini is a senior professor at The Hebrew University of Jerusalem, where he teaches modern Japanese history and Israeli foreign policy. He also teaches Israeli foreign policy at the Rothberg International School of The Hebrew University. His book *Golda — A Political Biography* won the 2010 Prime Minister's Prize.

Fiorina Mugione was the Regional Director ACP, GDSI (www.gdsi.ie) — one of Ireland's most respected international development consulting companies — in charge of business development and project management of trade, investment and entrepreneurship development from 2019–2022. An economist with an MBA in international trade, Fiorina Mugione has 30 years of experience in international organizations and has also had the opportunity to work in the private sector at the international level in marketing and export management functions. She worked primarily in the areas of research and analysis on enterprise, investment, and development issues at the United Nations Economic and Social Commission for Asia and the Pacific (ESCAP), Organisation for Economic Co-operation and Development (OECD), and United Nations Conference on Trade and Development (UNCTAD). Fiorina also managed the United Nations' EMPRETEC programme — the one-stop agency for small and medium-sized enterprise development in 40 countries worldwide (www.empretec.net). In addition, she led the teams to assist governments in formulating entrepreneurship and investment policies and coordinated business linkages and value chain development programs in Asia, Africa, the Middle East, and Latin America. She conducted several global and country-level research projects on youth, the green economy and women's entrepreneurship. Fiorina is also a trainer and enterprise coach with expertise in training trainers on youth and women entrepreneurship.

Mirjana Radovic-Markovic is a (Full) Professor of Entrepreneurship. She holds BSc, MSc, and PhD degrees in Economics, as well as Postdoctoral Studies in Multidisciplinary Studies from Lomonosov (Russia). She has served as a professor at a number of international universities, foundations, and institutes. Professor Mirjana is a founder and editor-in-chief of three peer-reviewed journals as follows: the *Journal of Women's Entrepreneurship and Education*, *International Review,* and *Journal of Entrepreneurship and Business Resilience*. She has written more than 30 books and more than 200 peer-reviewed journal articles. Her publications are published by top world publishing companies. Her article "Acceptance and use of lecture capture system (LCS) in executive business studies" published in *Interactive Technology and Smart Education* has been selected by the editorial team of Emerald as an Outstanding Paper in the 2018 Emerald Literati Awards. In other words, her article was chosen as a winner as it was one of the most exceptional pieces of work the team had seen throughout 2017.

Veland Ramadani is a Professor of Entrepreneurship and Family Business at Faculty of Business and Economics, South-East European University, North Macedonia. His research interests include entrepreneurship, small business management, and family businesses. He authored or co-authored around 170 research articles, 12 textbooks, and 24 edited books. He has published in the *International Journal of Entrepreneurial Behavior & Research, Journal of Business Research, International Entrepreneurship and Management Journal, Technological Forecasting and Social Change*, among others. Dr. Ramadani has recently published the book *Entrepreneurial Family Businesses* (Springer).

Mohammad Rezaur Razzak is an Assistant Professor of Strategic Management, Entrepreneurship and Family Business at the College of Economics and Political Science (EQUIS accredited) at Sultan Qaboos University in Oman. He obtained his bachelor's degree in mechanical engineering from the University of Texas at Austin followed by MBA from Southern Methodist University. He completed his Ph.D. with distinction from the University of Malaya specializing in strategy and family business. Dr. Razzak has over 36 years of experience that includes industrial and corporate positions followed by a full-time engagement in academia from 2006. At present, his research interests are in the areas of family business, senior entrepreneurship, digital transformation, emerging business models in the Industry 5.0 era, and sustainable supply chain practices.

Sally Shamieh is the Research Project Manager at the CRED Research Center of the ESA Business School in Lebanon. She holds a BA and an MA from the American University of Beirut, Lebanon, and an MA and a DBA from the SBS Swiss Business School in Zurich, Switzerland and has served as a Fulbright Scholar at the University of Kansas in the USA.

With over 15 years of experience in the private sector, Sally conducts research, teaches, trains, and consults in the fields of business development, entrepreneurship, sustainable development, and gender issues. She is an advocate of continuous learning, growth, and development. Sally is also a champion of women's empowerment and a supporter of women's entrepreneurship. She herself is an entrepreneur having established the consulting and training firm Maverick Partners in Dubai, UAE. She is also the Founder and Director of the civic institution Heart of Rachaya concerned with the human, social, and economic development of rural areas in the Bekaa region of Lebanon.

Ekaterina Vorobeva is a doctoral candidate at the Bremen International Graduate School of Social Sciences and an EU researcher at the Research Centre for East European Studies, the University of Bremen. She previously worked on several research projects on forced migration, transnationalism, and migrant entrepreneurship in Finland and Malta.

Ekaterina co-authored scientific articles and book chapters published by International Migration, SAGE Business Cases, GeoJournal, Palgrave Macmillan, and Springer.

Naveed Yasin is a (Full) Professor of Entrepreneurship at the Canadian University Dubai, United Arab Emirates. He has extensive experience working in the UK and the Gulf region delivering British and North American Higher Education curricula. The award winner of the highly acclaimed 'Outstanding All-Round Academic Award 2015' conferred by the Teaching and Learning Institute (UK), Dr. Yasin has an extensive record of impactful publications in entrepreneurship and business management journals and has also examined doctorates (PhD) as a lead external examiner for Cranfield University (UK) and the University of Pretoria (South Africa). He has also been a member of the Babson College's (USA) enterprise educators' global consortium. Prof. Yasin graduated with an MSc and a PhD in Cross-National Entrepreneurship from the University of Huddersfield (UK) and an MA in Higher Education from Manchester Metropolitan University (UK).

Rasim Zuferi is engaged as a lecturer at South-East European University, Tetovo, North Macedonia. His research interests includes marketing, consumer behavior, and entrepreneurial marketing. He has published several papers and attended many international conferences.

https://doi.org/10.1142/9789811283499_fmatter

Contents

Foreword		vii
Acknowledgment		ix
Disclaimer: Author's Responsibility		xi
About the Editors		xiii
About the Authors		xv
Chapter 1	Introduction to the Middle East *Dina Modestus Nziku, Léo-Paul Dana, and Aidin Salamzadeh*	1
Chapter 2	Entrepreneurship Ecosystems in the Middle East *Helene Balslev Clausen and Léo-Paul Dana*	15
Chapter 3	Women Entrepreneurship in the Middle East *Dina Modestus Nziku, Fiorina Mugione, and Aidin Salamzadeh*	23
Chapter 4	Women Entrepreneurs in Bahrain *Aidin Salamzadeh and Léo-Paul Dana*	53
Chapter 5	Women Entrepreneurs in Egypt *Ekaterina Vorobeva*	67
Chapter 6	Women Entrepreneurs in Iran *Aidin Salamzadeh and Léo-Paul Dana*	85

Chapter 7 Women Entrepreneurs in Israel 107
Osnat Akirav, Léo-Paul Dana, A. Allan Degen, Bella L. Galperin, and Meron Medzini

Chapter 8 Women Entrepreneurs in Jordan 141
Haya Al-Dajani

Chapter 9 Women Entrepreneurs in Lebanon 169
Sally Shamieh and Roula Gergess

Chapter 10 Women Entrepreneurs in Oman 193
Mohammad Rezaur Razzak and Suaad Jassem

Chapter 11 Women Entrepreneurs in Palestine 221
Doaa Althalathini

Chapter 12 Women Entrepreneurs in the Kingdom of Saudi Arabia 253
Wassim J. Aloulou, Veland Ramadani, Mohammad Alarifi, and Rasim Zuferi

Chapter 13 Women Entrepreneurs in Syria 283
Aidin Salamzadeh, Mirjana Radovic-Markovic, and Slimane Ed-Dafali

Chapter 14 Women Entrepreneurs in the United Arab Emirates 303
Sayed Abdul Majid Gilani, Naveed Yasin, and Abdullah Alshammaa

Chapter 15 Toward the Future 317
Dina Modestus Nziku

Index 329

https://doi.org/10.1142/9789811283499_0001

Chapter 1

Introduction to the Middle East

Dina Modestus Nziku[*,‖], **Léo-Paul Dana**[†,‡,§,**], **and Aidin Salamzadeh**[¶,††]

[*]*School of Business and Creative Industries, University of the West of Scotland, Glasgow, Scotland*
[†]*ICD Business School Paris, Paris, France*
[‡]*Dalhousie University, Halifax, Canada*
[§]*Lappeenranta University of Technology, Finland*
[¶]*Faculty of Management, University of Tehran, Tehran, Iran*
[‖]*dina.nziku@uws.ac.uk*
[**]*lp762359@dal.ca*
[††]*salamzadeh@ut.ac.ir*

Abstract

This chapter introduces this book that describes the reality of women's entrepreneurship in the Middle East while summarizing and reviewing each country presented in this book. All chapters have a similar structure in introducing the reader to the status of women's entrepreneurship, historical frameworks, entrepreneurial ecosystems, and future perspectives. These have been based on the authors' scientific analysis and recommendations based on the history, the current trends, and the country's government entrepreneurship policy and strategies in supporting startups, growth, and development of women entrepreneurship toward the future.

Keywords: Women entrepreneurship; historical frameworks; ecosystem; future perspectives; analysis; the Middle East.

1. Introduction

Women entrepreneurs are becoming the fastest-growing entrepreneurial population in the world (Ojong *et al.*, 2021; Nziku and Henry, 2020). The most important dimensions of this growth include job creation, developing local economies, and supporting families. For several decades, women entrepreneurship in the Middle East has been stunted due to the lack of comprehensive peace in the region, with countries spending more resources on the military (UNIDO, 2015).

There has been a diverse treatment of women in different countries within the Middle East due to different traditions and cultures whereby Christian, Druze, Jewish and Muslim women in Israel became the first to obtain the right to vote with their role in the community changing more rapidly compared to their neighboring countries within the region (Dana, 2000; IFC, 2007). Nonetheless, the Jordanian constitution gives women equal rights, and the national charter gives women equal opportunities as men regarding work, education, training, and employment. Regrettably, women in the Middle East and North Africa (MENA) region have continued to remain with the lowest rates of total entrepreneurial activity (TEA), at merely 4% of the population (IFC, 2007).

Thus far, in some countries in the region, local culture views women's economic independence as disruptive to family life. Therefore, the participation of women in the labor force is still low with the unemployment rate being higher among women than it is among men. The past study (Dana, 2000; IFC, 2007; Bastian *et al.*, 2018) reveals that some countries in the region still had labor laws dictating policy for equal work while making economic sense on employing men rather than women due to the fact of paid maternity leave. Therefore, the proposed edition will critically explore individual countries' historical framework, women's entrepreneurial ecosystems, and future perspectives. This will be highly based on an intensive assessment of each country's current policy and strategies for supporting women entrepreneurs (GWEP-OECD, 2021). Each chapter is expected to be written by native research experts with clear knowledge of the field of women's entrepreneurship.

The Middle East has long been a crossroads of trade and, hence, an important center for entrepreneurship (Dana, 2000). As stated by Dana,

"Across Western Asia, cultural, linguistic, and religious factors are still profoundly dominant, and they affect the context of business. A reminder of Islam's early days is the privileged social status accorded to self-employed merchants and artisans (Dana, 2022, p. xviii)." Dana elaborated, "Prophet Muhammad was personally impressed by the camel caravan voyages of traders, and on several occasions, he travelled with them in his youth. He spent over a decade in caravan trading, covering a wide territory from the Mediterranean to the Indian Ocean. His first wife Khadija was a successful merchant whom he worked for and later worked with (Dana, 2022, p. xix)." This book is for and about the women entrepreneurs of this region.

2. Structure of the Book

This book, *Women's Entrepreneurship in the Middle East*, consists of 15 chapters. This *Chapter* 1 is an introduction to the Middle East. This chapter has been written by editors to guide readers on the contents and flow of the book as well as its development and the authorship of each chapter. *Chapter* 2 has been authored by Balslev Clausen and Dana and depicts the *entrepreneurial ecosystems in the Middle East.* The chapter discusses the notion of an entrepreneurial ecosystem conceived first in 1930 to denote the physical and biological components in an environment and their relationship to each other. The authors in this chapter have gradually discussed the entrepreneurial ecosystem based on the definition, which captures the agglomeration of interrelated individuals, institutions, organizations, and regulatory entities in a geographical area that promotes entrepreneurial initiatives and actions.

Chapter 3 contains a general discussion on *women entrepreneurs in the Middle East.* Here Nziku, Mugione, and Salamzadeh have presented the overall introduction of the book in the context of the Middle East. The authors of this chapter have stressed the importance of developing strategies for achieving women's economic empowerment as a critical aspect of achieving sustainable development goals and fostering high-quality entrepreneurial activities in the region. Nevertheless, an overview of women entrepreneurship in the Middle East and Africa (MEA) (*FinTech Times*, 2021) implies that the region is home to the world's highest and lowest rates of female entrepreneurship.

Although the World Economic Forum (WEF, 2021) reports that the MENA region needs almost 143 years to close the gender gap at the most current rate, the authors in this chapter have noted that the number of women entrepreneurs in the Middle East has steadily risen in some economies like Israel, the United Arab Emirates (UAE), and Jordan. Women entrepreneurs are currently engaged in establishing foundations in the arts, education, and health sectors, thereby creating role models for these entrepreneurial activities and hence contributing toward closing the gender gap (Gadi, 2022; Nziku, 2014, 2016).

Chapter 4 is about women entrepreneurs in *Bahrain* and has been authored by Salamzadeh and Dana. The country relied highly on date farming and pearl fishery until the discovery of oil and gas, with a wide range of people from various ethnic groups living in peace, though there have been some religious conflicts between Shi'a and Sunni Muslims in some periods. Like any other country in the region, Bahraini women have never been immune to problems caused by a lack of proper social status, violence against women, and other legal problems.

Yet, women in this country are said to be more pulled into entrepreneurial activities apart from challenges like family commitments, lack of focus on enterprising activities, and high market competition against their male counterparts. Women entrepreneurs in this country are known to start up small-scale enterprises. Besides, the Bahrain Vision 2030 seems to set a pathway toward creating a better future with more attention given to the development of human capital for the long-term sustainability of the economy, which currently is highly reliant on oil and gas. The authors recommend more action from policymakers to develop the entrepreneurial ecosystem for improving the state of women entrepreneurs.

Chapter 5 covers women entrepreneurs in *Egypt* with a very interesting history from the Ptolemaic and Roman periods of the country with the involvement and significant role played by women in entrepreneurial activities and contribution to the general economy of the country. In this chapter, Vorobeva has discussed the considerable progress made by the government toward gender equality and empowerment of women in the country. Nevertheless, the International Labor Organization (ILO, 2016) has described the number of women entrepreneurs in Egypt as being the lowest in the MENA region and Sub-Saharan Africa.

Hassan and Zaharia (2021) argue on the roles of Egyptian women in society being reduced to simply those of mothers and housewives with the professional capabilities being so often called into question. Following, the Doing Business 2020 report of the World Bank, Egypt was ranked 114 out of 190 world economies on the ease of starting and running an enterprise in the country (World Bank, 2020). The analysis presented in this chapter shows that Egypt has improved its position in the ranking during the last few years. In 2016, Egypt Vision 2030 was just introduced by President el-Sisi, and the country occupied the 131th place among the other 190 states globally (World Bank, 2016).

Chapter 6 is about women entrepreneurs in *Iran*. In this chapter, Salamzadeh and Dana present the reality of women entrepreneurs in the country following the women's employment index of war-torn countries like Syria, Iraq, Afghanistan, Yemen, and Palestine. The index shows a slow increase in women's employment back in the 1970s, which then broke in the mid-1980s, continuing to remain low since, despite unsuccessful efforts at restoration. Apart from the scarcity of the national research on women's entrepreneurship in the country, women's employment in Iran has always faced problems, with women's entrepreneurship continuing to face increasing problems (Bahramitash and Esfahani, 2014). Sarfaraz and Faghih (2011) indicate that there has not been any improvement in the Iranian women's employment ratio for almost 20 years with the ratio of employment among men becoming five times that of women despite the number of female students being higher than that of male students within the country.

Nonetheless, the analysis indicates that the annual growth rates of the ratios of employment to the female population in the last 30 years show that Iran is in an optimistic situation and if it maintains a continuous growth trend and uses the existing capacities, it can add an average of 1% to its female employment ratio annually (Sarfaraz, 2017). According to WEF (2021), Iran needs almost 28 years to cover this distance from 12% to 40%.

Chapter 7 "Women Entrepreneurs in *Israel*", by Akirav, Dana, Degen, Galperin, and Medzini, indicates how education, science, and industry had become important elements of Israel's culture before the birth of the Israel nation, with explosive growth in the past two decades. According to

Yin (2017), foreign investors seem to be attracted to Israel and motivated by their workforce and industrial parks that are highly concentrated on technology. This chapter indicates how Israel's law provides strong protection for trade patents, copyrights, and trademarks.

The chapter discusses the changing role of women within Israel and other neighboring countries. This is not only because of the Kibbutz's movements, but also the equal participation of both men and women on a rotational basis in various jobs. Telles (2020) indicates how the Israelites' law contemplates numerous scenarios for distressed companies together with voluntary liquidations and court-supervised voluntary liquidations and reorganizations of business ventures.

Chapter 8, "Women entrepreneurs in *Jordan*", by Al-Dajani starts by presenting the state of women's entrepreneurship research in the Kingdom of Jordan, its challenges, and the opportunities. While citing Metcalfe, Bastan, and Al-Dajani, (2022), the state of policy and practices that support and advance women's entrepreneurship in the Arab world over the last five years is on the sharp rise with no exceptions in Jordan. According to the Global Entrepreneurship Monitor (GEM), the ratio of women's to men's TEA increased from 0.26 in 2016 to 0.59 in 2019, an improvement of around 127% in three years (GEM, 2020). Such an achievement is aided by the Kingdom's young and evolving entrepreneurship ecosystem (El Kharouf *et al.*, 2022), and the legal gender equality regulations and policies for women's and men's engagement in entrepreneurship (World Bank Group, 2022). However, the rate of women's labor force participation remains among the lowest in the world at 14% (Robbin, 2022), and lower than neighboring Lebanon (23%), Saudi Arabia (22%), and Palestine (18%) (ILO, 2022). The analysis of women entrepreneurs in Jordan within this chapter indicates that Jordan is not immune to the economic and social repercussions of the measures put in place locally, regionally, and internationally, to combat the COVID-19 pandemic, nor to the regional political and economic affairs.

Following the World Bank report (2022), the Kingdom's economic rebound during the first nine months of 2021 was steady but below expectations at 2.1% growth. Chapter analysis on the future of the kingdom indicates that organizational performance within Jordan's entrepreneurial ecosystem might be affected since projections show that economic growth might remain modest for the foreseeable future, coupled with stubbornly high rates of unemployment, and low rates of labor force participation, especially among women. Given the growth and developments in women's entrepreneurship in Egypt, Saudi Arabia, and the United Arab Emirates (UAE), Jordan cannot afford to stagnate as it will fall behind in the region. This is important for Jordan's economy as the trend of employment in the GCC is diminishing given that those nations are now prioritizing their own citizens who have become equally qualified.

Chapter 9, "Women Entrepreneurs in Lebanon," authored by Sally Shamieh and Roula Gerges, presents a comprehensive examination of the entrepreneurial ecosystem in Lebanon, with a specific focus on the role of women entrepreneurs. The chapter provides a historical overview and a current reality check, delving into the evolution of the ecosystem in a challenging environment. It highlights the significant role of women entrepreneurs in specific sectors, despite various challenges and barriers.

The chapter emphasizes the resilience and active engagement of women entrepreneurs in Lebanon. It details the challenges faced by female entrepreneurs, including societal and cultural constraints, and the impact of Lebanon's economic, political, and social turmoil on entrepreneurship. Despite these challenges, women entrepreneurs have shown remarkable resilience and have been integral to the economic growth and stability of Lebanon, even as they contend with ongoing economic collapse and the impacts of geopolitical circumstances. Hence, the term "the Lebanese iron woman."

Chapter 10, "Women Entrepreneurs in *Oman*," presents women as the fastest-growing segment in the realm of entrepreneurship. The authors of this chapter, Razzak and Jassem, reveal the growth of the state of women's entrepreneurship in Oman following the case study conducted in the country by Mustafa *et al.* (2021), which revealed that women business owners had tremendous resilience for general adversities, a quality that is of great value in the entrepreneurial process. Although, the overall percentage of women who embark on the entrepreneurial journey is significantly lower than that of men (PwC, 2017), this difference is greater depending on the cultural context (GEM Report, 2019–2021). Nonetheless, culture plays a significant role in determining the likelihood of women embarking on the entrepreneurial journey. The authors of this chapter have used examples of East Asians in discussing the significance and high involvement of women in entrepreneurship when compared to the MENA.

The situation seems very distinct in the most conservative societies that dominate in the Gulf Cooperation Council (GCC), which includes Bahrain, Oman, Saudi Arabia, Kuwait, Qatar, and the UAE. Furthermore, the authors in this chapter provide a general analysis of the Oman Vision 2040, which seems to underlie the overall theme of Omanization as the program not only looks to replace foreign workers with Omani citizens but also emphasizes the growth of business ownership by women who are the most underrepresented in the society. Therefore, Tanfeedh, a shared business services community, has been created in Oman for the purpose and the priority of developing the general entrepreneurship agenda (Al Sinani *et al.*, 2021). This has been along with an improvement in women's participation in business and other economic activities in the society. Andriamahery and Qumruzzaman (2022) present a significant change in most of the Formal Financial Institutions (FFI) that formally had a poor record of gender diversity in their loan portfolio but now seem to have gained confidence and are comfortable with providing finance to some women entrepreneurs. Following the analysis of the past and current states of women entrepreneurs in Oman, their future seems hopeful, though it might take a little longer for the gender gap within the region to close.

Omani women are now receiving significant support from their families with encouragement for young Omani women deciding to pursue the entrepreneurial path likely to be given more easily considering the low barrier to entry into the business through Internet platforms. In fact, the authors of this chapter reveal that many women can start their businesses in parallel with their household responsibilities and their regular jobs. Family restrictions to younger Omani women starting their own businesses could be considerably less of a factor in the age of digitalization.

In *Chapter* 11, "Women Entrepreneurs in *Palestine*", Althalathini has presented with clarity the reality of women entrepreneurs in the country by analyzing the historical background of women entrepreneurs, their framework, and ecosystem. The author has then presented with analysis the government policies and strategies for supporting women's entrepreneurial activities as well as recommendations for the future. Women entrepreneurs in this country are said to engage in entrepreneurial activities out of necessity due to the high level of unemployment and poverty. The author has provided a very detailed discussion of the country's socio-economy and the reality of the state of women entrepreneurs tracing their history from the foundation of the Palestinian Women's Union in 1921 with the role of challenging the patriarchal structure. This was accompanied by the Palestine Reform and Development Plan (PRDP).

Althalathini further reveals the weak and outdated legal system, lack of financing opportunities, and lack of access to the market. The state of the entrepreneurial ecosystem in Palestine is still said to be in the infancy stage with many women entrepreneurs facing institutional constraints that are an hindrance to entrepreneurial intention and behavior. Nonetheless, the extensive informal participation of Palestinian women in politics has been presented as among the causes of women's underrepresentation in formal politics and decision-making though women remain at the forefront and highly contributing to agriculture with most employed women being in service and agriculture industries.

Chapter 12, "Women Entrepreneurs in the *Kingdom of Saudi Arabia* (KSA)", by Aloulou, Ramadani, Alarifi, and Zuferi discusses the reality of women entrepreneurship in the country and the entrepreneurial ecosystem. GEM's 2020/2021 National Expert Survey ranked Saudi Arabia first among 44 economies surveyed in terms of COVID-19 *entrepreneurial response rank* and *government response rank*. The ranking reflects confidence in the government's ability to maintain strong entrepreneurial conditions despite the turmoil arising from the pandemic. Women in the Kingdom of Saudi Arabia (KSA) are free to start their own businesses without the permission of a husband or any male guardian. The participation of Saudi women in the labor market is currently a top priority of the KSA national development plan among other priorities and initiatives.

Chapter 13, "Women Entrepreneurs in *Syria*", is the chapter that has been authored by Salamzadeh, Markovic, and Ed-dafali, providing a discussion on the reality of women entrepreneurs in Syria and how historically the situation has been affected by wars that have had a significant impact on the business environment. The authors of this chapter have presented the level of Syrian women in entrepreneurial activities as of 2009 being only 5% with a slow increase to 23% in 2018 as confirmed and acknowledged by the Syrian National Report on Entrepreneurship.

The systematic policies of marginalization and impoverishment pursued by the ruling regime, which is said to have not paid any respect to their political, social, economic, and legal rights, are among the problems that Syrian women are said to have suffered for decades. The role of the Syrian revolution of March 2011 in women realizing their rights leading to participation in demonstrations and human rights, media, politics, and the general community has been well acknowledged by the authors of that chapter. This is accompanied by the impact of the transformation of the popular movement in the country into an armed conflict, which left lots of women facing various forms of outbreaks of violence. Against the odds, Syrian women are said to still operate in traditional jobs and activities that perpetuate stereotypical roles imposed by patriarchal authority, customs, and traditions. The Syrian International Business Association, which was founded for the purpose of assisting both social and economic integration of Syrian refugees and immigrants, has been found to have played a significant role in furthering the participation of women in business.

In *Chapter* 14, "Women Entrepreneurs in the *United Arab Emirates (UAE)*", the contributing authors Gilan, Yasin, and Alshammaa have presented and explained the overview of women entrepreneurs in the UAE through the historical summary of women entrepreneurs in the country and the entrepreneurial ecosystem as well as their success. The UAE governments initiatives and strategies to promote women in entrepreneurial ventures and their implications for the future of women entrepreneurship in UAE and the overall economy of the nation are also discussed. Considering the UAE government's firm commitment toward internationalization and retaining its position as a global hotspot, this chapter presents a discussion of women's entrepreneurial ecosystem in the country while showcasing a few cases of successful women entrepreneurs.

Chapter 15, "Toward the Future" is the chapter that presents the general conclusion of the analyses and discussions on the women entrepreneurs in the Middle East, their history, frameworks, and ecosystems.

Within this chapter, the author provides recommendations based on the analyses of the current government policies and strategies and what can be anticipated for *the future* of women entrepreneurs in the Middle East region based on the countries' histories, current trends plus any government strategies and initiatives in place for promoting entrepreneurial activities and motivating women to engage in entrepreneurial activities based on the discussions from each country presented in this edition.

3. Conclusions and Toward the Future

The overall expectations of both editors and chapter contributors for this edition is that readers will find this book to be more resourceful in providing both general and specific knowledge about women entrepreneurship in the Middle East. This edition encompasses the wide range of diversity present within the Middle East such that readers will be able to learn the uniqueness of each country presented in each chapter.

Although this edition provides a wide range of scientific evidence on women entrepreneurship from across the Middle East, the region still has a lot to be uncovered both theoretically and empirically. It is expected that not only academics and researchers in the field but also postgraduate research students, practitioners, and government policymakers will find this book a very important resource for their study backgrounds and literature reviews.

Readers are recommended to explore further similar book editions that provide rich discussions, evidence, and research in *Women Entrepreneurs in Sub-Saharan Africa* (Dabić *et al.*, 2022) and "The environment for women entrepreneurship in the Middle East and North Africa" (World Bank, 2023). Both resources cover the historical framework, entrepreneurial ecosystem, and the anticipation of the future perspectives for these regions based on the scientific analyses of women's history, initiatives for promoting and motivating women's involvement in economic activities as well as assessment of countries potential policies and strategies for the future sustainable entrepreneurial ecosystem with women at the forefront.

References

Andriamahery, A. & Qamruzzaman, M. (2022). “Do Access to Finance, Technical Know-How, and Financial Literacy Offer Women Empowerment Through Women’s Entrepreneurial Development?” *Frontiers in Psychology*, **12**, 776–798.

Bahramitash, R. & Esfahani, H. S. (2014). “Gender and Entrepreneurship in Iran”. *Middle East Critique*, **23**(3), 293–312.

Dabić, M., Dana, L.-P., Nziku, D. M., & Ramadani, V. (2022). *Women Entrepreneurs in Sub-Saharan Africa: Historical Framework, Ecosystem, and Future Perspectives for the Region.* Springer.

Dana, L. P. (2000). *Economies of the Eastern Mediterranean Region: Economic Miracles in the Making.* Singapore, London, and Hong Kong: World Scientific.

Dana, L. P. (2022). “Preface”. In Léo-Paul Dana, Aidin Salamzadeh, Veland Ramadani, and Ramo Palalic, eds., *Understanding Contexts of Business in Western Asia: Land of Bazaars and High-Tech Booms.* Singapore: World Scientific, pp. xvii–xxiv.

El Kharouf, A., Abualbasal, A., Abbadi, H., & Weir, D. B. (2022). “The Entrepreneurship Ecosystem for Enhancing Women’s Entrepreneurship in Jordan”. In Metcalfe, B., Bastian, B., & Al-Dajani, H., eds., *Women, Entrepreneurship, and Development in the Middle East.* London: Routledge, pp. 133–151.

Gadi, N. (2022). “Increasing Women’s Employment Opportunities in Digitalizing Saudi Arabia’s Economy”. *Open Journal of Business and Management*, **10**, 2869–2902. doi: 10.4236/ojbm.2022.105142.

Global Entrepreneurship Monitor (GEM, 2020). *Jordan National Report 2019–2020.* Amman, Jordan: Global Entrepreneurship Monitor.

Global Entrepreneurship Monitor (GEM, 2021). “Sultanate of Oman: National Report”. Retrieved from: https://www.unizwa.edu.om/Final%20Oman%20GEM%20National%20report2019_2020_Oct%2020.pdf.

International Labor Organization (ILO, 2022). “STAT Database”. Retrieved from: https://data.worldbank.org/indicator/SL.TLF.CACT.FE.ZS?locations=ZQ&most_recent_value_desc=false (Accessed on 16 March 2022).

Metcalfe, B., Bastian, B., & Al-Dajani, H. (2022). “The Mosque and the Satellite: Exploring the Multi-Level and Multi-Agency Dynamics of Women’s Entrepreneurship Development in the Middle East”. In Metcalfe, B., Bastian, B., & Al-Dajani, H., eds., *Women, Entrepreneurship, and Development in the Middle East.* London: Routledge, pp. 3–32.

Mustafa, F., Khursheed, A., Fatima, M., & Rao, M. (2021). “Exploring the Impact of the COVID-19 Pandemic on Women Entrepreneurs in Pakistan”. *International Journal of Gender and Entrepreneurship*, **13**(2), 56–72.

Nziku, D. M. (2014). "Tanzania Female Entrepreneurship: Strategies for Sustainability and Growth". Doctoral Thesis, Southampton Solent University, United Kingdom.

Nziku, D. M. (2016). "Strategies and policies influencing entrepreneurship start-up decisions: Evidence from Tanzania". In Diaz-Garcia, C., Brush, C. G., Gatewood, E. J. & Welter, F., eds, *Women's Entrepreneurship in Global and Local Contexts*. Cheltenham, UK: Edward Elgar.

Nziku, D. M. & Henry, C. (2020). "Policies for Supporting Women Entrepreneurs in Developing Countries: The Case of Tanzania". *Journal of Entrepreneurship and Public Policy*, **10**(1), 38–58.

OECD & Global WEP. (2021). "Entrepreneurship Policies Through a Gender Lens". In Henry, C., Orser, B., Coleman, S. (Global WEP), Potter, J., & Halabisky, D., eds., OECD. Retrieved from: https://www.oecd-ilibrary.org/industry-and-services/entrepreneurship-policies-through-the-gender-lens_71c8f9c9-en.

Ojong, N., Simba, A., & Dana, L.-P. (2021). "Female Entrepreneurship in Africa: A Review, Trends, and Future Research Directions". *Journal of Business Research*, **132**(2), 233–248.

PricewaterhouseCoopers (PwC) Report (2017). *Women Unbound: Unleashing Female Entrepreneurial Potential*. Retrieved from: https://www.pwc.com/gx/en/diversity-inclusion/assets/women-unbound.pdf.

Robbin, Z. H. (2022). *Women's Labor Force Participation And COVID-19 In Jordan*. Washington D.C.: Middle East Institute.

Sarfaraz, L. (2017). *Women's Entrepreneurship in Iran*. Switzerland: Springer.

Sarfaraz, L. & Faghih, N. (2011). "Women's Entrepreneurship in Iran: A GEM Based-Data Evidence". *Journal of Global Entrepreneurship Research*, **1**(1), 45–57.

The FinTech Times (2021). "Why the Right of Partnership a Win for Fintech, Banks and Consumers?" *The FinTech Times*. Retrieved from: https://thefintechtimes.com/an-overview-of-women-entrepreneurship-in-the-middle-east-and-africa/ (Accessed on 15 January 2022).

The World Economic Forum (WEF, 2021). "The World Economic Forum Gender Gap Report".

World Bank (2022). "The World Bank in Jordan". Retrieved from: https://www.worldbank.org/en/country/jordan/overview#1 (Accessed on 16 March 2022).

Yin, D. (2017). "What Makes Israel's Innovation Ecosystem So Successful". *Forbes Asia*. Retrieved from: https://www.forbes.com/sites/davidyin/2017/01/09/what-makes-israels-innovation-ecosystem-so-successful/?sh=595e9ab270e4 (Accessed on 15 May 2023).

https://doi.org/10.1142/9789811283499_0002

Chapter 2

Entrepreneurship Ecosystems in the Middle East

Helene Balslev Clausen[*,¶] **and Léo-Paul Dana**[†,§,||]

[*]*Aalborg University, Denmark*
[†]*ICD Business School Paris, Paris, France*
[‡]*Dalhousie University, Halifax, Canada*
[§]*Lappeenranta University of Technology, Lappeenranta, Finland*
[¶]*balslev@hum.aau.dk*
[||]*lp762359@dal.ca*

Abstract

The notion of the ecosystem was coined by Roy Clapham in 1930 to denote physical and biological components in an environment and their relationship to each other. Today, entrepreneurial ecosystems are defined as the agglomeration of interrelated individuals, institutions, organizations, and regulatory entities in a particular geographic area that acts upon and promotes entrepreneurial initiatives and actions. Governments influence activities within these ecosystems.

Keywords: Middle East; women entrepreneurs; ecosystem; entrepreneurship.

1. Entrepreneurship

Entrepreneurship is a remarkable and critical path for economic growth and development and the expanding body of scholarly literature suggests that a dynamic and self-sustaining entrepreneurial ecosystem can significantly enhance the opportunities for entrepreneurs. Brush *et al.* (2018)

suggest that the reasonable yet rudimentary underlying assumption of the ecosystem framework is that entrepreneurs have equal access to support, resources, and finance; yet, the literature indicates that entrepreneurial participation, access to resources, and outcomes from ecosystems are gendered (Martins *et al.*, 2021; Ojong *et al.*, 2021).

2. Entrepreneurship Ecosystems

The notion of the ecosystem was coined by Roy Clapham in 1930 to denote physical and biological components in an environment and their relationship to each other. Since then the concept has developed, and central to the idea of ecosystems is that they are dynamic, interdependent, and can be bounded within a small or large scope. Within the business ecosystems, Alfred Chandler's work (Chandler, 1969) describing the automobile-centric ecosystem pointed to complementary goods and services necessary for cars to be efficient, for instance, gasoline, roads, tire makers, etc. Entrepreneurial activities are not to be viewed as part of a single sector but as an ecosystem cutting across a variety of companies, products, and services, which according to Prahalad and Hammond (2002) is paired to networks or business structures.

There is a need to address and dive further into how entrepreneurship ecosystems potentially influence or are influenced by female entrepreneurial activities. While there is robust literature on entrepreneurship in Western societies (Dana, 2018), and an increasing interest in drivers, processes, and outcomes related to entrepreneurial activities in the Middle East (Dana, 2000), there remains limited literature on female entrepreneurship ecosystems. Aljuwaiber (2021) suggests that research on women entrepreneurship in the Middle East mainly focuses on prosperous and stable economies such as the UAE and Saudi Arabia. Therefore, there is still a knowledge gap regarding the experiences of women entrepreneurs in the contexts of the Middle East region (Althalathini *et al.*, 2021); moreover, entrepreneurship is contextual and regional in essence and develops at various levels and still the dynamics surrounding entrepreneurship and in particular female entrepreneurship in the Middle East overall remain relatively understudied as compared to Western countries.

Factors that shape the conditions of the system, and constitute various interconnected nodes, are mutually reinforcing, facilitating innovation and the growth of entrepreneurial endeavors (Aulet, 2008; Brush 2014; Fetters *et al.*, 2010; Kantis and Federico, 2012). Malecki (1997) contributed to the conceptualization by describing the continued concentration of innovative entrepreneurial activities in concrete regions, revealing that these environments emerged in strong entrepreneurial cultures and knowledge-creating organizations such as universities and significant public and private resources. These studies became important in the creation of the Global Entrepreneurship Monitor (GEM) National Expert Survey (NES), which collected information from experts on national framework conditions to identify the relevant determinants for increasing the growth of new enterprises. Ideas of entrepreneurial ecosystems as regional economic development strategies that foster innovative startups and associated with regional clusters and regional innovation systems were not new (Porter, 1998), also the idea that certain regional social and economic environments are conducive to entrepreneurship ecosystems have been approached earlier from the geographical perspective (among others Sorenson and Audia, 2000) and the sociological perspective (by Bahrami and Evans, 1995). These considered the relationships between entrepreneurial activities and local economic and social contexts to be central.

The increase in ecosystem research has led to a variety of conceptualizations originating from work on clusters (Bell *et al.*, 2009) and economic geography (Audretsch and Feldman, 1996), in which entrepreneurial ecosystems are defined as the agglomeration of interrelated individuals, institutions, organizations, and regulatory entities in a particular geographic area that acts upon and promotes entrepreneurial initiatives and actions (Isenberg, 2010; Mason and Brown, 2013). Efforts to develop theories about entrepreneurship ecosystems are ongoing but have as entrepreneurship literature in general derived from Western contexts that do not necessarily reflect or are applicable to the context of the Middle East. The difference in the institutional context, historical and political development, economic performance, and sociocultural legacies of these countries emphasize the need for contextually appropriate theory.

Governments' support through regulations and creating an environment that fosters innovation to strengthen entrepreneurship growth contributes to the entrepreneurial ecosystems, but even though the governmental institutional policy support is strengthened, studies by Dana (1990) and Clausen (2017) explore contexts in which cultural barriers might hinder the development of female entrepreneurship.

A significant model of entrepreneurship ecosystem often referred to is the BEEP model proposed by Isenberg (2011) in which he suggests that six central domains or elements need to be in place to sustain an ecosystem; these are: policy, finance, markets, human capital, support, and culture, and importantly the element's political standing in entrepreneurship is determined by a large number of variables that interact in a complex manner. Isenberg's studies (2011) also suggest that entrepreneurship ecosystems are not similar, yet critics point to the fact that this model assumes that all domains have equal importance and therefore overlooks context for instance.

Existing studies address ecosystems from a triple helix model in which it is the role of, and interrelations among, government, university, and industry that define the existence of entrepreneurship ecosystems. However, these studies fail to account holistically for the numerous influences on the emergence of entrepreneurial activities and how the differentiated access to technology, network density, and organizational variety impact the ecosystem (Zahra and Nambisan, 2012).

Dana (1995) pioneered the concept that understanding context is of vital importance. Manolova *et al.* (2020) demonstrate that there is significant heterogeneity within female ecosystem composition and dynamics as well.

Clausen (2017) as well as Clausen and Velázquez (2017) define the context in terms of the sociocultural, historical, and political, in which it becomes clear that findings from experiments are largely non-generalizable across contexts but immensely useful in their specific contexts. For instance, studies by Clausen examining the Palestinian entrepreneurial networks in tourism-related activities bring insights into how the impact of tourism provided access to establish entrepreneurial ecosystems and the conditions to sustain specific circuits of small services and goods to tourists and the residents.

An entrepreneurship ecosystem does not increase the number of new businesses established or stimulate economic development, whereas according to Isenberg (2014) on the contrary, economic development stimulates new business creation and startups. The studies further identify that many stakeholders must benefit in order for an entrepreneurship ecosystem to be self-sustaining (Isenberg, 2014).

2.1 *Informal ecosystems*

A significant contextual aspect is the informal sector in this region. Research has been done on the composition and consequences of informal economic activity and informal labor market participation, but understanding informal entrepreneurship ecosystems remains yet another open research avenue to be explored. The challenge to record-keeping and reporting on informality entrepreneurship is the nature of this kind of entrepreneurship being "invisible" to official measurements.

3. Components of an Entrepreneurship Ecosystem Framework

According to the Global Entrepreneurship Monitor (GEM, 2017) report, there are 12 major components of an entrepreneurship ecosystem framework: entrepreneurship finance, government policies and supports, taxes and bureaucracy, government programs for entrepreneurship development, education and training (pre- and post-secondary education), research and development (R&D) transfer, commercial and legal infrastructures, local markets dynamism and openness, physical and service infrastructures, and cultural and social norms (Faghih and Zali Reza, 2018). The GEM report from 2016 demonstrates a keen interest in entrepreneurial activities in the Middle East and reports that 30.28% of Turks are contemplating starting up a new business soon while 45.26% of Iranians, 48.26% of Emiratis, and 63.75% of Egyptians have intentions to start their own business. Several Middle Eastern countries face profound transformation processes and seek to foster entrepreneurship ecosystems or try to build entrepreneurship ecosystems mainly through encouraging startups and mandates and funding the industry to collaborate with startups and support them.

Moreover, the government seeks to strengthen the relationship with academia as well as the industry and create a triple helix that provides a framework for an entrepreneurship ecosystem, yet the lack of understanding of the other sectors often seems to hinder further collaboration. The cultural aspects play a particular role in the way the social network works as a means of managing and conducting entrepreneurial activities in the Middle East alongside other social networking practices. Importantly in emergent economies, entrepreneurial activities are vital as they lead to economic efficiencies, and the role of female entrepreneurs in the development of the economy is pivotal and often central to the government's inclusive economic policies. However, some parts of the region still struggle a lot with poverty, social exclusion, and gender inequality.

References

Aljuwaiber, A. (2021). "Entrepreneurship Research in the Middle East and North Africa: Trends, Challenges, and Sustainability Issues". *Journal of Entrepreneurship in Emerging Economies*, **13**(3), 380–426.

Althalathini, D., Al-Dajani, H., & Apostolopoulos, N. (2021). "The Impact of Islamic Feminism in Empowering Women's Entrepreneurship in Conflict Zones: Evidence from Afghanistan, Iraq and Palestine". *Journal of Business Ethics*. https://rdcu.be/ci0ku.

Audretsch, D. B. & Feldman, M. P. (1996). "R&D Spillovers and the Geography of Innovation and Production". *The American Economic Review*, **86**, 630–640.

Aulet, B. (2008). "How to Build a Successful Innovation Ecosystem: Education, Network and Celebrate". Xconomy.com. Retrieved from: https://www.xconomy.com/national/2008/10/14/how-tobuild-a-successful-innovation-ecosystem-educate-networkand-celebrate/?single_page=true (Accessed on 07 March 2023).

Bahrami, H. & Evans, S. (1995). "Flexible Re-cycling and High-Technology Entrepreneurship". *California Management Review*, **37**, 62–89.

Brush, C. (2014). "Exploring the Concept of an Entrepreneurship Education Ecosystem. Innovative Pathways for University Entrepreneurship in the 21st Century". In Kuratko, D., ed., *Advances in the Study of Entrepreneurship, Innovation and Growth* (Vol. 24, pp. 25–39). Bingley: Emerald.

Brush, C., Greene, P., Balachandra, L., & Davis, A. (2018). "The Gender Gap in Venture Capital — Progress, Problems, and Perspectives". *Venture Capital*, **20**(2). doi.org/10.1080 /13691066.2017.1349266.

Bell, S. J., Tracey, P., & Heide, J. B. (2009). "The Organization of Regional Clusters". *Academy of Management Review*, **34**(4), 623–642.

Chandler, A. (1969). *Strategy and Structure*. Boston, MA: MIT Press.

Dana, L. (1990). "Saint Martin/Sint Maarten: A Case Study of the Effects of Politics and Culture on Economic Development". *Journal of Small Business Management,* **XXVIII**(4), 91–98.

Dana, L. (1995). "Entrepreneurship in a Remote Sub-Arctic Community: Nome, Alaska". *Entrepreneurship: Theory and Practice*, **20**(1), 55–72. [Reprinted in Norris Krueger, ed., *Entrepreneurship: Critical Perspectives on Business and Management*, Vol. IV. London: Routledge, 2002, pp. 255–275].

Dana, L. (2000). *Economies of the Eastern Mediterranean Region: Economic Miracles in the Making,* Singapore, London and Hong Kong: World Scientific (ISBN: 981-02-4474-6).

Dana, L. (2018). *Entrepreneurship in Western Europe: A Contextual Perspective,* Singapore & London: World Scientific.

Faghih, N. & Zali Reza, M. (2018). *Entrepreneurship Ecosystem in the Middle East and North Africa (MENA). Dynamics in Trends, Policy, and Business Environment*. Cham: Springer.

Global Entrepreneurship Monitor (2017). "2016 Data of Global Entrepreneurship Monitor". Retrieved from: http://www.gemconsortium.org/data.

Isenberg, D. J. (2010). "How to Start an Entrepreneurial Revolution". *Harvard Business Review*, **88**(6), 40–50.

Isenberg, D. J. (2011). "The Entrepreneurship Ecosystem Strategy as a New Paradigm for Economic Policy: Principles for Cultivating Entrepreneurship". Presentation at the Institute of International and European Affairs, Dublin, Ireland, May 12.

Kantis, H. D. & Federico, J. S. (2012). "Entrepreneuerial Ecosystems in Latin America: The Role of Policies". International Research and Policy. Entrepreneurial Development Programme, Institute of Industry, Universidad Nacional de General Sarmiento (Argentina).

Malecki, E. J. (1997). "Entrepreneurs, Networks, and Economic Development: A Review of Recent Research". In Katz, J. A. (ed.), *Advances in Entrepreneurship, Firm Emergence, and Growth*. Greenwich: JAI Press.

Martins, O., Simba, A., Dana, L., & Liguori, E. (2021). "Women Entrepreneurship in Developing Economies: A Gender-Based Growth Model". *Journal of Small Business Management.* doi:10.1080/00472778.2021.1938098.

Mason, C. & Brown, R. (2013). *Entrepreneurial Ecosystems and Growth-Oriented Entrepreneurship*. Netherlands: OECD.

Ojong, N., Simba, A., & Dana, L. (2021). "Female Entrepreneurship in Africa: A Review, Trends, and Future Research Directions". *Journal of Business Research*, **132**, 233–248. doi.org/10.1016/j.jbusres.2021.04.032.

Prahalad, C. K. & Hammond, A. (2002). "Serving the World's Poor, Profitably". *Harvard Business Review*, **80**(9), 48–59.

Sorenson, O. & Audia, P. G. (2000). "The Social Structure of Entrepreneurial Activity: Geographic Concentration of Footwear Production in the United States, 1940–1989". *American Journal of Sociology*, **106**, 424–461.

Zahra, S. A. & Nambisan, S. (2012). "Entrepreneurship and Strategic Thinking in Business Ecosystems. *Business Horizons*, **55**, 219–229.

https://doi.org/10.1142/9789811283499_0003

Chapter 3

Women Entrepreneurship in the Middle East

Dina Modestus Nziku[*,§], Fiorina Mugione[†,¶], and Aidin Salamzadeh[‡,||]

[*]*School of Business and Creative Industries, University of the West of Scotland, Glasgow, Scotland*
[†]*Senior International Advisor, Versoix, Geneva*
[‡]*Faculty of Management, Department of Business Management, The University of Tehran, Tehran, Iran*
[§]*Dina.Nziku@uws.ac.uk*
[¶]*Fiorinamugione@gmail.com*
[||]*salamzadeh@ut.ac.ir*

Abstract

The authors provide a broad view of the entrepreneurial ecosystem and women entrepreneurship in the Middle East, emphasizing the importance of a development strategy to achieve women's economic empowerment as a critical aspect of attaining sustainable development goals, and fostering good-quality entrepreneurial activity. After framing these issues and reviewing the most relevant academic literature, the authors discuss the differences between the region's historical and current entrepreneurial conditions and the characteristics of women's entrepreneurial activity. They also consider the status of the entrepreneurial ecosystems, the policy dimensions, and their potential impact on creating new business activities for women entrepreneurs. Finally, the analysis identified the main strengths and weaknesses, opportunities and threats, reflecting in depth on which policies to adopt to modernize these ecosystems and further engage women in business in the Middle East.

Keywords: Women entrepreneurship; socioeconomic; government initiatives; family business; private sector development; the Middle East.

1. Introduction

Gender equality and women's empowerment are amongst the issues that run through the 2030 Agenda for Sustainable Development. They are among the most explicit and essential conditions for meeting most of the Sustainable Development Goals (SDGs) (UNCTAD, 2018). For several decades, the lack of comprehensive peace in the Middle East has curbed growth in the region, with the highest expenditure on the military keeping economic development lagging (Looney, 1991). However, an overview of women entrepreneurship in the Middle East and Africa (MEA) (*FinTech Times*, 2021) implies that the region is home to the world's highest and lowest rates of female entrepreneurship. According to the Global Entrepreneurship Monitor (GEM, 2017), there are several factors in the region determining the low participation of women in economic activities: (1) lower levels of formal education in some countries; (2) higher levels of domestic responsibilities; (3) lack of social networks (Nziku and Struthers, 2018; Nziku, 2016, 2014); (4) lack of capital and assets; (5) lack of successful women entrepreneur role models; and (6) cultural factors that affect women's confidence in succeeding in a wide range of entrepreneurial ventures.

Furthermore, Gatti *et al.* (2013) argued on the gender gap in the Middle East with evidence that it would take almost 150 years for the region to reach the current global average of women labor force participation. Similarly, the most recent study by the World Economic Forum, the Gender Gap Report (WEF, 2021), reports that the Middle East and North Africa (MENA) might need almost 143 years to close the gender gap at the most current progress rate.

However, the number of women entrepreneurs in the Middle East has steadily risen in some economies, including Israel, the United Arab

Emirates (UAE), and Jordan. As a result, the role of women has rapidly changed (Avivi, 2019) as most women in these countries experienced emancipation.

Cultural aspects also affect the ability of women to participate in economic activities. For example, Bedouin men expected women to carry out traditional roles of sewing and repairing tents. The local culture views the economic independence of women as a disruption of family life. Hence, the participation of women in the labor force remains low. Likewise, unemployment among women continues to be higher than among their male counterparts. The low rate of economic engagement among women in the region can partially be explained by the lack of conducive business environments and policies as well as the incomplete and misinterpreted laws and regulations that, in turn, cause current regulatory institutions to be ineffective in enhancing women's economic participation.

Moreover, an entrenched patriarchal context plays a significant role in such discrepancies, particularly in rural areas where society expects women to fulfil social duties as wives and mothers rather than work as active economic agents who are remunerated (ESCWA, 2022). In addition, many organizations and employers negatively perceive the fact that the labor law dictates a policy of equal pay for equal work and paid leave-of-absence during childbirth for women. Consequently, such policies lead to most employers narrowly looking at the short-term bottom-line, choosing to employ more men than women. The situation leaves more women with little choice but to be self-employed, though some official statistics are misleading because they do not report on women who work in their own homes. Working from home informally is very common for women in villages who produce handcrafts like embroidered pillowcases and dresses from the comforts of their own homes while remaining officially unregistered.

2. Historical Overview

The Middle East consists of a heterogeneous group of countries ranging from high-income oil-exporting countries to impoverished countries torn by wars and internal conflicts. This diverse region has consistently shown the highest unemployment rates for over 25 years (Kabbani, 2019), reaching

30% in 2017, and with one of the highest youth population shares in the world.

The economy of the Middle East is very diverse, with national economies ranging from hydrocarbon exporting based on natural resources extraction, high-tech manufacturing, and agricultural-based economies. It boasts different forms of governments, from religious states and centralized social economies to free market economies. In recent years, many of the countries in the region have undertaken efforts to diversify their economies. Implementing these economic reforms became more urgent in the region as oil price volatility threatened the economic stability of major oil-exporting countries. The new policies were aimed mainly at attracting foreign investment in an integrated global economy. Reforms also called for liberalizing the trade sector and entering into regional and international agreements. The lack of participation in regional and multilateral frameworks had prevented most trade (other than oil exports). Noting trade openness as a significant contributor to higher productivity in per capita income growth, several countries in the Middle East recognized the importance of membership in the WTO. Kuwait (January 1, 1995), Bahrain (January 1, 1995), Egypt (June 30, 1995), Qatar (January 13, 1996), and the United Arab Emirates (April 10, 1996) became members at early stages (A.P. Consulting, 2016). Saudi Arabia, Jordan, Oman, and Yemen accessed the WTO in 2000–2005, while Iran, Iraq, and Lebanon began their accession process and have obtained observer statuses (WTO, 2022).

In order to decrease resource dependency within the Gulf states, reforms and policy proposals for the future have been implemented and follow a plan of economic development, signaling the move from natural resources to a globally integrated diversified economy. Examples of such plans to diversify include the Saudi Arabia Vision 2030 and the United Arab Emirates Economic Vision 2030, each of which outlines these countries' goals to reach the desired economic growth and development level by 2030. In addition, the UAE is working on establishing a national culture that encourages innovation and entrepreneurship through partnerships between the public and private sectors with seven foci: renewable energy, transport, education, health, information technology/software, water, and space.

Religion is heavily integrated into the economic policy for many Middle Eastern countries and has proved to be a significant obstacle to effective economic reform. Political instability in the region has also deterred foreign investment and global economic integration. In addition, continuous regional conflicts (such as the Palestine–Israeli conflict) prevent the region from achieving its highest potential. The uprisings of 2010/2011 in several Arab countries were motivated by a widespread popular desire to remove the incumbent autocratic rule. However, as of late 2022, the desire for freedom and justice has not led to a genuine democratic transformation. Political transparency, institutional quality, and governance are important factors in stimulating growth and entrepreneurship.

In a worsening global environment, economies in the Middle East suffered multiple shocks: a global slowdown, the COVID-19 pandemic, high and volatile food and energy prices, and faster and stronger-than-expected tightening of financial conditions. Entrepreneurship has come to be considered one key to countries' economic development. Although high levels of unemployment, corruption, lack of government accountability, education, and political participation have been crucial issues in the region, it is now imperative to resolve them. In this respect, Ismail *et al.* (2017) assert that these macroeconomic and social situations in the region are the background for the new era of an innovative entrepreneurial economy.

Historically, cultural practices in the Middle East have played a most significant role in influencing and shaping entrepreneurial activities and economic development. These include the Islamic sharia, family dynamics, and the role of public and private sector institutions. According to Mugione and Penaluna (2018), the private sector is the driving force behind sustainable economic growth. Yet, many women in the Middle East face unique constraints in starting up, formalizing, and growing their businesses to contribute to their national economies fully. We describe in the following section the entrepreneurial ecosystem in the region and how it affects the women entrepreneurs there.

3. Entrepreneurial Ecosystem

Throughout these last two decades, many authors have researched the topic, and there are different definitions of the concept of an entrepreneurship ecosystem (Isenberg, 2011; OECD, 2008; Mason and Brown, 2014;

Neck *et al.*, 2004). In all of them, a set of actors, domains, and processes come into play in a specific geographic region. For example, Mason and Brown (2014) define the ecosystem as a set of interconnected entrepreneurial actors, organizations, institutions, and entrepreneurial processes that formally and informally coalesce to connect, mediate, and govern the performance within the local entrepreneurial environment, involving a dynamic and systemic nature, within a supportive environment. According to Isenberg, the ecosystem has six parts: Culture, Markets, Human Capital, Finance, Support, and Policy (Isenberg, 2011).

The United Nations Conference on Trade and Development (UNCTAD) also considers six elements in the ecosystem: the national entrepreneurship strategy, the regulatory framework, skills and education, finance, awareness, and networking (UNCTAD, 2014). Furthermore, an ecosystem is not merely a collection of isolated elements, rather the connections between the elements matter just as much as the elements themselves (Maliki and Benghalem, 2019; Mugione and Farinelli, 2017). Connectivity shows the density of connections between programs and resources for entrepreneurs, entrepreneurs themselves, and between the two groups. The more the interactions between entrepreneurs, investors, and other actors in an ecosystem, the better the ecosystem facilitates the flow of information and money (Bell-Masterson and Stangler, 2015). Connectivity is crucial to building an entrepreneurial ecosystem and is a gauge of entrepreneurial vibrancy.

Thus, building an entrepreneurial ecosystem within the Middle East requires the consistent, understandable, and predictable rule of law; the free movement of ideas, goods, and people across markets; a world-class technological infrastructure; and easy access to growth capital. In order to address these concerns, first, governments, especially in the Gulf, have passed procurement laws intended to encourage domestic business, such as requiring that local SMEs fulfil 10% or more of all government contracts, and granting SMEs exemptions from customs taxes for equipment, raw materials, and goods for production purposes. Significantly, these measures are present in most countries in the region, with well over two-thirds of the non-oil and non-government jobs found in SMEs, but they have no impact on tech-enabled startup opportunities (Laffineur *et al.*, 2018).

Nevertheless, initiatives such as the UAE's eGovernment effort, which puts most government services, information, regulatory filings, and fee payments online, are encouraging steps that make often-confusing and unclear processes more transparent for knowledge-based businesses. Second, governments often focus on creating and enabling businesses with investment capital and support services in *free zone* areas like the Dubai Media City or Saudi Arabia's King Abdullah Economic City with preferred tax statuses and special regulatory structures. While these facilities can be a constructive first step, isolated measures often displace or delay attention to broader, state-wide legal and regulatory reform. Still, even in cases where governments have ratified good national laws, they have taken an extremely long time to realize, and enforcement is often inconsistent. For example, the Gulf Cooperation Council (GCC) recently enacted laws to streamline customs formalities and allow visa-free travel between its constituent states; however, they took nearly a decade to pass, and getting permits can be a long process.

Entrepreneurs in the region are predominantly males. Apart from less involvement of women in big cooperations, most women entrepreneurs as indicated in the previous sections are highly concentrated on Micro, Small, and Medium Enterprises (MSMEs) that are prone to less financial support. The literature indicates that the region has both migrants and diaspora women entrepreneurs engaged in five key areas for fostering entrepreneurship, namely: networking, training, mentoring, investment, and venture capital partnerships (WEF, 2021). The five identified elements describe ascending levels of commitment to the entrepreneurial project. Migrants connected to the Middle East and several diaspora networks originating from Middle East countries living abroad tend to provide solid and valuable networks with the diaspora networking in their country of origin, providing opportunities for both migrants and refugee entrepreneurs.

Cultural and positive societal norms and attitudes toward entrepreneurship have been recognized as key components of entrepreneurial ecosystems (Isenberg, 2011). Women do not pursue their entrepreneurial aspirations because their societal contribution is not valued, determining a low social status. In addition, when failure is a stigma and viewed negatively, it will inhibit women entrepreneurs from developing new plans and learning from their setbacks. Perceptions of entrepreneurship measured in the Global Entrepreneurship Monitor (GEM) survey for the

Middle East are stable over time, suggesting that these negative attitudes toward entrepreneurship are deeply ingrained. There are, however, positive changes in selected countries. The adoption of a development strategy on women's economic empowerment has made possible the access of women to education and skills, improving at the same time their access to networks and business development services, including in some cases, access to grants and financing to start their businesses. We briefly summarize the entrepreneurial ecosystem in selected countries in the region.

Qatar: The government of Qatar has empowered women through access to education, economic participation, and career opportunities supporting growth. Qatar's higher education system includes over seven American-based universities. There are twice as many female students enrolled in universities as males, with nearly two-thirds of all graduates in Qatar being women. To support more women in business, the Qatari Businesswomen Association (QBWA) was established in 2000 to highlight women's contributions to economic activity and to provide a networking platform to empower professional women. Additionally, the Supreme Council for Family Affairs established the Women's Affairs Committee in 1998 to propose policies, plans, and programs to upgrade the potential of women culturally, economically, and politically. Qatari women in business also receive important incentives and assistance to grow their businesses. In 2021, 60% of grant recipients from the Qatar Business Incubation Center were women. These initiatives, among others, have resulted in Qatari women achieving the second-lowest women's unemployment rate in the world (*The Peninsula*, 2022).

Saudi Arabia: GEM's 2020/2021 National Expert Survey ranked Saudi Arabia first among 44 economies surveyed in terms of COVID-19 *entrepreneurial response rank* and *government response rank*. This ranking is favorable as it reflects confidence in the government's ability to maintain strong entrepreneurial conditions despite the turmoil arising from the pandemic.

Although women tend to be disproportionately underrepresented as business owners, business leaders, professionals, and labor force participants, they have made notable progress in knowledge acquisition and have access to high *government SME support* (rank 2, MIWE 2021), *general access to finance* (rank 4, MIWE 2021), and *availability of venture capital* (rank 3, MIWE 2021). Here, the society is supportive and has positive regard for entrepreneurship (rank 3, MIWE 2021), especially in terms of *attitude to entrepreneurial risk* (rank 7, MIWE 2021) (Gad, 2022).

Women are free to start their own businesses without the permission of a male guardian, and the number of commercial registers held in the name of Saudi businesswomen reached 98,853 in July 2018. Their enterprises are mainly in the services sector, operating in small businesses such as fashion, interior design, jewellery, cosmetics, clothing, art, and other professional services in education, event management, exhibition organization, public relations, and marketing. Other areas include commerce, information and communication technology (ICT), real estate, tourism, the restaurant business, and manufacturing.

Women's participation in the labor market is a top priority in the kingdom's national development plan, and many national and private initiatives are taking place. The Saudi government's Vision 2030 aims for bold economic reform, replacing the traditional reliance on oil with creating a dynamic private sector generating jobs for the young population. It focuses on developing an education system in line with the market and boosting SMEs as vital agents of economic development.

The newly established SME Authority adopted a new strategy, an up-to-date Kafala loan guarantee program, and a law to reduce the administrative burden on smaller companies. These measures will help to increase employment by facilitating access to funding, introducing business-friendly regulations, providing specialized training institutions, and encouraging venture capital funding. These reforms will also help young entrepreneurs to market their ideas and products and export them through e-commerce and international partnerships. The goal is to encourage Saudi financial institutions to allocate up to 20% of overall funding to SMEs by 2030. Many universities, (among others Effat, Dar Al Hekma, Princess Nourah Bint Abdul Rahman, and King Abdulaziz University) have established innovation and entrepreneurship centers and launched plans to educate and train young Saudi women in entrepreneurship development.

Similarly, MISK, The Prince Mohammed Bin Salman Bin Abdulaziz Foundation, promotes entrepreneurship among young Saudi men and women. In cooperation with the Bill and Melinda Gates Foundation, MISK launched the Grand Challenge initiative of $10 million to empower and motivate young Saudis to bring change for a better community. 100 young innovators selected will receive an award of $100,000 to find innovative solutions to crucial global challenges. The non-profit Centennial Fund helps young women with financial loans for their projects in their cities and villages. The Badir Program for Technology Incubators, an initiative by the King Abdul Aziz City for Science and Technology, promotes an entrepreneurial culture through workshops and training programs for women university students. With the Human Resources Development Fund, it has launched the 9/10th Startup Accelerator Program, which develops early-stage young entrepreneurs into potential high-flyers.

Israel: Education, science, and industry have been important elements of Israeli culture even before Israel's birth as a nation, yet explosive growth has only become evident in the past two decades, therefore, time is also an important factor. A combination of factors is critical in generating an entrepreneurial culture: (1) hunger for innovation, (2) lack of natural resources, (3) educational and technological infrastructure, (4) infusion of new immigrants who are trained engineers and scientists, (5) efficient government support through incubators and other mechanisms, and (6) the availability of private investments. Foreign investors are attracted to Israel's highly educated and motivated workforce, and the industrial parks wherein technology is highly concentrated. Incubators, such as the Nielsen Innovate Fund, have been important in supporting the entrepreneurial ecosystem in Israel (Yin, 2017). The Ministry of Economy and Industry supports numerous technological incubators, including the Meytav Technological Incubator that focuses on the life sciences sector. Entrepreneurs can also apply for public funding. In addition, the law provides strong protection for trade secrets, patents, copyright, trademarks, trade dresses, and designs. Commercial entities in Israel commonly enter into licensing agreements, including in-licensing agreements, cross-licensing agreements, and technology dispositions. The government also provides market research grants and subsidies for preparing business plans. The Marketing Encouragement Fund, for instance, offers financial support to enterprises seeking to enlarge their international marketing efforts. Bi-national funds are also available in Israel. Finally, the law contemplates various scenarios for distressed companies, including voluntary liquidation, court-ordered liquidation, court-supervised voluntary liquidation, and reorganization (Telles, 2020).

Palestine: The Palestinian Reform and Development Plan (PRDP) 2008–2010 was the first governmental plan that significantly impacted women's economic empowerment. Moreover, the National Development Plan (NDP) 2014–2016 aimed to promote women's entrepreneurship for economic development. It offered credits and training programs, but their efficiency was questioned (Sadeq *et al.*, 2011). These plans lacked mechanisms for monitoring and evaluating the impact. Thus, some strategies have not resulted in policy adoption and implementation. They did not create a sustainable, supportive environment for women's empowerment. For example, there are no Palestinian laws regulating the microfinance sector, and women find it difficult to meet their conditions and required guarantees (Elnamrouty *et al.*, 2013). With two separate governments in Palestine, the parliament has failed to pass legislation or make further amendments to laws and regulations. In addition, the labor laws on workforce protection still do not cover women's entrepreneurship.

Although the Palestinian government established the Ministry of Entrepreneurship and Empowerment in 2019, its activities and roles are still limited (Karaki, 2021). Hence, informal entrepreneurship and tax avoidance became a necessity for women's business survival in Palestine, which inhibits business growth (Althalathini *et al.*, 2020). Moreover, women's inability to formalize their businesses limits their access to finance or bank accounts. Although there are 16 banks and 8 specialized lending institutions in Palestine (Palestine Monetary Authority, 2021), the absence of a national currency and an independent monetary policy makes the Palestinian credit market lag behind developed markets (Sarsour, 2012). The Palestinian government borrows from domestic banks to meet its expenditures (Karaki, 2021). The political instability and high level of unemployment and poverty force the Palestinian banks to apply cautious and conservative lending policies to women (International Monetary Fund, 2018). They impose difficult criteria and ask for guarantees and high-interest rates to minimize the risks of funding, limiting women entrepreneurs' access to formal finance. This could be a severe challenge for women in Palestine where resources and collateral are constrained and owned mainly by men (Althalathini, 2015).

Besides infrastructure deficiencies (access and cost of electricity, ICT, roads, shipping), a significant weakness of the entrepreneurial ecosystem is that the education system is geared to the needs of the public sector and does not enhance the entrepreneurial intention and critical thinking of graduates (Khatib *et al.*, 2013). Therefore, entrepreneurship is still not attractive to young, educated people in Palestine, and education advancement negatively influences entrepreneurial entry (Morrar *et al.*, 2022). Nevertheless, significant efforts have been taken to support the Palestinian entrepreneurial ecosystem, including establishment of training programs to promote entrepreneurship among female graduates. Entrepreneurship is a donor-driven activity in Palestine, where international organizations support the creation of business incubators and accelerators to change attitudes and leverage entrepreneurship activities, particularly in the ICT sector. There are different accelerators and incubators in the West Bank and Gaza Strip whose main aim is to create an entrepreneurial-friendly environment. They provide training, mentoring, and networking to motivate students and graduates, mainly women, to pursue entrepreneurial behavior (World Bank, 2018) and create startups that address society's challenges and needs (Owda *et al.*, 2019). Indeed, these business incubators play a role in decreasing the high unemployment rate among the young graduates, especially women.

Jordan: There are 28 organizations in Jordan's entrepreneurial ecosystem, and of these 22 support women entrepreneurs through offering incubation, training, and funding primarily. Building on Caputo *et al.*'s (2016) research, El Kharouf *et al.* (2022) undertook a further mapping of Jordan's entrepreneurial ecosystem by adopting Isenberg's (2011) widely utilized model and its following six interrelated domains: (1) a conducive culture: (2) enabling policies; (3) financing provision; (4) qualified human capital; (5) markets for products and services; and (6) a suite of institutional support. In doing so, they also sought to identify the effectiveness of Jordan's entrepreneurial ecosystem, specifically for women entrepreneurs, and found that Jordan's entrepreneurial ecosystem had grown to comprise 74 organizations. Most of the institutions facilitate access to finance and offer business development services. In addition, many tracks of the National Entrepreneurship Policy offer entrepreneurial and vocational skills development, particularly for vulnerable groups, including women, youth, migrants, and refugees.

Egypt: In the Egypt Vision 2030, the current government outlined its main goal to promote and sustain entrepreneurship in the country. The document presents eight main objectives toward the goal of building a Robust Economy, including that the Egyptian economy should embrace science, innovation, and digitalization. It also outlines the crucial importance of the promotion of small- and medium-sized entrepreneurship. Promoting entrepreneurial activities is linked to lower unemployment rates and stable economic growth in the country.

With the support from the relevant authorities as well as private companies, the startup ecosystem of Egypt is rapidly evolving; many incubators, capital venture firms, and entrepreneurship support initiatives have been created lately (*FinTech Times*, 2021). For example, in 2010, the Egyptian government established the Technology Innovation and Entrepreneurship Center (TIEC). It aims at financially and otherwise assisting businesses in the sector of ICT. As a part of TIEC, Egypt Innovate was launched later. The incubator offers funding, networking opportunities, and business development counseling to would-be entrepreneurs. The "Fekretak Sherketak" initiative provides funding, mentorship, education, and other resources to prospective businesspersons. Flat4Labs is one of the early-stage venture capital firms that actively invests in new innovative businesses in the country. In addition, the universities also actively promote entrepreneurship through education; for example, Nile University and Cairo University offer relevant training and incubation programs.

All these efforts have already given the first results. The Egyptian Startup Ecosystem Report 2021 stated that Egypt accounts for 20% of all active technology startups in Africa, with the number of tech companies exceeding half a thousand (*FinTech Times*, 2021). Those new firms employ around 13,000 individuals, making a feasible contribution to eliminating unemployment in the country (*FinTech Times*, 2021). 94% of Egyptian startups are in the capital of the country, Cairo (*FinTech Times*, 2021). The main industries where technology startups operate are e-commerce, fintech, e-health, ed-tech, recruitment, and logistics (*FinTech Times*, 2021). The Report also accounted that 39% of the new technology companies received support from accelerators and incubators, underlining the significance of the introduced governmental initiatives (*FinTech Times*, 2021). Availability of funding remains a serious impediment on the way to entrepreneurship (Rizk and Rashed, 2019). Business owners also experience difficulties with access to information, technology, and general governmental assistance (Handoussa, 2010). However, the share of people who have started seeing more business opportunities in the Egyptian market has been increasing (Aboutaleb, 2020).

UAE: A recent study found that the UAE government is the strongest player in the ecosystem and the main driver of the current entrepreneurial movement. The government mandates strategies to the private sector and academia, such as the UAE's National Innovation Strategy and Abu Dhabi Economic Vision 2030, which in turn creates a kind of reliance on the government to initiate the growth in the ecosystem (Aljarwan *et al.*, 2019).

The ecosystem's strongest support elements are the excellent infrastructure, the legal framework, national and international networks and relations, an accessible market, and incubation and acceleration programs. Conversely, some of the ecosystem's weakest support elements include the risk-averse investment culture, a lack of angel investors due to the predominant social culture and mindset, and limited research and development.

Hamade (2016) identifies that free zones are developed by the UAE government as a convenient location for entrepreneurs to start their businesses, as such locations offer business owners a more streamlined setup process. This is due to such locations giving business owners the ability to set up customizable as well as flexible offices/workstations, and these locations may act as one-stop resource hubs for government services. Assi and Marcati (2020) highlight that many opportunities are currently available to women entrepreneurs in the UAE, regardless of ethnic origin or original place of birth. Several initiatives have been authorized and executed by the UAE government to aid women entrepreneurs in becoming successful. One of the widely known initiatives is the Dubai Businesswomen Council (DBWC), which is a non-profit organization that offers education, funding as well as training opportunities to aid and support the entrepreneurial aspirations of businesswomen based in the UAE (Embassy of the United Arab Emirates, 2021; UAE Gender Balance Council, 2020).

The integrated and innovative business incubator for UAE-based women offered by the Abu Dhabi Businesswomen Council (ADBWC) supports new business ideas. This is another example of an initiative implemented by the UAE government to support the growth of women entrepreneurs in the region (Embassy of the United Arab Emirates, 2021; UAE Gender Balance Council, 2020). Additionally, this incubator aids women in identifying their latent creative potential, which may lead to translating ideas into productive projects (Sharjah Media City, 2022; UAE Gender Balance Council, 2020). It should be noted that this initiative also offers technical support, advice, and guidance, as well as funding opportunities for aspiring women entrepreneurs (Hamade, 2016; UAE Gender Balance Council, 2020).

The Dubai Women Establishment (DWE) is a long-term initiative that hosts an annual Women Leadership Exchange Program. It provides guidance and support on sustainable leadership practices and networking opportunities for aspiring women entrepreneurs in the UAE, regardless of ethnic or social background (Sharjah Media City, 2022; UAE Gender Balance Council, 2020). Another option to support the growth and development of women entrepreneurs in the UAE is partnerships between private and government institutions based in the UAE, which offer the opportunity for in-depth training and increased capital to women entrepreneurs (Embassy of the United Arab Emirates, 2021; Hamade, 2016).

Lebanon: Initiatives to develop the entrepreneurship ecosystem focused on four key areas: legal and regulatory framework improvements, capabilities building, market structure development, and access to capital. By design, these efforts target the whole territory and many of them cater to all sectors, but with priority given to Agriculture, Industry, and ICT. The private sector development institutions focused on providing capital, developing capabilities, and to some extent to promoting the entrepreneurial culture. The low rates of economic engagement among women in Lebanon can be explained by incomplete and misinterpreted laws and regulations and an entrenched patriarchal system. These shortcomings are further exacerbated by the country's financial and economic crisis and compounded by the COVID-19 pandemic and the August 2020 Port of Beirut explosion. As part of the recovery plan, the government will execute a comprehensive program of structural reforms as part of its development agenda.

The major goal is to unlock the state's growth potential in an environmentally sustainable way, address long-term growth impediments (namely, inefficiencies and corruption), develop a diverse production base, increase exports, and create well-paid jobs to reduce unemployment and attract talented Lebanese back to the country (ESCWA, 2022). There are several prominent entrepreneurial accelerators and incubators in the entrepreneurial ecosystem, including the UK Lebanon Tech Hub (UKTH) and Speed, which were launched in 2015, and Flat6Labs and Smart ESA, established in 2016. Prominent universities like USJ, USEK, AUB, and LAU were among the most active in venture development and acceleration. There are also several venture capital and private equity funds, including Berytech Funds, Venture Partners, and Middle East Venture Partners. Simultaneously, the World Bank supported a private equity fund entrusted to Kafalat, which provided SME bank loan guarantee programs. These facilities attracted overseas talent from the Lebanese diaspora, supporting one of the main aims of reversing the brain drain. Despite the initial lack of tech talent in the Lebanese market, the industry picked up quickly, with institutions opening up courses and certificates in areas like coding, artificial intelligence, and cryptography.

Iran: The women's employment index shows a slow increase in women's employment back in the 1970s, which then broke in the mid-1980s continuing to remain low since, despite unsuccessful efforts at restoration. Apart from the scarcity of national research on women's entrepreneurship in the country; women's employment in Iran has always faced problems, with women's entrepreneurship continuing to face increasing problems (Bahramitash and Esfahani, 2014). Sarfaraz and Faghih (2011) indicate that there has not been any improvement in the Iranian women's employment ratio for almost 20 years with the ratio of employment among men becoming five times that of women despite the number of female students being higher than that of male students within the country.

Syria: The systematic policies of marginalization and impoverishment pursued by the ruling regime, which is said to have not paid any respect to their political, social, economic, and legal rights, are among the problems that Syrian women are said to have suffered for decades. The role of the Syrian revolution of March 2011 in women realizing their rights leading to participation in demonstrations and human rights, media, politics, and the general community has been well acknowledged by the authors of the chapter. This was accompanied by the impact of the transformation of the popular movement in the country into an armed conflict, which left lots of women facing various forms of outbreaks of violence.

Oman: The situation in this country seems very distinct in the most conservative societies that dominate in the GCC, which includes Bahrain, Oman, Saudi Arabia, Kuwait, Qatar, and the UAE. Furthermore, the authors in this chapter provide a general analysis of the Oman Vision 2040, which seems to underlie the overall theme of Omanization as the program for not only replacing foreign workers with Omani citizens but also emphasizes the growth of business ownership among women who are the most underrepresented in the society. Therefore, Tanfeedh, a shared business services community, has been created in Oman for the purpose and the priority of developing the general entrepreneurship agenda (Al Sinani *et al.*, 2021). This has been done along with an improvement in women's participation in business and other economic activities in their society. Andriamahery and Qumruzzaman (2022) present a significant change in most of the Formal Financial Institutions (FFI) that formally had a poor record of gender diversity in their loan portfolio but now seem to have gained confidence and are comfortable with providing finance to some women entrepreneurs. Following the analysis of the past and current state of women entrepreneurs in Oman, their future seems hopeful, though it might take a little longer for the gender gap within the region to close.

Notwithstanding the national characteristics of the entrepreneurial ecosystem, according to WEF (2021) data, most women's entrepreneurial ventures receive less financial support, making them more susceptible to economic shock and unable to pivot in case of any crisis. A study of women entrepreneurs in seven Sub-Saharan African countries reported similar outcomes: during the global pandemic and lockdowns crises, women-led businesses, i.e., beauty, retails, and social care, as well as arts and culture, were at the highest rate of closure due to lower productivity (Irene *et al.*, 2022). Furthermore, like any other ecosystem, the Middle East entrepreneurial ecosystem has processes in which entrepreneurs identify market opportunities, allocate resources, consider priorities, and create value for societies. The region has social enterprises with a wide range of business models that tend to reinvest most of their profits while focusing on value creation for the community and shareholders. Such social enterprises involve inclusive entrepreneurial activities like those highly run by women entrepreneurs (Figure 1).

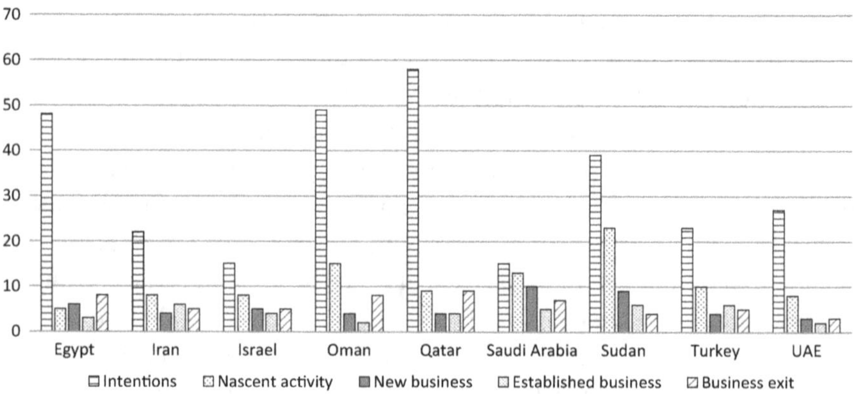

Figure 1: Entrepreneurial lifecycle for adult women in selected Middle East countries.
Source: GEM (2022).

4. Women Entrepreneurs

The most current reports (GEM, 2022; WEF, 2021) report that the region has more emerging social entrepreneurs than commercial ones. Social entrepreneurship engagement originates from an ongoing rising interest in achieving sustained social impact and increasing volunteerism among the youth, including the young women in the region. There is an increased social commitment and rejection of profit-motivated traditional business models. Most of the social enterprises in the Middle East fill the gaps in public services provision, address community challenges, and promote economic inclusion through job creation and upskilling. Furthermore, women's engagement in establishing foundations in the arts, education, and health sectors create role models for these entrepreneurial activities, hence, contributing toward closing the gender gap (Gadi, 2022; Nziku, 2014, 2016).

According to the WEF (2021) gender gap report, the 20th century has witnessed significant growth in the role of women in economic development and societies across the Middle East. These changes have spurred more research studies on women entrepreneurship in the region, which is yet said to need over a hundred years to close the gender gap. This gap is due to various cultural, social, legal, and regulatory barriers faced by women entrepreneurs who wish to participate in national, regional, and global value chains. Notwithstanding these obstacles, some countries in the region have spearheaded various reforms between 2019 and 2022, while accelerating government changes in policy during the lockdowns due to the COVID-19 pandemic. Most of these changes led to growth opportunities despite the additional challenges of economic recovery in sectors highly affected by the lockdowns, slow growth, and restructuring of value chains.

According to the enterprise survey of the World Bank (2022), the majority of women surveyed in Bahrain 59% are sole business owners of firms, which compares to 48% of the sole owners in Jordan and the UAE as well as 41% in Lebanon. The same survey recorded job creation: Jordanian women entrepreneurs employ six workers per firm. Almost 281 initiatives per annum promote entrepreneurship in the Arab countries: Jordan accounts for 17%, Lebanon represents 13%, and UAE, 9%.

According to the World Bank (2022), Saudi Arabia and Lebanon issued new legislation in entrepreneurship to facilitate business startups, ownership, and finance of women's businesses. Correspondingly, GEM (2022/2022) indicates the variation of entrepreneurial intentions for women from a low of 15% in Saudi Arabia to 58% in Qatar, while UAE indicates the most significant gender differences where women are two-thirds less likely to start up their businesses.

Characteristics of Women Entrepreneurship in the Middle East

The Middle East countries have a general population of 436 million, of which 214 million live in the Arab world. Women constitute 48% of the total population of which 20% are young women. Among this young population, 91.5% have a formal level of education. However, women's participation in the formal workforce is still low, with only 1 in 6 working-age women actively working (15% vs 65% for men) (World Bank Development Indicators, 2022).

(i) **Strengths**: The presence of a young and educated female workforce constitutes a positive determinant for entrepreneurship. Women entrepreneurs in the Middle East start their own business ventures mostly between the ages of 25 to 34 years (GEM, 2022). A study also stated that the region's women entrepreneurs possess extensive work experience that equips them with valuable skills and market knowledge. This prior work experience ranges from 6 years in the United Arab Emirates to almost 11 years in Lebanon. In addition, recovered economic growth and increased openness to trade and investment regionally and globally give nascent female startups market access and a consumer base.

(ii) **Weaknesses**: Women entrepreneurs in the Middle East still face many challenges, and cultural and social barriers hinder women from joining the labor market. We want to highlight the following obstacles:

- Women, Business, and the Law Report identifies where and which laws and regulations restrict women's economic inclusion, providing an important resource for achieving their full and equal participation. Israel, Saudi Arabia, and UAE score 82.80. Lebanon and Egypt are in the middle with a score of 50. Afghanistan, Oman Yemen, West Bank, and Gaza score among the lowest ranks, between 26 and 30. New data from the World Bank's We-Data project also show that a more discriminatory legal environment is associated with a greater probability that women-led businesses will commence operations in the informal sector. Within the legal framework, inheritance law, land ownership and access to the judicial system are the areas of most concern (World Bank, 2022).

- Some banks may require women in certain countries in the region to include their husbands as co-signers when applying for loans, even if the latter do not have the funds or are not involved in the business.
- Gender-discriminatory policies and norms may mean women-supported projects face higher interest rates.
- As in many parts of the world, women in the Middle East tend to command lower wages, which may lead to a lack of personal collateral that can be pledged to seek personal or business loans.
- Nascent female entrepreneurs who do not have a track record as entrepreneurs may be declined credit cards, loans, or business financial services altogether.
- There is no doubt that the lack of encouragement from families, mentors, and business advisors is an obstacle to the start up and growth of women's businesses.

(iii) **Opportunities for women entrepreneurs in the Middle East**: Notwithstanding the restraints, relatively low growth of business ventures, and challenges facing women in the Middle East, according to GEM (2022), any opportunity provided for women to participate in the labor market at an equivalent rate to that of men can raise the Gross Domestic Product (GDP) by 47% in the next decade. Both entrepreneurship and innovation play significant roles in the region's economy. We identified the following growing opportunities in the region:

- **Family businesses**: In these parts, family businesses are more influential than corporates. The majority of large family businesses in the Middle East tend to operate in traditional industries like franchizing, distribution, hospitality, real estate, and construction. According to PricewaterCoopers (PwC, 2021), family businesses contribute approximately 60% of the region's GDP and 80% of the workforce. In the past decades, these family businesses passed up to $1 trillion from one generation to another; this decade experienced new challenges due to disruptions caused by the COVID-19 global pandemic. However, *Forbes* (2022) reported the Middle East as having the top 100 family firms, with 87% as diversified business conglomerates that invest in a variety of sectors and geographies with the majority being led by men. Thanks to reforms and the new acceptance of women inheriting the family business, there will be opportunities for female leadership in family businesses in the Middle East.

- **Innovative digital firms**: Despite the gender gap and social challenges, women entrepreneurs in the Middle East are paving the way by tapping into the power of the digital economy for growth and success. Digital platforms bring women greater control over their personal schedules, reducing external childcare-related costs, eliminating the need to physically travel to work each day, and promising relief from the dual burdens of formal work and child care. Mastercard (2022) revealed that Middle East women entrepreneurs are leading in the digital footprint with 55% having some presence on social media and 71% having a company website. The Dubai International Financial Centre (DIFC) has a DIFC FinTech Hive program called *AccelerateHer*. It is a female-focused career mentorship accelerator aiming to provide young aspiring executives with the necessary tools and experience to help in shaping the future of the financial landscape. The *AccelerateHer* program has enabled almost 50 women with 104 mentorship pairings and presented around 80 workshops. Similarly, within Saudi Arabia, Mastercard founded an initiative called Girls4Tech, which is the company's signature Science, Technology, Engineering, and Mathematics (STEM) program, officially reaching its initial goal of educating one million girls worldwide. The most current and inspiring ambition of Girls4Tech is to reach five million girls by 2025. As a result, Saudi Arabia has increased the number of female entrepreneurs in the wider fintech industry.

- **Conducive development strategies**: The Arab world, particularly in the GCC region, is currently undergoing the implementation of large economic development and diversification strategies, namely: Saudi Vision 2030, Bahrain Vision 2030, Qatar National Vision 2030, Kuwait Vision 2035, UAE Vision 2021, and Oman Vision 2040, for instance. All these strategies aim to boost their youth working in the private sectors like financial services and fintech. In addition, there are multiple initiatives to educate and promote young Arab women to get into innovation and entrepreneurship across the region.

(iv) **Threats**: Political instability, unemployment, and religious predominance in determining the role of women in society may influence the pace of reforms. In addition, the lack of a multipronged national strategy to address barriers to female representation in the workplace, including addressing the double burden of work and family care, and negative perceptions around women abandoning the care system to work, make it difficult to break gender norms and deep-rooted biases. Gender norms begin to break down when girls and young women take on more traditionally male activities such as studying technology or pursuing self-employment and entrepreneurship.

Bikorimana and Nziku, (2022) reveal the importance of both national and transnational diasporic networks in providing both migrants and refugee entrepreneurs with information, financial resources, as well as access to potential markets. A digitally well supported diasporic network tends to be more helpful, though they still cannot replace local community networks for aiding, guiding, and signposting on the day-to-day practicalities of entrepreneurs in their immediate environment, or with understanding and navigating through the systems, structures, and institutional and regulatory environments for business in the host country (Bikorimana and Nziku, 2022, 2023).

Based on some estimations done by International Organizations, Micro, Small and Medium Enterprises (MSMEs) constitute almost

80% to 90% of businesses in the MENA region with at least 97% in the Arab world, with the intensity of almost one enterprise per 1,000 people concentrated toward micro enterprises (IFC, 2019). Further data from the Development and Employment Fund (DEF) indicate that women entrepreneurs have been given some credits in a variety of fields. Most of the women entrepreneurs who benefited from some credits had sewing and knitting, poultry and goat raising, dairy processing, beekeeping, and baking enterprises. The Ministries of Agriculture in several countries have emphasized that women play more active roles in rural development.

5. Toward the Future

Women's empowerment is part of the SDGs drive for economic and financial inclusion, and specific measures support women's entrepreneurship. For example, SDG 2 seeks to end hunger, achieve food security, and improve nutrition by doubling the agricultural productivity and incomes of small-scale food producers by 2030. This goal explicitly identifies women as a key target group. SDG 5 focuses on gender equality and empowering women and girls, including *equal rights to economic resources*, the ownership and control of land and other property, financial services, inheritance, and natural resources. Accordingly, supporting women's entrepreneurship is essential for achieving these goals and targets. Governments, donor and development agencies, and the broader private sector should develop policies, programs, and services focused on nurturing women, including young women, into business. Furthermore, we need to create and apply gender-sensitive indicators when measuring the impacts of entrepreneurship and entrepreneurship policies and programs to capture the full extent to which these activities affect the lives and opportunities of women.

In a region where gender parity is among the lowest in the world, gender justice and women's economic empowerment are hard to achieve without a gender transformative approach. In the region and many countries in the world, policies supporting women entrepreneurs are either siloed or mainstream. Unfortunately, neither of these approaches has worked well. Policymakers may consider a holistic approach to create a virtuous sequencing to build confidence and capacity among women entrepreneurs. Governments should develop a national strategy, redesigning the regulatory framework and policies (e.g., laws and regulations, social protection programs, taxation, and financial access), and the formal and informal education, including the cultural systems that reduce women entrepreneurship Development. Besides the adoption of the national strategy, we recommend five priorities:

1. **Remove regulatory hurdles**: Information technology and e-services can facilitate the fast-track establishment and lean operations of women's businesses.
2. **Develop entrepreneurship and labor skills**: Providing education and skills development will enable women entrepreneurs to acquire the requisite competencies and in-demand skills to engage effectively in self-employment. Providing women with business knowledge, information, and advice through mentoring and coaching will support them to engage in business activities effectively. Special vocational training will also help women launch their small and medium-sized enterprises as a long-term production strategy, including planning for higher market reach through effective supply chains and branding strategies.
3. **Facilitate access to finance**: Banks traditionally require clients to provide collateral such as land or real estate to secure loans. However, many creditworthy women-owned SMEs in the Middle East do not have the type of collateral required by commercial lenders and therefore have trouble accessing finance. To remove this barrier, the government and financial institutions may relax collateral requirements and introduce different schemes for creditworthiness evaluation. Policymakers should consider providing financial incentives, ensuring access to innovative financing, and supporting the development of the necessary infrastructure such as incubators and accelerators, which can help to catalyze the development of startups, for example, funds to support female entrepreneurship have been established in several countries in the region. Venture capital is also playing an important role in catalyzing alternative energy and environmentally friendly

technologies, with venture capital funds being used to spur green entrepreneurship.

4. **Leverage social and green entrepreneurship**: Although social enterprises, like other businesses, require business support services, unlike other businesses they may require general business support as well as tailored support for enterprise-specific needs. Social innovation parks, incubators, and hubs that promote collaboration and innovation among individuals working to develop enterprises that will address pressing social and environmental challenges have emerged. Icecairo, a green innovation hub in Egypt is equipping young entrepreneurs with green skills as well as business support to enable them to pursue green entrepreneurship. Established in 2012 with funding from Germany's development agency, German Agency for International Cooperation GmbH (GIZ), Icecairo is addressing Egypt's environmental challenges through low-cost solutions.
5. **Develop networks**: For women entrepreneurs, the establishment and access to networks are imperative, especially in the early stages. Strong networks can facilitate access for women entrepreneurs to business advice, investors, customers, and mentors. For aspiring entrepreneurs who tend to have lower levels of entrepreneurship skills as well as greater difficulty in navigating the business and regulatory environment, access to networks can help them to overcome these challenges. Business networks can support women entrepreneurs as they embark on entrepreneurship by providing them with information and guidance to help them manage and grow their businesses. Increasingly, online business networks and virtual meetings are facilitating information exchange between women entrepreneurs and their established counterparts.

In conclusion, looking forward to the future of women entrepreneurs in the Middle East, all governments that have not yet done so should enact legislation that guarantees the full economic participation of women in accordance with international human rights frameworks and standards, particularly the Convention on the Elimination of All Forms of Discrimination against Women and the Beijing Platform for Action. In addition, governments should work with the private sector to regularly review the business environment and investment climate for entrepreneurship and business growth. It should include a regular and careful assessment of the informal economy's size and nature to reduce informality levels and remove barriers for women entrepreneurs to greater financial and economic inclusion. Regular, formalized public–private dialogue platforms and processes should be established to monitor entrepreneurship issues and devise appropriate responses to these, engaging collaborative and partnership efforts. Particular attention should be paid to inclusive financial and entrepreneurial education and training services. At the same time, policymakers must not lose sight of the transformational challenges required to build better going forward after the global pandemic to accelerate the creation of more inclusive, resilient, sustainable, and green economies. Regional and international cooperation will be key complements to strong domestic policies in this regard.

References

Aljarwan, A., Yahya, B. A., & Almarzooqi, B. M. (2019). "Examining Frameworks of Entrepreneurial Ecosystems: A Case Study on the United Arab Emirates". Paper presented at the *Conference of Entrepreneurship & Innovation Management 4th Track International Conference on Organisation and Management* (ICOM), 12th & 13th June, Abu Dhabi.

Andhov, A. & Pedro, T. (2020). *Start-Up Law in Israel*. Edward Elgar Publishing Ltd.

Avivi, T. (2019). "Female Representation in Israel Politics". *Policy Analysis* (*Fikra Forum*). Retrieved from: https://www.washingtoninstitute.org/policy-analysis/female-representation-israeli-politics (Accessed on 12 January 2022).

A. P. Consulting (2016). "The Middle East and The World Trade Organisation — Articles". Retrieved from: http://www.mideastlaw.com/article_middle_east and the_wto.html.

Bastian, B. L., Sidani, Y. M., & El Amine, Y. (2018). "Women Entrepreneurship in the Middle East and North Africa: A Review of Knowledge Areas and Research Gaps". *Gender in Management*, **33**(1), 14–29. doi.org/10.1108/GM-07-2016-0141.

Bastian, B. L., Metcalfe, B. D., & Zali, M. R. (2019). "Gender Inequality: Entrepreneurship Development in the MENA Region". *Journal: Sustainability* (Switzerland).

Bell-Masterson, J. & Stangler, D. (2015). "Measuring an Entrepreneurial Ecosystem". Available at SSRN: http://dx.doi.org/10.2139/ssrn.2580336.

Bikorimana, C. & Nziku, D. M. (2022). "New Approaches to Raising Entrepreneurial Opportunity: *Refugee Women Entrepreneurs in Glasgow, Scotland*". Submitted for the Institute for Small Business and Entrepreneurship (ISBE) Conference, 27th and 28th October 2022, York, England.

Bikorimana, C. & Nziku, D. M. (2023). "Gender and Entrepreneurship among Refugee Women Entrepreneurs in Glasgow-Scotland". *Journal of Studies in Law and Economics*, **2**(127). DOI: https://doi.org/10.26485/SPE/2022/127/7.

Commonwealth (2018). "Youth Entrepreneurship for the Green and Blue Economy: Policy Toolkit". Retrieved from: https://production-new-commonwealth-files.s3.eu-west-2.amazonaws.com/migrated/inline/Youth_Entrepreneurship_Informal_Toolkit.pdf.

ESCWA (2022). "Women's Economic Participation in Lebanon: *A Mapping Analysis of Laws and Regulations*". E/ESCWA/CL2.GPID/2022/TP.27.

Forbes (2022). "The Middle East's Top 100 Arab Family Businesses".

Gadi, N. (2022). "Increasing Women's Employment Opportunities in Digitalizing Saudi Arabia's Economy". *Open Journal of Business and Management*, **10**, 2869–2902. doi:10.4236/ojbm.2022.105142.

Global Entrepreneurship Monitor (GEM, 2022). "Women's Entrepreneurship Report From Crisis to Opportunity".

Handoussa, H. (2010). "Key Development Challenges Facing Egypt". *United Nations Development Project (UNDP)*. Cairo, Egypt.

Irene, B., Nziku, D. M., Tesfaye, A., & Forson, C. (2022). "Having Nothing and Giving Much: Sub-Sahara African Women Entrepreneurs Thriving Under Covid-19 Pandemic". Full Paper presented at 36th *Annual Conference of British Academy of Management (BAM)* on 31st August–2nd September, Alliance Manchester Business School, Manchester, England.

Isenberg, D. (2011). "The Entrepreneurship Ecosystem Strategy as a New Paradigm for Economic Policy: Principles for Cultivating Entrepreneurship". *Institute of International and European Affairs* (Dublin, Ireland).

Ismail, A., Schott, T., Herrington, M., Kew, P., & de la Vega, I. (2017). "Global Entrepreneurship Monitor Founding and Sponsoring". In *Global Entrepreneurship Monitor* (Issue MENA Region Report).

Kabbani, N. (2019). "Youth Employment in the Middle East and North Africa: Revising and Reframing the Challenge". Brookings Institution. Retrieved from: https://www.brookings.edu/research/youth-employment-in-the-middle-east-and-north-africa-revisiting-and-reframing-the-challenge/.

Kasseeah, H. (2016). "Investigating the Impact of Entrepreneurship on Economic Development: A Regional Analysis". *Journal of Small Businesses and Enterprise Development*, **23**(3), 896–916.

Laffineur, C., Tavakoli, M., Fayolle, A., Amara, N., & Carco, M. (2018). "Insights from Female Entrepreneurs in MENA Countries: Barriers and Success Factors". In Faghih, N., & Zali, M., eds., *Entrepreneurship Ecosystem in the Middle East and North Africa (MENA).* Dynamics in Trends, Policy and Business Environment, 351–397.

Looney, R. E. (1991). "The Economics of Middle East Military Expenditures: Implications for Arms Reduction in the Region", *Bulletin of Peace Proposals*, **22**(4), 407–417. http://www.jstor.org/stable/44481593.

Maliki, S. & Benghalem, A. (2019, October). Feedback effects of Entrepreneurship, Innovation, and Economic Development: Empirical evidence from selected MENA Countries. In *World Conference on Management and Economics* (pp. 24–26).

Mason, C. & Brown, R. (2014). "Entrepreneurial Ecosystems and Growth-Oriented Enterprises". In Background Paper Prepared for the Workshop Organised by the OECD LEED Programme and the Dutch Ministry of Economic Affairs. Discussion Paper, OECD. Retrieved from: http://eprints.gla.ac.uk/view/author/29097.html.

Mastercard. (2022) "The Mastercard Index of Women Entrepreneur 2021: How Targeted Support for Women-Led Business Can Unlock Sustainable Economic Growth". mastercard.com/news/miwe (Accessed on 12 November 2022).

Mugione, F. & Farinelli, F. (2017). Promoting Entrepreneurship for Development. In T. Rensmann (Ed.), *Small and Medium-Sized Enterprises in International Economic Law* (pp. 339–355). Oxford University Press. https://doi.org/10.1093/acprof:oso/9780198795650.003.0014.

Mugione, F. & Penaluna, A. (2018). "Developing and Evaluating Enhanced Innovative Thinking Skills in Learners". In James *et al.*, (eds.), *Entrepreneurial Learning City Regions*. Springer Press. Retrieved from: link.springer.com Entrepreneurial Learning City Regions: Delivering on the UNESCO 2013, Beijing Declaration on Building Learning Cities | SpringerLink.

Neck, H. M., Meyer, G. D., Cohen, B., & Corbett, A. C. (2004). "An Entrepreneurial System View of New Venture Creation". *Journal of Small Business Management*, **42**, 190–208.

Nziku, D. (2014). "*Tanzania Female Entrepreneurship: Strategies for Sustainability and Growth*". Doctoral Thesis, Southampton Solent University. United Kingdom.

Nziku, D. (2016). "Strategies and Policies Influencing Entrepreneurship Start-Up Decisions: Evidence from Tanzania". In Diaz-Garcia, C., Brush, C. G., Gatewood, E. J., & Welter, F., (eds.), *Women's Entrepreneurship in Global and Local Contexts*. Cheltenham, UK: Edward Elgar.

Nziku, M. D. & Struthers, J. J. (2018). "Female Entrepreneurship in Africa: Strength of Weak Ties in Mitigating Principal-Agent Problems". *Journal of Small Business and Enterprise Development*, **25**(3), 349–367. doi.org/10.1108/JSBED-03-2017-0115.

OECD (2008). "Measuring Entrepreneurship: A Digest of Indicators OECD-Eurostat Entrepreneurship".

PricewaterCoopers (PwC, 2021). "Family Businesses in the Middle East and the New Normal: Reflect, Reframe and Optimise". PwC Middle East Family Business Survey 2021, available at www.pwc.com.

The FinTech Times (2021). "Why the Right of Partnership a Win for Fintech, Banks and Consumers?" *The FinTech Times*. Retrieved from: https://thefintechtimes.com/an-overview-of-women-entrepreneurship-in-the-middle-east-and-africa/ (Accessed on 15 January, 2022).

The Peninsula (2022). "Qatar, U.S. Committed to Empowering Women in Business, say officials. Retrieved from: https://thepeninsulaqatar.com/.

The World Economic Forum (WEF, 2021). "The World Economic Forum Gender Gap Report".

UNCTAD (2012). "*Entrepreneurship Policy Framework and Implementation Guidance*". UNCTAD/DIAE/ED/2012/1. Retrieved from: https://unctad.org/system/files/offcial-document/diaeed2012d1_en.pdf (Accessed on 18 November 2022).

UNCTAD (2013). "A survey on Women's Entrepreneurship and Innovation".

UNCTAD (2015). "*Policy Guide on Youth Entrepreneurship*". UNCTAD/DIAE/ED/2015/1. Retrieved from: https://unctad.org/system/files/offcial-document/webdiaeed2015d1_en.pdf (Accessed on 12 December 2022).

World Bank (2022). *World Development Indicators* (Accessed on 18 November 2022).

World Trade Organisation (WTO, 2022). "List of Members and Observers". WTO Members and Obsercers. Retrieved from: https://www.wto.org/english/thewto_e/whatis_e/tif_e/org6_e.htm (Accessed on 13 January 2023).

Yin, D. (2017). "What Makes Israel's Innovation Ecosystem So Successful". *Forbes Asia*. Retrieved from: https://www.forbes.com/sites/davidyin/2017/01/09/what-makes-israels-innovation-ecosystem-so-successful/?sh=595e9ab270e4 (Accessed on 25 November, 2022).

https://doi.org/10.1142/9789811283499_0004

Chapter 4

Women Entrepreneurs in Bahrain

Aidin Salamzadeh[*,¶] and Léo-Paul Dana[†,‡,§,||]

[*]*The University of Tehran, Tehran, Iran*
[†]*ICD Business School Paris, Paris, France*
[‡]*Dalhousie University, Halifax, Canada*
[§]*Lappeenranta University of Technology, Lappeenranta, Finland*
[¶]*salamzadeh@ut.ac.ir*
[||]*lp762359@dal.ca*

Abstract

Women entrepreneurs have become key drivers of entrepreneurial changes, especially in Middle Eastern countries where they have recently unleashed their distinguished power. Bahrain is not an exception. Even though women entrepreneurs in Bahrain struggle with a male-dominated culture, they have been successful in starting their own small businesses. Therefore, it is necessary to explore the context of doing business for women entrepreneurs. Then, this chapter reviews the historical aspects of Bahrain and then explores its entrepreneurial ecosystem. Finally, it provides some directions for the future of entrepreneurship in Bahrain.

Keywords: Women's entrepreneurship; women entrepreneurs; female entrepreneurship; Bahrain.

1. Introduction

The Kingdom of Bahrain (Bahrain), the third smallest country in Asia, is located in the Persian Gulf. The origin of the name is the Arabic term *al-baḥrayn* which means "two seas" (Turner, 2000). Bahrain is an oil-producing country with small amounts of reserves. But, it is mostly focused on processing the crude oil exploited from other neighboring countries (Nuruzzaman, 2013). They provide other services such as financial and commercial services and host international tourists. The capital of the country is Manama, which is a main destination for tourists from other countries, especially Saudis (Samer, 2017). Family is considered the most critical issue in the country, which is historically rooted in the customs of the Persian Empire that ruled over the region for centuries, before its independence in 1971 (Alvandi, 2010). Based on current estimations in 2022, the population is around 1.6 million (Abuzeyad, 2020).

Bahrain's economy was a traditional economy before the discovery of oil and gas. The economy relied highly on date cultivation and pearl fishery (Carter, 2019). However, many believe that Bahrain was home to the Dilmun civilization and served as the commercial gateway in ancient times (Gotoh *et al.*, 2020). People from various ethnic groups live in peace here; although there were conflicts between Shi'a and Sunni Muslims in some periods. Arabic is the official language of the majority of the population, and Bahrainis learn English at schools. Also, People speak Persian/Farsi, Urdu, Hindi, and Tagalog in some regions. As the country was separated from Iran before its independence, many Bahrainis still speak Persian/Farsi at their homes. Life expectancy is almost high (male = 77, and female = 81) (Wirayuda *et al.*, 2023). The country is culturally rich and hospitality is an advantage for the tourism industry (Exhibit 1). Creative industries have always been an integral part of Bahrain's economy (Al Sahaf and Al Tahoo, 2021).

This chapter provides an overview of the historical aspects of Bahrain. Then, the entrepreneurial ecosystem is explored, and the role of women entrepreneurs is discussed. Finally, the chapter concludes with some remarks about women's entrepreneurship in Bahrain.

2. Historical Overview

Bahrain is an old country with a fascinating history that is connected to ancient Persia. The country was civilized by the Dilmuns, and in the Bronze Age it turned into a trade center, especially due to its geopolitical

Exhibit 1. Bahrain's palm trees.

Source: https://pixabay.com/photos/bahrain-palm-tree-pool-arab-sea-1369259.

situation (Gotoh *et al.*, 2020). For thousands of years, Assyrians and Babylonians ruled over this region. Bahrain was governed by Achaemenids for around three centuries (Belgrave, 1952). After those centuries, Parthias expanded the Great Persia and ruled over other regions such as Oman. They turned Bahrain into a trade zone for expanding their span of authority and improving the regional economy. It was a major trade zone for pearl, cotton, and other products to various countries that were accessible through the Persian Gulf and the Gulf of Oman. Persians, Christians, Zoroastrians, Jews, and Arameans are the majority of the people living in this country. Bahrainis converted to Islam after the Muslims' conquest in wars, yet they still stick to many of their own religious beliefs and customs. Muslim rulers ruled over the country afterwards, even though Bahrain underwent many ups and downs during the governance of the Portuguese Empire, which lasted almost 80 years (1521–1602). In 1602, the Safavid Empire expelled Portuguese rulers and promoted Shi'a Islam in the country. For two centuries, Persian Emperors ruled over Bahrain. But this peace did not last longer, and in 1717 and 1738, Oman invaded them. In 1783, the Bani Utbah tribe from Qatar defeated Al-Madhkur, and their Khalifa moved to the country in 1799 (Alhoori, 2018). This change was brought forth mainly by the Ottomans as they became powerful. In the early 19th century, Omanis and Al Sauds invaded the country. It is noteworthy that these invasions were mainly due to the unique geopolitical situation of Bahrain (Ramadani *et al.*, 2022).

The UK recognized Al Khalifa as the ruler of Bahrain and supported their rulership over the country in 1820. Although they signed many agreements to protect the country, still many neighboring countries were struggling to invade Bahrain. Besides, the UK became more powerful in the country and Bahrain was dominated by them. This made Bahrainis sad and led to multiple unrests afterwards. The main business of Bahrainis was pearl fisheries, which was changed after the exploitation of petroleum. In 1911, some protestors, who were merchants, protested against the dominance of the British over the country, but they were exiled to India (Friedman and Friedman, 2020). This was a sign for other protestors to stop their protests against the British. In 1927, Reza Shah, the King of Iran, sent some forces against the British and asked for sovereignty over Bahrain (Mueller, 2016). Britain's pressures along with several conflicts between Shi'a and Sunni citizens, which were also pushed by the British, were among the major reasons to pull the trigger. The modern era of Bahrain was initiated after the discovery of oil and gas in 1932, and a major revolution unfolded — a transition from a traditional a pearl-based economy to an oil-based economy (Tuson, 1945). The modernization era tightened Bahrain's relationship with Britain, but it diversely affected the trend, as Bahrain joined the Allied side in World War II. Italians bombarded the country accordingly and ruined infrastructural facilities, although thankfully the damages were limited and it did not take long for them to recover. After the war, many Arab countries faced anti-Britain protests, and many communities such as the Jewish communities of Bahrain left Bahrain and immigrated to India and then Israel. The King of Iran, Mohammad Reza Shah, son of Reza Shah, held a referendum, which was managed by the UN, and Bahrain declared its independence in 1971. The country joined the UN and a new era started (Zuid, 2016).

The new economy of the country relied highly on oil and gas exploitations, which were affected by the oil boom and its impacts in the 1970s.

The Bahraini authorities, then, opted to diversify their investment portfolio to manage the possible risks. They managed to become a new trade zone in the Middle East, especially after the Lebanese Civil War. They took Beirut's place and expanded their relationships with several allies (Dana *et al.*, 2022). This new approach of the Bahraini authorities led to several negotiations and agreements, and their economy flourished. They formally changed the name of the country from the "State of Bahrain" to the "Kingdom of Bahrain" in 2002. The Bahraini economy continued to grow in the following years. But, the sociopolitical issues remained. For instance, the conflicts between Shi'a and Sunni tribes continued. In 2011, the Shi'a majority protested against the rulers who were mainly Sunni, and the Arab Spring accelerated the conflicts. But, the rulers cracked down on the protests and many people were killed. This sad incident was not covered by the Arab media, and the rulers continued their dominance (Al-Rawi, 2015; Karolak, 2017; Ramadani *et al.*, 2022).

Bahrain has become a destination for tourists and has highlighted its historical heritage to the world (Exhibit 2). It represents the modern Arab

Exhibit 2. Bahrain's night view.

Source: https://pixabay.com/photos/city-night-bahrain-skyline-evening-6758248.

Exhibit 3. Bahrain's traditional bazaars.
Source: https://pixabay.com/photos/bahrain-tropical-fruits-arabia-51182.

culture and entertains many visitors annually — more than five times its population. The Bahrain National Museum, the Al Khamis Mosque, the Qalat Al Bahrain, the Beit Al Quran, the Barbar temple, the A'ali Burial Mounds, the Arad Fort in Muharraq, and the Saar temple as well as the four-hundred-year-old Tree of Life are the major tourist destinations. The country has also invested in infrastructural facilities to host tourists. Simultaneously, the petroleum industry has grown dramatically during the last few decades. Their investments range from financial services to new technology-based industries. Many multinational corporations operate in the country and offer their products to the countries in the region. Bahrain's biocapacity is lower than the world's mean and it heavily relies on the imports of food and exports of oil products. The country has also a distinguished history of bazaars, as it was once a part of the Persian Empire, which was the inventor of the traditional bazaars (Exhibit 3). The economy has been growing in the last few years and has witnessed several changes (Dana *et al.*, 2022b; Ramadani *et al.*, 2022).

3. Entrepreneurial Ecosystem

Bahrain's entrepreneurial ecosystem relies highly on the state for the ease of doing business and its business history. The geopolitical state of the country provides entrepreneurs with a handful of opportunities to be identified, evaluated, and exploited both nationally and internationally (Meero *et al.*, 2021). As a critical hub for doing business in the Middle East, entrepreneurs can take advantage of such opportunities and business indicators in the business environment are also improved accordingly (Darwish *et al.*, 2020). The country signed agreements with multiple international organizations and improved its socioeconomic indicators. They proposed a vision for 2030 in 2008, i.e., The Economic Vision 2030, and introduced their visionary path toward creating a better future for Bahrainis (Amara and Albastaki, 2021). They offered a new slogan, i.e., "From Regional Pioneer to Global Contender", to initiate and navigate the new waves of change. The vision is focused on various aspects of the socioeconomic development of Bahrain, including sustainable development and competitiveness. The Bahraini officials believe that this plan can make significant changes in the trajectory path of the country and will lead to shaping a more prosperous and peaceful Bahrain (Omar, 2021). The vision pays careful attention to human capital and its development in order to reach a sustainable status in the long term. As the country must become less reliant on oil and gas resources in the future, they have offered several scenarios to improve the entrepreneurial ecosystem.

The current priorities of the country are to reduce national poverty indexes and to decrease the unemployment rates, especially youth unemployment (Salamzadeh, 2014). Therefore, they have proposed several initiatives for facilitating business operations, especially in the non-oil and gas sectors. In terms of doing business (2020), the country has experienced significant growth, which is planned to be better in the future. The following table reveals the facts and figures (Table 1). As it is shown in the table, Bahrain is ranked first in terms of paying taxes and ranked 17th in terms of dealing with construction permits and registering properties (Ramadani *et al.*, 2022; Batrancea *et al.*, 2019, 2022). However, in some cases, such as getting credit, the country still needs to improve its status.

Table 1. Ease of doing business in Bahrain.

Topics	DB 2020 Rank	DB 2020 Score	DB 2019 Score	Change in Score (% Points)
Overall	43	76.0	70.1	5.9
Starting a business	67	89.6	89.6	—
Dealing with construction permits	17	83.1	73.4	9.7
Getting electricity	72	79.7	74.8	4.9
Registering property	17	86.2	81.1	5.1
Getting credit	94	55.0	45.0	10
Protecting minority investors	51	66.0	64.0	2
Paying taxes	1	100	93.9	6.1
Trading across borders	77	78.7	77.8	0.9
Enforcing contracts	59	63.8	57.3	6.5
Resolving insolvency	60	58.2	44.6	13.6

Source: The World Bank.

The entrepreneurial ecosystem in Bahrain is a newly investigated topic that is not sufficiently discussed and investigated in the extant literature. Nevertheless, the promise of an entrepreneurial approach is evident in the business environment, as the government has already offered a set of initiatives, the startup ecosystem is growing, and entrepreneurship has become a hot topic for realizing The Economic Vision 2030 (Nakibullah, 2018). Generally speaking, the entrepreneurial ecosystem is flourishing in light of the recent changes in the legal, corporate, and economic aspects of firms. Besides, as mentioned earlier, the government has offered a set of initiatives for helping startups. For instance, they have reduced the minimum capital investment for startups and for setting up new ventures. This led to an increased propensity to invest in various startups and startup projects. The establishment of the Al Waha Venture Capital Fund is another sign of supporting such movements. This fund attracts angel investors and empowers entrepreneurs to help them realize their entrepreneurial dreams (Darwish *et al.*, 2021). Besides, Bahrain has also facilitated entrepreneurial efforts by revisiting its existing rules and regulations.

4. Women Entrepreneurs

Women in Bahrain, like many other regions, are exposed to many legal problems and violence. Issues such as the lack of proper social status, violence against women in prisons and police offices, and the radical religious system can be considered vital problems of women in Bahrain. The average political participation of women in Bahrain is 2.3%, which is very low compared to other countries in the region (Al-Ghazali *et al.*, 2013). Bahraini women were allowed to vote in the country's political elections after 2002. In the same year, Bahraini women gained the right to be candidates in the parliament of the country. The first woman who was able to appear in the parliament of Bahrain by winning the popular vote was Latifa al-Gaoud, who entered the parliament in 2006 (Maheep and Jahanghiri, 2022). In September 2017, for the first time, a woman was appointed to an important government position. Afaf Zainalabedine was the first woman who was appointed to the position of General Manager for Finance and Admin at Nogaholding[1] (Capello and Borisly, 2019).

Based on some recent studies (e.g., Alexandre and Kharabsheh, 2019), Bahraini women are more in the pull, not push situation of entrepreneurship. However, they need to have some female role models to act entrepreneurially. Bahraini women suffer from a lack of knowledge and experience in being enterprising and venturing. Moreover, most of their firms are small and medium-sized enterprises (SMEs) and one can barely find a female entrepreneur who has established a large firm. According to another study (Alnefaiei and Aziz, 2020), several challenges have been identified that decrease the level of entrepreneurial activities among Bahraini women entrepreneurs. These include issues such as family commitments and lack of focus on enterprising activities due to their family-related responsibilities, intense market competition with their male counterparts, and high rates of facilities and rent. Governmental rules and regulations as well as customs are also against them to some extent. While some of these issues were not strongly the reasons for a decreased rate of female entrepreneurship, some other studies have revealed that they are vital (Shaver *et al.*, 2022).

[1]National Oil and Gas Authority (NOGA).

Despite all the mentioned barriers, Bahraini women entrepreneurs struggle to unleash their entrepreneurial power and make significant changes in their society. For instance, Sofia Al-Asfoor is the founder of her own brand and produces colourful handmade bags and accessories. She uses Instagram to promote and sell her products. Roaya Saleh is another Bahraini female entrepreneur who has established a modern Middle Eastern restaurant, and she used her initiative and creative mind to offer creative recipes on her restaurant's menu. She won the Global Enterprise of the Year prize. Another exemplar is Latifa Al-Khalifa, who founded a startup in the field of education and personal development. She is among the few Bahraini female entrepreneurs who have established startups. Aisha Abdulmalik is another female entrepreneur who has established her own amazing jewellery line. She also uses social media platforms such as Instagram to promote and sell her products. Bahraini female entrepreneurs also offer creative services. For example, Abeer Al Matooq is a well-known life coach and a human resources expert who provides various services to her customers (Darwish *et al.*, 2021).

As mentioned in the previous examples, one can witness that most Bahraini female entrepreneurs have established small-scale enterprises to exploit entrepreneurial opportunities. This might be due to the context of doing business in Bahrain and the pressures enforced by society on those distinguished entrepreneurs (Kharabsheh *et al.*, 2021). This has led to a lack of enough role models for other potential female entrepreneurs. Besides, the entrepreneurial aspects of female entrepreneurs are not developed well, and the policymakers and officials still need to take significant actions to improve the entrepreneurial ecosystem for women entrepreneurs. Hopefully, entities like Tamkeen[2] are changing the entrepreneurial ecosystem and its dynamics in the business environment (Palalić *et al.*, 2021).

5. Toward the Future

Bahrain has a diverse culture that brings people from different walks of life and religions together. A special sign of this fact is that the country has various Hindu and Sikh temples, Maatams, Shiite and Sunni mosques, and

---

[2] See: https://www.tamkeen.bh/about-us.

churches (Ramadani *et al.*, 2022). Despite some disputes between the Shi'a majority and Sunnis, the general culture respects various perspectives. The business environment has undergone a significant change during the last two decades and social ties have improved the ease of doing business. Deregulations and major changes in the existing rules and regulations have led to creating a more ready environment for an improved enterprising culture. Historically, women have been under great pressure owing to the traditional culture, more specifically after the dominance of Islam. There is historical evidence that women were doing business more freely before being forced to convert to Islam. The Islamic and male-dominant culture of Bahrain, like most Arab countries, has put great pressure on potential women entrepreneurs. Hopefully, the government follows a new approach considering the proposed Economic Vision 2030. Recently, the entrepreneurial ecosystem of Bahrain has been changing as new players such as Tamkeen, have come to the scene and are promoting an entrepreneurial lifestyle among [potential] Bahraini entrepreneurs. Nevertheless, according to previous studies, there is a significant need to change the formal and informal institutions in line with devising soft and hard policies to support SMEs, entrepreneurs, and enterprising communities (Alexandre and Kharabsheh, 2019).

References

Abuzeyad, F. H., Al Qasim, G., Alqasem, L., & Al Farras, M. I. (2020). "Evolution of Emergency Medical Services in the Kingdom of Bahrain". *International Journal of Emergency Medicine*, 13, 1–8.

Al Sahaf, M. & Al Tahoo, L. (2021). "Examining the Key Success Factors for Startups in the Kingdom of Bahrain". *International Journal of Business Ethics and Governance*, 4(2), 9–49.

Alexandre, L. & Kharabsheh, R. (2019). "The Evolution of Female Entrepreneurship in the Gulf Cooperation Council, the Case of Bahrain". *International Journal of Gender and Entrepreneurship*, **11**(4), 390–407.

Al-Ghazali, B. M., Yusoff, R. M., & Sadi, M. A. (2013). "Women Entrepreneurs in Bahrain: Motivations and Barriers". *Sains Humanika*, **64**(2), 1–12.

Alhoori, A. A. (2018). *Citizenship Education in Bahrain: A Study of Textbooks and Public Debates (2001–2017)*. Doctoral dissertation. Qatar: Hamad Bin Khalifa University.

Alnefaiei, A. A. & Aziz, W. A. (2020, November). "Overcoming Challenges of Women Entrepreneurship in Bahrain: Evidence from the Events Planning Sector". In *2020 Second International Sustainability and Resilience Conference: Technology and Innovation in Building Designs (51154)* (pp. 1–7). IEEE.

Al-Rawi, Ahmed, K. (2015). "Sectarianism and the Arab Spring: Framing the Popular Protests in Bahrain". *Global Media and Communication*, **11**(1), 25–42.

Alvandi, R. (2010). "Muhammad Reza Pahlavi and the Bahrain Question, 1968–1970". *British Journal of Middle Eastern Studies*, **37**(2), 159–177.

Amara, A. B. H. & Albastaki, N. K. (2021, September). "The Role of Entrepreneurship Ecosystem in Fostering Startups Growth: Insight From Bahrain Entrepreneurship Ecosystem". In *ECIE 2021 16th European Conference on Innovation and Entrepreneurship Vol.* 1 (p. 89). Academic Conferences Limited.

Batrancea, L. M., Nichita, A., De Agostini, R., Batista Narcizo, F., Forte, D., de Paiva Neves Mamede, S., ... & Budak, T. (2022). "A self-Employed Taxpayer Experimental Study On Trust, Power, And Tax Compliance In Eleven Countries". *Financial Innovation*, **8**(1), 96.

Batrancea, L., Nichita, A., Olsen, J., Kogler, C., Kirchler, E., Hoelzl, E., ... & Zukauskas, S. (2019). "Trust and Power as Determinants of Tax Compliance Across 44 Nations". *Journal of Economic Psychology*, **74**, 102191.

Belgrave, J. H. (1952). "A Brief Survey of the History of the Bahrain Islands". *Journal of the Royal Central Asian Society*, **39**(1), 57–68.

Capello, M. A. & Borisly, N. (2019, September). "The Blooming of Women's Leadership in Oil and Gas in the GCC, Middle East, and Key Enablers for their Growth". In *SPE Annual Technical Conference and Exhibition*. OnePetro.

Carter, R. (2019). "Pearl Fishing, Migration, and Globalization in the Persian Gulf, Eighteenth to Twentieth Centuries". *Pearls, People and Power: Pearling and Indian Ocean Worlds* (pp. 232–262).

Dana, L. P., Salamzadeh, A., Ramadani, V., & Palalic, R., eds. (2022a). *Understanding Contexts of Business in Western Asia: Land of Bazaars and High-Tech Booms* (Vol. 4). Singapore: World Scientific.

Dana, L. P., Salamzadeh, A., Ramadani, V., & Palalić, R. (2022b). "The New Economy with Aspects of the Bazaar". In *Understanding Contexts of Business in Western Asia: Land of Bazaars and High-Tech Booms*, Singapore: World Scientific (pp. 521–534).

Darwish, S., Ahmed, U., Bunagan, V. D., & Sison, S. M. (2021). "Women Entrepreneurs (WE): Reshaping and sustaining the Gulf Cooperation Council (GCC) Economy". In *Artificial Intelligence Systems and the Internet of Things in the Digital Era: Proceedings of EAMMIS 2021* (pp. 455–466). Cham: Springer International Publishing.

Darwish, S., Raman, R., Gomes, A. M., & Nawaz, N. (2020). "Entrepreneurship Ecosystem in GCC and India: A Perspective". *Journal of Statistics Applications and Probability an International Journal*, **9**(2), 245–256.

Friedman, B. & Friedman, B. (2020). "One Step Forward, One Step Back". *The End of Pax Britannica in the Persian Gulf, 1968–1971*, 51–81.

Gotoh, T., Saito, K., Abe, M., & Uesugi, A. (2020, August). "Excavations at Wādī al-Sail, Bahrain 2015–2019". In *Proceedings of the Seminar for Arabian Studies* (Vol. 50, pp. 171–187).

Karolak, M. (2017). "Social Media and the Arab Spring in Bahrain: From Mobilization to Confrontation". In *The Arab Spring, Civil Society, and Innovative Activism* (pp. 81–119). New York: Palgrave Macmillan.

Kharabsheh, R. A., Ensour, W., Aldulaimi, S. H., & Alazzawi, A. (2021, December). "Bahraini Female and Social Entrepreneurs Networking Behavior". In *2021 International Conference on Sustainable Islamic Business and Finance* (pp. 24–32). IEEE.

Maheep, M. & Jahanghiri, Y. (2022). "Whither Arab Women? The Arab Feminist Legacy and The Role of Women in The Arab Spring". *Al-Mada: Jurnal Agama, Sosial, dan Budaya*, **5**(1), 63–80.

Meero, A., Rahiman, H. U., & Rahman, A. A. A. (2021). "The Prospects of Bahrain's Entrepreneurial Ecosystem: An Exploratory Approach". *Problems and Perspectives in Management*, **18**(4), 402.

Mueller, C. (2016). "Anglo-Iranian Treaty Negotiations: Reza Shah, Teymurtash and the British Government, 1927–32". *Iranian Studies*, **49**(4), 577–592.

Nakibullah, A. (2018). "Economic Diversification in Bahrain". *Applied Economics and Finance*, **5**(5), 67–74.

Nuruzzaman, M. (2013). "Politics, Economics and Saudi Military Intervention in Bahrain". *Journal of Contemporary Asia*, **43**(2), 363–378.

Omar, K. M. (2021). "Measuring the Entrepreneurship Characteristics and Its Impact On Entrepreneurial Intentions". *Open Journal of Business and Management*, **9**(2), 672–687.

Palalić, R., Kahwaji, A. T., Eddin, H. N., & Riđić, O. (2021). "Entrepreneurship in Bahrain". In *Entrepreneurship in the Gulf Cooperation Council Region: Evolution and Future Perspectives,* Singapore: World Scientific (pp. 7–23).

Ramadani, V., Palalić, R., Salamzadeh, A., & Dana, L. P. (2022). "The Context for Business in Bahrain". In *Understanding Contexts of Business in Western Asia: Land of Bazaars and High-Tech Booms,* Singapore: World Scientific (pp. 243–257).

Salamzadeh, A. (2014). "Youth Entrepreneurship in Developing Countries: Do Young People Know Their Potentials?". In *The International Conference on Youth and Our Cultural Heritage,* 15–18 May, Samsun, Turkey.

Samer, B. (2017). "Tourism Development in Bahrain: Dealing with Flux and Transformation". In *International Tourism Development and the Gulf Cooperation Council States* (pp. 95–110). Routledge.

Shaver, K. G., Al-Ubaydli, O., & Wegelin, J. (2022). "A Gulf in the Gulf? Gender Differences in Entrepreneurial Mindset in Bahrain". In *Academy of Management Proceedings* (Vol. 2022, No. 1, p. 10624). Briarcliff Manor, NY 10510: Academy of Management.

Turner, B. (2000). "Bahrain: Dawlat al Bahrayn (State of Bahrain)". *The Statesman's Yearbook: The Politics, Cultures and Economies of the World 2001* (pp. 250–254).

Tuson, P. (1945). "Records of Bahrain 1820–1960". *American History,* **1861**(1900).

Wirayuda, A. A. B., Al-Mahrezi, A., & Chan, M. F. (2023). "Factors Impacting Life Expectancy in Bahrain: Evidence from 1971 to 2020 Data". *International Journal of Social Determinants of Health and Health Services*, **53**(1), 74–84.

Zuid, A. Y. (2016). "Bahrain Between British and Iranian Occupations Allegations Unit Independence in 1971". *Basic Education College Magazine For Educational and Humanities Sciences*, **29**, 1–12.

https://doi.org/10.1142/9789811283499_0005

Chapter 5

Women Entrepreneurs in Egypt

Ekaterina Vorobeva

The Research Centre for East European Studies,
the University of Bremen, Germany
vorobeva@uni-bremen.de

Abstract

Recently, Egypt has been making considerable progress on its path to gender equality and the empowerment of women. The current government acknowledged the crucial role of women in the sustainable development of the country. This realization led to the creation of various initiatives to unleash the economic potential of the Egyptian female population. Nevertheless, despite some positive improvements, women remain severely underrepresented in the entrepreneurial ecosystem of the country. Moreover, they still face numerous barriers to full participation in the business market of Egypt. Social and structural gender discrimination poses a serious impediment to women's entrepreneurship in the state. Furthermore, women often lack sufficient human, social, and economic capital to establish and successfully expand their enterprises. By adopting a gender-sensitive lens in relevant policymaking, and engaging the private sector and education institutes, the government should continue working on the improvement of the position of women in the country.

Keywords: Women entrepreneurship; minority entrepreneurship; gender discrimination; gender equality; Egypt, Africa.

1. Introduction

In the last few years, Egypt has been steadily moving toward becoming a market-oriented economy. In the Egypt Vision 2030, introduced in 2016 by the current president Abdel Fattah Saeed Hussein Khalil el-Sisi, the overall goal of sustainable development was set for the country. Achieving this goal appears to be impossible without enhancing the private sector and unleashing the economic potential of women in the country. Therefore, in the mentioned document, the government announced its commitment to the promotion of entrepreneurship as well as the empowerment of women. The political stance chosen by the government has demonstrated its first positive results — unemployment and poverty have been on the decline lately, and Egypt was the only country in the Middle East and North Africa (MENA) region in 2020 that had a positive GDP growth rate (IMF, n.d.). The Doing Business reports of the World Bank have also moved Egypt up in the ranking on the ease of establishing and managing an enterprise in Egypt.

Although women's entrepreneurship entered the agenda of the state relatively recently, many steps have already been taken on the way to better inclusion of women in the business market. The support was delivered through a variety of initiatives and programs on providing better access to funding, networks, and crucial information. However, previous research demonstrated that women still face impediments on their way to entrepreneurship due to existent sociocultural norms, gender discrimination, and their economic positions. Indeed, the number of women entrepreneurs in Egypt is the lowest in the MENA region and Sub-Saharan Africa (ILO, 2016). Their roles in society are reduced to those of a mother and a housewife (Hassan and Zaharia, 2021), and their professional capabilities are often called into question. Limited access to the generation of crucial human, economic, and social capital is one of the main factors negatively affecting women's entrepreneurship in Egypt (Salman *et al.*, 2020). Women enterprises concentrate in rural areas and present low-profit, micro-, and informal businesses with limited potential for growth.

The current chapter intends to present an overview of literature devoted to women entrepreneurship in Egypt, summarizing the main findings of relevant articles and reports. It starts with a historical perspective on economic activities in the country. Then, it describes the current entrepreneurial ecosystem of the state with its major characteristics and the role of the government in entrepreneurship assistance. Later, the chapter touches upon women's entrepreneurship in Egypt and highlights the main features of women's businesses. The main impediments that women face in their entrepreneurial activities are discussed in detail. The chapter concludes with a summary of policy recommendations and potential directions for further development outlined by previous studies.

2. Historical Overview

Egypt has been involved in international trade for several thousands of years. For example, already during the Old Kingdom of Egypt, which existed between 2700 and 2200 BC in the Nile Valley, trade connections were established with Lebanon, Anatolia, and African kingdoms such as the Kingdom of Punt (which probably occupied the territory of modern Somalia). The Old Kingdom sold ebony, mirth, and metals, and received aromatic resins and cedar from its neighbors. The expanding trade networks of the Old Kingdom had a direct impact on shipbuilding, traveling, and exploration of the sea.

In those days, almost everyone had to act at least a little as an entrepreneur; one had to master a certain skill and sell it to his or her compatriots. The diversity of existing economic activities in the territory of modern Egypt around four thousand years ago was beautifully described in the work of Dua-Kheti from Sile. The piece of literature received the name *The Satire of the Trades* and dates to around 2000 BC. In this work, a scribe, Dua-Kheti, explains to his son Pepy the advantages of the profession of a scribe in comparison to other jobs. The text elaborates on the variety of economic activities in the Egypt of those days and mentions the professions of a sculptor, jeweller, barber, bricklayer, carpenter, gardener, mat-weaver, weapon-maker, bird-catcher, and trader (Exhibit 1). Therefore, a very rich economic life was a distinctive feature of Ancient Egypt.

During the Ptolemaic and Roman periods in Egypt, Alexandria was founded by Alexander the Great and later turned into the capital and the center of education, art, and governance of the enormous Ptolemaic Kingdom. In the period between 305 and 30 BC, Alexandria also became the main place of commercial activities in the Mediterranean.

Exhibit 1. Pyramids of Giza.

Source: https://pixabay.com/photos/pyramids-egypt-egyptian-ancient-2371501/ (free for commercial use).

The trade links expanded and reached the Arabian region, Indian shores as well as China. Already in those days, although facing numerous barriers, women could play a significant role in the economy of the state (Salman *et al.*, 2020). For example, a female ruler of Egypt, Cleopatra, was actively involved in the economic affairs of the country; she attempted to introduce price control and regulate exchange rates for foreign currencies coming to the busy port of Alexandria from all corners of the world. Later, in the 1st century AD, Saint Mark the Evangelist visited and promoted Christianity in Egypt, which laid the foundation for the emergence of the Egyptian Coptic Church.

In the 7th century AD, Islam was brought to Egypt by Sassanids and gained extreme popularity, creating a unique fusion with local beliefs and rituals. This event marked the beginning of Islamic control in Egypt, which lasted until the 16th century. During this period, Egypt developed its economic and cultural connections to other Muslim states. It was one of the main countries exporting wheat and barley to the Near East. Moreover, Egypt was involved in two busy trade zones — one in the Indian Ocean and the other in the Mediterranean Sea, and significantly benefited from both (Humphreys, 1998).

In 1517, Egypt became a part of the Ottoman Empire, whose rule de jure lasted until 1914, when the United Kingdom imposed a protectorate over Egypt for the next 8 years. In 1922, Egypt declared its independence in the form of a monarchy; however, the country stayed under the influence of Great Britain for a few more decades. Due to various reasons including the tariff restrictions imposed by the United Kingdom, industrialization started developing only in the 1930s in the country. At the beginning of the 20th century, successful enterprises in Egypt were mostly owned and run by foreigners. It was only after World War II that the first factories were established by Egyptian entrepreneurs. However, the culture of bazaars continued to flourish in Egypt (Exhibit 4). Dana (2012, p. 151) describes the uniqueness of the type of economic activity: "The bazaar is a social and cultural system, a way of life and a general mode of commercial activity, with a focus on the relationship between the buyer and the seller."

Dissatisfaction with the privileged position of Westerners in Egypt resulted in anti-Western riots, a military coup, and the abdication of Farouk I in 1952 (Dana, 2000). The new government attempted to industrialize the state. During the 1960s, when socialism impacted economic policies in Egypt, monopolies got formed, preventing the realization of the economic potential of the country in full (Dana, 2000). In 1970, Anwar Sadat became the president, and the following year marked creation of the Arab Republic of Egypt, which exists to the present day. Sadat tried to encourage foreign investments with the help of the Infitah program directed at reducing the domination of the public sector and transferring the initiative to the private sector in Egyptian economic life. The increasing global demand for oil made the Egyptian GDP grow at an astonishing 11% a year between 1975 and 1980 (Elmusa, 1991).

Following Sadat's assassination, Hosni Mubarak's regime between 1981 and 2011 witnessed increased economic difficulties such as low wages and high unemployment. Falling oil prices in the late 1980s negatively affected the Egyptian economy. The Economic Reform and Structural Adjustment Program undertaken in 1991 resulted in a devaluation of the Egyptian pound, the rise of interest rates, and a worsening of the standards of living among the poor. Authoritarianism grew in the state as well as the public's dissatisfaction with corruption, deteriorating freedom of speech, and economic policies. This resulted in the 2011 Revolution in Egypt and Mubarak's stepping down. In 2014, the current president el-Sisi was elected. As a part of his structural adjustment, he introduced the aforementioned Egypt Vision 2030 agenda in 2016. The document sets several ambitious goals in front of the Egyptian population, such as the elimination of poverty, reduction of public debt, promotion of innovations, digital transformation, and active use of renewable energy, to name a few. Closely related to the topic of the current chapter, Egypt Vision 2030 aims at empowering women and youth and supporting small and medium-sized entrepreneurship.

3. Entrepreneurial Ecosystem

Located in the north of Africa in the Nile Valley with direct access to the Mediterranean Sea and the Red Sea, Egypt has a rich variety of economic activities (Exhibit 2). Agriculture, manufacturing, oil and gas extraction, and tourism are among the well-developed sectors in the state. The transport system includes an expanding railway network and the airline EgyptAir. The Suez Canal connects the Mediterranean Sea and the Red Sea, enabling easy trade between Europe and Asia. A duty-free port Said is an important harbor in Egypt allowing exports of cotton and rice, it attracts new logistics companies every year. Moreover, the country receives a significant number of remittances from Egyptians working abroad. The Central Agency for Public Mobilization and Statistics (CAPMAS) of Egypt reported an extraordinary increase in remittances; in 2015, remittances accounted for \$18.3 billion, while in 2021 this number reached \$31.5 billion (State Information Service, 2022).

After many years of turbulence, Egypt is currently enjoying political stability, which has a positive impact on the state's economy. In recent years, with the help of multiple structural reforms, the country has been steadily moving toward becoming a market-oriented economy. Since 2017, the gross domestic product (GDP) of Egypt has been increasing, from \$235 billion in 2017 to \$365 billion in 2020 (The World Bank, n.d.a). GDP at purchasing power parity (PPP) per capita also grew steadily, demonstrating improvements in the standards of living of the state's population — in 2017 the indicator accounted for \$11 014, while by 2020 it increased to \$12 607 (The World Bank, n.d.b). Unemployment and poverty rates have also been gradually declining in Egypt in recent years.

In 2020, the Doing Business 2020 report of the World Bank ranked Egypt 114 out of 190 world economies on the ease of starting and running an enterprise in the country (World Bank, 2020). It should be noted that Egypt has improved its position in the ranking during the last few years.

Exhibit 2. Nile Valley.

Source: https://pixabay.com/photos/map-land-egypt-geography-11043/ (free for commercial use).

In 2016, when Egypt Vision 2030 was just introduced by President el-Sisi, the country occupied the 131st place among the other 190 states globally (World Bank, 2016). However, during the next few years, the position of Egypt gradually improved, which points to the effectiveness of the taken political stance. By 2020, Egypt had made significant progress in eliminating barriers to starting a business, protecting investors, and enhancing its infrastructure (World Bank, 2020). However, serious difficulties continue to be experienced by businesspersons with regard to paying taxes, enforcing contracts, and trading across borders (World Bank, 2020).

However, previous studies have noted that entrepreneurship in Egypt is generally identified as "necessity or subsistence-driven" rather than "opportunity-driven" (Hassan and Zaharia, 2021). Indeed, Handoussa (2010), as well as El-Fiky (2021), mentions that high unemployment rates push young individuals to start enterprises to secure incomes. Micro-, small-, and medium-sized enterprises (MSMEs) in the country account for 99% of the entire private sector and mostly operate in trade, services, and manufacturing (Handoussa, 2010). Around 80% of micro and small-sized businesses work informally, which makes them vulnerable to shocks and limits their possible growth (Handoussa, 2010). Availability of funding remains a serious impediment on the way to entrepreneurship (Rizk and Rashed, 2019). Business owners also experience difficulties with access to information, technology, and general governmental assistance (Handoussa, 2010). However, the share of people who have started seeing more business opportunities in the Egyptian market has been increasing (Aboutaleb, 2020).

Several laws regulate business activities in Egypt including The Commercial Register Law, the Anti-Trust Law, International Trade Laws, and others. In the Egypt Vision 2030, the current government outlined its main goals to promote and sustain entrepreneurship in the country. The document presents eight main objectives among which the Robust Economy goal was set. The section mentions that the Egyptian economy should embrace science, innovation, and digitalization. It outlines the crucial importance of the promotion of small- and medium-sized entrepreneurship. Entrepreneurial activities are linked to lower unemployment rates and stable economic growth in the country.

At the moment, with the support from the relevant authorities as well as private companies, the startup ecosystem of Egypt is rapidly evolving; many incubators, capital venture firms, and entrepreneurship support initiatives have been created lately (Disrupt Africa, 2021). For example, in 2010, the Egyptian government established the Technology Innovation and Entrepreneurship Center (TIEC). It aims at financially and otherwise assisting businesses in the sector of Information and Communication Technology (ICT). As a part of TIEC, EgyptInnovate was launched later. The incubator offers funding and networking opportunities as well as business development counseling to would-be entrepreneurs. The "Fekretak Sherketak" Initiative offers funding, mentorship, education, and other resources to prospective businesspersons. Flat4Labs is one of the early-stage venture capital firms that actively invests in new innovative businesses in the country. In addition, universities also take an active part in the promotion of entrepreneurship through education; for example, Nile University and Cairo University offer relevant training and incubation programs.

All these efforts have already given the first results. In the Egyptian Startup Ecosystem Report 2021, it is mentioned that Egypt accounts for 20% of all active technology startups in Africa with the number of tech companies exceeding half a thousand (Disrupt Africa, 2021). Those new firms employ around 13,000 individuals making a feasible contribution to the elimination of unemployment in the country (Disrupt Africa, 2021). 94% of Egyptian startups are in the capital of the country, Cairo (Disrupt Africa, 2021) (Exhibit 3). The main industries where technology startups operate are e-commerce, fintech, e-health, ed-tech, recruitment, and logistics (Disrupt Africa, 2021). The Report states that 39% of the new technology companies received support from accelerators and incubators, underlining the significance of the introduced governmental initiatives (Disrupt Africa, 2021).

Exhibit 3. The Capital of Egypt, Cairo.

Source: https://pixabay.com/photos/nile-river-cairo-nile-river-egypt-4600719/ (free for commercial use).

4. Women Entrepreneurs

4.1. *Describing women's entrepreneurship in Egypt*

Looking over the history of Egypt, scholars acknowledged that women in the country always suffered from inequality and inferior position in comparison to men (Salman *et al.*, 2020). Traditionally, women were assigned the roles of housewives and mothers. However, the position of women cannot be fully understood without looking at its intersection with other social categories such as class; for instance, the generation of capital was possible only for rich women (Salman *et al.*, 2020; Vorobeva, 2022). This demonstrates the especially vulnerable position of poor women.

Despite recent positive improvements in gender equality in Egypt, women's participation in both the labor market and entrepreneurship is still significantly constrained (Hassan and Zaharia, 2021). Indeed, the number of women entrepreneurs in Egypt is the lowest in the MENA region and Sub-Saharan Africa (ILO, 2016). In 2014, women accounted for 9% of the entire number of business owners in the country (ILO, 2016). In the Egyptian Startup Ecosystem Report 2021, it was stated that only 12.5% of all tech startups are founded or co-founded by women (Disrupt Africa, 2021). The abilities of women to perform professionally are still questioned, which is reflected in the high unemployment rates among women (Hassan and Zaharia, 2021; Aboutaleb, 2020).

Economic participation of women is even lower in global comparison; Egypt ranks 146 out of 156 countries with only 18.3% of women involved in the labor market (World Economic Forum, 2021). In The Global Gender Gap Report 2021, Egypt ranked 129 out of 156 countries (World Economic Forum, 2021). The number of women in managerial positions remains extremely low; only 7.4% of managerial positions are occupied by women in the country (World Economic Forum, 2021). "These inequalities are also reflected in wage and income gaps: the estimated earned income of a woman is currently 22% of that of a man" (World Economic Forum, 2021, p. 36).

Women entrepreneurship in Egypt has several distinct features. Those few businesswomen who managed to open their own firms operate as micro-enterprises or work informally (Hassan and Zaharia, 2021;

Aboutaleb, 2020; Rizk and Rashed, 2019). The size of their businesses negatively affects profits and prospects for growth (Aboutaleb, 2020). In 2018, the number of women who didn't have any starting capital was twice as that of men (Rizk and Rashed, 2019). The age of starting an enterprise proved to be higher for women in comparison to men in Egypt (Rizk and Rashed, 2019). The businesses of women are concentrated in rural areas, where 82% of all female entrepreneurs work (ILO, 2016). They choose agriculture, retail, and wholesale trade most often as industries for entrepreneurial activities (ILO, 2016) (Exhibit 4). Interestingly, illiterate women in Egypt proved to be more likely to own enterprises. Rizk and Rashed (2019) stated that 4% of illiterate women had companies, while only 1–2% of women with education degrees did so. Despite all the limitations, curiously, in comparison to male ones, female enterprises proved to grow their revenues faster (El-Hamidi, 2011).

Concerning motivations to engage with entrepreneurship, Egyptian women were characterized as "necessity entrepreneurs" rather than opportunity ones, in line with a general trend in the country (Hassan and Zaharia, 2021). "Unpaid work, low job quality, lack of safe work conditions, the burden of family duties, lack of market opportunities and other factors push women in Egypt to seek self-employment as a last resort for survival" (Hassan and Zaharia, 2021, p. 13). However, empowerment through autonomy and learning was also mentioned as both a motivation as well as the outcome of entrepreneurial activities of women (Hassan and Zaharia, 2021). The research of Aboutaleb (2020) mentions that the main motivations for Egyptian women to start their own companies were opportunity recognition, passions and interests, autonomy, and better home–work balance. Finally, women were also motivated by bringing up positive changes to their communities through the creation of jobs (Hassan and Zaharia, 2021).

During the last year, the Egyptian government proved to be very committed to the improvement of the position of women in the labor market and the entrepreneurship ecosystem. As it was mentioned above, in Egypt Vision 2030, empowerment of women and better gender equality are set as crucial goals. Moreover, 2017 was announced as the "Year of Egyptian Women" and in the same year the National Strategy for the Empowerment

Exhibit 4. A bazaar in Cairo.

Source: https://pixabay.com/photos/bazaar-cairo-egypt-egyptian-market-2499786/ (free for commercial use).

of Egyptian Women 2030 was released (Hassan and Zaharia, 2021). The Strategy acknowledges that sustainable development of the country is impossible to achieve without the empowerment of women. It is based on four main pillars: women's political empowerment and leadership; women's economic empowerment; women's social empowerment; and women's protection. These goals are expected to be achieved through a variety of initiatives on networking, training, funding, and counseling of women entrepreneurs in different industries as well as regions of Egypt. The National Council for Women in Egypt (NCW) is ensuring that gender equality in politics, healthcare, education, labor market, and social life is implemented and enhanced (El-Fiky, 2021). Additionally, private sector companies and NGOs have been launching several women's economic empowerment initiatives. For instance, the Social Innovation Hub under the Microsoft project "Aspire Woman", seeks to unlock young women leaders' potential via soft and business skills training (Aboutaleb, 2020,

p. 20). Public banks such as, for instance, Misr Bank, support the direction followed by the government and contribute to the improvement of access of women to loans and funding (Rizk and Rashed, 2019).

4.2. *Main constraints to women entrepreneurship*

However, despite the aforementioned positive changes in the political narrative, women entrepreneurs in Egypt still encounter numerous constraints in their business activities. Due to a variety of reasons, women in Egypt are not accepted as equal economic actors; their legitimacy in the role of entrepreneurs is constantly being challenged. Elimination of this attitude may assist in unleashing the great business potential females can present in the country. That is the rationale behind the detailed discussion of barriers to women entrepreneurship in Egypt. In a nutshell, "women continue to face significant challenges however, such as the difficulty of balancing between entrepreneurship and family responsibilities; a lack of access to financial and non-financing services; lack of access to markets and technology; business networks; and a weak voice in the policy dialogue process" (ILO, 2016, p. 12). The crucial impediments are described in depth in the following.

One of the most acute problems that any businesspersons but especially women entrepreneurs experience in Egypt is limited access to credit and financial resources (Hassan and Zaharia, 2021). Only 10% to 25% of banks' clients are women, and only 7% of women entrepreneurs get loans for business purposes (ILO, 2016). Women do not usually own valuable property or land, which makes them miss the formal criteria for loans (El-Hamidi, 2011). Due to these reasons, banks consider women a high-risk category of borrowers and impose high-interest rates and additional collateral on them (Hassan and Zaharia, 2021). In some cases, acquiring a loan requires a male cosignatory, which discourages women from applying. Moreover, women face higher rejection rates for receiving credit than men (ILO, 2016). 60% of women mentioned that high-interest rates were the main impediment to getting loans (Hassan and Zaharia, 2021). 42% of women were also unsatisfied with the small size of loans offered to them by banks (Hassan and Zaharia, 2021). Therefore, most businesswomen still must rely heavily on their own savings or borrow money from family and friends (Hassan and Zaharia, 2021). Hassan and Zaharia (2021) state that in their study, to finance their own firms, 57.5% of women entrepreneurs had to use savings, 37.5% borrowed money from relatives and friends, and 18.5% had to liquidate an asset.

Another important impediment for women entrepreneurs is the prevalent set of sociocultural norms in Egypt. Islamic Shari'a promotes "relative equality" between genders where women are expected to be financially dependent on men (ILO, 2016). Thus, it remains uncommon and barely acceptable for a woman to run her own firm (Dana, 2000; Hassan and Zaharia, 2021). Women often must seek approval from their husbands as well as extended family members to engage in entrepreneurship (Hassan and Zaharia, 2021). The main roles that women are expected to perform in society are reduced to those of a wife and a housekeeper. Thus, managing a household and raising kids, women might have limited time for entrepreneurial activities (Hassan and Zaharia, 2021). They are expected to prioritize family and kids over personal development and pursuing their own passions (Hassan and Zaharia, 2021).

The aforementioned sociocultural norms lead to gender discrimination and have a negative impact on the image of women as professionals and entrepreneurs. Despite the fact that women have been shown to seek higher education more often than men in Egypt, their professional capabilities are believed to be lower than those of men (Hassan and Zaharia, 2021). The situation can be even worse for women who reside in more traditional rural areas. Women may face extreme hostility from their competitors who tend to turn a business competition into a gender competition (Hassan and Zaharia, 2021). Male employees may disobey and question the orders of their female leaders (Hassan and Zaharia, 2021).

The generation of social and human capital is another crucial constraint to women's entrepreneurship in Egypt. Due to the low number of women in managerial positions as well as gender socialization, women, as a rule, lack the necessary leadership skills to successfully run a company (World Economic Forum, 2021). ICT skills of women, crucial for the expansion of business nowadays, remain underdeveloped (Hassan and

Zaharia, 2021; Aboutaleb, 2020). Bureaucracy, the legal side of business registration, and management have also proved to be challenging for women — 29.5% of women reported that they have close to no knowledge about business registration steps (Hassan and Zaharia, 2021; ILO, 2016). Due to scarce free time, high fees, and lack of relevant information, women rarely join business associations and, thus, have difficulty developing beneficial business networks and getting crucial insights into the markets (Hassan and Zaharia, 2021). Women are often not aware of the programs and initiatives available to them (ILO, 2016). In addition, women are underrepresented in relevant business authorities and organizations and, therefore, have little influence over policies directly concerning them (Hassan and Zaharia, 2021; ILO, 2016). The lack of female mentors in incubators and business hubs prevents the spreading of gender-specific crucial business information.

Hence, women have significant difficulties in growing their enterprises due to the lack of financial resources and necessary information (Hassan and Zaharia, 2021). Women find it difficult to take part in export markets (ILO, 2016). They have little knowledge about the needs of foreign consumers. Struggling with the legal side of business management within Egypt's borders and obtaining the necessary licenses and certificates to export their products abroad appear to be very challenging for women (ILO, 2016). In addition, limited in their financial resources, women are often unable to cover high travel costs abroad to develop networks and attend business events (ILO, 2016).

5. Toward the Future

The current political stance adopted by the Egyptian government toward gender equality in the labor market and the entrepreneurship ecosystem appears to be very promising. Moreover, the first positive results in some spheres are encouraging signs to continue in the chosen direction. For example, Egypt improved women's position in power: the number of women in parliament increased from 14.9% in 2020 to 27.4% in 2021 (World Economic Forum, 2021). However, previous research demonstrated that most women are still very sceptical about whether their businesses will survive in the long run, pointing to the necessity for tailored support (Hassan and Zaharia, 2021).

Indeed, women specified the need for various kinds of governmental assistance (Hassan and Zaharia, 2021). The International Labor Organization (ILO) (2016) suggested the creation of a special governmental body that focuses on connecting all key actors to empower women and support their entrepreneurial activities more effectively. Legislation concerning women's economic rights such as property rights and inheritance should be strengthened (ILO, 2016). There is an urgent need for all kinds of financial assistance for women enterprises; banks should be encouraged to develop a gender-sensitive approach in decision-making on loans (ILO, 2016). Moreover, the government could guarantee compensation for the lack of collateral (ILO, 2016). Training in financial literacy, business-related law, and regulations as well as utilization of ICT for business purposes were proved to be in high demand among businesswomen (ILO, 2016). A better spread of information about already existing initiatives and support programs is necessary so they can reach the intended audience. Intersectionality should also find its way into relevant policymaking in Egypt — previous studies have pointed out that older women, divorced women, or women in rural areas experience distinct challenges (El-Hamidi, 2011; Vorobeva, 2022). For instance, women with small children can benefit from tax relief on childcare (El-Fiky, 2021). In addition, networking events for women shall be organized; they can cluster by industry to provide the most valuable insights for participants. Finally, women should be better involved in policymaking that concerns them in both business associations and more general governmental institutions (ILO, 2016).

Apparently, none of the aforementioned is possible without the effective elimination of gender discrimination. Gender equality should be enhanced through education, labor market participation, and a shift in gender roles. Women should get accepted as equal economic and social actors. The proposed measures should unleash the great entrepreneurial potential of the Egyptian population and lead the country to the desired goal of sustainable development.

References

Aboutaleb, G. A. (2020). *Social Media Potentials in Supporting Women Entrepreneurship: The Case of Egypt.* Master's Thesis, the American University in Cairo. AUC Knowledge Fountain. Retrieved from: https://fount.aucegypt.edu/etds/1524 (Accessed on 26 April 2022).

Dana, L.-P. (2000). "Economic Sectors in Egypt and Their Managerial Implications". *Journal of African Business*, **1**(1), 65–81.

Dana, L.-P. (2012). "Learning from Lagnado about Self-employment and Entrepreneurship in Egypt". *International Journal of Entrepreneurship and Small Business*, **17**(1), 140–153.

Disrupt Africa (2021). *The Egyptian Startup Ecosystem Report 2021.* Retrieved from: https://mcit.gov.eg/Upcont/Documents/Reports%20and%20Documents_26102021000_Egyptian-Startup-Ecosystem-Report-2021.pdf (Accessed on 27 April 2022).

El-Fiky, S. (2021). *Gendered Entrepreneurship Contextualization in Egypt: An Empirical Study on Policies for Women Entrepreneurship Empowerment.* Master's Thesis, the American University in Cairo. AUC Knowledge Fountain.

El-Hamidi, F. (2011). *How Do Women Entrepreneurs Perform? Empirical Evidence from Egypt.* The Economic Research Forum. Working Paper No. 621.

Elmusa, S. S. (1991). "The Economy". In Metz, Helen Chapin (ed.), *Egypt: A Country Study*, 5th Edition. Washington, D.C.: Federal Research Division, Library of Congress, pp. 157–159.

Handoussa, H. (2010). *Key Development Challenges Facing Egypt.* Cairo, Egypt: UNDP.

Hassan, H. & Zaharia, R. M. (2021). Women Entrepreneurship in Egypt: Is It Just as Challenging for All Women? *European Journal of Interdisciplinary Studies*, **13**(1), pp. 11–30.

Humphreys, R. (1998). Egypt in the world system of the later Middle Ages. In C. Petry (ed.), *The Cambridge History of Egypt* (pp. 445–461). Cambridge: Cambridge University Press.

ILO (2016). *Women's Entrepreneurship Development Assessment.* ILO DWT for North Africa and ILO Country Offices for Egypt and Eritrea. Cairo.

IMF (n.d.). The *Arab Republic of Egypt.* Retrieved from: https://www.imf.org/en/Countries/EGY (Accessed on 25 April 2020).

Rizk, R. & Rashed, A. (2019). *Trends and Patterns of Women's Entrepreneurship in Egypt.* The Economic Research Forum. Working Paper No. 1369.

Salman, D., Rashdan, A., & Amr, L. (2020). "Egyptian Female Entrepreneurship As Driving Factors in the Digital Era, A Hope or a Challenge". *Economics and Law*, **2**(2), 33–49.

State Information Service (2022). *Remittances of Egyptians Abroad Hit a Record in 2021.* Retrieved from: https://www.sis.gov.eg/Story/164954/Remittances-of-Egyptians-abroad-hit-a-record-in-2021?lang=en-us (Accessed on 26 April 2022).

The World Bank (n.d.a). *GDP (Current US$) — Egypt, Arab Rep.* Retrieved from: https://data.worldbank.org/indicator/NY.GDP.MKTP.CD?locations=EG&most_recent_value_desc=false&year_high_desc=true (Accessed on 26 April 2022).

The World Bank (n.d.b). *GDP per capita, PPP (current international $) — Egypt, Arab Rep.* Retrieved from: https://data.worldbank.org/indicator/NY.GDP.PCAP.PP.CD?locations=EG (Accessed on 26 April 2022).

Vorobeva, E. (2022). "Chapter 11: Intersectionality and Minority Entrepreneurship: At the Crossroads of Power and Vulnerability". In Maalaoui. A., Khachlouf, N., Dana, L.-P., Ratten, V., (eds.), *Disadvantaged Minorities in Business: Entrepreneurship for Everyone.* Springer.

World Bank (2016). *Doing Business 2016.* Retrieved from: https://www.doingbusiness.org/content/dam/doingBusiness/media/Annual-Reports/English/DB16-Full-Report.pdf (Accessed on 26 April 2022).

World Bank (2020). *Doing Business 2020. Economy Profile: Egypt, Arab Rep.* Retrieved from: https://www.doingbusiness.org/content/dam/doingBusiness/country/e/egypt/EGY.pdf (Accessed on 26 April 2022).

World Economic Forum (2021). *Global Gender Gap Report 2021.* Retrieved from: https://www3.weforum.org/docs/WEF_GGGR_2021.pdf (Accessed on 26 April 2022).

https://doi.org/10.1142/9789811283499_0006

Chapter 6

Women Entrepreneurs in Iran

Aidin Salamzadeh[*,¶] **and Léo-Paul Dana**[†,‡,§,||]

[*]*Faculty of Management, Department of Business Management, University of Tehran, Tehran, Iran*
[†]*ICD Business School Paris, Paris, France*
[‡]*Dalhousie University, Halifax, Canada*
[§]*Lappeenranta University of Technology, Lappeenranta, Finland*
[¶]*salamzadeh@ut.ac.ir*
[||]*lp762359@dal.ca*

Abstract

Women entrepreneurs are brilliant change-makers in societies as they have proven this statement by offering innovative solutions to various problems. Iranian women have contributed to the socioeconomic development of the country and this chapter provides more detailed insights into the history of women's entrepreneurship and their challenges. Besides, the authors elaborate on the entrepreneurial ecosystem and the role of women entrepreneurs as an integral part of it. Finally, the chapter concludes with some remarks on the future directions of women's entrepreneurship in Iran.

Keywords: Women entrepreneurship; female entrepreneurship; entrepreneurial ecosystem; challenges; Middle East, Iran.

1. Introduction

The success of women entrepreneurs in societies not only causes economic development but also creates sociocultural outcomes. Typically, women become entrepreneurs for many reasons, including unemployment, reduced wages, and dissatisfaction with their previous jobs. According to official statistics, in recent years the share of women's employment in Iran has only been 14%, and the unemployment rate among women, especially educated ones, has increased significantly. The unemployment rate in 2021 was even higher than the average unemployment rate in the country, especially due to the shocks imposed by the COVID-19 pandemic (Bouzari *et al.*, 2021). Therefore, due to the necessity of increasing the share of women in the national economy and dealing with their unemployment crisis, it is mandatory to provide the necessary conditions for their development and provide a basis for them to become entrepreneurs (Pereira *et al.*, 2021; Salamzadeh and Dana, 2022). In this way, they can create businesses and job opportunities for themselves and others so that they can alleviate a major current problem of society.

In today's world, the existence of widespread economic competition at the global level has forced countries to create the necessary foundations to remain in the economic arena (Salamzadeh *et al.*, 2022). Besides, to strengthen the economic base of the country, we will need women's participation in all economic activities (Dana *et al.*, 2022). In this connection, empowering women and increasing their economic power as they comprise half of society is very critical. There are many ways to achieve this. For instance, one of the ways is to increase their access to financial support. Such initiatives can help empower women in the family and community through low-interest loans and establishing of small businesses managed by women (Radovic Markovic *et al.*, 2012, 2013). Moreover, women's microcredit funds are supported through national credit organizations and non-governmental organizations, but in this connection, it is worth noting that microcredit alone cannot create justice in economic opportunities (Modarresi *et al.*, 2016).

The national statistics show that the status of women has improved compared to the past, especially based on the policies of the ninth government. Nonetheless, in many areas still there is social inequality and discrimination, which shows that society needs to establish a new attitude toward justice, to make social, organizational, and individual interests more transparent (Ramadani *et al.*, 2013; Ojong *et al.*, 2021). In this connection, one of the issues that needs the attention of the officials and those involved in women's affairs is increasing women's health status and social security. This can be achieved through the promotion of culture and literacy of women and girls, as well as their health education, promotion of health awareness in families, access of female heads of households to special insurance policies, and cheap housing, cultural, and sports complexes (Rahman *et al.*, 2022).

In a situation where the national goal is to strengthen the competitiveness of the country's economy and interact with the global economy, this issue can be raised as an obstacle on the way to achieving the desired vision (Salamzadeh *et al.*, 2017). Creating a suitable environment for the development of women's economic participation through increasing the government's share in providing free/low-cost financial facilities, long-term and low-interest loans to women, establishing the necessary support for the development of entrepreneurship and innovative activities, as well as laying the groundwork for creating stability, development, and empowerment (Bastian *et al.*, 2021). Women's cooperatives and the reform of the payment system in accordance with the level of productivity and quality of services, regardless of their gender, are possible in line with the national privatization programs and within the constitutional frameworks.

In addition, revisiting the structure and modernization of women's research and education processes to develop the quality and professionalization of research and respond to the decision-making needs of the country's executive bodies to access equal educational opportunities, expand skill knowledge, and improve the productivity of human capital are among the policies that can affect all the socioeconomic sectors (Ramadani *et al.*, 2022) (Exhibit 1). Therefore, in this chapter, the authors provide an overview of the historical trends in Iran. Then, the entrepreneurial ecosystem is explained and women entrepreneurs' status in the country is explored. Finally, the chapter concludes with some remarks on the future of women's entrepreneurship in Iran.

Exhibit 1. Iranian female students.

Source: https://pixabay.com/photos/yazd-gardens-iran-persia-asia-6304402.

2. Historical Overview

Women in ancient Iran were not only highly respected but in many cases were considered equal to men. An Iranian woman had the right to own land, could own a business, receive equal pay, was free to travel alone, and if she was a member of the royal family, could meet with advisers to discuss political matters. The official titles of the court women of ancient Iran were most likely derived from the older Elamite culture and the Median Empire, which was chronologically just before the Achaemenid Empire (about 550 to 330 BC) and its founder, Cyrus the Great (reigned about 550 to 530 BC). Cyrus established the Persian model of freedom of religion and expression of opinion in his empire, and protecting the dignity and independence of women in all social classes was considered a part of this model (Chavalas, 1996). This pattern was also followed in the Parthian (or Arsacid; 227 BC to 224 AD) empire, but due to the loss of writings and works of art after the fall of the Parthians to the Sassanid government (224 to 651 AD), there is no clear evidence of the living conditions of women in that period. However, there are many pieces of evidence left from the Sassanid period that show that women's rights were still protected at the same level or higher than in the Achaemenid period (Sarfaraz, 2017; dos Santos *et al.*, 2019).

For instance, Irdabama (5th and 6th century BC) was an Iranian merchant woman during the reign of Darius the Great (who ruled from 522 to 485 BC). She is the most well-known and richest businesswoman who is mentioned in the documents of the Achaemenid Empire in Persepolis. She was clearly a very wealthy person and was likely to be from the nobility or royalty class. Several seals relating to her business dealings have been found. The historical literature describes how goods and food rations were distributed among the employees of Irdabama and how she supervised her vast assets (Tuplin, 1998). She traveled widely in Iran and Mesopotamia with her servants. Irdabama had 480 workers, mainly in what is now called Shiraz. She is the most prominent example of Iranian women of this period, who owned land and real estate in Iran as well as in other lands such as Babylon, Syria, and Egypt. She was mainly active in wine and grain trading and supervised her commercial businesses, production centers, and real estate (Bahadori, 2017; Brosius, 2020).

Iranian women always had a high position in the culture of ancient Iran until the fall of the Sassanid Empire with the invasion by Muslim Arabs in 651 AD. After that, the longtime dignity of a woman as an independent human being and the owner of her own destiny was replaced by assumptions that placed women as second-class citizens, in need of a man's supervision and guidance. Nevertheless, Iranian women entrepreneurs still continued their participation in the socioeconomic development of the region in various parts of the country (Forouharfar, 2021).

Since the beginning of the past century, the world has seriously faced a socioeconomic phenomenon called women's economic participation in jobs outside the home (Modarresi *et al.*, 2017). The employment situation of women in Iran is similar to that in developing countries, i.e., it is not a favorable situation, and women always have fewer job opportunities and often work in the informal sector with low pay (Javadian and Singh, 2012). In fact, it can be said that according to the statistics, only 14% of women are economically active, with the most activity in the service sector (45.8%) and about 16.7% in the industrial sector (manufacturing).

About 71% of the employees in the service sector participate in educational, health, and social activities. Most of the female employees are in the group of employees and only 0.9% of them are employers. Working women mostly live in urban areas (56%) and are in the age group of 25–29 years. Besides, the majority of them are engaged in marriage and raising children and in general family affairs. It is noteworthy that Iran's employment rate is low compared to other countries. The unemployment rate of the population is also increasing day by day in a way that currently 26.1% of active women in urban areas are unemployed (Bagheri *et al.*, 2022). The unemployment rate of educated women has been constantly increasing, especially in recent years. Therefore, in trying to improve the current situation and get rid of such problems and obstacles, a collective responsibility has been raised among policymakers and activists in recent years. Unfortunately, national research in the field of women's entrepreneurship is very limited due to the newness of the subject, and since even women's employment in Iran has always faced problems, women's entrepreneurship is facing increasing problems (Bahramitash and Esfahani, 2014).

From 1991 to 2007, the employment rate in Iran changed from 39% to 41%, then it decreased to 35% until 2011, After that, it started an increasing trend that continued almost until the start of the COVID-19 pandemic and brought the employment rate back to 39% in 2018 and 2019 (Salamzadeh and Dana, 2021). With the start of the pandemic, the employment ratio decreased again and within a year it decreased by nearly 2.8%. This amount of change in one year is completely unprecedented in the last three decades. The changes in the employment of women and men after 2005 are more or less similar to the general changes in the index that were described. The trend of changes in women's employment from 1990 to 2006 was increasing and continuous, and its amount increased from 8% to 15% during this period (Salamzadeh and Ramadani, 2021). Iran's employment rate in 1990, i.e., the years after the war, was lower than all other countries. This position improved until 2005, but it decreased again. If we do not consider Yemen, in 2013, 2014, and 2015, Iran had the lowest percentage of female employment among all countries in the region. In addition, considering the lack of change in the overall index currently and the existing single points, it seems that the ratio of men's employment has also experienced a downward trend in this period (Khyareh, 2018).

The best years of women's employment in Iran were the years 2003 and 2004, as well as the years 2015, 2016, and 2017. In most of the other years, the growth amount is less than 1%. However, in both periods, the growth that had occurred was offset by subsequent declines. Another noteworthy point is the greater fragility of the women's employment market. The impact of the COVID-19 pandemic on the labor market showed that women's employment is not only smaller than men's employment market but also more vulnerable (Dheer and Salamzadeh, 2022). The ratio of employment to the population in 2020, i.e., the first year of the pandemic, among women, has decreased by more than twice that of men. Of course, it is better to use the absolute number of employees to study the impact of the pandemic on men's and women's markets, which is out of scope of this chapter. Considering that this phenomenon seems to be global, it is better to consider this issue at the global level (Bagheri *et al.*, 2022; Bouguerra *et al.*, 2015).

The ratio of employment to the population of women in countries belonging to different income groups — based on the ranking proposed by the World Bank — has significant differences. The percentage of women's employment in high-income countries such as Sweden, Japan, Canada, and England is around 52% (Salamzadeh and Ramadani, 2020). In countries with upper middle income such as Turkey, Azerbaijan, Malaysia, and Brazil, the index is spread around a lower value, i.e., nearly 40%, but in two countries of this category, Jordan and Iraq, the employment ratio of women is less than 20% (Ottesen *et al.*, 2022; Yenilmez, 2019). Maybe because there are still fewer opportunities for women to work in these countries. In low-income countries, there are two types of behaviors regarding the employment rate of women. In some of them, such as Rwanda, Madagascar, North Korea, and Mozambique, the ratio of women's employment to their population is very high, that is, women have to work side by side with men and in some cases more than them, although in some other countries such as Sudan and Somalia, the percentage of female employment is very low. Lower-middle-income countries such as Iran are seen everywhere in the distribution, and the ratio of employment to the population in them does not focus on specific values (Afolabi *et al.*, 2022).

It seems that it is possible to explain the diversity of women's employment rates in countries by using the income group of countries and some other factors such as access to natural resources like oil and gas and some other factors such as historical, cultural, and political factors. As mentioned earlier, the ratio of employment to the population of women in Iran is one of the lowest employment ratios in the world, and in the last two years only in Yemen, Iraq, Jordan, Palestine, and Djibouti has the ratio of employment of women been lower than in Iran. But to have a broad understanding of the phenomenon of low employment of women in Iran, we enlargen the circle of comparison a little and compare the ratio of women's employment in Iran with that in other countries. Among the high-income countries, the ratio of employment to its female population is not close to that of Iran (Salamzadeh and Ramadani, 2020). The employment rate of women in Iran is similar to small clusters of middle-to-high-income countries (Iraq and Jordan), low-income countries (Yemen, Syria, Afghanistan, Somalia, and Sudan), as well as some low-middle-income countries (Palestine, Djibouti, Egypt, Algeria, Lebanon, India, Morocco, Tunisia, and Pakistan). In all these countries, the ratio of employment to the population of women is less than 20% (Cheratian *et al.*, 2022; Ogundana *et al.*, 2021; Rezaei *et al.*, 2017).

Considering that the group of countries seems to partially explain the ratio of employment to the population of women, it is possible to compare countries, not the ratio of employment to the population of women, but the inequality of employment between men and women. For this comparison, some studies divide the ratio of employment to the population of men by the ratio of employment to the population of women and call it the gender inequality index of employment. If the result is equal to 1, it means that the ratio of employment in men and women is equal, and if it is greater than 1, it means that the ratio of men's employment is higher than the ratio of women's employment. The advantage of this index compared to the previous index is that it is less dependent on the economic group of countries (Naderi *et al.*, 2022).

Examining this index shows that the distance between Iran and the world is greater than what was shown until now. The index of gender inequality of employment in Iran in all the years that are included in the study period has a gap with the countries of the world that is worthy of reflection, and in some years it is higher than all the countries in the World Bank data. In a recent year, when the data were fully available, i.e., 2020, the value of this index in Iran was 5.6. In other words, the employment rate of men in this year in Iran was 5.6 times the employment rate of women. Meanwhile, according to the latest statistics, this ratio is 1.29 in selected countries (Cheratian *et al.*, 2022).

3. Entrepreneurial Ecosystem

An entrepreneurial ecosystem is a collection of people, organizations, methods, laws, events, etc. in a geographical area that affects entrepreneurial activities (and not necessarily job creation) in that area. Any institution that actually or potentially encourages and supports entrepreneurship is considered a beneficiary of an entrepreneurial ecosystem, such as government bodies, universities, banks, entrepreneurs, growth centers, acceleration centers, social leaders, labor representatives, etc. Therefore, it is necessary to recognize and design suitable policies for the development of entrepreneurship, paying attention to all the existing elements of the ecosystem and their interactions. It is noteworthy that any weakness in an institution or a subsystem affect the overall functioning of the ecosystem. Thus, a successful entrepreneurial ecosystem develops as a function of what happens in different areas (Khavarinezhad and Jafari-Sadeghi, 2022). Figure 1, which is borrowed from Salamzadeh and Ramadani (2021), illustrates the main components of the entrepreneurial ecosystem in Iran.

Although the economic participation rate of women in Iran has doubled compared to 70 years ago, women still have a very small share in the economy and labor market of Iran. As economic surveys show, the economic participation rate of women in Iran is about 16%. The latest report of the Statistics Center on the unemployment situation of women in Iran shows that this summer the share of women in the labor market was less than 20%, while the unemployment of women in this season is much higher than that of men and is reported to be more than 18%. Official reports show that women's economic participation has increased from

International level

- International venture capitalists/venture capital funds
- International startup studios
- Non-resident Iranian experts and entrepreneurs

National level

- Vice-Presidency for Science and Technology
- Ministries
- Universities
- Funds such as the Iran National Innovation Fund and its subsidiaries, the Export Development & Technology Exchange Fund, Iran National Science Foundation, and VC Fund Association;
- National Elites Foundation
- Iran Lab Expo
- National Technomart of Iran
- Iranian Knowledge-based Leaders Federation
- Iran Lab Expo
- Export Development & Technology Exchange Corridor
- Labs' Net
- Center for Progress and Development of Iran

Industrial level

- Innovation centers
- Innovation factories
- Sector-specific accelerators, venture capital funds, and incubators

Firm level

- New technology based firms (NTBFs) — Knowledge-based firms
- Startups
- Creative firms

Team level

- Independent teams
- Supported teams

Individual level

- Freelancers
- Intended/potential entrepreneurs
- Young talented individuals

Figure 1. The major players in the Iranian entrepreneurial ecosystem.

Source: Salamzadeh and Ramadani (2021).

9.2% in 1956 to more than 16% in 2018 (Salamzadeh and Ramadani, 2020). However, this progress is not suitable for the social, cultural, and economic changes required in society, except in the category of education, where in recent decades many women have been added to the Iranian educated population. At times, it has been reported that the number of women who have entered university is more than men (Salamzadeh and Kawamorita Kesim, 2017).

The low economic participation and the high unemployment rate of women show that half of Iran's population still has many problems participating economically. The scope of these barriers is wide ranging from social to cultural problems. Although the approaches to the category of women's entrepreneurship have changed a lot, this is still the dominant approach that gives priority to men. Employers consider men to be the breadwinners of the households and if they have to make a choice, they choose a male labor force in equal conditions between men and women. In some cases, they go beyond this and even demand the employment of women with a lower salary than men. In their opinion, because women are not the breadwinners of the house, they can do with lower salaries. In addition, some employers are still of the opinion that women have less power, ability, and skills to work. A mentality that is fundamentally wrong and looks more like a justification for destroying women's rights (Modarresi *et al.*, 2016, 2017).

The set of problems that exist in the field of women's entrepreneurship has prompted women to start special activities in the field of entrepreneurship and self-employment. When they see that they are facing various obstacles to work, they try to start and run their own businesses by themselves. Now many women are looking to be their employers and we see that women have made great strides in various jobs, including freelancing jobs. Meanwhile, there is an important point that should be considered. There have been many analyses about the work situation of women and almost all of them agree that women face social, cultural, and economic obstacles to economic participation (Mohamadi, 2020). These challenges are mentioned in the next section.

With greater globalization, in the last 15 years the Iranian startup ecosystem has seen different faces and brands. Brands that are mostly associated with the names of young men wearing t-shirts. Ironically, Iran's startup ecosystem is one of the few business environments where Iranian girls and women have had a successful and impressive presence in comparison to other sectors and other economic areas of the country (Golzard, 2020). The flexible working environment of startups, the lack of well-defined frameworks and gender restrictions in startup workplaces, the need for new skills, and, most importantly, the desire to follow the successful examples from other countries of the world, in which women have played a prominent role, have led to the success of Iranian women in startups (Salamzadeh, 2018).

4. Women Entrepreneurs

Most of the development indicators in Iran do not have such a distance from other countries in the world. As a result, it can be said that improving any index might not be a priority. However, the women's employment index in Iran is similar to that of the war-torn countries such as Syria, Iraq, Afghanistan, Yemen, and Palestine. In the last few decades, other economic issues such as inflation have been controlled, even if in a temporary manner, and in some cases, they have become single digits and have approached their conventional values in the world, but the employment ratio of women in Iran has not changed much in 30 years. In the past, it has never been close to its conventional values in the rest of the world and Iran has always been among the worst performers from the point of view of women's employment. The slow increase in women's employment in the 1970s was broken in the mid-1980s, and efforts to restore it in the mid-1990s were also unsuccessful. The result is that the employment ratio of Iranian women has not improved even to a little extent in over 20 years (Exhibit 2). Besides, the ratio of employment to population among men is about 5 times that of women, and in many years the number of female students has been more than the number of male students (Sarfaraz and Faghih, 2011).

Another reason that can raise the issue of women's employment as an effective entry point to Iran's development path is that employment is a basic and comprehensive issue. When a person does not have a job, s/he does not have independence and support, and when s/he does not have support, s/he does not have a voice in society. Raising issues such as inflation control as the most important economic issue in the country and focusing on it has created a discourse and confused social groups. In fact, inflation is a technical and complex issue, its nature is such that it depends more than anything on the decisions of the government and managers, and people cannot participate in its realization. When the population of a

Exhibit 2. Iranian female model.

Source: https://pixabay.com/photos/woman-beauty-culture-traditional-7372855.

society does not have jobs, talking about controlling liquidity, controlling the monetary base, economic growth, and raising economic literacy is nonsense. Hopefully, the national slogan of creating employment has a lot of capacity to start the engine of development in the country. The main issue of employment in Iran, as shown in detail in the extant literature, is primarily nothing but increasing the employment of women. However, this issue is not addressed as much as it should be in the public domain (Makizadeh *et al.*, 2022; Mahdipour, 2022).

Women make up half of Iran's workforce, but their potential has not yet been used in the development of the country, and until a solution is devised, Iran will not find its way to development. In this section, we review the main barriers to women's employment and entrepreneurship. It can be clearly said that environmental factors play a very critical role compared to individual factors because personality traits and psychological abilities are greatly influenced by environmental factors. The social, cultural, legal, religious, political, and economic situations of society certainly play a significant role in strengthening or weakening activities in different manners, especially entrepreneurship (Exhibit 3). We categorized the obstacles to women's entrepreneurship as follows (Borna *et al.*, 2022; Sadrnabavi and Daneshvar, 2022):

- **Cultural barriers**: These barriers are related to the shared values, beliefs, norms, and, in a single word, the culture. These include (i) the existence of gender discrimination in the workplace in job promotion,

Exhibit 3. Iranian female photographers.

Source: https://pixabay.com/photos/mashhad-girls-mellat-park-winter-1702209.

education, social participation, and the like; (ii) the negative attitude of people and those involved in women's entrepreneurship; (iii) the negative reactions of officials, organizations, and economic and social institutions; (iv) The existence of a patriarchal culture and men not accepting women as leaders; (v) Lack of trust in women entrepreneurs and avoiding cooperation with them; (vi) The existence of religious and stereotyped beliefs about women; (vii) Social insecurities (for example, intercity business trips and staying in hotels and places); and (viii) The existing inequality in the education system in families, schools, and universities.

- **Individual barriers**: Some barriers are related to women workers and entrepreneurs themselves. These include (i) Fear of failure and more irritability of women than men; (ii) Not having the right role model; (iii) Being satisfied with the current job conditions and fearing risk (resistance to change); (iv) Low self-confidence and lack of courage; (v) Lack of women's physical ability to bear more work pressures; (vii) Age and number of children; and (viii) The effect of marriage (unmarried women have more freedom of action for economic and social activities).
- **Social barriers**: In Iran, and some parts of the world, society imposes a set of barriers on women entrepreneurs, namely: (i) Intersection of company affairs with family issues and inconsistency of role expectations; (ii) Lack of encouragement of women by families and lack of support from other sources; (iii) Absence of entrepreneurship counseling centers in universities from government institutions; and (iv) Parents' or spouse's opposition to female entrepreneurship.
- **Legal barriers**: Rules and regulations can also be barriers for women entrepreneurs in Iran. Among these, the following are of paramount importance: (i) The existence of cumbersome administrative rules and existing bureaucracy; (ii) Lack of sufficient laws regarding the protection of women entrepreneurs; (iii) Laws governing the family, such as prohibiting a woman from working if her husband does not consent, a written lease to leave the country; (iv) Lack of adequate facilities in the field of maternity leave and related issues; (v) Lack of necessary rules and regulations for business development; and (vi) Difficulty in obtaining permits.

- **Information barriers**: Women entrepreneurs might not have enough access to information and also may lack relevant skills. These barriers include (i) The component of lack of guidance in the field of marketing and lack of awareness of the business environment and the environmental factors; (ii) Low level of technical knowledge in women and lack of professional skills; (iii) Lack of legal information; and (iv) Lack of management skills.
- **Economic and business barriers**: Last but not least is economic and business barriers, which can affect the level of women's entrepreneurship to a great extent. These include: (i) Providing initial capital and necessary liquidity; (ii) Difficulty in entering and developing the presence of women in the competitive market; (iii) Limits of women's economic freedom (freedom to choose the place of investment, type of activity, etc.); (iv) The negative attitude of banks and financial institutions toward granting loans and facilities to women entrepreneurs; (v) Banks' delay in the timely provision of financial resources needed by women entrepreneurs; (vi) Problems related to getting the right suppliers, raw materials, and the like; (vii) Women's inability to provide the collateral required by banks and financial institutions; (viii) Inability to gain the trust of customers, suppliers, investors, etc; (ix) Problems related to paying taxes, insurance costs, controlling and managing costs, etc.; and (x) Lack of suitable business locations, hardware and software facilities, transportation, etc.

5. Toward the Future

Global information shows that women-owned small and medium-sized enterprises (SMEs) mostly tend to operate in low-profit or low-growth sectors. Retail services, beauty, and food are some of the sectors that women focus on. In Africa and Asia, about 75% of women are in these customer-oriented sectors (Salamzadeh and Ramadani, 2020). They are rarely employed in the mining, construction, electronics, or software industries. The problem is that usually women concentrate on businesses with low income and have a limited economic perspective for themselves. Accordingly, they usually choose jobs and businesses for themselves, which reinforces this gender-based income gap. As a result, focusing on these sectors limits women's financial opportunities, and unfortunately, banks also consider these jobs as lesser investment opportunities. This is while SMEs are of great importance because they have a specific performance in all economies of the world. Thus, encouraging more women to have SMEs and entrepreneurial lifestyles will increase job prospects and create an opportunity for their economic development. However, studies have also shown that when women are transferred to male-dominated sectors, they can earn three times more than in female-dominated sectors.

If Iran wishes to step up along the path of development and evolve from being a lower-middle-income country to an upper-middle-income country, it should increase the employment of its women to the level of the latter class of countries. The average ratio of employment to the population of women in these countries is 40%. Besides, the annual growth rates of the ratio of employment to the female population in the last 30 years show that Iran is in an optimistic situation and if it maintains a continuous growth trend and uses the existing capacities, it can add an average of 1% to its female employment ratio annually. At this rate, according to some studies, Iran needs almost 28 years to cover this distance from 12% to 40% (Salamzadeh and Ramadani, 2020). It goes without saying that high self-confidence, creative thinking, a positive outlook on life, anticipating the future, not being afraid of failure, having a sense of solving problems, a sense of helping others, concern for serving others, honesty and balance between one's role at home and outside the family, defining a clear entrepreneurial goal, training, and having a long-term plan and goal are among the features that woman entrepreneurs should consider in order to succeed in any niche markets.

References

Afolabi, J. A., Raifu, I. A., & Aminu, A. (2022). "Entrepreneurship and Unemployment Nexus in MENA: Does Institutional Quality Matter?". *Journal of Small Business & Entrepreneurship*, 1–33.

Bagheri, F., Ghaderi, Z., Abdi, N., & Hall, C. M. (2022). "Female Entrepreneurship, Creating Shared Value, and Empowerment in Tourism; The Neutralizing Effect of Gender-Based Discrimination". *Current Issues in Tourism*, **26**(21), 1–18.

Bahadori, A. (2017). "Achaemenid Empire, Tribal Confederations of Southwestern Persia and Seven Families". *Iranian Studies*, **50**(2), 173–197.

Bahramitash, R. & Esfahani, H. S. (2014). "Gender and Entrepreneurship in Iran". *Middle East Critique*, **23**(3), 293–312.

Bastian, B. L., Hill, S., & Metcalfe, B. D. (2021). "Gender, Culture and Entrepreneurship in the Middle East and North Africa (MENA)". In *Women's Entrepreneurship and Culture* (pp. 20–46). Cheltenham, UK: Edward Elgar Publishing.

Borna, E., Afrasiabi, H., Kalate Sadati, A., & Kermani, M. (2022). "Women's Perception of Barriers and Facilitators of Success: A Grounded Theory Study". *Woman in Development & Politics*, **20**(3), 501–527.

Bouguerra, N. (2015). "An Investigation of Women Entrepreneurship: Motives and Barriers to Business Start Up in the Arab World". *Journal of Women's Entrepreneurship and Education*, **1–2**, 86–104.

Bouzari, P., Salamzadeh, A., Soleimani, M., & Ebrahimi, P. (2021). "Online Social Networks and Women's Entrepreneurship: A Comparative Study between Iran and Hungary". *Journal of Women's Entrepreneurship and Education*, **3–4**, 61–75.

Brosius, M. (2020). "Achaimenid Women". In *The Routledge Companion to Women and Monarchy in the Ancient Mediterranean World* (pp. 149–160). London: Routledge.

Chavalas, M. W. (1996). *Women in Ancient Persia (559–331 BC) Brosius* (258 p.). Maria: New York: Clarendon Press. [*History: Reviews of New Books*, **25**(1), 40–40].

Cheratian, I., Goltabar, S., & Calá, C. D. (2022). "The Unemployment–Labor Force Participation Linkage In Iran's Women Labor Market". *International Journal of Development Issues*, **21**(2), 218–236.

Dana, L. P., Salamzadeh, A., Ramadani, V., & Palalic, R., (eds.) (2022). *Understanding Contexts of Business in Western Asia: Land of Bazaars and High-tech Booms* (Vol. 4). Singapore: World Scientific.

Dheer, R. J. & Salamzadeh, A. (2022). "Pandemic Threats: How SMEs Can Respond to the Challenges from Global Crises". *International Journal of Globalisation and Small Business*, **13**(1), 1–17.

dos Santos, V. F., Morais, G. M., de Araújo Ribeiro, F. F., & Jardim, D. (2019). "Female Entrepreneurship: Evolution, Current Challenges, and Future Prospects". *International Journal of Business Administration*, **10**(5), 1–21.

Forouharfar, A. (2021). "The Institutional History of Women Entrepreneurship in Modern Persia: A Socio-historicism Approach", Rezaei, S., Li, J., Ashourizadeh, S., Ramadani, V. and Gërguri-Rashiti, S. (Ed.) The Emerald

Handbook of Women and Entrepreneurship in Developing Economies, Emerald Publishing Limited, Bingley, pp. 165–189. https://doi.org/10.1108/978-1-80071-326-020211010.

Golzard, V. (2020). "Economic Empowerment of Iranian Women Through the Internet". *Gender in Management: An International Journal*, **35**(1), 1–18.

Javadian, G. & Singh, R. P. (2012). "Examining Successful Iranian Women Entrepreneurs: An Exploratory Study". *Gender in Management: An International Journal*, **27**(3), 148–164.

Khavarinezhad, S. & Jafari-Sadeghi, V. (2022). "The Context for Business in Iran". In *Understanding Contexts of Business in Western Asia: Land of Bazaars and High-Tech Booms* (pp. 61–90), Singapore: World Scientific Publishing.

Khyareh, M. M. (2018). "Determinants of Female Entrepreneurship in Iran: An Institutional Approach". *Economic Annals*, **63**(216), 111–129.

Mahdipour, F. (2022). "Instagram as a Means of Empowering Iranian Women by Focusing on Home-based Businesses". *Journal of Women's Entrepreneurship and Education*, **2022**(3–4), 223–245.

Makizadeh, V., Yousafzai, S., Jamshid, S. A., & Nasiri, M. (2022). "Iranian Women Entrepreneurs: Creating Household Value Through Entrepreneurship". In *Research Handbook of Women's Entrepreneurship and Value Creation* (pp. 211–233). Bingley, UK: Edward Elgar Publishing.

Modarresi, M., Arasti, Z., Talebi, K., & Farasatkhah, M. (2016). "Women's Entrepreneurship in Iran: How Are Women Owning And Managing Home-Based Businesses Motivated to Grow?" *International Journal of Gender and Entrepreneurship*, **8**(4), 446–470.

Modarresi, M., Arasti, Z., Talebi, K., & Farasatkhah, M. (2017). "Growth Barriers of Women-Owned Home-Based Businesses in Iran: An Exploratory Study". *Gender in Management: An International Journal*, **32**(4), 244–267.

Mohamadi, K. (2020). *In-Depth Analysis of Women Entrepreneurs in Turkey, Germany and Iran*. Doctoral dissertation.

Naderi, N., Khosravi, E., Azadi, H., Karamian, F., Viira, A. H., & Nadiri, H. (2022). "Barriers to Developing Social Entrepreneurship in NGOs: Application of Grounded Theory in Western Iran". *Journal of Social Entrepreneurship*, **13**(2), 221–243.

Ogundana, O. M., Simba, A., Dana, L. P., & Liguori, E. (2021). "Women Entrepreneurship in Developing Economies: A Gender-Based Growth Model". *Journal of Small Business Management*, **59**(sup1), S42–S72.

Ojong, N., Simba, A., & Dana, L. P. (2021). "Female Entrepreneurship in Africa: A Review, Trends, and Future Research Directions". *Journal of Business Research*, **132**, 233–248.

Ottesen, A., Banna, S., Alzougool, B., & Simović, V. (2022). "Driving Factors for Women's Switch to Electric Vehicles in Conservative Kuwait". *Journal of Women's Entrepreneurship and Education*, **3–4**, 46–67.

Pereira, J., Braga, V., Correia, A., & Salamzadeh, A. (2021). "Unboxing Organisational Complexity: How Does it Affect Business Performance During the COVID-19 Pandemic?" *Journal of Entrepreneurship and Public Policy*, **10**(3), 424–444.

Radovic Markovic, M., Salamzadeh, A., & Razavi, M. (2013). "Women in Business and Leadership: Critiques and Discussions". In *The Second International Scientific Conference on Employment, Education and Entrepreneurship* (pp. 19–31). Belgrade, Serbia.

Radovic Markovic, M., Lindgren, C., Grozdanic, R., Markovic, D., & Salamzadeh, A. (2012). Freedom, individuality and women's entrepreneurship education. Entrepreneurship Education-A Priority for the Higher Education Institutions, Kiten, Bulgaria.

Rahman, M. M., Salamzadeh, A., & Tabash, M. I. (2022). "Antecedents of Entrepreneurial Intentions of Female Undergraduate Students In Bangladesh: A Covariance-Based Structural Equation Modeling Approach". *Journal of Women's Entrepreneurship and Education*, **1–2**, 137–153.

Ramadani, V., Gërguri, S., Dana, L. P., & Tašaminova, T. (2013). "Women Entrepreneurs in the Republic of Macedonia: Waiting for Directions". *International Journal of Entrepreneurship and Small Business*, **19**(1), 95–121.

Ramadani, V., Rahman, M. M., Salamzadeh, A., Rahaman, M. S., & Abazi-Alili, H. (2022). "Entrepreneurship Education and Graduates' Entrepreneurial Intentions: Does Gender Matter? A Multi-Group Analysis Using AMOS". *Technological Forecasting and Social Change*, **180**, 121693.

Rezaei, S., Dana, L. P., & Ramadani, V., (eds.) (2017). *Iranian Entrepreneurship: Deciphering the Entrepreneurial Ecosystem in Iran and in the Iranian Diaspora*. Cham: Springer.

Sadrnabavi, F. & Daneshvar, H. (2022). "Lived Experiences of Successful Women Entrepreneurs (Smes) in Iran: A Feminist Phenomenological Study". *Qualitative Research in Financial Markets* (Ahead-of-print).

Salamzadeh, A. (2018). *Start-up Boom in an Emerging Market: A Niche Market Approach* (pp. 233–243). Cham: Springer International Publishing.

Salamzadeh, A. & Dana, L. P. (2021). "The Coronavirus (COVID-19) Pandemic: Challenges Among Iranian Startups". *Journal of Small Business & Entrepreneurship*, **33**(5), 489–512.

Salamzadeh, A. & Dana, L. P. (2022). "A Systematic Literature Review of Crisis Management in and by Small and Medium-Sized Enterprises". *Small and Medium Sized Enterprises and the COVID-19 Response*, (38–61). UK: Edward Elgar Publishing.

Salamzadeh, A. & Kawamorita Kesim, H. (2017). "The Enterprising Communities and Startup Ecosystem in Iran". *Journal of Enterprising Communities: People and Places in the Global Economy*, **11**(4), 456–479.

Salamzadeh, A. & Ramadani, V. (2021). "Entrepreneurial Ecosystem and Female Digital Entrepreneurship–Lessons to Learn From An Iranian Case Study". In *The Emerald Handbook of Women and Entrepreneurship in Developing Economies* (pp. 317–334). Bingley, UK: Emerald Publishing Limited.

Salamzadeh, A., Arasti, Z., & Elyasi, G. M. (2017). "Creation of ICT-Based Social Start-Ups in Iran: A Multiple Case Study". *Journal of Enterprising Culture*, **25**(01), 97–122.

Salamzadeh, A., Radović-Marković, M., & Ghiat, B. (2022). "Women Entrepreneurs in Algeria. Women Entrepreneurs in North Africa: Historical Frameworks, Ecosystems and New Perspectives for the Region", pp. 87–102, Singapore: World Scientific.

Sarfaraz, L. (2017). *Women's Entrepreneurship in Iran*. Switzerland: Springer.

Sarfaraz, L. & Faghih, N. (2011). "Women's Entrepreneurship in Iran: A GEM Based-Data Evidence". *Journal of Global Entrepreneurship Research*, **1**(1), 45–57.

Tuplin, C. (1998). *Women in Persia-M. Brosius: Women in Ancient Persia 559–331 BC*, Oxford Classical Monographs (pp. xx + 258). Oxford: Clarendon Press, 1993. Cased, £ 35. ISBN: 0-19-815009-1. *The Classical Review*, **48**(1), 104–106.

Yenilmez, M. I. (2019). "Women on Boards Improving Women's Empowerment Through Entrepreneurship in Turkey". In *Handbook of Research on Entrepreneurial Leadership and Competitive Strategy in Family Business* Pennsylvania, United States (pp. 22–41). IGI Global.

https://doi.org/10.1142/9789811283499_0007

Chapter 7

Women Entrepreneurs in Israel

Osnat Akirav[*,††], Léo-Paul Dana[†,‡,§,‡‡], A. Allan Degen[¶,§§], Bella L. Galperin[‖,¶¶] and Meron Medzini[,‖‖]**

[*]*Western Galilee College, Israel*
[†]*ICD Business School Paris, Paris, France*
[‡]*Dalhousie University, Halifax, Canada*
[§]*Lappeenranta University of Technology, Lappeenranta, Finland*
[¶]*Ben Gurion University, Israel*
[‖]*University of Tampa, USA*
[**]*Department of Political Science, Hebrew University of Jerusalem, Jerusalem, Israel*
[††]*osnatak@bezeqint.net*
[‡‡]*lp762359@dal.ca*
[§§]*degen@bgu.ac.il*
[¶¶]*bgalperin@ut.edu*
[‖‖]*mmedzini@zahav.net.il*

Abstract

Some nations are secular in that they have a separation between church and state, while others have declared themselves to be Christian states, and yet others are Islamic states. There is only one Jewish state though, and that is Israel, the subject of this chapter. Jewish women have continuously lived in Israel, before either Christianity or Islam was established. The Virgin Mary was among them. In Israel today, women entrepreneurs are very active and the ecosystem encourages women entrepreneurship.

Keywords: Bedouin; Druze; Jews; m-commerce; startup nation; technology.

1. Introduction

Israel covers slightly over 20,000 km^2. Its neighbors are Egypt, Jordan, Lebanon, Syria, and the Palestinian Authority territories.

The Land of Israel is the historical homeland of the Jewish people, and the State of Israel is the nation-state of the Jewish people, in which it realizes its natural and historical right to self-determination. That said, it has a heterogeneous population; the country is home to Bahai, Christians, Druze, Jews, Muslims, Samaritans, and others. Immigrants come from around the world. Exhibit 1 shows women learning Hebrew in Ethiopia before immigrating to Israel.

Savta Gamila (Exhibit 2), a Druze industrialist who manufactures soap, employs 50 women in Israel and 60 disabled people at her packaging plant in the Netherlands; she has been a leader in the emancipation of women in the Druze community (Akirav, 2019).

Women like her have long been at the forefront of the business ecosystem in Israel (Kurlander and Efrati, 2019). Other well-known women

Exhibit 1. Ethiopian women preparing to immigrate to Israel.

Source: Photo © Léo-Paul Dana.

Exhibit 2. Druze industrialist Savta Gamila.
Source: Photo © Léo-Paul Dana.

entrepreneurs are Pnina Rosenblum, who founded *Pnina Rosenblum* an Israeli cosmetics and care company (blue-and-white brand) with 30 years of experience. Yafit Greenberg is a businesswoman specializing in advertising. When commercial television began broadcasting in 1993, she offered low-cost advertisement slots in a similar style to the newspaper adverts. Her unusual advertising style sees her front the advert herself to talk about the product. Ofra Strauss is an industrialist and the chairperson of the Strauss group, which is the second largest food product manufacturer in Israel. In addition, she is the president of Jasmin NGO, promoting Jewish and Arab Israeli women's entrepreneurship. Yasmin Lukat, is the founder of the Israel Collaboration Network (ICON), an organization linking Israeli entrepreneurs with venture capitalists and key connections in Silicon Valley. Kira Radinsky sold her consumer analytics company "SalesPredict" to eBay for millions of dollars and today is the Israeli Chief Scientist at eBay. Yozmot Atid (a nonprofit organization) was established in 2015 to reduce the social gaps in Israel by empowering the underprivileged and providing them with tools to help them establish and develop small businesses, with an emphasis on women's entrepreneurship, in the geographic and social periphery of Israel. So far, over 5,000 women have undergone the empowerment process and are part of the 'Yozmot Atid' alumni.

The Israeli innovation authority, which is a government statutory corporation responsible for Israel's innovation policy, initiated a project

Exhibit 3. Trilingual sign at a bank in Israel.
Source: Photo © Léo-Paul Dana.

called "Women in Tech" to reduce the gender gap in high-tech. Its first step was to produce a comprehensive report with current data about women in high-tech and suggest action items to begin with.

Arabic and Hebrew are widespread languages in Israel; Amharic, English, French, Spanish, and Russian are also common. Exhibit 3 shows a trilingual sign at a bank in Israel featuring Arabic, English, and French.

From its independence in 1948 to the 1970s, Israel was governed by the Labor Party with socialist policies. During the past 50 years, its economy has shifted to one focused on high value-added, technology-based products and services. Israelis have reached the position of being third in the world in terms of university degrees per capita.

Israel was the first nation to launch m-commerce, allowing Israelis to use mobile phones to activate fuel dispensers and to pay for petrol at service stations. The level of venture capital is second only to the US (Hartz, 2018). Israel also has more startups per capita than any other country in the world (Coleman, 2018). Some successful examples that have gained attention globally include Fiverr, StoreDot, and Wix

(Bussgang and Stern, 2015). In 2017, Intel purchased Mobileye, an Israeli startup, for $15 billion.

Israel has been responsible for many innovations, for example, the invention of the USB stick and the development of WAZE. There is also a brain-drain as successful Israelis often use their talents and networks elsewhere; Gurau, Dana, and Katz-Volovelsky (2020) focus on Israelis in China's industrial markets.

Prudent fiscal and monetary policies, liberalization of trade, de-regulation, privatization, and removal of exchange controls boosted the economy that became characterized by a per capita gross domestic product (GDP) at par with western European economies, and growth rates as high as Asia's tigers.

2. Historical Overview

> The Land of Israel was the birthplace of the Jewish people. Here their spiritual, religious and national identities were shaped... Here they wrote and gave the Bible to the world....
>
> — Declaration of the Establishment of the State of Israel published in the *Official Gazette*, May 14, 1948

In Biblical times, the Jewish kingdoms of Judaea and Israel (Samaria) were founded here, and the tribe of Zebulun specialized in commerce. Foreign trade accelerated economic development, especially under King Solomon. In 586 BC, Jewish sovereignty ended when the Babylonians captured Judea and Samaria and exiled the citizens. King Cyrus of Persia later permitted Jews to return to Judea. The country then came under the rule of Alexander the Great's descendants and was ruled by Greeks until a Jewish rebellion, headed by the Hasmonean family, created an independent Jewish state, but that ended when the Romans occupied it in 63 BC. The Romans ruled the country through a series of proxy kings; the most famous was Herod, during whose reign Jesus preached his sermons. A rebellion in 70 AD ended the autonomous existence of Judea, launching centuries of exile until re-establishment of Israel in 1948. During occupation by foreign troops, Jerusalem came to be known as *Aelia Capitolina*, and the Jewish kingdom of Judaea was renamed *Syria Palaestina*.

Exhibit 4. Safed.

Source: Photo © Léo-Paul Dana.

The Jewish community that remained in the country after 70 AD lived predominantly in the cities of Jerusalem, Hebron, Tiberius, and Safed (Exhibit 4). This land later fell under the influence of the Byzantine Empire. Then came the Muslim conquest in the 8th century, lasting until 1089, when the Crusaders arrived, established a Christian state, and exterminated many Muslims and Jews. In Jerusalem, the Crusaders transformed the Dome of the Rock (Exhibit 5) — an Islamic shrine — into a church and the Al-Asqa Mosque into a royal residence. Saladin defeated the Crusaders in 1281, and the country was then ruled by the Egyptian Mamelukes from 1291 until the Ottomans arrived.

Exhibit 5. Gold-covered Dome of the Rock in the walled city.
Source: Photo © Léo-Paul Dana.

Ben-Zvi (1966) noted that the Jewish community, already vibrant during the 15th century, was enthusiastic about the arrival of Ottoman rule in 1517. He noted that sultans "refrained completely from meddling in the lives of their Jews" (1966, p. 229). On Ottoman-era maps, the area making up the modern State of Israel is divided into the Ottoman: (i) Mutasarrifate of Jerusalem — also referred to as Jerusalem Sanjak (Yazbak, 2017) — and (ii) Syria Vilayet, which was subdivided into prefectures, including the Acre Sanjak (Late Ottoman Galilee, successor to the Safed Sanjak) and the Nablus Sanjak, among others. In 1888, these were transferred to the Beirut Vilayet.

In exchange for guaranteeing a substantial increase in the yearly tax revenues, Sultan Suleiman the Magnificent granted a long-term lease on the Tiberias region to Dona Gracia (Mendes) Nasi — in 1558 she, thus, obtained ruling authority over the region. With the help of the sultan, she began to rebuild the area's abandoned towns to make them available to refugees from Spain, so they could settle there. Her aim was to turn

Tiberias into a major new center of Jewish settlement, trade, and learning. This venture was one of the earliest attempts at a modern Zionist movement.

As of 1840, the majority of the population of Jerusalem was comprised of Jews. From the early 1840s, Jews emerged from the walled Old City of Jerusalem, establishing new neighborhoods.

Until 1864, Haifa was a district in the prefecture (sanjak) of Acre, with a rapidly developing port on the Mediterranean Sea. In 1869, Templers (rooted in Lutheranism) established a German Colony in Haifa. Between 1876 and 1908, Ottoman Sultan Abdul Hamid II initiated reforms and encouraged the migration of Muslims to the Acre prefecture, and in 1878, he exempted migrants from land taxes for 12 years. This encouraged Muslims from North Africa and the Caucasus Mountains as well as from Bosnia to settle in Haifa.

The Bedouins — tribal groups whose traditional lifestyle was nomadic pastoralism — raised camels,[1] goats, and sheep for a livelihood. As explained by Degen, El-Meccawi, and Kam (2019), camels were used as pack animals, for transportation, and for ploughing. Tribal rulers — powerful leaders at the time — charged caravans for passage across the desert. There were two principal communities of Bedouins in the region. Those in the north were of Syrian ancestry, while Bedouins in the south (Exhibit 6) had their origins in tribes that came from Saudi Arabia. The two groups were not related; they spoke dissimilar dialects. The Bedouins in the Negev Desert did not register their lands; this exempted them from paying taxes and serving in the army. By the late 19th century, the traditional pastoral economy of the Bedouins had evolved into a mixed agricultural and pastoral economy. As the Ottomans began building the railroad to Egypt, many Bedouins were attracted to wage labor.

Meanwhile in Europe, "A whole series of special taxes were invented and enforced against Jews ... meat cost a third more to the Jews ... a percentage tax was levied upon all rents received by Jews and on profits ... printing presses owned by Jews paid annually ... the Jewish head of a family had to pay a special tax ... Jewish youths were stripped of practically

[1]Degen *et al.* (2019) found that although transportation and ploughing were replaced by motorized vehicles, there is still a desire to maintain camels for traditional reasons.

Exhibit 6. Bedouin woman weaving.

Source: Photo © Léo-Paul Dana.

all safeguards and legal reservations ...” (Harold, 1892, pp. 28–29). Following large-scale pogroms against Jews in the Russian Empire in 1882, numerous Jews felt anti-Semitism was so rife that there was no future for them in that empire. A student group, the *Bilu'im*, arrived in Syria Vilayet and established villages on land they purchased from local Arabs.

Harms and Ferry noted that at the time, “Jews already resided in Palestine, some of whom had been there as long as any of the native Arabs” (2012, p. 60). The old Jewish communities were known as the

Old Yishuv. During the 19th century many Jews here were self-employed artisans and peddlers. Harms and Ferry elaborated that these Jews "were Arabic-speaking Ottoman citizens who were integrated into the culture and, for all intents and purposes, had decent relations with the native Christians and Muslims (2012, p. 61). A few of them became middlemen facilitating trade between Arab growers and European industrialists. For a detailed discussion of the Old Yishuv, see Meron (2022).

In 1894, Theodore Herzl, who came from a Hungarian Jewish family, began to ponder the fate of the Jews. Very much under the influence of nationalism in the various parts of the Austro-Hungarian empire, he argued that the Jews had an ancestral homeland from which they were driven out centuries ago.

In 1897, he called for a Zionist Congress in Basle, which proclaimed that the Zionism's goal was a recognized Jewish state. He established the World Zionist Organization as its governing structure, which would authorize him to negotiate with the Ottoman Empire for a concession of land for the purpose of a Jewish state. He also sought the support of the major European powers. In 1901, the World Zionist Organization created the Jewish National Fund (JNF) to raise funds to purchase land under Ottoman rule and later administered by the British (Exhibit 7). Financial assistance came from Jewish philanthropists, including Sir Moses Montefiore. In his novel, *Altneuland* (Herzl, 1902), Herzl envisioned the return of Jews to the land of their origin, still under Ottoman rule.

In 1903, the British proposed the creation of an autonomous Jewish area in Uganda, but Jews wanted to return to the historical land where they had their roots — not an imperialist colonialization. With Albert Einstein's support, the Technion was established in 1912; today, it is the leading university for engineering in Israel (Beyar *et al.*, 2017).

Zionist aspirations were achieved during the First World War when under the command of General Sir Edmund Allenby, the British captured Ottoman territories: Beersheba was captured on October 31, 1917, and on November 2, the British Foreign Secretary — Arthur James Balfour — signed the document that came to be known as the Balfour Declaration. (See: https://avalon.law.yale.edu/20th_century/balfour.asp.) A major power, now on the verge of capturing a substantial area of land from the retreating Ottoman Empire, committed itself to sponsoring the creation of a national Jewish homeland. The British proceeded to capture Gaza on

Exhibit 7. JNF "blue box" to collect funds to purchase land and re-create a country.
Source: Photo © Léo-Paul Dana.

November 7 and Jaffa on November 16. Finally, the British occupied Jerusalem on December 11, 1917.

The Treaty of Versailles set up a system of mandates, for the administration of former possessions of Germany and the Ottoman Empire, and to prepare them for future independence. Based on this promise, in 1920, the newly created League of Nations awarded the British the mandate over land from the Mediterranean Sea to Iraq (henceforth Mandatory Palestine) — an area of 120,466 km^2 — with the understanding that the mandatory government would implement the Balfour Declaration. On April 25, 1920, the San Remo Conference confirmed the Balfour Declaration's pledge concerning the establishment of a Jewish national home in Palestine. At this conference, the mandate for Palestine — including the Golan Heights — was presented to the United Kingdom; the basis for the British regime in Palestine was the Balfour Declaration. The mandate was ratified by the Council of the League of Nations on June

24, 1922. France backed the establishment of a Jewish homeland in Palestine, and the United States followed suit.

Although the League of Nations recognized the legality of the Balfour Declaration, the British were not pressed to conform to it. In 1922, most of the land for Palestine (89,213 km^2 of the 120,466 km^2) was designated to form the Emirate of Transjordan,[2] and Jewish settlement was prohibited there. In 1923, the United Kingdom ceded the Golan Heights to the French Mandate of Syria.

Jerusalem developed rapidly in Mandatory Palestine and the city's business sector grew (Exhibit 8). In 1924, the High Commissioner for Palestine opened King George V Avenue, which became a major artery.

In 1930, a British Commission recommended that immigration be curtailed to fit the country's absorptive capacity. Nevertheless, during the mandate, the Jews managed to slowly create their own administrative,

Exhibit 8. Businesses in Jerusalem.

Source: Photo © Léo-Paul Dana.

[2]Severed from British Mandatory Palestine, Transjordan later became the Hashemite Kingdom of Jordan.

Exhibit 9. Tel Aviv.

Source: Photo © Léo-Paul Dana.

educational, medical, and financial institutions, trade unions, industrial bases and, above all, advanced agriculture. In 1932, 1934, and 1936, the Levant Fair was held in Tel Aviv (Exhibit 9) to promote trade.

The British kept a tight hold on the economy. They went as far as disallowing Bedouin Arabs from collecting salt from Sodom. Meanwhile, camel trade dwindled with the arrival of the automobile. Formerly wealthy people became impoverished, and many worked for wages in Jewish agricultural settlements. By now, Jews had established institutions including banks and trade unions, economic arrangements ranging from small businesses to collective communities, and several forms of settlements including *moshavim* (the singular of which is *moshav,* or settlement), and communal *kibbutzim* (the singular of which is *kibbutz*, or cooperative).

The ideology of the *kibbutz* involved a communal sharing of work (as per one's ability), profit (as per one's needs), child-rearing, and leisure time, on communal grounds. Meals and child-care were provided. The *kibbutz* economy was based originally only on agriculture. Today, *kibbutzim* have highly developed industries, producing a wide variety of products, including plastics, irrigation systems, metal products, and even computer components — 60% of the output is exported. In addition, urban *kibbutzim* have been established, most of which provide services (e.g., education), and have reformed the communal structure.

In 1939, the United Kingdom was strategically concerned about retaining, and even strengthening, its friendship with Arabs as it would be a valuable asset to have them as allies on the eve of a war. The MacDonald White Paper of 1939 restricted Jewish immigration and land purchase, and, thus, confirmed the pro-Arab policy of the British.

World War II resulted in the extermination of 6,000,000 Jews. Following the war, the Jews of British Mandatory Palestine, whose population reached 600,000, engaged in anti-British acts, eventually forcing the British government to abandon the mandate. In 1947, the UK asked the UN to propose a solution for the future of Palestine. Resolution 181 was adopted to partition the country into two states, terminate the mandate, and internationalize Jerusalem. Nine percent of the area of the land received by the British as Mandatory Palestine was allotted to the Jews, while the rest would yield the Arabs two states, namely Jordan and Palestine. While the Jews accepted, the Palestinian Arabs and the neighboring Arabs states rejected the resolution and vowed to undo it by war, which broke out on November 30, 1947, as Egypt, Iraq, Jordan, Lebanon, and Syria united to fight against the possibility of a Jewish state. Azzam Pasha, Secretary-General of the Arab League, exclaimed: "This will be a war of extermination and momentous massacre." Egypt occupied the Gaza Strip and Jordan occupied East Jerusalem and the West Bank of the Jordan River. The Israelis were able to withstand the war because they had a well-organized army, a working economy, a robust financial system, reserves of food, a highly motivated population, and first-class civilian leadership embodied in its founding father David Ben-Gurion. Thus, British Mandatory Palestine was carved up, but not according to Resolution 181. On May 14, 1948, the State of Israel was declared. War raged on and one of its consequences was the creation of a Palestinian refugee problem.

As a result of hostility against Jews in Arab countries (Browne, 1948), there also came to be Jewish refugees. Beginning in 1948, approximately 850,000 Jews were forced to leave Arab countries in which they had lived for millennia, and became Jewish refugees. Many arrived in Israel to escape religious persecution in their countries of origin, with a large number identifying themselves as Arabic-speaking Jews rather than as Israelis. Julius (2018) argued that the Jewish exodus from Muslim lands and the flight of Palestinian refugees constituted an unfinished population exchange, with Jewish rights yet to be addressed.

In 1949, armistice agreements between Israel and Egypt, Lebanon, Jordan, and Syria ended the war, but failed to promote peace; Arab nations violated the agreements, blocked Israeli shipping from using the Suez Canal and the Straits of Tiran, proclaimed an economic boycott of Israel, and launched cross-border raids. Incidents became common and the situation deteriorated rapidly toward another war. Israel's economy survived this massive challenge with the help of world Jewry and German reparations. Concomitantly, the state regulated many sectors, and taxes were high, as military expenditures placed a high toll on the economy. The socialist policies of the Labor-led government were not conducive to private business.

El Al became the first airline based outside North America and Europe to offer scheduled flights over the North Atlantic in 1951. These were operated by Lockheed Constellations (see Exhibit 10), stopping in Gander, Newfoundland.

In 1956, Egypt nationalized the Suez Canal, the result of which was a new conflict — France and the UK angered by Egypt. It was the start of a second war with Israel, during which Israel captured and occupied the entire Sinai. As a result of American pressure, Sinai was returned to Egypt in 1957.

Israel's thriving economy, expanding international ties, growing tourism, and the completion of its nuclear facility in Dimona, a city in the Negev desert, alarmed neighboring states. During the 1960s, the Arab

Exhibit 10. Constellation at London Heathrow.
Source: With permission from the Marvin G. Goldman Collection.

countries created a unified command, absorbed massive quantities of Soviet weapons, and sought to halt Israel's water works. In January 1965, the newly created Palestine Liberation Organization (PLO) launched its first military operation against Israel. Also in 1965, a new harbor was built at Eilat.

A third war brewed in 1967, with the re-establishment of the Arab High Command, a joint effort of Iraq, Syria, and the United Arab Republic (UAR) — as Egypt was called at the time. On May 19 — at the request of the UAR's President Nasser — the UN began withdrawing its peacekeeping forces from the Gaza Strip, a stretch of land which the UN had allocated to the Palestinians but which was controlled by Egypt since 1948. Despite the accord confirming that the Gulf of Aqaba was an international waterway, on May 22, 1967, the UAR blocked the Straits of Tiran, preventing all Israeli cargo from reaching or leaving Eilat, Israel's only port on the Red Sea. That day, Israeli Prime Minister Eshkol publicly declared to Cairo and Damascus that Israel had no desire to wage war against them. On June 5, 1967, Eshkol sent a communication to Jordan's

Exhibit 11. General Moshe Dayan.
Source: Photo © Léo-Paul Dana.

King Hussein, "We shall not initiate any action whatsoever against Jordan. However, should Jordan open hostilities we shall react with all our might" (Mann, 1973, p. 185). Israel's General Moshe Dayan (Exhibit 11) had already declared that a threat of invasion from Jordan would be "a move which would oblige the Israel Army to capture the West Bank of the river Jordan" (Dayan, 1966, p. 36). What came to be known as the Six-Day War broke out on June 5, 1967. Israel occupied the Gaza Strip, the Golan Heights, and the West Bank. On June 5, 1967, Israeli forces cut off the Gaza Strip from Egypt; later that day, Jordan opened a second front, with fighting in Jerusalem. On June 6, the Israelis penetrated the West Bank; that same day, the UN Security Council approved a cease-fire resolution. On June 7, on the Egyptian front, Israeli troops occupied Sharm el Sheikh, thereby putting an end to the blockade of the Gulf of Aqaba. The Israelis reached the Suez Canal on June 8, 1967, and this ended the war with Egypt. During the next two days, Israel took control of the Golan Heights, from which the Syrians had been shelling Israeli civilian targets.

The Israeli offer to withdraw from Sinai and the Golan Heights in return for full peace was rebuffed by Egypt and Syria. Various attempts to bring about a resolution of the crisis failed. With the failure of diplomacy, Egypt's new president Anwar Sadat, felt he had to engage Israel in a war that would start a political process. His gamble paid off.

Meanwhile, as a result of the Six-Day War, Israel's economy boomed and there was massive immigration. The Gaza Strip, the Golan Heights, and the West Bank were integrated into the Israeli economy. East Jerusalem became increasingly heterogenous, but integration was costly, and discontent was on the rise. In 1973, biophysicist Ephraim Katzir became president of Israel. Exhibit 12 shows him shaking hands with a young graduate.

The state of ceasefire between Israel and its Arab neighbors ended when Syria and Egypt launched an attack on Israeli forces in the Sinai and

Exhibit 12. Ephraim Katzir in red.

Source: Photo © Léo-Paul Dana.

the Golan Heights on the most sacred Jewish Holy Day, Yom Kippur. At first (October 6–9, 1973), Israel was caught by surprise and was unprepared, thus suffering many casualties and the loss of weapons. The tide turned on the Golan Heights on October 10 and in Sinai on October 15 when Israeli forces crossed the Suez Canal and reached some 101 kilometres from Cairo. At this point, the Soviet Union intervened and demanded an immediate cease-fire, which was accepted on October 22, 1973 (Security Council Resolution 338).

The war cost Israel 2,600 lives, and 1.5 years of its national product. Israel was forced to accept the proposals of US Secretary of State Henry Kissinger; Israeli forces withdrew from their previous positions. Prime Minister Yitzhak Rabin, whose policy was to oversee the rehabilitation of the Israeli economy, accepted an agreement with Egypt on further withdrawal in Sinai. During these turbulent times, taxes were high in order to pay for a high national defence budget. With the Labor Party in power, the state was deeply involved in the heavily regulated economy characterized by powerful unions.

Led by Menachem Begin (Exhibit 13), the Likud Party was elected in 1977, and the Camp David Accords established the framework for peace with Egypt. On March 26, 1979, Prime Minister Menachem Begin signed a peace treaty with Egypt's President Sadat. Under the terms of this accord, Israel returned the entire Sinai Desert to Egypt.

In 1982, Israel found itself engaged in another war, this time against the PLO in Lebanon. Its forces reached Beirut and destroyed PLO infrastructure; the PLO relocated to Tunisia.

By 1984, Israel was on the verge of economic collapse. The overprotected economy needed massive restructuring, so the government launched a comprehensive economic stabilization program. This emergency measure included a wage freeze, cuts in public spending and pegging of the national currency to the US dollar. In September 1985, a new currency was introduced; one thousand Israeli shekels became one new Israeli shekel (NIS).

During the first Gulf War, Israel yielded to American demands and did not respond to 39 scud missile attacks from western Iraq. During the early 1990s, many Jews arrived from the former Soviet Union; they were mostly well-trained, educated people who contributed enormously to

Exhibit 13. Menachem Begin.
Source: Photo © Léo-Paul Dana.

Israel's growing high-tech industries and medical services. Israel also absorbed 30,000 immigrants from Ethiopia.

June 1993 marked the launch of the "First Entrepreneurship Course in the Arab Sector." Also, the American Jewish Joint Distribution Committee (JDC) launched an entrepreneurship course for single mothers.

In September 1993, Israel and the PLO signed their first accord. In 1994, Israel and Jordan signed a peace agreement and, for the first time since 1948, borders opened (Exhibit 14). At the Casablanca Conference, the Arab boycott of Israel crumbled. Fast-growing markets opened to Israel, while foreign investment rushed in.

Exhibit 14. Open border between Israel and Jordan.
Source: Photo © Léo-Paul Dana.

As less capital was being spent on defence, more was available for research and development (R&D) in technology. During the 1990s, Israel was characterized by high-tech activity (Almor and Heilbrunn, 2013). According to Frucht-Eren (1996), Israeli researchers were responsible for major contributions, including: the discovery of a bacterium that is toxic only to mosquito larvae, and was adopted by the World Health Organization to control malaria; the first demonstration of the effectiveness of deprenyl in treating Parkinson's disease; the first clinical diagnosis of amniocentesis, used to identify abnormalities in a foetus; affinity chromatography; an instrument to scan and sort cells to detect cancer at an early stage; a strategy to fight parasitic weeds, which has already saved crops in Africa and the Middle East; an encoding technology for protecting computer-generated data, used in smart-cards; crystallization of the ribosome; and revelation of the three-dimensional structure of the enzyme responsible for nerve impulses. Additionally, Israeli researchers developed the following: a drug for Alzheimer patients; a new method of transplanting bone marrow from non-compatible donors; a pediatric heart surgery technique; lithium substitutes for psychiatric use; a protein to treat chronic hepatitis and herpes; a medical procedure to treat earthquake victims crushed under rubble; a method to heal shattered bones; and a drug to control multiple sclerosis.

Formerly agricultural cooperatives, *kibbutzim*, diversified to produce computer chips and software (Dana, 1999). Heilbrunn (2008) found a substantial increase in innovative activity among *kibbutzim*. At *Kibbutz Sde Eliyahoo*, farmers use barn owls for pest control of organic produce, a safer solution than pesticides for crops. This project has brought together Israelis, Jordanians, and Palestinians, supported by the Ministry of Agriculture and the Ministry of Cooperation.

By 2000, *Wired* had ranked Israel as the fourth most influential high-tech hub in the world, after Silicon Valley, Boston, and Stockholm-Kista. According to DeFontenai and Carmel (2001), Israel had 135 scientists, technicians, and engineers in engineering and life sciences per 10,000 employees — compared to 80 per 10,000 in the US. Coupled with high expenditures on R&D, this transformed Israel into a highly advanced country, with a technology-driven economy, a mere 2% of which was derived from agriculture — although agriculture still provides much to the local market (Exhibit 15).

In 2005, a Likud-led coalition headed by Ariel Sharon unilaterally decided to remove all Israeli presence in the Gaza Strip. In 2008, Innovation Africa was founded as a nonprofit social enterprise to bring Israeli agricultural, solar energy, and water innovations to villages in Africa.

As of 2009, under the leadership of Netanyahu, Israel focused on building an ecosystem to propel itself into a startup hub. The Israel Innovation Authority, formerly known as the Office of the Chief Scientist, became a central governmental agency responsible for fostering innovation; in 2013, it worked with Nielsen and Partam Hi-Tech, an Israeli venture capital fund, to create the Nielsen Innovate Fund.

As Israel's economy flourished, Fraiberg (2017, p. 353) examined this nation's startups as the result of innovation systems or "constellations of resources" (e.g., technologies, knowledge workers, regulations, policies) that increase economic growth. Exports grew, including military hardware,

Exhibit 15. Making juice from locally grown oranges.
Source: Photo © Léo-Paul Dana.

high-tech products, pharmaceuticals, and electronics. Ousset-Krief (2018) reported that Israel had become the world's second innovation hub after Silicon Valley.

In 2020, COVID-19 hit Israel seriously. In July, Israel Aerospace Industries and Rafael signed an agreement with the Emirati Group 42 to cooperate toward a technology to combat COVID-19. The following month, Donald Trump announced a deal he had brokered between Israel and the United Arab Emirates (UAE), culminating in an agreement calling for Israel and the UAE to establish mutual diplomatic relations and the inauguration of flights between Tel Aviv and Abu Dhabi. The deal drew immediate support from Bahrain, Egypt, and Oman. In September, Israel signed the Abraham Accords signaling peace and cooperation with Bahrain and the UAE. Economic consequences were seen as unlimited. Israel and the UAE agreed to allow 28 direct flights weekly between the countries. This was in addition to unlimited flights to and from the

Eilat-Ramon Airport. The Migal Galilee Research Institute https://www.migal.org.il/en — a regional R&D center of the Israeli Science and Technology Ministry — was among the first in Israel to cooperate with the UAE.

In October 2020, Israel announced normalization of relations with Sudan. In December, an Israeli delegation met with King Mohammed VI of Morocco and full diplomatic relations with Morocco became official.

3. Entrepreneurial Ecosystem

While the traditional bazaar, as an institution, is alive and well in Israel, this country has been focusing on high-tech innovation. Israel has an unusual combination of high growth and a stable economic infrastructure. The state traditionally did relatively little to encourage enterprise or economic growth; rather, private initiatives did so (Dana, 1999).

More than half of Israel is a desert, but much is cultivated, even under arid conditions. Over 60 years ago, Catarivas (1957) argued that "impossible" does not exist in the Hebrew language. Drip irrigation was an Israeli invention, Israel built the world's largest water desalination plant, and much agriculture in this country thrives on recycled water and water purified by ultra-violet light. While Water-Gen extracts water from the air, Israel also developed technology that allows potatoes and tomatoes to be irrigated with salt water. It is the only country in the world with a net gain in its number of trees. Israeli technology allows blind people to see virtually (Dana, 2018), and Israel leads the world in medical patents.[3] In Haifa, MeMed has regulatory approval on a point-of-care medical device that determines within minutes if an infection is bacterial or viral. This innovation will greatly reduce the inappropriate use of antibiotics, and thus lower the risk of antibiotic resistant microbes.

As the late Lord Rabbi Jonathan Sacks suggested, one can change the world not by the idea of power but by the power of ideas and that is the essence of Judaism. The Jews are people whose heroes are teachers, whose citadels are houses of study, and whose passion is learning.

[3] The PillCam (camera in a pill that is swallowed) for endoscopy was invented in Israel.

During the first decades following independence, enterprises were hindered by bureaucratic red tape, punitive tax rates, and required payments to the national insurance scheme, *Bituah Leumi*. In 1987, reforms were instituted to help small businesses, and corporate tax rates fell from 61% to 45%, but Israel still had neither a venture capitalist network nor loan funds for small firms (Katzenstein, 1991). Bijaoui and Regev (2015) concluded that most entrepreneurs in Israel were ready to cooperate with an open incubator. Beyar *et al.* (2017) summarized: "The explosive growth in startup companies is fairly recent in Israel's history. Education, science, and industry have been important elements of Israeli culture even before Israel's birth as a nation, yet the explosive growth is only evident in the past two decades, therefore, time is also an important factor. It is difficult to delineate and isolate specific factors and their impact on the growth and success of the life sciences industry in Israel. Clearly, a combination of factors is key in generating an entrepreneurial culture: hunger for innovation, lack of natural resources, educational and technological infrastructure, infusion of new immigrants who are trained engineers and scientists, efficient government support through incubators and other mechanisms, and the availability of private investments" (p. 2567).

Foreign investors are attracted to Israel's highly educated and motivated workforce and the industrial parks wherein technology is highly concentrated. Incubators, such as the Nielsen Innovate Fund, have been important in supporting the entrepreneurial ecosystem in Israel (Yin, 2017).

The Ministry of Industry and Trade supports numerous technological incubators, including the Meytav Technological Incubator that focuses on the life sciences sector.

The government has a very positive attitude toward foreign investment; foreigners can participate in all sectors of the economy, except those concerning national defence. At the Ministry of Industry and Trade, the Investment Promotion Center is a full-service, "one-stop shop" providing information and contacts for firms considering expansion in Israel. To enhance matters, Israel offers tax holidays, tax allowances, tax reductions, and accelerated rates of depreciation.

With approximately 200 venture capital firms in Israel, finance is no longer a problematic issue. Furthermore, special financial incentives are offered to industries that contribute to employment and to exports. From its capital in Jerusalem, the state offers a variety of grants. Among these are grants for developing innovative products (50% of approved expenditures) and for new ventures (66% of approved expenditures). Assistance is available to train employees and to reduce the cost of rent. Besides, the government provides market research grants and subsidies toward the preparation of business plans. The Marketing Encouragement Fund, for instance, provides financial support to enterprises seeking to enlarge their international marketing efforts. Bi-national funds are also available in Israel, including the Singapore Israel Industrial Research and Development Fund. Complementing the many grants, loans are also readily available. There are several loan funds in Israel, including government, philanthropic, and private funds, some described by Dana (1999). Now that the historical context and entrepreneurial ecosystem in Israel has been discussed, we turn to the role of women entrepreneurs.

4. Women Entrepreneurs

Women in Israel — regardless of religion — were the first in the Middle East to obtain the right to vote. Subsequently, the role of women in Israel changed more rapidly than in neighboring countries. The *kibbutz* movement contributed to this, as men and women participated equally on a rotational basis to various jobs. Defence considerations also emancipated the women in Israel. Since boys and girls were sent to the army, both men and women gained various skills, i.e., assets to be used in the non-military economy. Women in Israel have, on average, more academic degrees than the men.

Nevertheless, in some traditional families, women continue to help their husbands in the family business. Exhibit 16 features an Arab Israeli woman.

Yazamiyot, established in 2012 by Hilla Ovil Brenner and Shiran Melamdovsky, is the largest community of women entrepreneurs in Israel, helping women in all stages of their entrepreneurial journey. The overall goal of *Yazamiyot*, according to Melamdovsky, is "to meet, network, learn and help each other, and our vision is to dramatically increase the presence of women entrepreneurs across these industries in the next few years.

Exhibit 16. Shepherding sheep.
Source: Photo © Léo-Paul Dana.

In Tel Aviv, there is much awareness as to the gender gap, but our community aims to combat this by creating great collaborations and opportunities" (Batsheva, 2022). The organization has mentorship programs and office hours, develops and manages courses for different startup stages, and cooperates with tech corporates and institutions including Google Tel Aviv on Google Campus for Moms, a program designed to empower new mothers to pursue entrepreneurial roles, Microsoft Accelerator, Rise — Barclays innovation program — WIX, and the US Embassy. It also leads early stage courses at Tel Aviv University. In some municipalities, *Yazamiyot* is working with women who did not previously believe they could become entrepreneurs. The program has been exemplary in training and also mentoring women to be entrepreneurs in Israel, which is greatly increasing the number of women in the high-tech and biotechnology sectors.

The program appears to be quite successful. In 2015, according to the Global Startup Ecosystem, Tel Aviv was in fifth place in the world for the proportion of businesses founded by women. Approximately 20% of businesses were founded by women, whereas the global percentage was approximately 18%.

In 2019, a report by the Mastercard Index of Women Entrepreneurs (MIWE) named Israel as the fourth best country in the world for women entrepreneurs, and in 2020, it named Israel as the top country. This recognition was based mainly on the support provided to Israeli women in small and medium-sized enterprises. The report also stated that: "Israeli women are more driven (by 2.3% on average) than Israeli men to pursue business opportunities and gain independence and economic self-reliance" (Eve Young, 2020).

More recently, the 2021 MIWE report ranked Israel in the top 10 economies in the world (ranked 8th) for women entrepreneurs. The 2021 MIWE report is composed of 12 indicators and 27 sub-indicators to create three "Components" including women's advancement outcomes; knowledge assets and financial access; as well as entrepreneurial supporting conditions. These dimensions rank factors and conditions that support and drive the female share of business owners across 65 economies (The Mastercard Index of Women Entrepreneurs, 2022).

While mainstream women in Israel experienced emancipation, Bedouin men continued to expect their women to fulfil traditional roles; for instance, Bedouin women are expected to bear many children, care for them, and even to arrange marriages. Bedouin women are responsible for the upkeep of the home, including preparing traditional bread (Exhibit 17), cooking, cleaning and sewing — and they also take care of livestock kept near the home and help in harvesting dates and olives. However, many Bedouin women are attending schools of higher education, comprising approximately 75% of the Bedouin students in Israeli universities and colleges (El-Meccawi and Degen, 2016) and many women drive cars.

In addition, Bedouin women have demonstrated initiative as entrepreneurs. Women sell poultry, eggs, occasional lambs, some dairy products, and artifacts at the weekly Bedouin market held regularly at different sites in the Negev Desert. These women have been selling these items prior to the establishment of the State of Israel.

In 1991, two Bedouin sisters residing in Lakiya, a Bedouin town in the Negev Desert, established a women's cooperative, "Lakiya Negev Bedouin Weaving", to preserve traditional weaving and provide employment for Bedouin women. Today, there are 30–60 Bedouin women employed at the cooperative, with most of them working from their homes. The Lakiya weaving project produces a variety of woven wool

Exhibit 17. Making bread.
Source: Photo © Léo-Paul Dana.

items, including carpets, pillow covers, pouches, and bags, which are sold on the premises, but are also marketed in Europe, USA, and Arab states. The products can be bought online, and most sales today are commissioned from Europe. In 1998, the two sisters established "Sidreh", a non-profit organization, also located in Lakiya, that supported the cooperative. Sidreh's aims were to improve the status and empowerment of Bedouin women in four fields: "(1) access to knowledge: improving the educational levels of Bedouin women; (2) access to resources: promoting economic resilience of Bedouin women by increasing income and maximizing the use of available resources; (3) gender equality and participation: improving the social position of women and advancing women's rights; and (4) sustainable development: professionalization and organizational development" (Degen and El-Meccawi 2022). At about the same time, and also in Lakiya, Huda Alsana established "Desert Embroidery", a project designed to preserve traditional handicrafts and to generate income for Bedouin women. Today, approximately 12 Bedouin women, wearing embroidered dresses, weave and stitch colorful designs for dresses, scarves, and wall-hangings in a workshop next to a woven Bedouin tent (D'Ignoti 2018).

In 2005, Miriam Abu-Reqaik established "Desert Daughter", which produces cosmetics, soaps, and remedies from desert herbs and natural products such as camel milk. Miriam received a BA in marketing from a University in London. She returned to her hometown, Tel Sheva, in the Negev Desert, where she started producing products from herbal components using formulae that were passed on to her from her grandmother. Today, Miriam grows these herbs and sells her products in Israel and abroad; orders can be placed online as well. Desert Daughter employs four Bedouin women in this successful enterprise (Kloosterman 2012).

5. Toward the Future

During its first 50 years of independence, the State of Israel transformed itself from a poor, agriculture-based country into a world leader in innovation and technology development. Inbound foreign investment in Israel rose from a mere $24 million in 1994 to $18 billion in 2019.

During its 50th year of existence, Israel exported software amounting to $1.5 billion. Since then, international agencies have upgraded the financial and business rankings of Israel. While financial investments are being prompted by opportunities in local capital markets, industrial investments are being attracted to the high level of technological skills available in Israel. Among successful investors are Apple, AT&T, IBM, Intel, IBM, Motorola, Microsoft, and Phillips.

Israel has an impressive number of qualified engineers per capita. While the US has eight engineers per 1,000 workers, and Japan has 7.5, Israel has 14 engineers per 1,000 workers. While the nation is host to important foreign investors, local new ventures are highly visible in its export-oriented high-tech industry. Israel's economy is being led by scientific and industrial R&D.

A favorable environment for enterprise — coupled with a highly-educated workforce and free trade agreements — has been beneficial for the economy; yet, economic development in Israel has been hindered by the need for heavy defence expenditures. Thus, Israel has not benefitted fully from its potential. Peace with all its neighbors would allow efforts to be more focused on the economy. Diplomatic relations with neighbors can open new markets. When Israelis sub-contract to enterprises in other countries, this is beneficial in at least two ways. First, employment in host countries is created, enhancing the buying power of people who can then be better positioned to purchase Israeli products. Second, producing in low-cost environments allows Israeli products to become increasingly competitive in world markets; lower costs lead to lower prices, which, in turn, lead to more demand, allowing for greater opportunities of scale, and further cost reductions.

Entrepreneurial ecosystems are defined as the interacting elements that foster new firm creation in a specific context (Neck, Meyer, Cohen, and Corbett, 2004) and research on entrepreneurial ecosystems contributes to our understanding of entrepreneurship (Neck *et al.*, 2004), while the literature focuses on gaining an understanding of components within these systems (Bahrami and Evans, 1995; Cohen, 2006). Likewise, the Global Startup Ecosystem Ranking provides a framework to understand entrepreneurship (Compass, 2017), and, in 2020, the entrepreneurship ecosystem in Tel Aviv ranked 6th in the world.

In the future, it is likely that women entrepreneurs in Israel will continue to play a central role in unlocking sustainable growth on a global level. Understanding and supporting women in an entrepreneurial ecosystem can play a critical role in the success of women. In Israel, there are several organizations that support women business owners including: (1) *Jasmine*: An organization that promotes economic development of all Israeli women, regardless of creed, class, socioeconomic status, race, or ethnicity. (2) *Netta*: An organization that promotes public dialog on women in the workplace. (3) *Temech*: A nonprofit organization that is committed to empowering and training Orthodox women in Israel to maximize their employment opportunities and financial success. Other organizations include: The Israel Women's Network, The Women's International Zionist Organization, *Yazamiyot*, and Woman2Woman.

Only women Israeli entrepreneurs are eligible to receive services from these organizations that promote the professional development of women as business owners and leaders (Women Helping Women, 2019).

References

Akirav, O. (2019), "The Lioness from Peki'in," *International Journal of Entrepreneurship and Small Business*, **37**(2), 232–249.

Almor, T. & Heilbrunn, S. (2013), "Entrepreneurship in Israel: Theory and Practice," *American Journal of Entrepreneurship*, **6**(2), 16–36.

Batsheva (2022), *Israel's Startup Nation: The Flourish of Female*. Retrieved from: https://batsheva.tv/iIsraels-startup-nation-the-flourish-of-female-entrepreneurs/ (Accessed on 13 November 2022).

Ben-Zvi, I. (1966). "Under Ottoman Rule 1517–1917". In David Ben-Gurion, ed., *The Jews in Their Land.* London: Aldous House.

Beyar, R., Zeevi, B., & Rechavi, G. (2017). "Israel: A Start-up Life Science Nation. *Lancet*, **389**, 2563–2569.

Bijaoui, I. & Regev, D. (2015). "Entrepreneurship and Viral Development in Rural Western Negev in Israel". *Journal of Research in Marketing and Entrepreneurship*, **17**(1), 54–66.

Browne, M. (1948). "Jews in Grave Danger in all Muslim Lands: Nine Hundred Thousand in Africa and Asia Face Wrath of Their Foes". *New York Times*, 16 May, Section E, p. 4.

Bussgang, J. & Stern, O. (2015). "How Israeli Start-ups Can Scale". *Harvard Business Review*, September 10.

Catarivas, D. (1957). *Israel.* Paris: Editions du Seuil.

Cohen, B. (2006). "Sustainable Valley Entrepreneurial Ecosystems". *Business Strategy and the Environment*, **15**, 1–14.

Coleman, A. (2018). "Tel Aviv Tech Startups to Watch in 2018." *Forbes*, March 6, 2018, Retrieved from: https://www.forbes.com/sites/alisoncoleman/2018/03/06/the-tel-aviv-tech-startups-to-watch-in-2018/#54270ee26011 (Accessed on 25 November 2022).

Compass (2017). *The Global Start-Up Ecosystem Ranking 2017*. Retrieved from: https://startupgenome.com/thank-you-enjoy-reading/ (Accessed on 25 November 2022).

Dana, L.-P. (1999). "Small Business in Israel". *Journal of Small Business Management*, **37**(4), 73–79.

Dana, L.-P. (2018). "Computers for the Blind". In R. D. Hisrich, & V. Ramadani, (eds.), *Entrepreneurial Marketing: A Practical Management Approach* (pp. 97–98). Cheltenham: Edward Elgar.

Dayan, M. (1966). *Diary of the Sinai Campaign.* London: Wiedenfield & Nicolson.

DeFontenai, C. & Carmel, E. (2001). "Israel's Silicon Wadi: The Forces behind Cluster Formation". SIEPR Discussion Paper No. 000–40. *Stanford Institute for Economic Policy Research*, http://www-siepr.stanford.edu/papers/pdf/00–40.pdf (Accessed on 25 November 2022).

Degen, A. A. & El-Meccawi, S. (2022). Ground Loom Weaving Among Negev Bedouin Women". In L-P. Dana, V. Ramadani, R. Palalic & A. Salamzadeh, (eds.), *Artisan and Handicraft Entrepreneurs: Past, Present, and Future* (pp. 3–32). Cham, Switzerland: Springer Nature.

Degen, A. A., El-Meccawi, S., & Kam, M. (2019). "The Changing Role of Camels among the Bedouin of the Negev". *Human Ecology*, **47**(2), 193–204.

D'Ignoti, S. (2018). "Bedouin Women of the Negev Fight Stereotypes One Business at a Time". *The New Humanitarian*. Retrieved from: https://www.deeply.thenewhumanitarian.org (Accessed on 13 November 2022).

El-Meccawi, S. & Degen, A. A. (2016). "Higher Education among Bedouin of the Negev: Tel Sheva as a Case Study". *Nomadic Peoples*, **20**(1), 88–107.

Fraiberg, S. (2017). "Start-up Nation: Studying Transnational Entrepreneurial Practices in Israel's Start-up Ecosystem." *Journal of Business and Technical Communication*, **31**, 350–388.

Frucht-Eren, L. (1996). *Israel: A Scientific Profile.* London: The British Council.

Gurau, C., Dana, L.-P., & Katz-Volovelsky, E. (2020). "Spanning Transnational Boundaries in Industrial Markets". *Industrial Marketing Management*, **89**, 389–401. doi.org/10.1016/j.indmarman.2020.01.008.

Harms, G. & Ferry, T. M. (2012). *The Palestine-Israel Conflict: A Basic Introduction*, 3rd Edition. Ann Arbor: Pluto Press.

Harold, F. (1892). *The New Exodus*. London: C.P. Putnam's Sons.

Hartz, B. (2018). "From Israel, with Innovation". *Business Observer*, February 16.

Heilbrunn, S. (2008). "Factors Influencing Entrepreneurial Intensity In Communities". *Journal of Enterprising Communities: People and Places in the Global Economy*, **2**(1), 37–51.

Herzl, T. (1896). *The Jewish State: An Attempt to Solve the Jewish Question.* Leipzig & Vienna: Verlags-Buchhandlung.

Julius, L. (2018). *Uprooted: How 3000 Years of Jewish Civilization in the Arab World Vanished Overnight.* Elstree, UK: Vallentine Mitchell.

Katzenstein, L. (1991). "The Ten Commandments for the Beginning Entrepreneurs". In John C. Oliga, ed., *Proceedings of the ENDEC World Conference on Entrepreneurship and Innovative Change* (pp. 142–143). Nanyang Technological University, Singapore.

Kloosterman, K. (2012). "Cosmetics from the Desert's Daughter". Israel 21c, Retrieved from: http://www.Cosmetics from the desert's daughter—ISRAEL21c (Accessed on 13 November 2022).

Kurlander, Y. & Efrati, N. (2019). "Our Herstory: Beit Hillel's Founding Mothers". *International Journal of Entrepreneurship and Small Business,* **37**(4), 573–581.

Mann, P. (1973). *Golda.* New York: Washington Square Press.

Meron, O. C. (2022). "The Economy of the Sephardic Old Yishuv in Eretz Yisrael, 1830–1917". In Yaron Ben-Naeh, & Michal Held Delaroza, eds., *The Sephardim in Erets Israel: Jewish Communities of the East in the 19th and 20th Centuries.* Jerusalem: Ben Zvi Institute and Israel's Ministry of Education.

Neck, H. M., Dale Meyer, G., Cohen, B., & Corbett, A. C. (2004). "An Entrepreneurial System View of New Venture Creation". *Journal of Small Business Management*, **42**(2), 190–208.

Ousset-Krief, A. (2018). "Israel a la Pointe des Decouvertes Scientifiques". *Magazine LVS*, **September**, 26–27.

The Mastercard Index of Women Entrepreneurs (2022). "The Mastercard Index of Women Entrepreneurs: How Targeted Support for Women-Led Business Can Unlock Sustainable Economic Growth". March 2022. Retrieved from: https://www.mastercard.com/news/media/phwevxcc/the-mastercard-index-of-women-entrepreneurs.pdf.

Women Helping Women (2019). "Resources for Women Business Owners in Israel". Retrieved from: https://successfulwomenofisrael.com/16-israeli-nonprofit-organizations-that-help-women-business-owners/.

Young, E. (2020). "Israel Named Best Country in World for Women Entrepreneurs". *Jerusalem Post*, November 24, 2020. Retrieved from: https://www.jpost.com/israel-news/israel-named-best-country-in-world-for-women-entrepreneurs-650051 (Accessed on 13 December 2022).

Yin, D. (2017). "What Makes Israel's Innovation Ecosystem So Successful". Forbes Asia. Retrieved from: https://www.forbes.com/sites/davidyin/2017/01/09/what-makes-israels-innovation-ecosystem-so-successful/?sh=595e9ab270e4 (Accessed on 25 November 2022).

https://doi.org/10.1142/9789811283499_0008

Chapter 8

Women Entrepreneurs in Jordan

Haya Al-Dajani

Mohammed Bin Salman College of Business and Entrepreneurship
haldajani@mbsc.edu.sa

Abstract

The growing interest in studying and researching women's entrepreneurship in Jordan is welcomed as the Kingdom continues to grapple with one of the lowest rates in the world for women's entrepreneurship, and one of the highest rates for unemployment. To better understand the opportunities, challenges, and prospects for women entrepreneurs in Jordan, this chapter covers the past, present, and future of women entrepreneurs in Jordan. This is achieved by first presenting a contextual overview of Jordan and a historical overview of the development of the entrepreneurial ecosystem in the Kingdom. Secondly, a discussion of the current and maturing entrepreneurial ecosystem, and how it relates to women entrepreneurs operating in the Kingdom, is presented. Third, and finally, the chapter offers a set of potential prospects for the future of women entrepreneurs in Jordan. In doing so, the chapter highlights that the entrepreneurial ecosystem in Jordan began with a "gender neutral" approach assuming that men and women entrepreneurs shared the same barriers, challenges, and opportunities. However, as it developed, there was a growing awareness of the lack of engagement from women entrepreneurs, which led to an awareness of gendered barriers to women's entrepreneurship and business growth. Strategies and remedies have been activated to address this, but this could be too little, too late.

Keywords: Women entrepreneurs; entrepreneurial ecosystem; entrepreneurship opportunities; entrepreneurship challenges; entrepreneurship engagement; Jordan.

1. Introduction

The growing interest in studying and researching women's entrepreneurship in the Arab world highlights both women's increasing engagement in entrepreneurship as well as the challenges and opportunities that shape this engagement throughout the region. This research is important as it can inform and shape the policies and practices that support and advance women's entrepreneurship, especially as women's entrepreneurship rates in the Arab world over the last 5 years have seen sharp rises (Metcalfe *et al.*, 2022). The rate of women's entrepreneurship in Jordan is no exception. According to the Global Entrepreneurship Monitor (GEM), the ratio of women's to men's total entrepreneurial activity increased from 0.26 in 2016 to 0.59 in 2019, an improvement of around 127% in 3 years (GEM, 2020). Such an achievement is aided by the Kingdom's young and evolving entrepreneurship ecosystem (El Kharouf *et al.*, 2022), and the legal gender equality regulations and policies for women's and men's engagement in entrepreneurship (World Bank Group, 2022). Nevertheless, the rate for women's labor force participation remains among the lowest in the world at 14% (Robbin, 2022), and lower than neighboring Lebanon (23%), Saudi Arabia (22%), and Palestine (18%) (ILO, 2022).

To better understand the opportunities, challenges, and future prospects for women entrepreneurs in Jordan, and consistently with other chapters in this book, this chapter begins with a contextual overview of Jordan, and then presents a historical overview of the development of the entrepreneurial ecosystem in Jordan, followed by a presentation and discussion of the current entrepreneurial ecosystem in Jordan, and how it relates to women entrepreneurs operating in the Kingdom. The chapter then presents an overview of the challenges and opportunities that women entrepreneurs in Jordan are facing, before concluding with a discussion on what the future holds for women entrepreneurs in Jordan.

Located in a rough neighborhood, Jordan gained its independence from the British in 1946 and was declared the Hashemite Kingdom of Jordan in 1949. The majority of Jordan's population of 10.4 million (Worldometer, 2022) live in urban centers and are ethnically Arab and religiously Muslim. Armenians, Circassians, and Chechens make up Jordan's main ethnic minorities, totaling approximately 5% of the population.

Additionally, 6% of Jordan's population is religiously Christian (CIA, 2022). Comprising 35% of Jordan's population of 10.4 million, equating to approximately 2.9 million, are non-citizens comprising Iraqi, Libyan, Palestinian, Syrian, Yemeni, and other refugees as well as legal and illegal immigrants (Ghazal, 2016). Indeed, Jordan ranks among the world's top 10 refugee host nations (Statista, 2019).

Similarly to other countries in the Arab world, the majority of the Jordanian population is under the age of 30 — the median age is 22.5 years (World Population Review, 2022) — and highly educated with a youth literacy rate of 99% for both girls and boys. With regards to schooling, the net enrolment rate for secondary schooling is 89.4% for girls and 86.5% for boys (UNESCO, 2017), and similarly to other Arab nations, female students also outnumber male students at the university level (World Bank, 2013). Despite such achievements within the education sphere, Jordan has one of the highest youth unemployment rates in the Arab world at 33.3% (El Kharouf *et al.*, 2022), reflecting the state of its struggling economy. As an emerging economy among the most water-poor countries in the world, Jordan has limited natural resources and is heavily dependent upon the import of fossil fuels, as well as foreign aid, remittances from Jordanians working abroad, and income generated in the services sector, which accounts for over 70% of gross domestic product (GDP) (Mehtap, Caputo and Pellegrini, 2017). Jordan's economy had been struggling even before the COVID-19 pandemic locked down its economy. With its GDP growth averaging approximately 2% between 2016–2019, it was impossible to create sufficient jobs for its youthful labor force. This was exacerbated in 2020 when GDP grew by only 1.6%, and most recently in 2021, by 2.2% (World Bank, 2022). As expected, the COVID-19 pandemic has exacerbated the unemployment trends as businesses reduced employee numbers or shut down.

Young university graduates on average wait for 3 years before securing their first job in Jordan (OECD, 2021). The burdensome unemployment rate results from structural problems within Jordan's economy and the higher education sector, as well as the economic impact of the COVID-19 pandemic. First, the economy is unable to create new jobs to absorb the new graduates, and second, the university education there is not equipping its graduates effectively with the vocational or employability skills needed in Jordan's labor market. With regards to the impact of the COVID-19 pandemic on the Jordanian economy, Raouf *et al.* (2020) report that the Jordanian government managed to reopen its economy following the COVID-19 pandemic lockdown by supporting the sectors that were hardest hit during its strict lockdown. They also reported that Jordanian households whose income was generated in Jordan's services, industry, tourism, or agriculture sectors were most severely affected, as these sectors came to a standstill due to local, regional, and international lockdowns. Unfortunately for the young Jordanian university graduates, these are the sectors where most employment occurred prior to the COVID-19 pandemic, and which will only recover fully through "fostering sustainable economic transformation and structural change" (Raouf *et al.*, 2020, p. 7) whereby policies and incentives are directed at creating greater resilience for withstanding economic shocks, diversification in economic activities, and job creation. Indeed, Jordan has been focusing its entrepreneurship policies to promote economic growth for over a decade (Mehtap *et al.*, 2017), and these have had some effect. For example, entrepreneurial ventures across the Kingdom led to the creation of 49,600 new jobs in 2019, but the number of job seekers that year exceeded 100,000 (El Kharouf *et al.*, 2022).

Relatedly, while Jordan prides itself on exporting highly qualified talent to other parts of the Arab world as a labor force management strategy offering some relief from the unemployment rates in Jordan, this strategy also increases the Kingdom's brain drain. Such migration is increasingly evident among both female and male graduates in Jordan, illustrating the increasing social and economic mobility of Jordanian women. However, such migration does not nurture entrepreneurship as the majority of these young Jordanians are contracted to jobs in nations within the Gulf Cooperation Council (GCC), where their economic engagement is limited to their contracting employer, and the conditions for starting and registering a business are not accessible to the majority of migrant employees. Given Jordan's economic woes and highly educated yet unemployed youth, a potential solution for driving Jordan's economy forward might lie in the adoption and growth of entrepreneurial ventures among Jordan's young women and men, in Jordan. The next section of this chapter presents a historical overview of the development of Jordan's entrepreneurial ecosystem and how this is linked to enhancing social and economic mobility and entrepreneurship.

2. Historical Overview

Originally coined by James Moore (1993), and defined by Mason and Brown (2014: 5) as "a set of interconnected entrepreneurial actors (both potential and existing), entrepreneurial organizations (e.g., firms, venture capitalists, business angels, banks), institutions (universities, public sector agencies, financial bodies) and entrepreneurial processes (e.g., the business birth rate, numbers of high growth firms, levels of "blockbuster entrepreneurship", number of serial entrepreneurs, degree of sell-out mentality within firms and levels of entrepreneurial ambition) which formally and informally coalesce to connect, mediate and govern the performance within the local entrepreneurial environment", the entrepreneurial ecosystem encompasses the formation of social network systems that support the local and regional economies, their sectors, and industries (Zacharakis *et al.*, 2003; Isenberg, 2011). As such, the purpose of the entrepreneurial ecosystem is to reveal how the interactions between the stakeholders in it support (or suppress) entrepreneurship and the entrepreneurial mindset (Auerswald, 2015; Malecki, 2011). It is also important to note that "Entrepreneurship ecosystems do not operate in a vacuum — they are socially, culturally, politically, economically, geographically, and historically situated, and are thus influenced, and possibly constrained, by such interwoven contexts, as are all the players operating within them" (El Kharouf *et al.*, 2022, p. 145).

To define and understand an entrepreneurial ecosystem, the context in which it operates as well as how it fosters or hinders entrepreneurship, its key actors and their respective roles need to be identified and analyzed. In doing so, we can better understand the strengths within the entrepreneurial ecosystem, and also analyze the existing gaps and/or weaknesses, and the potential for addressing them within the given context. Similarly to national economic development policies and strategies in developing economies, the government in Jordan remains highly motivated to improve its economic performance by first supporting entrepreneurship in the Kingdom, particularly among its youth population, to alleviate poverty, create jobs and reduce unemployment, and enhance innovation, and second, promoting its successes within the Kingdom and beyond.

Adapted from the German Agency for International Cooperation GmbH (GIZ) (2019), Table 1 highlights the historical development of Jordan's entrepreneurial ecosystem from its inception in the early 1990s, in advance of other nations in the Arab world (Omet, 2015). At that time, the focus was on launching organizations that offered business coaching, incubation, microfinance, entrepreneur networks, and seed funding. The National Strategy for Microfinance, for example, was launched by the Ministry of Planning and International Cooperation at this time to facilitate the distribution of microfinance programs through several established governmental and nongovernmental organizations, to alleviate poverty (Al-Maaitah, 2019). Having established these initial services, a decade later in the 2000s the entrepreneurial ecosystem was developing through a focus on angel investors, entrepreneurship training, business plan and

Table 1. Historical overview of Jordan's entrepreneurial ecosystem.

	Entrepreneurial Ecosystem Dimensions	Organizations
1990s	Business Coaching Incubation Microfinance Networks Seed Funding	Jordan Technology Group Riyada Tamweelcom Young Entrepreneurs Association (YEA)
2000s	Angel Investors Business Growth Programs Business Plan and Start Up Competitions Entrepreneurship Training	Endeavor Jordan iPARK INJAZ Jordan Enterprise Development Corporation (JEDCO) King Abdullah II Fund for Development National Fund for Enterprise Support (NAFES) Queen Rania Center for Entrepreneurship
2010s	Accelerators Entrepreneurial Ecosystem Development	Beyond Capital ISSF Oasis 500 Shamal Start

Source: Adapted from GIZ (2019).

startup competitions. Indeed, in 2003 the Jordan Enterprise Development Corporation (JEDCO) was mandated to provide a comprehensive suite of business support services to nurture and grow the Kingdom's entrepreneurial activity and to contribute to the development of national entrepreneurship policies (JEDCO, 2020). As the Kingdom's central organization for entrepreneurship, JEDCO has orchestrated a number of entrepreneurship support strategies such as the National Strategy for Entrepreneurship Development and small and medium-sized enterprises (SME) Growth (2015–2019). During this time and to combat the problematically high unemployment rate, several initiatives focusing on formal and informal entrepreneurship training for youth and especially university students, were initiated to encourage and prepare Jordan's youth to start up enterprises. As the entrepreneurial ecosystem established itself and matured its services, the 2010s decade witnessed the growth in the number of service providers and organizations in the entrepreneurial ecosystem, and the introduction of accelerators to support business growth alongside continuing to grow the number of startups.

This historical overview of the development of the entrepreneurial ecosystem in Jordan shows that it adopted a "gender neutral" approach rather than a "gender aware" one. The underlying assumption was that men and women entrepreneurs in Jordan shared the same barriers, challenges, and opportunities. This is despite Jordan's recognition of the existing historical gendered barriers to entrepreneurship and employment, and the many nonprofit and nongovernmental initiatives in the Kingdom working to advance gender equality and women's advancement. For example, Jordan joined the "Women and Girls Empowered" (WAGE) program in the late 1990s to encourage women in rural and poor areas of Jordan to engage in micro enterprise through training, mentoring, and the provision of women-only incubator facilities. WAGE is a global consortium sponsored by the United States State Department Secretary's Office of Global Women's Issues (S/GWI) with a mandate to promote the rights and empowerment of women and girls through American foreign policy. Furthermore, Tamweelcom — a Jordanian micro credit company — which was established in 1999 as a nonprofit organization with a grant from USAID, is the Jordanian partner of WAGE and provides financing and credit for poor and low-income individuals. Tamweelcom is owned by the Noor Al Hussein Foundation, one of the King Hussein Foundation's pioneering development entities, and has historically focused upon financially excluded citizens, particularly women. More recently however, they have expanded their beneficiaries to include youth and both registered and unregistered SMEs operating at the margins of the economy. While Tamweelcom and other agencies focusing on poverty alleviation and social development are now recognized stakeholders in Jordan's entrepreneurial ecosystem, historically they were not. This is likely due to the restricted definitions of an *entrepreneur* rampant in the 1990s, which excluded poor and marginalized individuals, especially women. Globally, they were considered "beneficiaries" of entrepreneurship, rather than potential entrepreneurs themselves.

Decades later, the Jordanian National Employment Strategy (NES) was launched in 2011 to address Jordan's economic and unemployment woes. Within this strategy, entrepreneurship was prioritized as a robust solution and was given a dedicated work stream focused specifically on nurturing an entrepreneurial culture and entrepreneurial mindset within the nation. The NES also specified the urban–rural divide with regard to entrepreneurial activity, and the underrepresentation of women in Jordan's entrepreneurship landscape. The barriers creating this underrepresentation and identified in the NES typically included the need to reform laws and regulations governing home-based employment, part-time employment, maternity leave and benefits, and childcare. In many ways, while the NES appeared to support women's entrepreneurship, this seemed to be limited to supporting them within the already saturated feminized sectors, rather than engaging them in the broader sectors of the economy.

As the entrepreneurial ecosystem in Jordan developed and grew, the definitions of the term entrepreneur widened to encompass a broader range of individuals and entrepreneurial activities. Alongside these developments, the awareness that the lack of engagement from women entrepreneurs in the Jordanian entrepreneurial ecosystem was due to gendered barriers to women's entrepreneurship and business growth also expanded. Strategies and remedies have been activated to address this, but this could be too little, too late especially given that the number of women engaging in entrepreneurship in Jordan is not increasing significantly (GEM, 2020), and due to the economic effects of the measures put in place to combat the COVID-19 pandemic.

3. Entrepreneurial Ecosystem

Given that entrepreneurial ecosystems are dynamic rather than static, regular mapping of the entrepreneurial ecosystem is needed as it enables the analysis of the capacities, relations, and interconnectedness within and between the myriad components comprising the entrepreneurial ecosystem. Similar to entrepreneurial ecosystems in the Arab world, Jordan's entrepreneurial ecosystem is maturing and continuing to grow, yet is largely under researched. As such, the available research about its effectiveness and impact on Jordan's social and economic development remains limited (Zayadin *et al.*, 2022). As has been acknowledged by Caputo *et al.* (2016, p. 395) among other researchers, the general "lack of systematic data collection is a typical characteristic of the Middle East and an impediment to carrying out deeper quantitative analysis of official data" about entrepreneurship trends. When embarking upon researching Jordan's entrepreneurial ecosystem, Caputo *et al.* (2016) found that a comprehensive database documenting the organizations that support and enable entrepreneurship in the Kingdom did not exist. As such, their research created the first such database, and therefore, the first official recognition of the organizations in Jordan's entrepreneurial ecosystem that support and enable women entrepreneurs. To summarize their results, they found 28 organizations in Jordan's entrepreneurial ecosystem, and of these, 22 supported women entrepreneurs through offering primarily incubation, training, and funding. Furthermore, "out of the 22 companies, we found that 14 were registered as non-profit organizations, four were private companies and four were public companies, either related to the Jordanian Government [such as JEDCO] or a foreign government [such as MEPI]. All the organizations are based in Amman but declare that they operate throughout Jordan" (Caputo *et al.*, 2016, p. 402).

Building on Caputo *et al.*'s (2016) research, El Kharouf *et al.* (2022) undertook a further mapping of Jordan's entrepreneurial ecosystem by adopting Isenberg's (2011) widely utilized model, and its six interrelated domains, namely: a conducive culture; enabling policies; financing provision; qualified human capital; markets for products and services; and a suite of institutional support. In doing so, they also sought to identify the effectiveness of Jordan's entrepreneurial ecosystem, specifically for women entrepreneurs and found that Jordan's entrepreneurial ecosystem had grown to comprise 74 organizations. Within this chapter, the Jordanian organizations mapped by El Kharouf *et al.* (2022) are highlighted to analyse the strengths of Jordan's entrepreneurial ecosystem as well as its areas for improvement. The chapter demonstrates the levels of activities of these organizations to support women's entrepreneurship in Jordan's entrepreneurial ecosystem, within the context of each of Isenberg's (2011) six domains. The findings are highlighted in Table 2 and the grey shaded areas in this table reflect the Jordanian organizations under each of the six domains.

Table 2. Organizations supporting women entrepreneurs in Jordan's entrepreneurial ecosystem.

Organization Supporting Women Entrepreneurs in Jordan	Isenberg's (2011) Six Domains					
	Policy	Finance	Markets	Human Capital	Support	Culture
1. Accelerator Tech		■				
2. ActionAid		■			■	
3. Afaq Jordan for Development and Training		■			■	
4. Ahli Bank (Nashmiat)		■				
5. Ahli Microfinance Company		■				
6. Almamlaka TV						■
7. AMIDEAST					■	
8. Arabreneur		■	■			
9. Aramex — RedLab					■	
10. ASEZA Aqaba	■					
11. Bank al Etihad (Shorouq)		■				

Table 2. (*Continued*)

Organization Supporting Women Entrepreneurs in Jordan	Isenberg's (2011) Six Domains					
	Policy	Finance	Markets	Human Capital	Support	Culture
12. Business Development Center			■	■	■	
13. Chamber of Commerce	■		■			
14. Chamber of Industry	■		■			
15. DAMA Ventures		■				
16. Dash Venture		■				
17. Development and Employment Fund		■				
18. Edraak					■	
19. EFE Jordan		■			■	
20. Endeavor Jordan						■
21. ERASMUS+				■		
22. Ethmar for Islamic Finance		■				
23. EU — Shamal Start		■				
24. Eureka		■				
25. FINCA		■				
26. For9a						■
27. German Jordanian University				■		
28. Greater Amman Municipality	■					
29. Growfin		■				
30. Hashtag Arabi						■

(*Continued*)

Table 2. (*Continued*)

Organization Supporting Women Entrepreneurs in Jordan	Isenberg's (2011) Six Domains					
	Policy	Finance	Markets	Human Capital	Support	Culture
31. Hikma Ventures		■			■	
32. iDare for Sustainable Development		■				
33. iMENA		■				
34. INJAZ		■		■		■
35. Intel Capital		■				
36. International Youth Foundation — Badir					■	
37. iPark		■				
38. Irada		■				
39. JEDCO		■				
40. Jordan Chamber of Industry					■	
41. Jordan River Foundation			■		■	
42. Jordanian Society for Business Entrepreneurship		■	■			
43. Jordan University of Science and Technology Center of Excellence and Innovative Projects				■		
44. KAFD					■	■
45. MENA Aps		■				
46. MENA Venture Investments		■				
47. MENATech					■	

Table 2. (*Continued*)

Organization Supporting Women Entrepreneurs in Jordan	Isenberg's (2011) Six Domains					
	Policy	Finance	Markets	Human Capital	Support	Culture
48. Microfund for Women		■	■			
49. Migrate		■				
50. Ministry of Labor	■					
51. Ministry of Planning and International Cooperation	■					
52. Ministry of Industry and Trade	■					
53. Ministry of Social Development	■					
54. National Microfinance Bank		■				
55. Oasis 500		■	■		■	■
56. Orange					■	
57. Princess Sumaya University for Technology				■		
58. Queen Rania Center for Entrepreneurship		■		■		
59. Ro'ya TV						■
60. Ruwwad MVF		■				
61. Shoman Foundation		■			■	
62. SilaTech		■			■	
63. Silicon Badia		■				

(*Continued*)

Table 2. (*Continued*)

Organization Supporting Women Entrepreneurs in Jordan	Isenberg's (2011) Six Domains					
	Policy	Finance	Markets	Human Capital	Support	Culture
64. Studio Be					■	
65. TAG Organization		■				
66. Tamweelcom		■			■	
67. Umniah					■	
68. UNICEF				■		
69. University of Jordan Innovation Center				■		
70. UNRWA		■				
71. USAID		■			■	
72. WAMDA		■				■
73. Zain					■	
74. ZOOMAAL		■				
Total	8	41	8	9	22	8

Source: Informed by El Kharouf *et al.* (2022).

As can be seen from Table 2, only 14 of the 74 organizations are active in more than one domain, and of those 14, only the Business Development Center is active across three domains, and only Oasis 500 is active across four. Perhaps surprisingly, given that one of the main barriers globally to women's entrepreneurship is access to finance (Marlow and Patton, 2005), the domain with the majority of organizations (41) in Table 2 is the Finance domain. Here, 18 of the 41 organizations provide financial advisory services only, and the remaining 22 offer funding, finance, and investment. As expected, however, the domain with the second largest number of organizations (22) is the Support domain. This is expected as Jordan continues to focus its efforts on growing the number of entrepreneurial ventures in the Kingdom as a strategy to create jobs and reduce unemployment. The one glaring gap where much more needs to be done lies within the Markets domain as evidently very few organizations offer or facilitate access to markets for the entrepreneurs' products and services.

Given the state of Jordan's economy, and the number of registered enterprises operating within it, the entrepreneurial ecosystem looks healthy. Not only is it enabling entrepreneurship in the Kingdom, it is itself an engine for job creation with its 74 organizations employing women and men. At the top end of the spectrum is Oasis 500 — the only organization in Jordan's entrepreneurial ecosystem to be active across four of Isenberg's (2011) six domains of the entrepreneurial ecosystem. Oasis 500 is a pre-seed and seed fund manager and business accelerator that provides startups with funding and business acceleration training as well as technical support and guidance from highly experienced business coaches and mentors, among other entrepreneurship services. The Chief Executive Officer (CEO) of Oasis 500 since 2018 is Luma Fawaz, who was named by *Forbes* as one of the Middle East's "Top 100 Power Businesswomen" for 2019 and 2020. Since she began leading Oasis 500, she has endorsed strategies to ensure that the organization is women-inclusive. To date, 80% of the employees at Oasis 500 are women, and 40% of the organization's 175 startups are also founded by women (Abukumail and Qanadilo, 2021). In this regard, Oasis 500 is unique rather than typical of organizations in Jordan's entrepreneurship ecosystem and ecosystems elsewhere in the Arab world with regards to being women-inclusive. However, it clearly illustrates the importance of the organization "walking the talk" in order to transform women's entrepreneurship, especially as the vast majority of the organizations in the entrepreneurial ecosystem offer their services to both men and women and are not for women only.

In addition to the number of organizations in Jordan's entrepreneurial ecosystem *vis-à-vis* the size of the Kingdom's economy and the number of businesses, the diversity of the organizations within it also signals its healthiness. Between them, they offer a wide array of services ranging from regulation, venture capital, seed funding, microfinance and microcredit, advisory services, training, entrepreneurship education, incubation and acceleration, co-working spaces, for networking, mentoring, and coaching. While this explains the role and contribution of Jordan's entrepreneurial ecosystem to the increasing total entrepreneurial activity in the Kingdom (GEM, 2020), the glaring gaps in supporting entrepreneurs to access markets for their products and services also explain the limitations of the entrepreneurial ecosystem. Additionally, in the absence of a national database and/or online platform that details the organizations within Jordan's entrepreneurial ecosystem, its organizations have a limited outreach as they fail to attract a wider net of nascent and established entrepreneurs who are familiar with them. Such poor marketing and communication practices have resulted in low subscriptions and uptake of the services provided, especially by women entrepreneurs.

4. Women Entrepreneurs

Despite the healthiness and strengths of Jordan's entrepreneurial ecosystem as shown in the section above, more needs to be done to ensure that women entrepreneurs benefit from the wide range of available services. The author of this chapter concurs with Caputo *et al.* (2016, p. 403) that "building a sound ecosystem in which female entrepreneurs can flourish is essential for the economic development of Jordan", and to achieve this, more effort on behalf of the organizations to be women-inclusive, and to address the existing gendered barriers, is needed. Such gendered barriers that limit the engagement of established and nascent women entrepreneurs in the Jordanian entrepreneurial ecosystem and consequently to establish, maintain, and grow their businesses have been identified in the literature on women's entrepreneurship in Jordan (El Kharouf *et al.*, 2022; Banihani, 2020; GEM, 2018; Mehtap *et al.*, 2017) and include:

1. Access to entrepreneurship education/training;
2. Access to finance;
3. Bureaucratic systems;
4. Cultural gendered stereotypes and expectations;
5. Lack of female entrepreneur role models, mentors, and coaches;
6. Lack of suitable childcare;
7. Limited market access;
8. Travel limitations for accessing support;

9. Unsuitable timings and locations for the available services;
10. *Wasta* (personal connections).

Clearly, many of these gendered barriers are embedded within access to the service, rather than the service itself, and the other identified gendered barriers relate predominantly to cultural practices (Banihani, 2020). This complements the GEM Jordan National Report (2018, p. 85) that concluded that "women in Jordan, when provided with the resources (i.e., training, finance, mentors), are risk-takers and not apprehensive about starting their own businesses". Failing to address these gendered barriers will result in wasted valuable resources and services, limited positive outcomes, and no transformation in Jordan's gendered entrepreneurial status quo. While service-providing organizations in Jordan's entrepreneurial ecosystem can easily address the gendered "access" barriers, addressing the cultural practices will be more challenging and requires partnerships with a wider range of regulatory, policy, and social development organizations. Recognizing and understanding the gendered barriers and their implications that hinder women's entrepreneurship and their business growth in Jordan will result in effective and responsive measures that will enhance the impact of Jordan's entrepreneurial ecosystem and the engagement of women entrepreneurs within it.

To start with, policies related to entrepreneurship in Jordan should be revised to be more women-inclusive by recognizing, validating, and accommodating the access needs of women entrepreneurs. For cxample, ensuring that entrepreneurship education and training are affordable, and accessible during the hours that suit the women entrepreneurs and that they are available at accessible locations throughout Jordan. Furthermore, ensuring that reliable and affordable childcare facilities are available at the training/education/mentoring/coaching/networking sessions and that these sessions are also available during hours that suit the women entrepreneurs. With regards to *wasta*, rather than enhancing access to *wasta* among women entrepreneurs in Jordan, policymakers and regulatory agencies within Jordan's entrepreneurial ecosystem must prevent and eliminate this practice based on favoritism and nepotism, which leads to discrimination, injustice, and inequity.

Additionally, as the COVID-19 pandemic revealed, there is an urgent need for the Jordanian government to invest in the information and communication technology (ICT) infrastructure to accelerate the transition to a more digital economy and facilitate telecommuting, remote working, and home-based enterprising. This is essential for the majority of women-owned, small, and/or home-based enterprises to expand their businesses within and beyond Jordan's physical borders. We must remain mindful of the extent to which micro and small businesses dominate women's entrepreneurship in Jordan (Al Wleidat and Al-Kharouf, 2019) similar to global trends. The vast majority of these enterprises operates within feminized, saturated sectors, where business growth is realistically unlikely (Banihani, 2020). Additionally, many women entrepreneurs in Jordan operate within the informal economy, running non-registered enterprises. While this offers an alternative to unemployment, and allows women entrepreneurs to engage in low-risk venturing, it does preclude them from accessing finance and other support services offered through Jordan's entrepreneurial ecosystem (Al-Dajani *et al.*, 2019).

In her study on empowering women through entrepreneurship in Jordan, Banihani (2020) argued that gendered barriers hinder women's entrepreneurship, and the traditional patriarchal gendered norms continue to reinforce a gendered division of domestic labor with women continuing to be responsible for their children, households, and extended families, while adhering to social and cultural norms that limit their mobility and economic engagement. Indeed, such traditional and patriarchal gendered norms not only impede women's entrepreneurship in Jordan, but also the overall economy, which becomes deprived of their talent, innovation, and entrepreneurial mindset (GEM, 2018). Thus, despite the huge strides made by successful Jordanian women entrepreneurs such as Luma Fawaz, Mary Nazzal-Batayneh, Nadia Dajani, and Reem Badran, much more needs to be done to support the diverse range of women entrepreneurs. Certainly providing business mentoring and coaching from other women entrepreneurs operating in Jordan such as Exhibits 1 and 3, promoting their successes, and recognizing them as entrepreneurs and role models will be welcomed.

As shown in Isenberg's (2011) entrepreneurial ecosystem model, and outlined in the GEM Jordan National Report (2018) and elsewhere in the

Exhibit 1. This picture shows Rana A. Safadi at the amphitheater in downtown Amman, the capital of Jordan. Rana is a Jordanian artpreneur and founder of Jordan's House of Culture (www.houseofculture.co).

Source: Haya Al-Dajani (2021).

literature, "it is important to note that all the components of the environment in which women and men act entrepreneurially (or cannot act proactively and innovatively) are mutually dependent. This dependency demands a holistic approach not only in research but also in designing appropriate policies for building a supportive environment in which entrepreneurial behavior can flourish" (GEM, 2018:24). Such a holistic approach however will remain ineffective if the patriarchal and traditional social and cultural gender norms are not reformed (Metcalfe, Bastian, and Al-Dajani, 2022). Indeed, "to disregard the differential limitations and pressures applied to women entrepreneurs, is to turn a blind eye to the realities of women's lives … until women [in Jordan] are freed from the psychological and practical bonds of sole domestic responsibility, their ability to participate in the labor force, either as employees or as

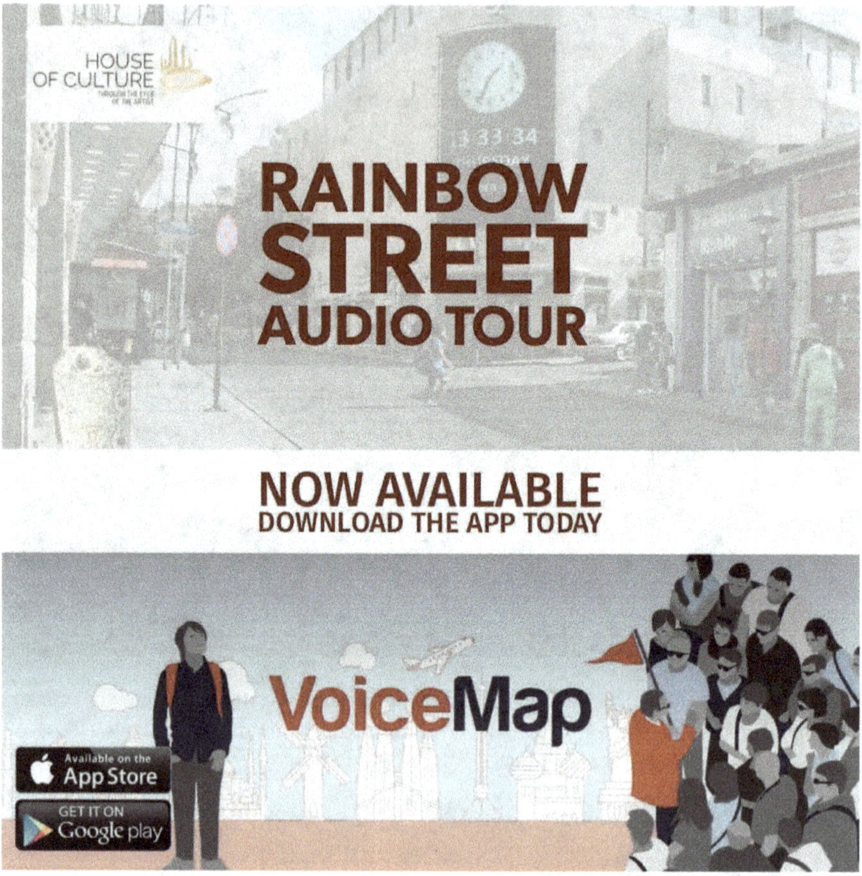

Exhibit 2. This picture shows a unique digital product for Jordan that artpreneur Rana A. Safadi developed to enable the digital transformation of her House of Culture enterprise (www.houseofculture.co).

Source: Haya Al-Dajani (2022).

entrepreneurs, will be severely curtailed" (El Kharouf *et al.*, 2022, p. 145). In other words, women's engagement in the labor force and/or in entrepreneurship in Jordan will remain around its current low rates if the social gender inequalities and the gendered barriers preventing women from economic participation persist. Signs of this persistence were reported by Mehtap *et al.* (2017) in their research exploring the entrepreneurial intentions of women university business studies students in Jordan. They found significant reservations from them toward entrepreneurial careers due to their fears about "the weakness of the Jordanian economy, lack of finance, fear of risk, gender inequality, and inability to maintain a work and private life balance" (Mehtap *et al.*, 2017, p. 207). The weakness of the Jordanian economy, lack of finance, risk and gender inequality have already been discussed in this chapter, however, with regards to the work–life balance, it is important to note that the average family size in Jordan is 4.7 (Department of Statistics [Jordan] and ICF, 2019), and the average age at marriage for women is 27, and 30 for men (Assaad *et al.*, 2021).

As such, the cumulative disadvantage resulting from the multiplicity of gender-based barriers in the form of gender inequalities, gendered stereotypes, patriarchal traditions, and norms at the micro, meso, and macro levels, and experienced by the majority of women in Jordan (Caputo *et al.*, 2016; Zayadin *et al.*, 2022), is already affecting future generations of potential women entrepreneurs in Jordan. This is disappointing as these women university students should be among the most likely women in the Arab world to engage in entrepreneurship (Al-Dajani *et al.*, 2020). It is also disappointing as it shows how little progress has been made globally to remove the gender-based barriers that prevent women's access to entrepreneurship (de Bruin *et al.*, 2007). It is important therefore for organizations in Jordan's entrepreneurial ecosystem to continue their efforts to be gender-aware, and women-inclusive, in order to contribute to the removal of the gendered barriers and the reform of patriarchal gendered norms. In doing so, Jordan's entrepreneurial ecosystem can effectively contribute to positive socio-behavioral change among both men and women.

5. Toward the Future

Looking ahead, Jordan is not immune to the economic and social repercussions of the measures put in place locally, regionally, and internationally, to combat the COVID-19 pandemic, nor to the regional political and economic affairs. The Kingdom's economic rebound during the first nine months of 2021 was steady but was below expectation at 2.1% growth (World Bank, 2022). As expected, the performance of the organizations within Jordan's entrepreneurial ecosystem will also be affected by this, especially as projections show that economic growth will remain modest for the foreseeable future, coupled with stubbornly high rates of unemployment, and low rates of labor force participation, especially among women. Given the growth and developments in women's entrepreneurship in Egypt, Saudi Arabia, and the United Arab Emirates (UAE), Jordan cannot afford to stagnate as it will fall behind in the region. This is especially important for Jordan's economy as the trend of employment in the GCC is diminishing given that those nations are now prioritizing their own citizens who have become equally qualified. As such, the return of the Jordanians from the GCC to Jordan may either further increase the bulging unemployment rates or enhance the entrepreneurship rates as the returnees invest their accumulated wealth into entrepreneurial venturing in Jordan. For the second more favorable scenario to occur, the entrepreneurship ecosystem in Jordan must be ready and willing to facilitate this through removing the gendered barriers and bureaucratic procedures that have hindered engagement in entrepreneurship to date and, as outlined earlier in this chapter center upon improved inclusive policies for entrepreneurs operating at all levels of the economy as well as engaging more women at all levels of the entrepreneurial ecosystem, especially within the leadership and management levels of its organizations. In many ways, the Jordanian returning from the UAE, for example, and wanting to start a business in Jordan will want to have a similar level of service and support as the Emirati entrepreneurs receive in their home country.

Another important area for looking toward the future is addressing the lack of accessibility of women entrepreneurs in Jordan, to the business support services offered to them through the entrepreneurial ecosystem. An updated and accessible platform with a database of all the organizations that support entrepreneurs in the Kingdom and the services they offer is urgently needed. Not only will this support the entrepreneurs and the would-be entrepreneurs in Jordan, but it will also enhance the profile of the Kingdom's entrepreneurial ecosystem and, potentially, investment in it. Such a platform can also open up market opportunities within the Kingdom as well as for export, and include a wider range of business growth services to complement those focusing on startups and the pre-startup stages. As we learned during the COVID-19 pandemic lockdown, a major hindrance affecting accessibility and lying beyond the remit of the organizations in Jordan's entrepreneurial ecosystem is the

ICT infrastructure. This needs rapid updating to guarantee entrepreneurs reliable internet and mobile connectivity throughout the Kingdom so they can actively and competitively engage in the digital entrepreneurship space as shown in Exhibit 2. Technology-based startups (TBS) operating in Jordan's knowledge economy are most affected by the Kingdom's ICT infrastructure and are important as they are more likely than other micro and small enterprises to create professional job opportunities and have accelerated growth (GIZ, 2019). Given that one in three TBS in Jordan and across the Arab world is women-owned, and employs women, this illustrates the leadership and growth prospects that women entrepreneurs have in this sector (Al-Dajani *et al.*, 2020).

As customers and businesses are increasingly expected to be present and engaged in social media outlets and digital entrepreneurship, it is encouraging to see the Jordanian government adopting the Jordan Source initiative to support its ICT sector and enhance the Kingdom's positioning as a hub for digital investments. Organisations within Jordan's entrepreneurial ecosystem can support this initiative by offering digital skills and social media training as shown in Exhibit 3, alongside other existing training offerings to ensure that entrepreneurs are not disadvantaged by their lack of skills in these areas. This is especially relevant to entrepreneurs operating micro and home-based enterprises who may have relied on face-to-face rather than digital operations and customer interactions to date. Additionally, the impact of the Jordan Source initiative needs to be monitored to determine its impact on women's entrepreneurship in Jordan in the future. Similarly, the Kingdom's economic visioning exercise and public sector modernization plan launched in 2022 to target growth and opportunities over the next 10 years in Jordan and guide inclusive and resilient growth and development efforts (Word Bank, 2022) should also be scrutinized to ensure that they are gender-aware, gender-inclusive, and entrepreneurship oriented.

Alongside improvements in entrepreneurship policy, ICT infrastructure development, enhancing the access of women entrepreneurs to the services offered within the entrepreneurial ecosystem in Jordan, and widening women's participation in the leadership and management of the organizations in the entrepreneurial ecosystem, engaged scholarship and research must be embedded within the future growth plans for Jordan's

Exhibit 3. This picture shows Amani Qaddoumi with her trainees. Amani is a Jordanian established and leading creative brand designer and strategist (https://www.amaniqaddoumi.com/). Alongside her award-winning design services, Amani provides training on branding and visual identity development for young entrepreneurs, through several **organizations** active in Jordan's entrepreneurial ecosystem.

Source: Haya Al-Dajani (2022).

women entrepreneurs and the entrepreneurial ecosystem. To avoid duplication of efforts, and to enhance transparency and impact as well as to widen dissemination of the findings, the engaged scholarship and research efforts need to be collaborative efforts involving academic researchers, gender specialists, think tanks, government agencies, local and international aid agencies, and a multitude of organizations operating within Jordan's entrepreneurial ecosystem and supporting women entrepreneurs in Jordan. A research-informed, research-led, gender-aware, and gender-inclusive entrepreneurial ecosystem will lead to a more prosperous future for Jordan's women entrepreneurs.

References

Abukumail, A. & Qanadilo, N. (2021). "5 Startups Led by Women that are Shaping the Future of Entrepreneurship in Jordan. World Bank Blogs". Retrieved from: https://blogs.worldbank.org/arabvoices/5-startups-led-women-are-shaping-future-entrepreneurship-jordan#:~:text=According%20to%20the%20Global%20Entrepreneurship,percent%20in%20only%203%20years (Accessed on 16 March 2022).

Al-Dajani, H., Bennett, D., Orser, B., Rambo, K., & Thomas, M. (2020). "Policy Brief: Advancing Enterprise Education for Women in Science, Technology, Engineering and Mathematics (STEM) among MENA Countries". *G20 Insights Journal*. Retrieved from: https://www.g20-insights.org/policy_briefs/advancing-enterprise-education-for-women-in-science-technology-engineering-and-mathematics-stem-among-mena-countries/.

Al-Dajani, H., Akbar, H., Carter, S., & Shaw, E. (2019). "Defying Contextual Embeddedness: Evidence from Displaced Women Entrepreneurs in Jordan". *Entrepreneurship & Regional Development*, **31**(3–4), 198–212.

Al Maaitah, N. (2019). "The Legitimacy of Profit of Microlending Institutions and Women's Empowerment: A Case Study from Jordan". *Theory, Methodology, Practice*, **15**(1), 3–17.

Al Wleidat, O. & Al-Kharouf, A. (2019). "The Role of Small Projects in Employment of Rural Women in Madaba Governorate". *Dirasat Journal of Human and Social Sciences*, **46**(1), 15–47.

Assaad, R., Krafft, C., Sieverding, M., Al-Hajj, L., Cheung, R., & Omar, I. (2021). *Policy Brief: The Transition to Adulthood in Jordan: Supporting Youth Aspirations*. Jordan: UNICEF.

Auerswald, P. E. (2015). "Enabling Entrepreneurial Ecosystems: Insights from Ecology to Inform Effective Entrepreneurship Policy". *Kauffman Foundation Research Series on City, Metro, and Regional Entrepreneurship*. Kansas City: Ewing Marion Kauffman Foundation.

Banihani, M. (2020). "Empowering Jordanian Women Through Entrepreneurship". *Journal of Research in Marketing and Entrepreneurship*, **22**(1), 133–144.

Caputo, A., Mehtap, S., Pellegrini, M., & Al Refai, R. (2016). "Supporting Opportunities for Female Entrepreneurs in Jordan". *International Journal of Entrepreneurship and Small Business*, **27**(2/3), 384–409.

CIA (2022). *The World Factbook, Jordan.* The World Fact Book. Retrieved from: https://www.cia.gov/the-world-factbook/countries/jordan/ (Accessed on 16 March 2022).

de Bruin, A., Brush, C., & Welter, F. (2007). "Advancing a Framework for Coherent Research on Women's Entrepreneurship". *Entrepreneurship Theory and Practice*, **31**(3), 323–339.

Department of Statistics [Jordan], & ICF (2019). *Jordan Population and Family Health Survey 2017–2018: Key Findings*. Amman, Jordan, and Rockville, Maryland, USA: DOS and ICF.

El Kharouf, A., Abualbasal, A., Abbadi, H., & Weir, D. B., (2022). "The Entrepreneurship Ecosystem for Enhancing Women's Entrepreneurship in Jordan". In Metcalfe, B., Bastian, B., Al-Dajani, H., (eds.), *Women, Entrepreneurship, and Development in the Middle East* (pp. 133–151). London: Routledge.

GEM (2018). *Jordan National Report 2016–2017.* Amman, Jordan: Global Entrepreneurship Monitor.

GEM (2020). *Jordan National Report 2019–2020.* Amman, Jordan: Global Entrepreneurship Monitor.

Ghazal, M. (2016). "Population Stands At Around 9.5 Million, Including 2.9 Million Guests". *The Jordan Times*. Retrieved from: http://www.jordantimes.com/news/local/population-stands-around-95-million-including-29-million-guests (Accessed on 16 March 2022).

GIZ (2019). *Jordan's Start-Up Economy: Assessing the Economic Contribution and Potential of Tech and Tech-Enabled Start-Ups*, Bonn, Germany: Deutsche Gesellschaft für Internationale Zusammenarbeit (GIZ) GmbH.

ILOSTAT Database (2022). Retrieved from: https://data.worldbank.org/indicator/SL.TLF.CACT.FE.ZS?locations=ZQ&most_recent_value_desc=false (Accessed on 16 March 2022).

Isenberg, D. (2011). *The Entrepreneurship Ecosystem Strategy as a New Paradigm for Economic Policy: Principles for Cultivating Entrepreneurship.* Babson Entrepreneurship Ecosystem Project, Babson College, Babson Park, MA.

JEDCO (2020). *About Us.* Retrieved from: http://jedco.gov.jo/Pages/viewpage.aspx?pageID=147 (Accessed on 16 March 2022).

Malecki, E. (2011). "Connecting Local Entrepreneurial Ecosystems to Global Innovation Networks: Open Innovation, Double Networks and Knowledge Integration". *International Journal of Entrepreneurship and Innovation Management*, **14**, 36–59.

Mehtap, S., Caputo, A., & Pellegrini, M. (2017). "Encouraging Female Entrepreneurship In Jordan: Environmental Factors, Obstacles and Challenges". In Ramadani, V. *et al.*, (eds.), *Entrepreneurship and Management in an Islamic Context* (pp. 207–225). Switzerland: Springer International Publishing.

Marlow, S. & Patton, D. (2005). "All Credit to Men? Entrepreneurship, Finance and Gender". *Entrepreneurship Theory & Practice*, 717–735.

Mason, C. & Brown, R. (2014). *Entrepreneurial Ecosystems and Growth Oriented Entrepreneurship: Final Report*. Paris: Organisation for Economic Co-operation and Development (OECD).

Metcalfe, B., Bastian, B., Al-Dajani, H. (2022). The Mosque and the Satellite: Exploring the Multi-Level and Multi-Agency Dynamics of Women's Entrepreneurship Development in the Middle East. In Metcalfe, B., Bastian, B., Al-Dajani, H., (eds.), *Women, Entrepreneurship, and Development in the Middle East*, Routledge, London, pp. 3–32.

Moore, J. (1993). "Predators and Prey: A New Ecology of Competition". *Harvard Business Review*, **May/June**.

OECD (2021). *Empowering Youth and Building Trust in Jordan*, OECD Public Governance Reviews. Paris: OECD Publishing. Retrieved from: https://doi.org/10.1787/8b14d38f-en.

Omet, G., Shami, M., Bino, A., & Abu Khalf, K. (2015). "Entrepreneurship in Jordan: Regional Analysis and Envisaged Role". *Research Journal of Business and Management*, **2**(3), 323–333.

Raouf, M., Elsabbagh, D., & Wiebelt, M. (2020). *Impact of COVID-19 on the Jordanian Economy Economic Sectors, Food Systems, and Households*. Regional Program Policy Note 9. Washington, D.C.: International Food Policy Research Institute.

Robbin, Z. H., (2022). *Women's Labor Force Participation and COVID-19 in Jordan*. Washington D.C.: Middle East Institute.

Statista (2019). Retrieved from: https://www.statista.com/statistics/263423/major-refugee-hosting-countries-worldwide/ (Accessed on 30 November 2020).

UNESCO (2017). Effective Literacy Programmes. UNESCO Institute for Lifelong Learning. Retrieved from: http://litbase.uil.unesco.org (Accessed on 16 March 2022).

World Bank (2013). *Hashemite Kingdom of Jordan Country Gender Assessment: Economic Participation, Agency and Access to Justice in Jordan*. Washington D.C.: The World Bank.

World Bank (2022). *The World Bank in Jordan*. Retrieved from: https://www.worldbank.org/en/country/jordan/overview#1 (Accessed on 16 March 2022).

World Bank Group (2022). *Women, Business and the Law Report*. Washington D.C.: International Bank for Reconstruction and Development/The World Bank.

World Population Review. Retrieved from: https://worldpopulationreview.com/countries/jordan-population (Accessed on 16 March 2022).

Worldometer (2022). Retrieved from: https://www.worldometers.info/world-population/jordan-population/ (Accessed on 16 March 2022).

Zacharakis, A. Shepard, D., & Coombs, J. (2003). "The Development of Venture-Capita-Backed Internet Companies: An Ecosystem Perspective". *Journal of Business Venturing*, **18**, 217–231.

Zayadin, R., Zucchella, A., & Anand, A. (2022). "Exploring The Emancipatory Role Of Entrepreneurship In A Developing Context". *International Journal of Entrepreneurial Behavior & Research*, **28**(2), 527–547.

https://doi.org/10.1142/9789811283499_0009

Chapter 9

Women Entrepreneurs in Lebanon

Sally Shamieh[*,‡] **and Roula Gergess**[†,§]

[*]*Research Project Manager, ESA Business School*
[†]*Lecturer ISC Paris and TBS Paris*
[‡]*shamieh.s@esa.edu.lb*
[§]*rgergessabourjeily@gmail.com*

Abstract

This chapter provides an in-depth examination of the entrepreneurial ecosystem in Lebanon, with a specific focus on the pivotal role played by women. Offering both a historical overview and a contemporary reality check, it establishes an overarching framework within which entrepreneurship in Lebanon is comprehensively described and explored. The narrative delves into the emergence and evolution of the ecosystem against the backdrop of a turbulent environment, shedding light on the progressively evolving role of women entrepreneurs. A detailed analysis of the current status of women in Lebanon highlights the challenges and barriers that female entrepreneurs encounter. This chapter also emphasizes the active engagement of women entrepreneurs in various sectors and concludes with an outlook on the future.

Keywords: Crisis; resilience; women entrepreneurship; entrepreneurship ecosystem; Lebanon.

1. Introduction

Lebanon is known for its thriving entrepreneurial scene, playing a pivotal role in laying the groundwork for numerous successful businesses in the region. In 2016, the ratio of total entrepreneurial activity

(TEA) in Lebanon reached its highest at 21.2% (GEM, 2016), attributed to the tradition of liberalism and the dominance of the private sector in the country. The open market and laissez-faire trade practices have historically fostered an environment conducive to entrepreneurial endeavors. Since 2005, there has been a strategic redirection of funds toward supporting entrepreneurial activities in small and medium-sized enterprises (SMEs).

Despite Lebanon's renowned entrepreneurial spirit, potential startup founders must carefully assess the intricacies of the local ecosystem. While the world has recently recovered from the COVID-19 pandemic, Lebanon still faces multiple challenges, including health, economic, political, social, and security concerns.

Although Lebanon is characterized by a conservative society, a patriarchal culture, a cumbersome bureaucracy, and a multitude of challenges that hinder entrepreneurial activity, women entrepreneurs have flourished and made their way. Lebanese women have always been active members of the society and proved to be resilient social pillars, strong and enduring in the face of conflict, disruption, and volatility. This has had a profound impact on women's social roles. The issuance of Circular 331 by the Central Bank in 2013 marked a positive step toward promoting entrepreneurship, leading to the flourishing of female-led businesses across diverse industries. The supportive ecosystem eventually contributed to economic upswing and improved the overall status of women, aligning with Sustainable Development Goal (SDG) number 5 on gender equality and women's empowerment. Today, women entrepreneurs remain integral to and the backbone of Lebanon's economic growth and stability, even as the country contends with the aftermath of economic collapse ongoing conflict along its southern border. Despite challenging circumstances, women persist in seeking opportunities to initiate businesses during crises, viewing Lebanon as an inspirational destination for their entrepreneurial ideas. Unfortunately, women in the Middle East and North Africa (MENA) region, while highly active, continue to have the lowest rates of TEA, comprising only 4% of the general population.

2. Historical Overview

Lebanon, the small mountainous country along the Mediterranean Sea (Exhibit 1), has been described as the Pearl of the Middle East and its capital Beirut as the Paris of the region. With an area of no more than 10,425 km^2 and a population expected to reach 6.7 million in 2022 (UNFPA, 2022), Lebanon's golden days were witness to prosperity, abundance, and opulence. With its wealth of culture and beautiful nature, multiplicity of religions and sects, and a hint of Western European influence, Lebanon was the place to be.

Despite this picturesque beauty, Lebanon suffered from consecutive shocks to its system ever since the 1970s, in the form of civil strife, foreign invasions, economic downturns, political instability, and massive population displacement. The situation has been aggravated by the influx of Palestinian, Syrian, and Iraqi refugees, making Lebanon the country hosting the largest number of refugees per capita in the world (UNHCR Lebanon, 2019), with over 2 million refugees out of the global total of 6.7 million. Despite all this, the resilient Lebanese spirit has always prevailed.

Exhibit 1. Mount Harmon in Lebanon.

Source: Photographer Marwan Maalouli, 2021.

2.1. *Current context*

More recently, Lebanon has plunged into a full-blown financial and economic crisis that has been described by the World Bank as potentially ranking among the top three worst crises worldwide since the mid-19th century (World Bank, 2021). In Transparency International's 2021 Corruption Perceptions Index, Lebanon ranked 154 out of 180 economies, despite adopting several anti-corruption measures (Schutter, 2022). The country has accumulated massive national and international debts and has a drastically devaluated local currency amid a fragmented sectarian political setup resulting in a political deadlock with excessively high levels of corruption. The resulting impact on the population has been devastating, robbing the Lebanese of their purchasing power, with over half the population plummeting into poverty amid soaring unemployment rates. Nearly 80% of the population now lives in poverty, as the value of the currency has fallen by 95% (Schutter, 2022). The economic crisis was accompanied by a social revolt movement in October 2019, where thousands took to the streets to express anger and frustration. The COVID-19 pandemic further aggravated the situation in early 2020, placing additional strain on the already weak infrastructure of the Lebanese government. To top it all, the traumatic explosion at the Port of Beirut on August 4, 2020 was a horrific blow to Lebanon with material damages estimated at close to US$3 billion, apart from the lives lost and the devastating social and psychological impacts on the population. The Beirut blast is considered the strongest non-nuclear explosion of the 21st century (Helou, 2021), resulting in over 6000 casualties. The combination of all the above-mentioned intense events and acute conditions provides Lebanon with an extreme context, generating a disruptive environment for individuals as well as businesses.

2.2. *Economy and the private sector*

Economically, Lebanon operates in a free economy characterized by a laissez-faire tradition, promoting an ultra-liberal stance and safeguarding private initiatives (Gaspard, 2004). Lebanon's liberal economy has been based on competitiveness and private property, with the banking and service sectors accounting for about 70% of the gross domestic product (GDP). Agriculture contributes 10% of the GDP, while the industrial sector accounts for the remaining 20% (IDAL, 2019). Nevertheless, the private sector is encumbered by government inefficiencies, including "red tape, corruption, arbitrary licensing decisions, complex customs procedures, high taxes, tariffs and fees, archaic legislation, and inadequate intellectual property rights protection" (CIA, 2022). However, since 2019, the Lebanese economy has been in a free fall. The United Nations Economic and Social Commission for Western Asia (ESCWA) estimated that private sector sales have diminished by 45% and that the Lebanese economy contracted by 20% in 2020 alone compared to the previous year, with further contraction expected in the years to follow (ESCWA, 2021). The country has been struggling severely, on economic, social, political, and financial spectrums, with each passing month marking worse figures than the previous one. With Lebanese authorities still unable to agree on a strategy to address the problem of the country's failed economic model, real GDP fell by 10.5% in 2021, following a 21.4% decline the previous year. Furthermore, real GDP is expected to decline by 6.5% in 2022, with extremely high uncertainty assuming that macroeconomic policies remain inadequate and the political and security scenarios remain stable (World Bank, 2022). According to the World Bank, Lebanon's GDP marked a 58.1% contraction, plunging from US$52 billion in 2019 to US$21.8 billion in 2021, the highest contraction in a list of 93 countries (World Bank, 2022). Added to this is the mounting unemployment rate. According to the International Labor Organization (ILO) and the Central Administration of Statistics Agency (CAS) study, the unemployment rate in Lebanon increased from 11.4% in 2018–2019 to 29.6% in January 2022, implying that more than one-third of the country's labor force is unemployed (ILO and CAS, 2022). This situation was worsened by COVID lockdowns, driving many businesses toward forced closures and layoffs; the explosion at the Beirut Port also contributed to the destruction and forced closure of enterprises and businesses.

2.3. *Ease of doing business*

In some countries, governments impose regulations that burden entrepreneurs (World Bank, 2020). Such regulations limit the ability of entrepreneurs to freely start their businesses. For startups and entrepreneurs, the ease of doing business is an important indicator as to the efficiency and effectiveness of the system, the freedom of conducting transactions, and the status of the regulatory changes and reforms implemented by the government to develop the private sector. The World Bank's Ease of Doing Business ranking is an index that compares economies based on how conducive the regulatory environment is to business and how much it has changed compared to other economies. The report looks at small and medium-sized businesses and measures the regulations that affect them throughout their life cycles. It can then assess the processes for starting a business, obtaining a building permit, obtaining an electricity connection, registering property, accessing credit, paying taxes, trading across borders, handling bankruptcies, hiring workers, and so on. According to the World Bank's Ease of Doing Business report for 2019, Lebanon ranked 143rd out of 190 economies[1], implying that Lebanon has more complex and less business-friendly regulations (World Bank Group, 2020). The complicated situation in Lebanon makes conducting and formalizing business even more complex than before. "With the current economic crisis, You cannot open a bank account for your business, take out a loan, transfer money, or even register your startup," says Tana Haidar, Deputy Director at Smart ESA (Haidar, 2022).

3. Entrepreneurial Ecosystem

3.1. *The rise of the entrepreneurial ecosystem*

The Lebanese entrepreneurial landscape started taking shape in the early 2000s, with individual entrepreneurs trying to make it on their own. However, the game-changer was the issuance of Circular 331 (C331) by the Lebanese Central Bank in August 2013, injecting US$400 million[2] into the Lebanese enterprise market through private equity funds, with the support of local banks (Banque Du Liban, 2013). With the objective of retaining human assets while boosting the country's economy, the circular aimed to create the foundations for a new Lebanese knowledge economy that is knowledge-based and tech-oriented. C331 made way for

[1]At the time of writing this chapter, the latest Ease of Doing Business report for Lebanon issued by the World Bank dated back to the year 2019.

[2]The limit was raised to $650 million in 2016.

entrepreneurs to make use of financial support from commercial banks or special venture capital funds, while guaranteeing funding organizations up to 75% of their investments and limiting potential losses to a mere 25% (BLOM Invest Bank, 2021). The policy development of C331 spurred the expansion of the entrepreneurship ecosystem in Lebanon through the entry of commercial banks into the equity market and the growth of new capital funds. At the same time, C331 addressed the equity gap by fostering a venture capital (VC) industry in Lebanon, facilitating the entry of several VC funds onto the scene by providing licenses.

The following years witnessed the launch of several prominent entrepreneurial accelerators and incubators, including the UK Lebanon Tech Hub (UKTH) and Speed in 2015, and Flat6Labs and Smart ESA in 2016 (Exhibit 2). Prominent universities like Saint Joseph University (USJ), Holy Spirit University of Kaslik (USEK), the American University of Beirut (AUB), and the Lebanese American University (LAU) were among

Exhibit 2. Young lady pitching at SMART ESA event.

Source: Smart ESA, ESA Business School, 2021.

the most active in venture development and acceleration. The circular also supported the launch of several venture capital and private equity funds, including Berytech Funds, Venture Partners, and Middle East Venture Partners. Simultaneously, the World Bank supported a private equity fund entrusted to Kafalat, which offered SME bank loan guarantee programs. The entrepreneurship ecosystem was flourishing and buzzing with new startups, platforms, and offerings. These facilities attracted overseas talent from the Lebanese diaspora, supporting one of the main aims of C331 of reversing the brain drain. Despite the initial lack of tech talent in the Lebanese market, the industry picked up quickly, with educational institutions opening up courses and certificates in areas like coding, artificial intelligence, and cryptography.

With all these happenings, the Lebanese newfound entrepreneurial ecosystem flourished with success stories materializing all around. There are many examples of successful ventures that could not have made it had it not been for the newly founded landscape, noting that many successes were funded outside C331. Next Automated Robots or NAR is one such tech startup to erupt from the ecosystem with the aim of developing drone-based solutions enabling drones to analyze and interpret data. The founders Nicolas Zaatar and Charlie El Khoury spotted the opportunity and made use of the ecosystem to launch their venture. NAR has since been acquired by US-based B3Bar Holdings. Anghami is another example of a Lebanese startup in the music industry, founded by Elie Habib and Eddy Maroun back in 2012, and is worth over $220 million today. Anghami is the first Arab music streaming platform to be listed on Nasdaq originating from the founders' passion for music combined with their expertise in the tech industry. Another instance is Ostaz, originally known as Synkers, founded by three dynamic women, Zeina Sultani Nakad, Audrey Nakad, and Sybille Nakad. Ostaz, the literal translation of the term *teacher*, is an online tutoring platform in the Ed-tech industry that aims to connect learners and tutors in schools as well as universities. FoodSight is another exciting tech startup in the food industry that provides a platform for consulting services to food manufacturers. It was founded by a motivated Lebanese agri-food entrepreneur Fidèle El Achkar within Berytech's Agrytech Accelerator Program. El Achkar capitalized on major gaps in the agri-food sector and has attracted thousands of users among food experts and manufacturers. There are countless success stories that are witness to the credibility of the nascent ecosystem.

By September 2018, the Governor of the Central Bank declared that the startup sector was worth almost a billion dollars, representing 1.5% of Lebanon's GDP (BLOM Invest Bank, 2021). As per the Global Entrepreneurship Monitor (GEM) report of 2018[3], Lebanon ranked first among eight MENA countries for new business ownership, early-stage entrepreneurial activity, and established business ownership, and "almost one in two adults in Lebanon were either starting a new business, running a new business or running an established business" (Hill, 2018, p. 10). Circular 331 was followed by several amendments and modifications to address flaws and blemishes in the original policy. Despite the mishaps, and although far from perfect, the ecosystem was starting to take shape and looked much more solid. There is no denying that the entrepreneurial landscape started taking shape following Circular 331. As the tech scene emerged, the environment became more hospitable as money was being injected. Nevertheless, the Global Entrepreneurship Monitor 2018 report confirmed the lack of government infrastructure support for the entrepreneurial ecosystem, highlighting that "Lebanon's open and supportive culture was the major factor supporting entrepreneurial activity in 2018" (Hill, 2018, p. 11).

4. Women Entrepreneurs

4.1. *Women issues in Lebanon*

The progression of women's status in Lebanon has gone through several phases, in direct relation to the country's economic, political, and social development. Historically, women in Lebanon have been the most progressive and liberal among the neighboring Arab countries. Lebanese women obtained suffrage in 1953 and have since shown great progress toward sustainable empowerment goals. Compared to their counterparts in the region, Lebanese women had more freedom and liberty to pursue

[3]At the time of writing this chapter, the latest Global Entrepreneurship Monitor (GEM), Lebanon national report issued dated back to 2018-2019 due to the lack of sponsors in crises' time (Hill, S. (2022). Professor & lead author of the GEM National Report for Lebanon and currently GEM Global (R. Gergess, Interviewer).

education, as well as work outside the home, express political views, and participate fully in all aspects of life. The increased economic participation of women took off in the 1990s when Lebanon witnessed a migration of its male workforce to the neighboring and lucrative Gulf countries. With increased access to education, women, who were left behind to take care of the families, took courageous initiatives toward their own careers and development, in light of the country's booming years at the time. They expanded their long-established habitual roles outside the traditional framework of solemn housework and duty. This opened new pathways as efforts toward income generation and women's empowerment proliferated into a new era of implemented gender equality practices. International conventions were signed and ratified in the mid-1990s, addressing women's concerns, gender equality, and women's empowerment. In 1997, Lebanon acceded to the Convention on the Elimination of All Forms of Discrimination Against Women (CEDAW), and in 1998 Lebanon established the National Commission for Lebanese Women (NCLW). Nevertheless, as is the case in many countries around the world, reality does not reflect great progress in women's access to employment opportunities, financial capital, and leadership positions. Women continue to experience marginalization in the context of the Lebanese economy within what is generally considered a patriarchal society.

4.2. *Patriarchal culture*

Women all over the world carry the added burden of family responsibilities, elder care, and home upkeep. Lebanon is no different in that regard. Lebanon is regarded as a patriarchal culture where social norms assign women as the main caregivers of the family and men as the financial providers. Lebanese women entrepreneurs continue to operate within societal and cultural constraints and limitations (Tlaiss and Kauser, 2019). Yet, several barriers still exist that hinder the development of new women-owned business ventures. Access to capital, salient sociocultural norms, and the economic meltdown have limited the advancement of those entrepreneurial activities. Entrepreneurial trends are still gendered, and "women are rarely seen in executive positions" confirmed Carla Saba, Deputy General Manager of Berytech.

In rural areas, constraining social and religious norms hinder women from joining the labor force and the economy as a whole. Lebanese women, amounting to ±50% of the population, contribute to a solemn 26% of the labor force (World Bank, 2020). The United Nations' fifth Sustainable Development Goal (SDG5), focusing on gender equality, explicitly addresses women's economic empowerment. However, the Lebanese government has not set ambitious goals to enhance women's political or economic participation, overlooking the substantial economic growth that could result from increased female involvement in the labor force. Although the Global Gender Gap Report 2021 highlights that the largest gender gap worldwide is in the MENA region, Lebanon managed to narrow its gender gap by 3.8 percentage points (World Economic Forum, 2022). The share of women ministers increased from 3.4% to 31.6% from January 2019 to January 2021. Nevertheless, women remain underrepresented in decision-making roles, exhibiting weak political participation. Their representation in parliament falls below expectations, standing at only 4.7% (World Economic Forum, 2021). In the corporate arena, leadership positions are still predominantly held by men, and the few women on boards or in C-level positions are primarily associated with family businesses where the woman has a close familial relationship with the male figure behind the business.

Women continue to experience marginalization and informal discrimination in the context of the Lebanese patriarchal society. In terms of existing legislation, there is a notable deficiency in providing adequate support for women to overcome informal discrimination and navigate challenges. While women have the legal right to obtain employment or pursue a trade or profession similar to men, they are restricted from entering certain industries as outlined in Lebanon's labor law code of 1946. Addressing this issue and eliminating constraints that hinder women from working in sectors such as mining, manufacturing, energy, agriculture, and transport necessitate a comprehensive modernization of the law to align with evolving societal and economic developments.

Another legal challenge in addressing various issues related to women in Lebanon is associated with the personal status laws, which are governed by the country's system of confessionalism within its political and social structure. This poses a complication related to women's empowerment and gender equality. Religious communities implement their own legal codes, and these can vary significantly based on one's religious affiliation and practices, often resulting in disadvantaged positions for women (World Economic Forum, 2021). Sectarian inheritance laws exhibit variations among different sects, leading to unequal rights for sons and daughters in inheriting assets from their parents. These assets are crucial for obtaining loans to support their entrepreneurial endeavors. While in some cases, inheritance is equal between men and women, cultural practices may still favor male heirs (World Bank, 2020). Women should have the legal capacity to register a business, open a bank account, and sign contracts on equal terms with men (Exhibit 3).

4.3. *Supportive ecosystem*

In Lebanon, conditions for female entrepreneurs are relatively favorable compared to neighboring countries, yet women-owned businesses predominantly operate in the informal sector, often in traditionally female

Exhibit 3. Citizens demonstrating for women's rights.

Source: CTRDA, 2020

roles such as agrifood, education and artisanal work. This sector poses significant challenges, especially in accessing formal financial channels and business expansion. However, the last decade has seen a supportive ecosystem evolve, buoyed by a plethora of programs, actors, and institutions dedicated to fostering women's economic participation.

Local and international non-governmental and nonprofit organizations are at the forefront of advocating for women's equity, empowerment, and entrepreneurship. These efforts have led to a notable increase in female entrepreneurs, particularly in rural areas where women, often unskilled and with limited income, face the added complexity of setting up new businesses in a patriarchal society. Motivated primarily by necessity, these women are gradually changing societal norms by leveraging their unique skills and creativity to create sustainable and commercially viable ventures. NGOs have played a crucial role in this transformation, launching empowerment programs that have boosted female and rural entrepreneurship. These organizations support women through microfinance, skill development, capacity building, and access to networks and finance, especially for those without formal finance options (Exhibit 4). The private sector, too, has joined in with corporate social responsibility initiatives aimed at nurturing female entrepreneurship.

The Lebanese scene is characterized by a large number of microfinance institutions. Al Majmoua, Ibdaa, Emkan, and Ameen have been specifically active in addressing women's empowerment and entrepreneurship. The World Bank has also been an active contributor in Lebanon, supporting microfinance programs and working with the Lebanese Council for Women, the Lebanese American University's Women's Studies Department, and the League of Lebanese Businesswomen to further develop gender studies. The United States Agency for International Development (USAID) has also participated in these microfinance initiatives to help women become more successful entrepreneurs, ensuring improved access to capital. Projects under the Council for Development and Reconstruction (CDR), such as the Assistance Program for Women's Empowerment in Lebanon, have also been supported by the European Union, the United Nations Development Fund for Women (UNIFEM), and the Economic and Social Fund for Development (ESFD).

Exhibit 4. Lebanese woman in a rural area making agri-food products, while caring for her grandson.

Source: CRED Research Center, ESA Business School, 2022.

United Nations agencies like UN Women, UNIFEM, UN Economic and Social Commission for Western Asia (ESCWA), EU for Women Empowerment (EU4WE), and UN Development Program (UNDP) provide financial and technical support programs to encourage women entrepreneurs to initiate businesses in regional and global economies. UN organizations collaborate with local players to initiate and implement projects. The Lebanese government and the World Bank also launched the We-Fi (Women Entrepreneurs Finance Initiative) project in 2019 to "help and empower women-led and women-owned small and medium enterprises (WSMEs) in Lebanon and to expand their access to domestic and export markets through e-commerce platforms" (World Bank, 2019). UKAID has also dedicated funds and extended support to women business owners and entrepreneurs. Many institutions and organizations have also backed various projects promoting women's economic involvement.

Agence Universitaire de la Francophonie (AUF) in partnership with Berytech plans yearly competitions and offers grants with the aim of supporting and empowering women entrepreneurs. Berytech "provides assistance in building/networking, policy reform, start-up and SME development, acceleration and incubation, technology transfer help, and women empowerment which managed to connect organizations across many European cities with the intention of offering business help to female entrepreneurs" (Berytech, 2022).

Associations like the Lebanese League of Women in Business (LLWB) offer a platform that brings together and supports professional women (Exhibit 5). LLWB was established in 2006 and has since "endorsed and embraced a number of female-led startups offering seed money and angel funds, while extending partnerships and collaborations with various stakeholders in the ecosystem that share similar goals of addressing socio-economic gaps" (Zein, 2022). Insure & Match Capital (IM Capital)/IM Ventures, a subsidiary of Berytech, works to encourage

Exhibit 5. LLWB Join and Grow event in the Bekaa supporting women entrepreneurs.

Source: Lebanese League of Women in Business (LLWB, 2022).

female entrepreneurs and "provide matching capital, equity guarantee and support programs to a broad spectrum of businesses ranging from seed stage to growth phase, as well as to investors in Lebanon" (Kiame, 2022). Funds worth US$10 million of investment were provided from 2015 through 2020, of which almost $3 million went to women-led startups.

The Lebanese Women Angel Fund (LWAF), created by IM Capital in partnership with LLWB and Go Beyond Investing, is a program that provides investment funds by women for women (Saba, 2022). Their sole investor, the United States Agency for International Development (USAID), always welcomes and promotes gender equality, and the fact that IM Capital's executive position is led by a woman helped in promoting women's entrepreneurial initiatives (Kiame, 2022). Saba (2022) asserted that efforts are concentrated on accompanying female entrepreneurs and empowering them throughout their programs. They are supported, trained, coached, and mentored until the pitching stage. "Although start-ups were the first to be hit by the crises in Lebanon, tech subsectors flourished and Lebanese companies became more competitive in terms of pricing and offering in ICT" says Saba (Saba, 2022). She continues, "Now, we are practicing a backward integration process by introducing USJ students to entrepreneurship courses in order to support more and more entrepreneurs."

Accelerators and incubators in general have a clear gender policy when it comes to taking on startups. Berytech, for example, is adamant about supporting Lebanese women in the pursual of their careers and startups in the technology sectors. Launched by the ESA Business School in 2018, Smart ESA has been one of the most successful accelerator programs in Lebanon, winning many awards across the region. Smart ESA has a 50/50 policy in every cohort, ensuring that women are equally represented (Haidar, 2022). Beirut Digital District (BDD) stands as a vibrant and dynamic tech hub in Lebanon, playing a pivotal role in bolstering women in tech startups. It offers a range of services, facilities, and innovative tools tailored for modern businesses. BDD maintains a high-tech, high-quality environment, fostering flexible lifestyle and work practices, all underscored by a commitment to eco-friendly practices.

Women in tech and in science have also received support. There has been a surge in women entrepreneurs in male-dominated sectors such as clean-tech, agri-food, energy, digital, STEM, and engineering industries.

Warrior women have emerged within the system and made their way through. There are countless examples of Lebanese women entrepreneurs who have rocked the boat, and it is not a novelty that Lebanese women make it to stardom. Female entrepreneurs from Lebanon have often made it to the *Forbes* top entrepreneurs list in the past years. Examples include Nadia Moussouni, the co-founder of Energy 24, a startup that seeks to create alternative energy storage and generators. Loulou Khazen is another young lady whose Bas startup was the Middle East's first online freelance work marketplace. Shahiya, the Lebanese recipe portal, is another success story by Hala Labaki, Carole Makhoul, Cezar Gemayel, and Daniel Neuwirth with investment from WAMDA, an entrepreneurship ecosystem accelerator in the MENA region.

In the Information and Communication Technology (ICT) field, young Lebanese women have been making substantial strides as well. ICT moderates modern computing by managing the infrastructure and components and is a field that has been typically dominated by men for quite a long time. Despite this male hegemony, there are several success stories of women. Siroun Shamigian, a Lebanese female entrepreneur, managed to create Kamkalima, an e-learning platform promoting the Arabic language. Manal Hakim, another woman of Lebanese origin, founded Geek Express, a multidimensional tech platform that provides coding courses for kids and adults. Myki is a cyber security startup established by Priscilla Elora Sharuk that can securely store passwords across devices for future reference. Eve Tamraz is another female Lebanese scientist and entrepreneur who co-founded Sensio Air with Cyrille Najjar. Sensio Air is a modernized healthcare analytics company that created the Sensio Air device, which monitors air quality and detects mold, dust, pet dander, and pollen in a room, and can also prevent symptoms of asthma and allergies. SE Factory is a leading coding program founded by Fadi Bizri and Zeina Saab in response to the large demand for coders in Lebanon and across the world. Digital Opportunity Trust (DOT) is yet another example, founded by Marianne Bitar Karam, which focuses on technology in education to groom young people into becoming impactful leaders within their communities.

Often enough, women incorporate a social aspect into their business, adopting and highlighting critical social issues within their environments and societies. Women-led enterprises, benefiting from a heightened awareness and sensitivity to women's issues, frequently embody a supportive element for other women. One example is Sara's bag through which Sarah Baydoun aims to empower underprivileged women and women in prison by incorporating their artisanal skills and needlework into her high-quality luxury handbags. Believing in the importance of women's empowerment and their social inclusion, her mission was to create luxurious handmade bags, while opening up a space for emancipation. Rana Khoury and Caroline Farra are also social entrepreneurs who established Phenomenal Women, a social enterprise that aims to empower survivors of gender-based violence by offering them training opportunities and providing job prospects in a diverse mix of sectors, including catering, fashion, nursing, construction, and even furniture-making. Their aim is to financially and psychologically empower survivors of violence, trafficking, and rape, and give them a space to be liberated, away from the austerity of life.

Women entrepreneurs have a natural caregiver instinct and Lebanese women take it to the next level. They embrace it and fly with it, even in the most dire situations. Aline Kamikian entered the food and beverage industry, yet another male-dominated industry, with a rebellious attitude that challenged social norms and representations. Realizing her father's dream, and combining her passion for food with her Armenian roots, Aline opened her first traditional Armenian restaurant for which she won the Brilliant Lebanese Awards in 2014. Today, Aline runs a chain of Armenian restaurants, Mayrig, Batchig, and Lahmajun, in Lebanon, KSA, UAE, Armenia, and the Maldives. Following the August 4 explosion at the Beirut Port, and despite the destruction of her business and being injured herself, Aline did what she knew best — food. As an emergency response, she set up an emergency kitchen to feed the victims and the families who lost their homes.

Although not an exhaustive compilation, the above-mentioned examples serve as a small sample illustrating the potential and capabilities of women entrepreneurs in Lebanon, even in the face of challenging circumstances. All of these success stories inspire and empower other women to take that leap of faith, face the hurdles, and rise up to the challenges. These women are leading the way, inspiring others, and contributing significantly to the economic and social fabric of Lebanon. Lebanon does not lack brilliant successful women entrepreneurs; however, it lacks the supporting environment that women need to shine.

5. Toward the Future

Like everything else, the journey is not always smooth, and there is still significant room for improvement on various fronts.

5.1. *The challenges*

Lebanon's economic ecosystem, while possessing potential for innovation, currently faces challenges due to the existing infrastructure and regulatory framework. The business environment requires certain fundamental elements to be conducive for growth, elements that are presently underdeveloped. The government's administrative and legal structures for business operations, particularly for startups, are in need of modernization. Issues such as outdated regulations, bureaucratic processes, and long-standing laws and policies present considerable challenges. These challenges are evident in various aspects, from banking policies to employment regulations, where the administrative burden and time needed to navigate the system can be significant. Recognizing these challenges, there is a clear and urgent need for a comprehensive reform of the regulatory and legal framework. Such reforms should aim to better support the development of a knowledge-based economy and address key issues like private equity investments and the facilitation of stock options and stock warrants. This approach could lay the groundwork for a more robust and dynamic economic environment in Lebanon.

Furthermore, Circular 331 of the Central Bank, while a step in the right direction, exhibits certain limitations that need to be addressed to fully rejuvenate Lebanon's entrepreneurial ecosystem. The circular primarily focuses on Series A funding, leaving a noticeable gap in the crucial Seed stage for startups. This gap is significant as it represents a pivotal phase for these companies. Despite the partial guarantees offered by the Central Bank, commercial banks and venture capital funds often adopt a conservative approach, preferring to invest in startups that have already gained some traction and show promising prospects. This conservatism places a substantial financial burden on startups during their critical early stages, often necessitating self-funding or bootstrapping. There is an evident need to cultivate a culture that views failure not as a setback but as a valuable learning experience and a stepping stone for future growth. Additionally, a significant aspect of the current economic climate in Lebanon is that Circular 331's support is limited to Lebanese companies operating within the country, which overlooks the crucial aspect of scaling businesses internationally. The anticipated electronic trading platform, intended to enable startups and SMEs to open their capital to public investment, has yet to be implemented. Consequently, Lebanese companies with growth potential are often inclined to establish operations outside of Lebanon to access better launch opportunities and broader markets. Addressing these issues could provide a more supportive environment for local startups and enhance Lebanon's overall economic landscape.

5.2. *Hope ahead*

The evolution of entrepreneurship ecosystems is a gradual process, often marked by challenges and learning opportunities. In the context of Lebanon, where recent economic and financial turmoil has been prominent, the entrepreneurial landscape is facing a period of necessary reinvention and adaptation. To foster growth and stability in this ecosystem, several strategies can be implemented, all of which hinge on effective collaboration and coordination among various stakeholders. One key area of focus is the development of accelerator programs. The current landscape, characterized by competing programs, can evolve into a more cohesive network of complementary and supplementary initiatives. These programs can extend beyond the typical three-month timeframe, which often falls short in preparing startups for investors. Longer, more comprehensive support systems are needed. Post-acceleration and incubation programs that offer continued coaching and mentoring will be instrumental in addressing these gaps. These initiatives can play a pivotal role in guiding startups through the critical phases following initial acceleration, providing sustained support and expertise. Another significant avenue for enhancing the entrepreneurial ecosystem is the emphasis on scale-up programs and fostering connections with international investors. These elements are crucial for startups looking to expand beyond local markets and gain access to broader investment opportunities. Moreover, universities in Lebanon are positioned to be key contributors to this ecosystem. Their involvement can range from providing educational resources, research support, mentorship, and networking opportunities, all of which are vital for nurturing entrepreneurial talent and ventures. The provision of physical resources such as workspace, along with coaching and mentoring services, is essential. These resources are fundamental in supporting startups and are key to rebuilding and strengthening the entire entrepreneurial framework in the country. Capitalizing on Lebanon's human capital is another significant aspect. By tapping into the rich pool of skills and expertise within the country and reaching out to the Lebanese diaspora, the ecosystem can gain access to a wealth of knowledge, experience, and potentially, investment. The diaspora can play a crucial role in providing insights, connections, and financial support, all of which are invaluable for a burgeoning entrepreneurial environment. The role of financial support cannot be overstated. It is imperative to attract and engage both local and international funding institutions. This financial backing is not just about providing capital but also about instilling confidence in the Lebanese market, encouraging further investments, and fostering a cycle of economic growth and innovation. These efforts collectively can build a more robust and resilient entrepreneurial ecosystem in Lebanon, capable of weathering economic challenges and fostering sustainable growth and innovation.

Amidst these efforts, the role of women in the entrepreneurial landscape of Lebanon is particularly noteworthy. There is an immense potential for women to lead and drive the resurgence of this sector. The concept of the 'Lebanese iron woman' symbolizes strength, resilience, and the ability to overcome challenges. By empowering women entrepreneurs, providing them with the necessary resources and support, and recognizing their potential as leaders and innovators, Lebanon can pave the way for a more inclusive and dynamic entrepreneurial ecosystem. The revival of this ecosystem, therefore, is not just about economic recovery; it's also about nurturing hope and promise in Lebanon. Through a collaborative, inclusive approach that leverages the country's human capital and empowers its entrepreneurs, especially women, Lebanon can look forward to a rejuvenated, robust, and resilient economic future.

References

Banque Du Liban (2013). "Circular 331". *Intermediate Circular No 331 Addressed to Banks and Financial Institutions*. Lebanon: Beirut.

Berytech (2022). Retrieved from: https://berytech.org/about/type-of-support/.

BLOM Invest Bank (2021). *BDL Circular 331 as a Local Opportunity for Lebanese Talent: An Update.* Retrieved from: www.blominvestbank.com: https://blog.blominvestbank.com/39961/bdl-circular-331-as-a-local-opportunity-for-lebanese-talent-an-update/#:~:text=In%20more%20details%2C%20the%20circular,to%2075%25%20of%20the%20investments.

CIA (2022). *The World Fact Book: Lebanon*. Retrieved from: www.cia.gov: https://www.cia.gov/the-world-factbook/countries/lebavnon/#government.

ESCWA (2021). *Lebanon's Formal Private Sector: The Bitter Reality of 2020.* Beirut: ESCWA.

Gaspard, T. (2004). *A Political Economy of Lebanon, 1948–2002. The Limits of Laissez-faire.* Leiden, Boston: Brill.

Haidar, T. (2022). Communications Director at Smart ESA (S. Shamieh, Interviewer).

Helou, M. E.-H. (2021). "Beirut Explosion: The Largest Non-Nuclear Blast in History". *Disaster Medicine and Public Health Preparedness,* (1–2), 1–2.

Hill, S. (2018). *Global Entrepreneurship Monitor Lebanon National Report 2018.* Global Entrepreneurship Monitor.

IDAL (2019). *Investment Development Authority of Lebanon (IDAL)*. Retrieved from: IDAL Invest Lebanon: https://www.investinlebanon.gov.lb/en/lebanon_at_a_glance/lebanon_in_figures/economic_performance.

ILO and CAS (2022). *Lebanon Follow-up Labor Force Survey.* Beirut: CAS. Retrieved from: file:///C:/Users/Baalbaki.C/Downloads/Lebanon%20FLFS%20Jan%202022%20EN.pdf.

Kiame, C. (2022). Former Chief Investment Officer, IM Funding (R. Gergess, Interviewer).

Saba, C. (2022). Deputy General Manager, Berytech (R. Gergess, Interviewer).

Schutter, O. D. (2022). *Report of the Special Rapporteur on Extreme Poverty and Human Rights.* Lebanon: United Nations. Retrieved from: https://lebanon.un.org/en/181582-report-special-rapporteur-extreme-poverty-and-human-rights-olivier-de-schutter.

Tlaiss, H.A. & Kauser, S. (2019). "Entrepreneurial Leadership, Patriarchy, Gender, and Identity in the Arab World: Lebanon in Focus". *Journal of Small Business Management*, **57**(2), 517–537.

UNFPA, U. N. (2022). *World Population Dashboard — Lebanon*. United Nations Population Fund. Retrieved from: https://www.unfpa.org/data/world-population/LB.

UNHCR Lebanon (2019). *Lebanon Fact Sheet*. Retrieved from: www.unhcr.org/lb: https://www.unhcr.org/lb/wp-content/uploads/sites/16/2020/02/UNHCR-Lebanon-Operational-Fact-sheet-January-2020.pdfnal-Fact-sheet-January-2020.pdf&usg=AOvVaw34Xf4RN_2bBk442Ocip_CX.

World Bank (2019). Retrieved from: https://www.worldbank.org/en/news/feature/2019/09/25/revolutionizing-women-led-businesses-in-lebanon-through-e-commerce.

World Bank (2020). *Women's Economic Participation in Iraq, Jordan and Lebanon*. Retrieved from: http://www.worldbank.org/en/news/press-relese/2020/06/23/addressing-the-barriers-that-hold-back-womens-economic-activity-in-the-mashreq-countries-would-boost-growth-and-prosperity.

World Bank (2021, June 1). *Press Release*. Retrieved from: www.worldbank.org: https://www.worldbank.org/en/news/press-release/2021/05/01/lebanon-sinking-into-one-of-the-most-severe-global-crises-episodes.

World Bank (2022). *Lebanon's Economic Update*. Lebanon: World Bank. Retrieved from: https://www.worldbank.org/en/country/lebanon/publication/economic-update-april-2022.

World Bank (2022). *Lebanon's Crisis: Great Denial in the Deliberate Depression*. Retrieved from: www.worldbank.org.

World Economic Forum (2021). Retrieved from: https://www.weforum.org/reports/global-gender-gap-report-2021.

World Economic Forum (2022). Global Gender Gap Report 2022. Retrieved from: World Economic Forum: https://www.weforum.org/reports/global-gender-gap-report-2022.

Zein, A. (2022). Advisor to the BOD, LLWB (S. Shamieh, Interviewer).

https://doi.org/10.1142/9789811283499_0010

Chapter 10

Women Entrepreneurs in Oman

Mohammad Rezaur Razzak[*,‡] **and Suaad Jassem**[†,§]

[*]*Assistant Professor of Strategic Management, Entrepreneurship & Family Business, Department of Management, College of Economics & Political Science, Sultan Qaboos University, Muscat, Sultanate of Oman*

[†]*Assistant Professor of Accounting, Modern College for Business and Science, Muscat, Sultanate of Oman*

[‡]*m.razzak@squ.edu.om*

[§]*suaadjassem@yahoo.com*

Abstract

Policymakers in most nations consider entrepreneurship to be a major driver of gross domestic product (GDP) growth as well as social development. In this context, women's entrepreneurship is one of the fastest-growing fields of study that has drawn wide attention from both policymakers and academics. However, not all societies have equally emphasized the importance of developing and nurturing the participation of women in entrepreneurial ventures. For instance, in many Middle Eastern countries such as Oman, the presence of women as business owners is substantially underrepresented. Nevertheless, Oman has undertaken an ambitious plan under *Oman Vision 2040*, to diversify and transform the economy of the country through numerous initiatives. One such focus area is the growth of women's entrepreneurship and their participation in the development of small and medium-sized enterprises (SMEs).

Despite the significant rise in the number of women entering the job market, the participation of women in entrepreneurship in Oman is quite dismal. Therefore, this study aims to take a nuanced look at the existing condition of women entrepreneurs in Oman, and the underlying reasons for their insufficient participation in entrepreneurial ventures. The findings narrated in this chapter are based on secondary sources from reliable academic literature, as well as reports and research work published by international organizations such as the Global Entrepreneurship Monitor, World Bank, United Nations, etc., and globally recognized consulting firms such as McKinsey and Company. The chapter identifies six major points that are being considered as factors that may impede the proliferation of entrepreneurial actions by women in Oman. Toward the end, the chapter presents an outlook for Omani women entrepreneurs in the age of digitalization.

Keywords: Women entrepreneurs; Omani women entrepreneurs; Oman Vision 2040, Oman.

1. Introduction

Entrepreneurship is widely acknowledged as a driver of economic development and drew wide attention mostly after World War II due to a need for developed countries to spur innovation and for developing countries to reduce unemployment through self-employment (Andriamahery and Qamruzzaman, 2022). As a result, in the last few decades, at an accelerating pace, entrepreneurship has become a buzzword among policymakers, academics, and economic planners (Abbasianchavari and Moritz, 2021). Empirical evidence indicates that new ventures created in the form of micro-, small-, and medium-sized enterprises are among the largest source of new employment creation (Sanyal and Hisam, 2018). Furthermore, a World Bank report on the association between innovation and entrepreneurship indicates that entrepreneurial ventures are linked to product and process innovation, and the development of new business models (The World Bank, 2021).

Women as entrepreneurs represent the fastest-growing segment in the realm of entrepreneurship globally. A recent report by the Global Entrepreneurship Monitor (GEM) indicates that policymakers around the world have realized the importance of gender diversity and inclusiveness in terms of the social impact of entrepreneurship. In fact, because of the COVID-19 pandemic, female entrepreneurs have been the hardest hit of all categories of business owners (GEM Report, 2019–2021). This is mainly attributed to the burden of balancing family responsibilities along with struggles related to business survival. Yet, case studies conducted by

Mustafa *et al.* (2021) among female entrepreneurs, indicate that women business owners have demonstrated tremendous resilience in the face of adversity.

In recent years, academic research related to women's entrepreneurship has drawn substantial traction. In fact, this stream of studies is among the most widely covered theme in the entrepreneurship literature (Abbasianchavari and Moritz, 2021). According to the extant literature, studies on women's entrepreneurship reveal many interesting discoveries, especially concerning poverty reduction, social inclusion, and women's empowerment (Cardella *et al.*, 2020). Nonetheless, the overall percentage of women who embark on the entrepreneurial journey is significantly lower than that of men (PwC, 2017), and this difference is greater depending on the cultural context (GEM Report, 2019–2021).

Culture plays a huge role in determining whether women are likely to pursue the entrepreneurial path. For instance, in East Asian nations such as China, Taiwan, Hong Kong, South Korea, etc., the involvement of women in entrepreneurship is significantly higher compared to in male-dominated societies such as the Middle East and North African (MENA) nations. This chasm is more visible in the more conservative societies prevailing in the Gulf Cooperation Council (GCC) region, which comprises the six wealthy nations of Bahrain, Oman, Saudi Arabia, Kuwait, Qatar, and the United Arab Emirates (UAE) (Alam and Alam, 2019). Furthermore, the difference in entrepreneurial intentions among women in the GCC region has been studied by researchers who found that the women in Oman and Bahrain showed the highest levels of participation in self-employment, compared to the other four GCC member countries (GEM Report, 2019–2021).

The importance of entrepreneurship is also a priority for policymakers at the highest levels in the Sultanate of Oman, where the country is pushing for diversification of the economy away from dependence on hydrocarbons (i.e., oil and gas) to other economic activities. Under the ambitious Oman Vision 2040, formulated under the leadership of His Majesty the Late Sultan Qaboos, the focus on entrepreneurship has been delineated as a thrust sector (Al Sinani *et al.*, 2021). Therefore, the key decision-makers in Oman have initiated multiple priority programs and projects to develop, nurture, and sustain entrepreneurship. A vital component of the entrepreneurship development program is the focus on bringing more Omani women toward pursuing entrepreneurship as a life choice (Ghouse *et al.*, 2017).

2. The Sultanate of Oman

The Sultanate of Oman is the third largest country in the Arabian Peninsula with a land area of 212,460 km^2. It shares land borders with the Kingdom of Saudi Arabia, Yemen, and the UAE, and the remaining border is the coastline with the Indian Ocean, the Gulf of Oman, and the Arabian Gulf (Belwal *et al.*, 2014).

The six member countries share a common language and religion. However, in terms of history, Oman is among the oldest civilizations, especially the Dhofar region of the country is home to many ancient civilizations. Strategically, Oman is situated in one of the most crucial trade routes in the world, the Hormuz Strait, which is the essential lifeline to the world's crude oil supply. Topologically, Oman is different from other GCC countries, as it has monsoon-type weather in the south, and a vast array of mountain ranges that rise to nearly 3,000 m. Culturally, it has a rich mix that resulted from its' heritage derived from multiple tribal values, and Arab, Zanzibari, and Balochi cultures. In terms of religious practices, the Omanis strongly value their Islamic culture but are extremely tolerant of other cultures (Kothaneth, 2019).

2.1. *Historical overview of Oman*

Oman as a nation is considered among the oldest of the civilizations in the Arab world. Evidence unearthed by Western archaeologists indicates that the ancient city of Al Wattih, which was in Oman, dates to over 10,000 years. Historians note that pre-Islamic Oman was dominated by Babylonians, Assyrians, and the Persian empire, because of it is strategic location on the Indian Ocean. The advent of the Islamic era started during the period of the Holy Prophet Muhammad (May Allah's Peace and Blessings be Upon him) in the early 7th century A.D. In fact, a letter from the Prophet Muhammad is exhibited in the National Museum in Oman, which invites the Omani people to Islam and mentions a prayer “Allah’s mercy be on the people of Al Ghubaira (Oman), they believed in me although they have not seen me” (Kothaneth, 2019).

Subsequently, Oman has been ruled by various dynasties, imamates (rule of imams or khalifas through the oath of allegiance), and foreign powers including the Persians, the Portuguese, and the British. The longest-serving dynasty was the Nathania dynasty, which ruled till 1470. By the 18th century, the empire in Oman stretched until the East African Coast of Zanzibar. After 1970, when Sultan Qaboos bin Said took over the reins of the country, a new era of development and modernization had taken root in the Sultanate of Oman (Landen, 2015; Risso, 2016).

2.2. *Entrepreneurial ecosystem in Oman*

Oman has been fortunate with the discovery of large deposits of oil and gas, making it a member of the GCC. However, compared to the other five GCC member nations, both Oman’s and Bahrain’s annual revenues from oil and gas are considerably lower. Furthermore, the ratio of Omani citizens to foreign workers is much higher than that of its’ neighbors. For instance, in Qatar and UAE, the composition of local citizens to foreigners is considerably low, while in Oman the majority of population are Omani citizens. This may be considered a boon for Oman both in terms of having a sustainable demographic mix as well as from the point of view of national security (Mahi and Thani, 2019).

The Late Sultan Qaboos ruled for five decades, and he was revered by his people as well as by foreigners living in Oman. He was a highly educated and enlightened man, whose priority was the prosperity and safety of Omanis. The discovery of fossil fuel and windfall profits from the sale of hydrocarbons enabled the Late Sultan Qaboos to transform Oman from a traditional to a modern nation. However, in the last decade, the Late Sultan Qaboos knew that he had to induce a second economic revolution to enable his nation to become an economically diversified and highly capable diaspora to meet the challenges of the future. With these goals in mind, Oman declared the Oman Vision 2040, where entrepreneurship development was a vital component. Within the framework of the Oman

Vision 2040 lies the underlying theme of Omanization. The Omanization program not only aims at replacing foreign workers with Omani citizens but also emphasizes growth in business ownership among underrepresented parts of society such as women. For driving the entrepreneurship development agenda, the government has created a body known as Tanfeedh. The new economic mission under the Oman Vision 2040 is being fully implemented under the able leadership of the present Sultan His Majesty Haitham bin Tariq, who succeeded his cousin Late Sultan Qaboos (Al Sinani *et al.*, 2021).

Under the ninth 5-year plan for the National Program for Enhancing Economic Diversification (Tanfeedh), the development of an entrepreneurial ecosystem has been given high priority. The Omani government has considered enhancing the role of the private sector as an engine of GDP growth. In this situation, the focus of the government has shifted toward SMEs, which involves strategic plans along with specific project initiatives. The programs were developed after examining the best practices of industrialized nations that have successfully diversified their economies through entrepreneurship and SME development, which have meta-morphed into complete ecosystems. Such ecosystems capture different factors of entrepreneurship ecosystem development at both macroeconomic and microeconomic levels. Key individuals who are tasked with executing Tanfeedh are working to update the entrepreneurship ecosystems in Oman to achieve economic diversity in the manner of the more advanced economies around the world. Hence, the first step toward driving entrepreneurship was mapping the present entrepreneurial ecosystem in the Sultanate. This enables the analysis of the challenges and opportunities for entrepreneurs so that the policymakers can address the issues that need attention with effective interventions (Sanyal and Hisam, 2018).

2.2.1. *Entrepreneurship in Oman*

Numerous studies have brought to the forefront Oman's increased need for entrepreneurship and SME development to ensure that the Omanization program moves forward steadily while also diversifying the economy (Alam and Alam, 2019; Mahi and Thani, 2019). For example, an empirical study by Echchabi *et al.* (2020) based on data from 250 entrepreneurs who started their businesses during the period 2000–2015 in Oman revealed that the entrepreneurship promotion initiatives of the government have led to substantial growth in the number of SMEs compared to previous decades. However, this growth in SMEs is not sufficient to meet the government's targets under the Oman Vision 2040. The following section presents the key entrepreneurial initiatives in Oman.

2.2.2. *Entrepreneurship policies and initiatives*

This section sheds light on the rationale for introducing entrepreneurship as a potential key driver for diversifying the Omani economy and the policies and efforts for enhancing the levels of entrepreneurial ventures in the country. The Oman Vision 2040 document reveals that there are several reasons that convinced policymakers to consider entrepreneurship development as a thrust sector (Al Sinani *et al.*, 2021).

First, Oman has a young population — in 2021, it was estimated that around 33% of Omanis were below the age of 18 according to the Oman National Center for Statistics and Information, 2022. A United Nations report suggests that nations with a high percentage of young population have the potential of converting this population into a demographic dividend if they manage their policies properly. This is a major issue now considering the fact that many Western nations are struggling with a growing aging population (UNCTAD Report, 2014).

Second, the rate of enrollment over the current decade in tertiary education in Oman has shown a significant rise compared to the rate of enrollment over a decade ago. This is particularly apparent among female students compared to males. A survey by the Ministry of Higher Education shows that the number of girls applying for admissions into universities in Oman is twice that of male applicants. This discovery is crucial for planners as they can target more women through entrepreneurship education in colleges and universities.

Third, the people of Oman by tradition have been traders for centuries, meaning that by creating the right conditions, the diaspora is likely to take the entrepreneurial path based on the traditions of their forefathers.

Fourth, having been a tax-free country for a long time, Oman has only very recently introduced some corporate income taxes and the value-added tax. Despite this change in taxation policy, the rate of taxes makes Oman a very attractive place to do business in.

Fifth, Oman has a fair ranking on the global economic freedom index, with a score of 76 for labor freedom, 61 for business freedom, and 65 for investment stability freedom (Chavali, 2016).

Sixth, the government of Oman has placed a high priority on an innovation-driven economy. In fact, two institutions, *The Research Council* and *Muscat Science Park,* promote high-impact research and development in partnership with the premier universities in the country such as the Sultan Qaboos University.

Finally, in 2014 the government set up a dedicated organization to develop, support, and nurture entrepreneurial organizations through the Public Authority of SME Development, also known as *Riyadah.*

Tables 1 and 2 show key initiatives undertaken through government and private sector-led initiatives. These programs were created to

Table 1. Key government initiatives for supporting entrepreneurship.

Program	Year	Driving Organization	Goal of the Initiative
Fund for the Development of Youth	1999	Ministry of Manpower	To promote entrepreneurship among Omani youth, offering equity financing, starting at OMR 20,000
SANAD	2001		To fund the establishment of small-scale enterprises for the public with maximum of OMR 20,000
Commercial loans	2013	The Central Bank of Oman	To allocate 5% of its commercial loans to SMEs
Land allocation	2013	Ministry of Housing	To allocate commercial and residential lands in different governorates to build business centers dedicated to entrepreneurship and offer them for use by SMEs
Payment expedition	2013	Ministry of Commerce	To expedite payments for SMEs who have government contracts
SME support	2013	The Tender Board	For no less than 10% of the value of purchases and government tenders to be provided to SMEs

Table 1. (*Continued*)

Program	Year	Driving Organization	Goal of the Initiative
SME support	2014	All government entities	For employees desiring to dedicate themselves to their own businesses full-time and receive salaries from the government for 1 year
Riyada and Al-Raffd Fund	2014	The Public Authority of SMEs	(1) To develop and accelerate the establishment of SMEs through collaboration with public and private authorities; (2) to instil the culture of entrepreneurship in Omani youth; (3) to create more renewable job opportunities for Omani youth through SMEs, and (4) to play a key role in diversifying the economy through SMEs, which add value to the national economy by supporting innovation, and through use of modern technologies
Entrepreneurs Award for SMEs			To recognize the Best Male Entrepreneur and Best Female Entrepreneur; Best Project/ Idea/Concept; Best Home Business, and Best Media

Source: Official Website of Riyada (2022).

Table 2. Key private sector initiatives for supporting entrepreneurship.

Program	Year	Driving Organization	Goal
Intilaaqah	1995	Shell Oil Company	To develop the entrepreneur trainee's ability to conceptualize the business environment by enabling him/her to acquire the necessary skills for running small businesses professionally
INJAZ	2005	Non-Government Organizations (NGOs)	To bring the business and education sectors together to educate future entrepreneurs
SME loans	2014	All Omani banks	To offer a low rate of interest to SMEs and startups run by Omani citizens

Source: Official Website of Riyada (2022).

undertake a variety of support strategies for entrepreneurship development through interventions such as education, training both locally and abroad, seed funding, growth funding, working capital support, and other support such as allocating land and consulting services, etc. (Riyada, 2022).

Alam and Alam (2019) have examined the numerous initiatives listed in the tables above. The study asserts that although the focus of most of the programs is on providing financing to the SME owners, in the GCC countries finance is not the critical obstacle. The real challenge is with issues such as the assessment of the feasibility of the business ideas, developing a proper business plan, and sufficient managerial capabilities to ensure the success of the business. The authors go on to say that funding in the GCC countries is the least of the impediments, in fact, the real problem is with sufficient entrepreneurial skills that need to be developed through a strategy that covers both higher education as well as trade schools. In another study by Echchabi *et al.* (2020), the author asserts that the entrepreneurial culture has not permeated through modern Omani society, especially among the youth who grew up in luxury and did not experience the struggles of their predecessors before the oil wealth. However, Oman has great potential for unlocking the talents of their young population, particularly young women, in terms of entrepreneurship. The government of Oman is sincere and has therefore made entrepreneurship development a core component of Vision 2040 (Sanyal and Hisam, 2018).

The function of monitoring the development of entrepreneurship through the growth of SMEs was established under the SANAD program launched by the Ministry of Manpower. Later in 2013, a Royal Decree was issued to establish a separate entity called the Public Authority of SME Development (PASMED). Not only was the SANAD program shifted to PASMED, but all subsequent SME development activities were managed under a new name *Riayada* (Khan *et al.*, 2021). This authority with the assistance of the Ministry of Commerce published a set of criteria for classifying enterprises under the categories of micro-, small-, and medium-sized (as shown in Table 3).

Although the above initiatives and policies appear to help promote entrepreneurship development in the country, there seems to be a lack of any exclusive program that is dedicated to encouraging entrepreneurship

Table 3. Classification of enterprises.

	Enterprise Size	Number of Employees	Annual Turnover (OMR)
1	Micro	1–4	<25,000
2	Small	5–9	25,000 to <250,000
3	Medium	10–99	250,000 to <1,500,000

Source: Website of Ministry of Commerce.

among women. This matter will be discussed at length in the subsequent sections.

3. Entrepreneurship Among Arab Women

The part of the world typically considered the Arab region comprises 25 countries starting from Oman situated in the Middle East on the shore of the Indian Ocean to Morocco, which is situated on the shore of the Atlantic Ocean in North Africa. These countries share Arabic as a common language and Islam as a common religion (Magd and McCoy, 2014). Despite the apparent similarities, there are significant differences in the cultures of these countries.

Risso (2016) classifies Arab countries into the Gulf region, which comprises the six countries of the GCC that share a somewhat common culture and customs, and the remaining Arab countries such as Algeria, Lebanon, Iraq, Syria, Egypt, Jordan, etc., which all have different political and cultural compositions that are quite idiosyncratic. The difference is at times quite stark, in that the Arabic dialect spoken in some parts of Arabia is not easily understood in other parts.

Academic research related to the role of Arab women in entrepreneurship is insufficient and quite scattered both geographically as well as over the period of the studies done (Assi and Marcati, 2020). Most of the studies are focused on the oil-rich states of the GCC, particularly Saudi Arabia and UAE, and with fewer studies on women in the context of non-oil-based economies such as Egypt, Tunisia, Morocco, etc. There appears to be a lack of both depth and breadth in the peer-reviewed literature on entrepreneurship among women in MENA, which is needed to draw generalizable inferences about the experiences of Arab women in being entrepreneurs (Khan *et al.*, 2021).

3.1. *Women entrepreneurs in Oman*

Gender equality is one of the 17 United Nation's Sustainable Development Goals (SDGs). The idea behind this SDG goal is to create equal opportunities for women and men to fully participate in economic activities through work and business (Smith, 2020). In this regard, Oman is in a fairly good position compared to other GCC members. During the reign of the Late Sultan Qaboos, the country witnessed many educated women flourishing in various government positions in the bureaucracy and at the ministerial levels. In fact, Oman is among the few GCC countries that have appointed a female ambassador to important foreign missions. For instance, Hunain Sultan Al Mughairy served as Oman's ambassador to the United States of America from 2005 (Al Wahaibi, 2020).

Over the last decade, leading higher educational institutions such as the Sultan Qaboos University accepted a larger proportion of female applicants compared to males, purely considering admissions on merit. A study by Al Harthy (2021) indicates that around 57% of the students on the merit list of graduating students from high schools are girls, which makes it easier for them to qualify for admission into universities and colleges compared to their male counterparts. This influx of young women into tertiary education has created a noticeable increase in the number of female participations in various professions in the country including medical science, engineering, information technology, finance, accounting, and also in general management areas (Al Harthy, 2021).

Despite the strides made by women in Oman in education and participation in the job market, the incidence of young women venturing into the entrepreneurial path is relatively rare unless the woman comes from an established business family. In that case, the participation of such women is more aligned with being involved in a family-owned business rather than becoming an entrepreneur (Khan *et al.*, 2021). To delve into the causes that are restraining women in Oman from pursuing entrepreneurship, a starting point would be to look at the academic literature available in the context of Omani women.

The extant literature indicates that the published studies in reputable peer-reviewed journals are very limited, scattered, and quite old, except for a few of the recent publications such as Ecchabi *et al.* (2020) and Khan *et al.* (2021). The earlier studies such as Al-Riyami *et al.* (2002) looked at challenges and opportunities for women entrepreneurs in Oman through face-to-face interviews with several women. Furthermore, Belwal *et al.* (2014) conducted a study of women in the Al-Dhahirah region of Oman to determine their perceptions about challenges and motivations in the context of entrepreneurship.

The relatively more recent studies are by Ghouse *et al.* (2017), who studied the perceptions of Omani women living in rural and mountainous parts of Oman. In a more recent study, Ecchabi *et al.* (2020) conducted a cross-sectional survey of 384 female students in major universities in Oman to determine the drivers of their entrepreneurial intentions. Using structural equation modeling, the authors found that factors such as attitude toward risk, subjective norms, and facilitating conditions had no statistically significant influence on the entrepreneurial intentions of Omani women. Hence, there appears to be a dearth of sufficient academically rigorous studies on women entrepreneurship in Oman from which to draw meaningful conclusions about the challenges that women in Oman perceive regarding pursuing self-employment through entrepreneurial ventures.

The next step is to examine research undertaken by globally renowned non-academic institutions with regard to female participation in entrepreneurship in Oman. The first significant study is by GEM, which was last updated in 2021. While the GEM report provides meaningful in-depth information about entrepreneurial behaviors and attitudes along with spider- and bar graphs, showing entrepreneurial framework conditions, etc., which are encapsulated within seven chapters covering various aspects of entrepreneurship, very little is mentioned exclusively about women entrepreneurship (GEM Report, 2019–2021). Another study by the United Nations Conference on Trade and Development (UNCTAD) reports on science, technology, and innovation policies in Oman. This report also sheds some light on opportunities for female participation in entrepreneurship in Oman and suggests that digitalization may address many obstacles faced by potential Omani women entrepreneurs (UNCTAD, 2014). Furthermore, there is no specific information on what specific challenges are being faced by female entrepreneurs in Oman, and how digital entrepreneurship would help overcome these challenges.

However, an in-depth study by the consulting firm McKinsey and Company was authored by Assi and Marcati (2020). This report focuses on the prospects of work for Arab women in the era of globalization and digitalization. This study provides some meaningful clues on perceived factors that may be potential determinants of entrepreneurship in the context of women in the GCC region. The next section delves into the salient features of this report by McKinsey and Company, and the manner in which it relates to women entrepreneurs in Oman.

3.1.1. *Factors that are likely determinants of perceptions toward entrepreneurship among Omani women*

In 2020, McKinsey and Company published a detailed report on work opportunities for women in the MENA region (which also includes Oman) in the era of the Fourth Industrial Revolution (Industry 4.0) (Assi and Marcati, 2020). In their report on women in the GCC countries, the report identifies several factors that provide clues to determining the challenges that Omani women are likely to perceive in pursuing self-employment through entrepreneurship. These factors are as follows:

1. Family support and encouragement have a significant influence on women, both in venturing into their own business and expanding their existing business operations.
2. The presence of female role models has an impact on the decisions and choices women make with regard to their careers, whether it is seeking employment or starting their own business.
3. Women tend to have a different view of business success compared to their male counterparts. For instance, women are happy with stable businesses that they like, rather than seeking high-growth scalable businesses such as manufacturing, construction, etc.
4. Since women in the GCC region seldom socialize with all strata of society, they usually have less access to external finance compared

to men. As a result, two issues emerge: (a) they have to rely on family money to start a business, and (b) they tend to focus on service sector businesses that require less capital.

5. Initiatives led by the government or private sector aimed at providing technical training and mentorship for building business management skills have no exclusive programs for women. Due to the conservative social structure in Oman, the women would rarely take part in such mixed training sessions. As a result, women typically lack sufficient knowledge of managing complex businesses.
6. Women have less access to market information. For detailed knowledge of markets and consumer behavior, there is insufficient sector-wise updated data available in Oman. Therefore, most businessmen rely on close personal networks to derive market intelligence. In the case of women, it is difficult to access such networks, as they are typically male-dominated.

Considering the above six points presented by the McKinsey report as a baseline for further exploration of the issues related to women entrepreneurs in Oman, the following are discussions presented by the authors of this chapter on each of the above points that are specific to the women in the Sultanate of Oman, and their challenges and opportunities for venturing into entrepreneurship.

(i) Family Support:

The Omani society is closely tied to family values and culture. Islamic values and tribal identities dominate the family culture. Omanis have always been proud of their Arabic and Islamic heritage. The government also tries to ensure that the traditional values that bind society together are still intact. Furthermore, it is to be noted that compared to Western society, the influence of the family over the behavior and aspirations of its members in Omani society is much more. Hence, before a man or a woman in Oman decides to undertake any work or journey in life that is not aligned with past practices of the family, one would normally consult with key decision-makers in the family and seek their blessings. This is also aligned with the Islamic family system that tries to create equilibrium within the family in terms of the rights of the parents, husband, wife, children, and other relatives. This is tied to the understanding that a family is a place of peace and stability.

As a result of the heavy influence of family oversight on the activities of family members, especially Omani women, it has always been difficult for girls to venture out into a work life that requires them to frequently interact with outsiders, especially men that are outside the family circle. However, with the effects of globalization and high rates of female education, Omani women have also experienced great transformation in their boundaries. In fact, greater numbers of women have gone into the job market in non-traditional sectors that were previously dominated by men. For example, positions in marketing and sales were exclusively occupied by men as they require frequent interaction with customers of all types. However, over the last decade, a large number of Omani women have been seen working in traditionally male-dominated positions such as sales position and customer service. This change is noticeable in all the major cities in Oman, especially in retail outlets.

Similarly, in the banking and finance sectors, Omani women have made great strides, as many women with sufficient skills and training are seen in important decision-making positions in banks as well as other financial institutions. Similarly, a large number of Omani women have gone into the tourism and hospitality industry. This change is an indication of the fact that their families have developed the flexibility necessary to allow their daughters to work in non-traditional business sectors where these women must interact with men and women from various backgrounds.

In terms of venturing into self-employment by urban Omani women, it is true that most of them are going into relatively easy-to-manage service businesses such as beauty salons, fitness consulting, fast food outlets, clothing boutique stores, etc. In terms of such women rarely moving into larger business ventures such as manufacturing, construction, logistics, etc., the explanation may be that the risk perceptions and feasibility of such businesses or the managerial skills experience required to manage such businesses may be the causes rather than lack of family support for Omani women. However, in the case of women living in rural parts of the country, family traditions may play a far greater role in restricting women from participating in self-employment.

(ii) Absence of Role Models in Women Entrepreneurship:

Abbasianchavari and Moritz (2021) conducted an in-depth study of the formation of entrepreneurial intentions through the presence of entrepreneurial role models. The authors conducted a meta-analysis of 86 articles published in top-tier journals on the topic of entrepreneurial role models and found that there is an overall consensus among researchers on the influence of entrepreneurial role models on the intentions of the younger generation particularly young women in deciding on whether to start their own business or not. However, they also discovered that for older women, with work experience, the presence of entrepreneurial role models was not a significant factor.

Drawing on the findings of the above study, one may conclude that for younger women without sufficient trade skills or knowledge of business, having role models to emulate is more important. Therefore, for Omani young women to decide whether to start their own businesses or to seek employment, entrepreneurial role models are likely to be crucial. In this sense, Omani society had been lagging in presenting sufficient names of successful self-made women in business. Most of the prominent women in ownership of businesses in Oman are heading organizations that are owned by their families, and they have taken over as natural successors.

Nevertheless, more and more younger women seem to be launching businesses through social media platforms in the areas of fashion, beauty, health consulting, etc. These women seem to be inspired by other Western women who are famous on YouTube. Therefore, the digitalization of society is likely to bring about changes (Chaudhry and Paqibuit, 2021). This matter will be discussed further in Section 4.

(iii) Women Seek Stable, Not High-Growth Businesses:

The most recent list of registered Omani SMEs available on the database of *Riyadah* shows that about 19.8% of the SMEs are shown to be owned exclusively by women. Out of this list, an overwhelming majority (93.2%) of these businesses are shown as micro- and small-sized service businesses, such as salons and spas, beauty and fitness consulting, boutique clothing stores, small fast-food outlets, small retail outlets, etc. The statistics appears to suggest that women entrepreneurs in Oman are either choosing the safety of businesses that require relatively low initial investment and may be considered as low risk since there are low exit barriers from such businesses if someone decided to wind up the business. Most such business organizations faced immense financial crunches during the prolonged lockdown periods enforced in 2020 due to the COVID-19 pandemic (Mustafa *et al.*, 2021). However, toward the 4th quarter of 2021, many businesses made a return hoping that 2020 style lockdowns were no longer expected.

The reasons for most women focusing on such businesses may be beyond just the risk-aversion hypothesis. One reason is that most Omani women set up these businesses and employ foreign female workers to work in these types of organizations. For getting foreign workers, business owners must typically arrange employment permits for their staff. This type of permit is at times challenging, especially if they have to employ female guest workers. For instance, for operating spas, beauty salons, and fitness businesses, the customers are women; as a result, the owners have to get female employees from the Philippines, Nepal, and India. In order to get employees for these operations, the Omani employer has to provide certain financial benefits along with guarantees to get permits to bring in such employees. This makes the process more challenging. On the other hand, a manufacturing or construction business owner would just employ male workers from the cheapest source available, and the processing of permits would be much easier.

Therefore, to take the position that Omani women business owners are simply averse to risk and only focus on small service businesses is not conclusive. In fact, this would require further in-depth investigation to unearth a more nuanced rationale. Hence, there may be other factors driving Omani female entrepreneurs toward such businesses that have not been sufficiently investigated.

(iv) Women Entrepreneurs Have Less Access to Finance

An insightful study was conducted by Andriamahery and Qamruzzaman (2022) across various Asian countries, on how access to finance for women stands as an impediment to women's empowerment. The research shows that in most Asian countries, Formal Financial Institutions (FFIs) have a poor record of gender diversity in their loan portfolio when it comes to funding startup businesses. In fact, most FFIs are comfortable in providing finance to men compared to women when it comes to startups but show more gender diversity when it comes to financing established businesses with a successful track record. The findings of the aforesaid study show that the context of Asia is different from Northern Europe, but somewhat similar to Southern Europe. For instance, Leitch *et al.* (2018) conducted a study on female entrepreneurs in Europe and found that women in Northern European countries such as Sweden and Germany had equal access to startup finance compared to Southern European countries such as Spain and Italy. Hence, social, cultural, and geographical contexts seem to have some bearing on access to finance for female entrepreneurs.

In terms of academic research publications related to access to finance for women in Oman or in the GCC, there are hardly any publications in Scopus-indexed or International Scientific Indexing (ISI)-indexed journals. Most of the publications on this topic currently available are in journals that are not well recognized yet. However, the World Bank Report dated March 2020 titled "GCC reforms are changing women's lives" narrates findings on access to finance for women entrepreneurs in GCC countries. The report shows that most of the startup ventures launched by women in GCC are with family money, and usually either the parents or the husbands provide access to funding.

An unpublished study developed by Professor Sami Khan and colleagues from Mazoon College in Oman mentions that there is a perception among Omani women that access to finance will be challenging for them without the intervention of a male member of the family. This notion arises from various reasons. The first is that there is no formal published information that is provided to potential female entrepreneurs about the sources of finance available to them if they choose to pursue the entrepreneurial path. Secondly, Omani women in general tend to consult with a senior male member of the family before they venture out to look for funding. Therefore, this matter needs further exploration in order to determine the exact barriers that women perceive with regard to entrepreneurial finance.

(v) No Exclusive Technical/Entrepreneurship Training for Women

One of the first recognized institutional programs for training Omani youth in entrepreneurship was launched in 1995 by the Shell Oil Company as a corporate social responsibility (CSR) initiative in Oman. This program is known as *Intiqallah*, which is part of Shell's LiveWIRE project that provides training, counseling, and consultancy services to potential entrepreneurs. Since then, the government of Oman has made great strides in entrepreneurship education. For instance, the SANAD program was launched under the Ministry of Manpower, which provides incubation services to young people coming out of technical schools with monetary as well as technical assistance (Belwal *et al.*, 2014; Ghouse *et al.*, 2017). Based on a Royal decree in 2013, the SANAD program was later placed under the Public Authority of SME Development (PASMED). Furthermore, Know About Business (KAB) has been launched in partnership with the International Labor Organization (ILO) to empower young people to acquire skills to establish their own businesses. Furthermore, Injaz is a program in conjunction with Junior Achievement (JA) Worldwide to provide young people with enterprise-level skills from school to university (Khan *et al.*, 2019).

Despite the numerous training and education programs, there does not appear to be any specific business incubator or technical training/education project that is purely aimed at female entrepreneurship development, though, with the promulgation of the Oman Vision 2040, higher education institutions are required to incorporate entrepreneurship as a core course in business and management degrees for all. Nevertheless, coursework through business degrees in higher education is unlikely to deliver any meaningful outcomes. What is needed is a fully woman-only program that provides technical training, mentorship, and consultancy for women who choose to start their own businesses.

(vi) Women have Less Access to Market Information

To assess the feasibility of a new business idea or to decide on further investment in an existing business, stakeholders driving the enterprise need to have sufficient information about the market dynamics of the industry. Such dynamics are related to information about customer demands, unexplored market niches, and competitive situations existing in the customer segment the entrepreneur plans to focus on.

Typically, such information is easily obtained by large companies through outsourcing to international firms such as Nielsen, which provides market intelligence at a substantial cost. However, for smaller companies, such investments are usually out of their reach. Therefore, SME owners usually obtain market knowledge through social interaction and personal networks (Wu, 2021).

For women in Oman, learning about business and markets through social interactions and personal networks is much more challenging, compared to men. This is due to the conservative nature of social interactions. For an Omani woman to openly venture out to gauge consumer perceptions through interactions with men in the market, who are outside their family circle, would be a difficult task. As a result, Omani women who start businesses usually observe other businesses in their neighborhood and make a subjective assessment of the likelihood of success of such a business. Many of these businesses are then launched with the assistance of a male member of the family, without any formal business feasibility analysis or plan. Eventually, the business either fails or barely survives through subsidies from the owner's family (Sanyal and Hisam, 2018).

The above situation is also exacerbated by the fact that there appears to be no publicly available database on market information on different products, commodities, and services in Oman that may be helpful to existing as well as potential new entrepreneurs. Particularly for women entrepreneurs a dynamic and updated digital database of market information will be crucial.

The next section of this chapter sheds light on the future and ways in which changes in technology may remove many of these obstacles that stand in the way of a large number of potential female entrepreneurs in Oman from participating in the entrepreneurial process.

4. Toward the Future for Omani Women through Digital Entrepreneurship

In recent decades globalization has pressured businesses to rapidly change, requiring them to adopt advanced digital technologies to integrate efficiencies into their processes through hyper-connected collaborative tools (Bouncken *et al.*, 2021). This process of organizational change has been accelerated by the COVID-19 pandemic, forcing organizations to transform their business models in ways that human direct interaction is rapidly replaced by the interaction between intelligent machines (Kraus *et al.*, 2021). The incorporation of technology-based in Industry 4.0 ecosystem has also fostered business model innovation (BMI) like never before (Kraus *et al.*, 2021).

Such disruptive changes in business models driven by digitalization have created a vista of opportunities, especially for underrepresented segments of society such as women to consider venturing into businesses that would be considered a man's realm in the conventional business setting (Assi and Marcati, 2020). A completely new stream of academic and applied research has emerged that is being referred to as *Digital Entrepreneurship* (Kollmann *et al.*, 2021).

Digital entrepreneurship basically entails the application of digital technologies in business processes. A simple definition of digital technologies is offered by Lyytinen *et al.* (2016, p. 49): "products or services that are embodied in information and communication technologies, or enabled by them." The extent of digitalization of the business depends on the business model. For instance, some companies (e.g., Meta, Google, Uber, AirBNB, etc.) are considered fully digitalized, while others (e.g., Amazon, Apple, etc.) use advanced digital technologies to manage a vast portion of their business processes (Kollman *et al.*, 2021). Whatever be the case, the fact is that digital entrepreneurship is being touted as a great *leveller*, where a person of any gender or any race can do business globally (Kraus *et al.*, 2021).

The idea is that instead of merely focusing on general entrepreneurship skills development through education and training, which are currently being provided and are mainly attracting young male participants, organizations such as *Riyada* need to focus more on information technology (IT) and digital skills development for all. This will likely enable women to find their own innovative business ideas, which could germinate into startup ventures driven by women entrepreneurs.

In the Mckinsey Report on the *Future of Work for Women in the Middle East*, Assi and Macati (2021) point out that digital inclusion is likely to be a catalyst for driving women's participation in entrepreneurship as well as more technology-based work. With the reshaping of the workplace in the post-pandemic era, greater opportunities will open up for women to venture into scalable business fields, such as manufacturing and logistics, that were not typically considered as women's realms.

With digital commerce taking center stage in business and trade, several new avenues have opened up for women. For instance, Ghalya* is a female restaurant owner in Muscat of a restaurant that started operations around 2018 and that serves Mexican cuisine. In the past, she would depend on her husband to deal with suppliers, promote the business, and deal with payments of fees and levies of the local authorities. However, with enhanced digital literacy, Ghalya made connections with suppliers in China through e-commerce sites such as Alibaba for products such as avocados, which are a large part of her cuisine, plus they are quite expensive when purchased from local fruit distributors. After importing a few containers of avocados from China at a much lower cost, Ghalya realized that she could become a distributor herself. She started importing and selling avocados to other restaurants as well as luxury hotels. This has now blossomed into another channel of revenue for her. Furthermore, now she makes all her tax and government fee payments through official e-governance channels. Last but not least, Ghalya spends a good part of her time promoting her business through social media platforms, which are creating a snowball effect by bringing in more customers both local and foreign. This is just one example of how digitalization has enabled Omani women to break through barriers that were holding them back.

In relation to the six factors discussed in Section 3.1.1, which were considered potential determinants of participation of Omani women in entrepreneurship, the move toward a digital marketplace addresses many of these issues quite effectively. The following are the possible implications of digital entrepreneurship for Omani women, in terms of each factor:

(i) Family support and encouragement for young Omani women deciding to pursue the entrepreneurial path is likely to be much easier considering the low barrier to entry into the business through Internet platforms. In fact, many women can start their businesses in parallel with their household responsibilities and their regular jobs. This has become a common theme globally, where people of all ages are trying to create multiple streams of income by leveraging social media and online delivery channels, and matching them with products and services that they are familiar with. Furthermore, the cost of winding up of such businesses is also not prohibitively high. Hence, family restrictions for younger Omani women to start their own businesses could be considerably less of a factor in the age of digitalization.

(ii) In terms of having role models to start a business, the Internet has created a borderless world where people from all geographic regions and cultures can learn from each other and follow those who are successful. The Internet is full of successful young and old women entrepreneurs, who share their successes with the world through various social media platforms. As a result, Omani women now have a much greater array of individuals they could look up to as role models in launching their own businesses.

(iii) Women shying away from scaleable businesses such as production is also going to be less of a factor. These days, one can look into the value chain of a product one wishes to sell, and outsource production almost anywhere one wants. This has been one of the reasons the numbers of business participants on the B-2-B platforms of Amazon and Alibaba have exploded. Entrepreneurs, whether men or women, can easily find manufacturers for any products they wish to develop, and have them shipped to their customers without them even touching the product. By training and educating Omani women in making proper use of these digital platforms, they can also venture into businesses that are high-growth and scalable.

(iv) Access to finance for women entrepreneurs is also another factor that is supposed to influence the entrepreneurial intentions of women entrepreneurs. Digital platforms now make it much easier to reach out to investors from all over the world, including the possibility of crowdfunding, venture capital, angel investors, etc. Women entrepreneurs would no longer be required to only bank on FFIs, which have more rigidity in their financing practices.

(v) There being no exclusive training for women entrepreneurs in Oman is unlikely to be a hindrance in a digitalized world. There are hundreds and thousands of online courses, training workshops, etc. offered by universities, private organizations, and even international organizations such as the United Nations Development

Program (UNDP), International Finance Corporation (IFC), etc. Furthermore, Massive Open Online Courses (MOOCs) such as Coursera, Udemy, Khan Academy, etc. offer various short and long training courses for anyone who wishes to learn about any topic. Many of these courses are free of cost.

(vi) Women in Oman not having sufficient access to market information will also not be a major impediment soon. In fact, these days AI-based algorithms are used by many technology companies that use the large flow of data to analyze consumer preferences and provide suggestions on precise and targeted advertisements and marketing campaigns. Access to this type of information is not difficult anymore. In fact, software companies are now providing services at a reasonable cost to micro- and small entrepreneurs who need data to be analyzed with artificial intelligence-based algorithms.

In light of the preceding discourse, it appears that shifting the focus of the women in Oman from traditional business models to a more digitally savvy workforce is likely to remove or at least minimize the obstacles that Omani women have been perceiving in the past with regard to entrepreneurship.

5. Toward the Future

The online marketplace created through digital platforms is a game-changer for female entrepreneurship, especially for women from conservative societies such as Oman. Not only are Omani women able to access market information and financial access through digitalized businesses, the new phenomenon is also giving women the flexibility they need to streamline their personal commitments at home with the demands of their work. With an increasing number of girls enrolling in higher education in Oman, and with the application of smart technologies in education, the upcoming generation of young Omani women is expected to look beyond the traditional employment market and consider starting their own businesses.

The encouraging statistics on more and more girls enrolling in STEM-related subjects and also into business and management programs in colleges and universities in Oman suggests that a wave of new young women entrepreneurs with highly developed digital capabilities is likely to start their own technology-driven ventures and choose to become entrepreneurs. This forecast is mirrored by the report presented by McKinsey and Company on the next generation of Arab women that are entering the workforce, especially in the era of Industry 4.0. Omani policymakers and planners have reasons to be optimistic about Omani women, who are expected to play a major role in achieving the Oman Vision 2040, through entrepreneurship.

References

Abbasianchavari, A. & Moritz, A. (2021). "The Impact of Role Models on Entrepreneurial Intentions and Behaviour: A Review of the Literature". *Management Review Quarterly*, **71**, 1–40.

Al Harthy, Y. S. (2021). *Modelling Student Flows in the Omani Higher Education System*. Ph.D Dissertation submitted at the University of Wollongong, Australia. Retrieved from: https://ro.uow.edu.au/cgi/viewcontent.cgi?article=1992&context=theses1.

Al Sinani, A. Z. M., Ayyapan, P., & Magd, H. (2021). "Corporate Governance Best Practices aligned with Oman Vision 2040 — Way Forward". *Global Business and Management Research*, **13**(3), 57–69.

Al Wahaibi, A. N. (2020). "Women's Empowerment from the Perspective of Female Omani Academic Leaders". In Papa, R., (eds.), *Handbook on Promoting Social Justice in Education*. Cham: Springer.

Alam, M. N. & Alam, N. (2019). "Impact of Small and Medium Enterprises on Oman Economy". *International Journal of Economics and Business Research*, **2019**(2), 140–152.

Andriamahery, A. & Qamruzzaman, M. (2022). "Do Access to Finance, Technical Know-How, and Financial Literacy Offer Women Empowerment Through Women's Entrepreneurial Development?" *Frontiers in Psychology*, **12**, 776–798.

Assi, R. & Marcati, C. (2020, March). *Women at Work in the Middle East*. McKinsey & Company, Retreived from: https://www.mckinsey.com/featured-insights/middle-east-and-africa/women-at-work-in-the-middle-east.

Belwal, S., Belwal, R., & Al Saidi, F. (2014). "Characteristics, Motivations and Challenges of Women Entrepreneurs in Oman's Al-Dhahira Region". *Journal of Middle East Women's Studies*, **10**(2), 135–151.

Bouncken, R. B., Gast, J., Kraus, S., & Bogers, M. (2015). "Coopetition: A Sytematic Review, Synthesis, and Future Research Directions". *Review of Managerial Science*, **9**(3), 577–601.

Cardella, G. M., Henandez-Sanchez, B. R., & Sanchez-Garcia, J. C. (2020). "Women Entrepreneurship: A Systematic Review to Outline the Boundaries of Scientific Literature". *Frontiers in Psychology*, **11**(1), 218–234.

Chaudhry, I. S. & Paquibut, R. Y. (2021). "Women Empowerment Through Microentrepreneurship in Online Business in The Sultanate of Oman". *Academy of Entrepreneurship Journal*, **27**(1), 113–127.

Chavali, K. (2016). "Dynamics of Women Enterpreneurs in Sultanate of Oman: Opportunities and Obstacles". *International Review of Management and Marketing*, **6**(1), 23–28.

Echchabi, A., Omar, M. P. S., & Ayedh, A. M. (2020). "Entrepreneurial Intention Among Female University Students in Oman". *Journal of International Business and Entrepreneurship Development*, **12**(4), 202–217.

Ghouse, S., McElee, G., Meaton, J., & Durrah, O. (2017). "Barriers to Rural Women Entrepreneurs in Oman". *International Journal of Entrepreneurial Behaviour and Research*, **23**(6), 998–1016.

Global Entrepreneurship Monitor (GEM). *Sultanate of Oman: National Report*. Global Entrepreneurship Monitor: Retrieved from: https://www.unizwa.edu.om/Final%20Oman%20GEM%20National%20report 2019_2020_Oct%2020.pdf.

Khan, S. A., Ghosh, A. P., & Myers, D. A. (2021). "Women Entrepreneurship in Oman". In *Conference proceedings of 50th World Conference of the International Council for the Small Business* (ICSBB), June 15–18, Washington, D.C. Retrieved from: https://www.researchgate.net/publication/274898251_Women_Entrepreneurship_in_Oman.

Kollmann, T., Kleine-Stegemann, L., de Cruppe, K., & Then-Bergh, C. (2021). "Eras of Digital Entrepreneurship: Connecting the Past, Present, and Future". *Business Information Systems Engineering*, **64**, 15–31.

Kothaneth, L. (2019). *Islam in Oman: A Precious Letter That is Pride of Nation*. Oman Observer. Retreived from: https://www.omanobserver.om/article/32249/Features/islam-in-oman-a-precious-letter-that-is-pride-of-the-nation.

Kraus, S., Jones, P., Kailer, N., Weinmann, A., Chaparro-Banegas, N., & Roig-Tierno, N. (2021). *Digital Transformation: An Overview of the Current State of the Art of Research* (pp. 1–15). Sage *Open*. Retrieved from: https://journals.sagepub.com/doi/full/10.1177/21582440211047576.

Landen, R. G. (2015). *Oman Since 1856*. Volume 2286 in the series Princeton Legacy Library.

Leitch, C., Welter, F., & Henry, C. (2018). "Women Entrepreneurs' Financing Revisited: Taking Stock and Looking Forward". *Venture Capital*, **20**(2), 103–114.

Lyytinen, K., Yoo, Y., & Boland, R. J. J. (2016) "Digital Product Innovation Within Four Classes of Innovation Networks". *Information Systems Journal*, **26**, 47–75.

Magd, H. A. E. & McCoy, M. P. (2014). "Entrepreneurship in Oman: Paving the Way for a Sustainable Future". *Procedia Economics and Finance*, **15**(1), 1632–1640.

Mahi, S. R. & Thani, J. K. N. A. (2019). "The Strategies Used by SMEs to Survive During the Economic Crisis in the Sultanate of Oman". *Journal of Student Research*, **4**, 131–142.

Mustafa, F., Khursheed, A., Fatima, M., & Rao, M. (2021). "Exploring the impact of the COVID-19 pandemic on women entrepreneurs in Pakistan". *International Journal of Gender and Entrepreneurship*, **13**(2), 56–72.

PricewaterhouseCoopers (PwC) Report (2017). *Women Unbound: Unleashing Female Entrepreneurial Potential*. Retrieved from: https://www.pwc.com/gx/en/diversity-inclusion/assets/women-unbound.pdf.

Risso, P. (2016). *Oman and Muscat*. London, UK: Routledge.

Sanyal, S. & Hisam, M. W. (2018). "The Role of Business Incubators in Creating an Entrepreneurial Ecosystem: A Study of the Sultanate of Oman". *Indian Journal of Commerce and Management Studies*, **9**(3), 52–67.

Scuotto, V., Nocotra, M., Guidice, M. D., & Gregori, N. K. (2021). "A Micro Foundational Perspective in Smes' Growth in the Digital Transformation Era". *Journal of Business Research*, **192**(1), 382–392.

Smith, M. J. (2020). "Sustainable Development Goals: Genuine Global Change Requires Genuine Measures of Efficacy". *Journal of Maps*, **16**(2), 2–4.

The World Bank Report (2021). *Innovation and Entrepreneurship are Recognized as Key Building Blocks of Competitive and Dynamic Economies*. Retrieved from: https://www.worldbank.org/en/topic/innovation-entrepreneurship.

UNCTAD Report (2014). *Science, Technology, and Innovation Policy Review: Oman*. Retrieved from: https://unctad.org/system/files/official-document/dtlstict2014d1_en.pdf.

Wu, K. (2021). "Market Research for Small Businesses: A Real-World Perspective". *Journal of Business and Finance Librarianship*. doi.org/10.1080/08963568.2021.1982566.

https://doi.org/10.1142/9789811283499_0011

Chapter 11

Women Entrepreneurs in Palestine

Doaa Althalathini

Oxford Brookes Business School
Oxford Brookes University
dalthalathini@brookes.ac.uk

Abstract

This chapter explores the experiences of, and challenges faced by, women entrepreneurs in Palestine. The critical review of available literature revealed that the politically unstable context resulted in the transformation of traditional gender norms. The high level of unemployment and poverty have pushed Palestinian women to engage in entrepreneurial activities out of necessity. Nevertheless, Palestine still has a very low number of women's entrepreneurial activities due to the structural and institutional challenges they face. Although many women are highly educated, they still face numerous barriers to entering the workforce, which have a negative impact on their human and social capital. Women entrepreneurs in Palestine not only fight the difficult political and security conditions but also patriarchal norms and structures. Therefore, they demonstrate resilience by defying their contextual embeddedness while contributing to social change. The advancements in technology and the affordability of using social media are creating more opportunities for Palestinian women to start and run businesses. This chapter contributes to the growing literature on women's entrepreneurship in the Middle East and mainly in under-researched contexts affected by political instabilities.

Keywords: Women's entrepreneurship; institutions; occupation; conflict contexts; technology; Palestine.

1. Introduction

Women entrepreneurs are becoming the fastest-growing entrepreneurial population in the world (Nziku and Henry, 2021). Promoting women's entrepreneurship has become a priority in many countries, recognizing their crucial role in economic development and social well-being of the society (Sajjad *et al.*, 2020). In particular, policymakers are interested in stimulating women's entrepreneurship in contexts of conflict and political instabilities as a key strategy for reducing poverty and promoting gender equality and peace (World Bank, 2020a). For example, there is a growing number of women entrepreneurs in Palestine (Althalathini *et al.*, 2020), where lack of job opportunities and high levels of poverty have pushed these women to start businesses out of necessity (Sabella and El-Far, 2019). Despite that Palestinian women have made significant progress in terms of education and employment, where statistics show that females have higher educational attainment than males (PCBS, 2021), their labor force participation is one of the lowest in the world, estimated at 18% compared to 70% for males in 2021 (PCBS, 2022). Similar to other patriarchal Middle Eastern countries (Tlaiss, 2019), Palestinian women still face barriers to engaging in economic activities, where the ascribed role of the man as the breadwinner and the woman as the housewife and mother are still prevalent norms (Al-Dajani and Marlow, 2010; Bastian *et al.*, 2018). Nevertheless, the high percentage of educated women and technological advancements are increasingly helping to grow the opportunities for entrepreneurship among Palestinian women (Ahmed, 2021).

While research on women's entrepreneurship in the Middle East is still limited (Al-Dajani *et al.*, 2019), it mainly focuses on prosperous and stable economies such as UAE and Saudi Arabia (Aljuwaiber, 2021). This is despite the fact that the Middle East is still one of the most conflict-affected areas in the world (Júlia *et al.*, 2020). A quarter of all violent conflicts over the past two centuries took place in the Middle East, including Syria, Yemen, and Iraq (Mundy, 2019). Necessity entrepreneurship — starting one's own business when there is no other option to make money — is highly prevalent in conflict contexts (Tommaso *et al.*, 2015) and among women (Bullough and Renko, 2017). Therefore, there is still a knowledge gap on the experiences of women entrepreneurs in the under-explored conflict contexts of the Middle East region (Althalathini *et al.*, 2022). In particular, Palestine has one of the most enduring conflicts in the world (Khoury and Prasad, 2016). Through critical analysis of academic and non-academic literature on gender, entrepreneurship, and conflict, this chapter aims at exploring the experiences of Palestinian women in their pursuit of entrepreneurship in a setting of a variety of inequalities such as constrained agency, role boundaries, and limited expectations for occupational pursuits. The chapter highlights the challenges women entrepreneurs face and the opportunities they have to promote their entrepreneurial activities. In doing so, the chapter answers the calls for more contextualization of women's entrepreneurship research (Yousafzai *et al.*, 2019) and contributes to the growing research in the Middle East region by focusing on the context of Palestine.

2. Historical Overview

2.1. *Political background*

The beginning of the *Nakba* (catastrophe) for Palestinians started with the establishment of the State of Israel in 1948 following the British occupation (Sa'di and Abu-Lughod, 2007). More than 700,000 Palestinians (nearly 60% of the population) were expelled from their homes and over 530 Palestinian villages were destroyed (Arda and Banerjee, 2021; UNRWA, 2022). Moreover, Israel occupied Gaza Strip and the West Bank including East Jerusalem in the 1967 war (United Nation, 2022). However, the formal conflict was brought to a "temporary" end by the Oslo Declaration of Principles in 1993 after the first *Intifada,* which began at the end of 1987 (Barber, 2008). Accordingly, the Palestinian Authority (PA) was formed and Israel withdrew from parts of the West Bank and Gaza Strip, which came under the leadership of a Palestinian government (Farsakh, 2002). Therefore, the Palestinian territories have been segregated into two districts, the West Bank and Gaza Strip (Barber, 2008). The international aid flow to the PA began pouring in from many counties, which has mainly come in the form of grants since the PA had a very limited capacity to repay loans (Barber, 2008). Later, economic indicators began to show stability due to the relative political stability in the region, and Israel also allowed an increasing number of Palestinian workers to work in its labor markets until 2000. In addition, the PA's strategy was to create jobs in their new institutions to absorb part of the workforce in providing public services and reducing unemployment.

However, the political situation flipped upside down once again after the second *Intifada* erupted in September 2000. On the eve of the second *Intifada*, 128,000 people, or 21% of employed Palestinians, worked in the Israeli labor market, accounting for about 21% of Palestinian incomes (World Bank, 2003). Nevertheless, the permit system was tightened up, and only 9% of Palestinian workers were still working in Israel and the settlements by the end of 2004, leading to severe unemployment and loss of income, especially in the absence of a viable Palestinian private sector as an alternative means of employment (World Bank, 2004). Reports of the largest international human rights NGOs such as Amnesty International (2022) and Human Rights Watch (2021) in addition to Israeli organizations such as B'Tselem (2021) recognize Israel's treatment of Palestinians as apartheid and a system of oppression and domination. Movement in the West Bank is subject to many checkpoints. Palestinians are often required to obtain permits for movement within the West Bank itself, limiting Palestinians' freedom to move home, obtain work, and invest in businesses or construction (Bashi and Diamond, 2015). Moreover, Israel has relied on imprisonment as one of its key strategies to control the Palestinian territories, where more than 40% of Palestinians including children have been imprisoned at least once (Beinin and Hajjar, 2014).

In 2005, Israel withdrew from Gaza Strip, and after the Islamic political party *Hamas* won the parliamentary elections in 2006, Israel implemented a blockade on Gaza and tightened its restrictions on the movement of people and goods. Therefore, Gaza not only became separated from the West Bank, it also became completely isolated from the rest of the world (World Bank, 2014a). A year later, *Hamas* — the Palestinian militant and nationalist organization — took over the control of Gaza Strip and governance has been divided between the political party *Fatah*-led PA in the West Bank and the Hamas-run PA in Gaza Strip since then. The international community responded by boycotting the Hamas-led government while supporting the Fatah-led PA, which in turn has deepened the conflict between the two political parties. Moreover, Gaza has suffered four consecutive wars, in 2008, 2012, 2014, and 2021, which caused significant damage to the infrastructure and the death of thousands of people. For example, the last attack on Gaza, which lasted 11 days, resulted in

US$ 380 million in physical damage and US$190 million in economic losses (World Bank, 2021a). Palestinians in Gaza have been left trapped in a cycle of poverty, unemployment, and food insecurity, where 80% of them are dependent on humanitarian aid (Human Rights Watch, 2019, p. 305). These political instabilities in addition to the tensions between the major Palestinian political parties have severely affected the social and economic climate in Palestine.

2.2. *Socio-economic conditions*

Palestine is a low-middle-income country with a 2020 per capita GDP of US$3,239.7 (World Bank, 2021b). The population size was 5.3 million in 2021, 3.2 million in the West Bank and 2.1 million in the Gaza Strip (PCBS, 2022). Severe political conflicts over many successive years have generated prolonged refugee situations (UNHCR, 2021). Nearly 7 million Palestinians live in the diaspora, where 6.3 million live in Arab countries and 750,000 in foreign countries (PCBS, 2022). The small Palestinian economy has been forced to grow dependent upon international aid, Israeli demand for goods and labor, and remittances from the Palestinian diaspora (Sarsour *et al.*, 2011). The prolonged occupation and its practices, where they control and restrict access to the land, air, and sea, have created an aid-dependent economy, with Palestine accumulating the "second-highest aid dependency in the world between 2002 and 2014" (Marktanner and Merkel, 2019, p. 265). Therefore, the PA struggles to sustain jobs and income for its people. Unemployment levels are high, with a significant difference between women and men in 2021 (42.9% and 22.4%, respectively) (PCBS, 2022). Figure 1 shows that the employment rate among women continued to increase remarkably over time as will be discussed later. Moreover, the unemployment rate is exceptionally high among the youth between 15 and 24 years (42.1% in 2021), leading to an inability to develop on-the-job skills and a colossal impact on the economy.

Moreover, the agricultural sector, which plays a key role in the Palestinian economy and food security, has been severely affected due to Israeli's restrictions on exports/imports and farmers' movements, land confiscation, the separation wall, and limited access to water resources (FAO, 2011). For example, Israel's restrictions on the importation of fertilizers have had a detrimental impact on agricultural productivity, which

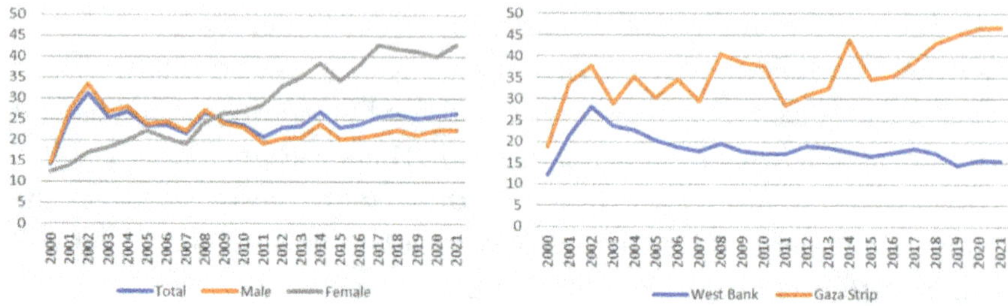

Figure 1. Unemployment rate participation based on gender and area, 2000–2021.

has declined by 20%–33% (UNCTAD, 2015). In the Gaza Strip, the worsening situation and the successive wars have resulted in a significant decline in economic conditions compared to the West Bank (Figure 1), where the poverty rate stands at 44.7% (10.6% in the West Bank) (UNCTAD, 2015). The Gaza's fishing industry is severely impacted due to Israeli's practices including access prevention of 85% of the fishing areas allocated to them under the Oslo Agreements, seizing and/or damaging fishing boats and equipment, restrictions on fishing exports and entry of raw materials, and attacking fishermen (Amnesty International, 2022; OCHA, 2019). These practices have resulted in 95% of Gaza's fishermen living under the poverty line (B'Tselem, 2018).

Nevertheless, the poverty context in Palestine is somewhat unique in that it "is not correlated with poor human development outcomes; Palestine is in fact a stellar performer on many dimensions of human development" (World Bank, 2011, p. 9). Despite the occupation, the literacy rate is one of the highest in the world, with 94.4% in 2020 (World Bank, 2021c). Palestinians have a long-standing tradition of spending generously on higher education. Although literacy and education are among the highest in the Middle East and North Africa (MENA) region, the 2021 labor force participation rate is very low at 43.4% (PCBS, 2022). Informal employment is high (62%) and mainly among males, 67%, compared to 36% for females (PCBS, 2021b). The brain drain of highly educated individuals to more stable countries has resulted in a loss of considerable human capital (Sharabati-Shahin and Thiruchelvam, 2013). The Palestinian economy is crippled, and the United Nations Relief and

Works Agency for Palestine Refugees in the Near East (UNRWA), a key employer in Palestine, remains underfunded (International Labour Organization, 2021). As a result of these socio-economic challenges, women in Palestine suffer from double marginalization: being part of the Palestinian people who live under Israeli occupation and living in a traditional, male-dominated society with cultural restraints that pose particular challenges for women seeking to get ahead (Muhanna, 2013).

2.3. *Women in Palestine*

Palestinian women have a rich history of participating in political and social life in Palestine, which can be traced back to at least 1921 with the foundation of the Palestinian Women's Union (Abdulhadi, 1998). Later, many women's organizations and unions were established to contribute to social work and resist the occupation, while women's participation has also expanded to military operations (Hiltermann, 1991). According to Holt (2003, p. 231), one of the most significant effects of the first *Intifada* (uprising) was the "transformation that took place in women's consciousness of their roles", challenging their position in the patriarchal structure. In contrast to the first *Intifada*, the escalation of militarization in the second *Intifada* has led to the decline of civil society and women's roles tended to be minimal (James, 2013). The society became more conservative, and the progress women made in the first *Intifada* was disrupted (Kuttab, 2014). Although women have extensive informal political participation, they are still largely underrepresented in formal political and public decision-making (Samaroo, 2018). Women still do not have equal access to political opportunities, where only 17 of 132 (13%) seats in the parliament are held by women (Inter-Parliamentary Union, 2019).

Despite an increase in female representation due to the quota system, the political conditions played a significant role in undermining women's activism. The permit system and mobility restrictions due to Israeli occupation curtail women's participation in political, economic, and cultural life (Griffiths and Repo, 2021). Moreover, the society is still conservative and not in support of gender equality, mainly among young males (Kostenko *et al.*, 2016). Nevertheless, despite the low engagement rates and the fluctuation in women's involvement in the labor market, their participation rates rose over the last two decades, from 12.9% in 2000 to 17.2% in 2021 as shown in Figure 2 (PCBS, 2000, 2021c). Table 1 shows that higher education has witnessed a significant increase in the number of female students from 2009 to 2019, which has led to increased participation in the labor market. Females are also studying majors in male-dominated sectors such as ICT, engineering, law, and business although they are still dominant in education, arts, and nursing (PCBS, 2021a). While women with higher education are more likely to participate in the

Figure 2. Labor force participation rate, 2000–2021.

Table 1. Number of students enrolled in Palestinian higher education institutions by gender, 2009/2008 and 2019/2018.

Gender	2008/2009	2018/2019
Males	80,007	84,513
Females	100,006	133,613
Total	180,013	218,126

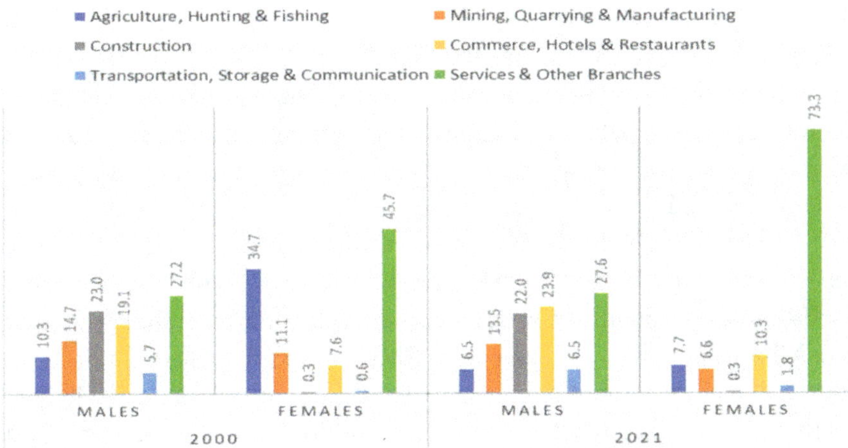

Figure 3. Percentage of employed males and females by economic activity, 2000 and 2021.

labor market than other educational groups, the political, economic, and social challenges means that these women can remain unemployed.

The contribution of women in agriculture was significant, with most of the employed women working in service and agriculture in 2000 (Figure 3). After two decades, and similar to other Middle Eastern countries, services still employ the highest percentage of women at 73.3%, compared to 29.4% for men (PCBS, 2021c). However, the limited available literature shows that an increasing number of Palestinian women are more willing to engage in entrepreneurial activities. The next section will discuss the entrepreneurial ecosystem in Palestine and how it impacts women entrepreneurship.

3. Entrepreneurial Ecosystem

Micro, small, and medium-sized enterprises (SMEs) constitute over 90% of the Palestinian economy (Abddullah and Hattawy, 2014). In particular, family businesses account for more than 70% of Palestine's businesses (Sultan *et al.*, 2017). The difficult political and economic situation has pushed men and women into necessity entrepreneurship with the hope that entrepreneurship might boost economic and social development.

However, the entrepreneurial ecosystem is yet in the infancy stage, with Palestinian entrepreneurs in general and women entrepreneurs in particular facing many institutional constraints which hinder their entrepreneurial intention and behavior (Khoury and Prasad, 2016). The lack of appropriate formal and informal institutions for the entrepreneurial ecosystem can inhibit women entrepreneurship (Hechavarría and Ingram, 2019). Palestinian women entrepreneurs run their businesses in a weak and outdated legal environment with tight resources, inefficient financing opportunities, limited market access, and weak marketing ability (Atyani and Alhaj-Ali, 2009). For example, SMEs are still treated similarly to large companies without any incentives or accounts for the considerable challenges they face (Sultan and Sultan, 2020). According to the World Bank (2020b), it takes 11 procedures, 44 days, and 40.3% of income per capita in order to legally start a business in Palestine. This is in comparison with the MENA region, which takes seven procedures, around 20 days, and 16.7% of income per capita. With insecurity situations and many checkpoints that restrict mobility of women entrepreneurs, the complicated legal environment severely affects their business start-up and survival (Althalathini and Al-Dajani, 2021). Therefore, women mostly start home-based businesses and are discouraged to move to the formal sector (Khoury *et al.*, 2018).

The Palestinian Reform and Development Plan (PRDP) 2008–2010 was the first governmental plan that proposed significant actions toward women's economic empowerment. Moreover, the national development plan (NDP) 2014–2016 aimed to promote women entrepreneurship for economic development. They offered credits and training programs but their efficiency was questioned (Sadeq *et al.*, 2011). These plans lacked mechanisms for monitoring and evaluating the impact and only some strategies were translated into policies. They did not create a sustainable supportive environment for women's empowerment. For example, there are no Palestinian laws regulating the microfinance sector, with women finding it difficult to meet their conditions and required guarantees (Elnamrouty *et al.*, 2013). With two separate governments in Palestine, the parliament has failed to pass any legislation or make any further amendments to laws and regulations. Also, the labor laws on workforce protection still do not cover women entrepreneurship. Although the Ministry of

Entrepreneurship and Empowerment was established in 2019, its activities and roles are still limited (Karaki, 2021). Hence, informal entrepreneurship and tax avoidance has become a necessity for women's business survival in Palestine, which inhabits business growth (Althalathini *et al.*, 2020).

Moreover, women's inability to formalize their businesses limits their access to finance or to have a bank account. Although there are 16 banks and 8 specialized lending institutions in Palestine (Palestine Monetary Authority, 2021), the absence of a national currency and an independent monetary policy makes the Palestinian credit market lag behind developed markets (Sarsour, 2012). The Palestinian government depends on borrowing from domestic banks to meet its expenditures (Karaki, 2021). The political instability and high level of unemployment and poverty force the Palestinian banks to apply cautious and conservative lending policies to women (International Monetary Fund, 2018). They impose difficult criteria and ask for guarantees and high-interest rates to minimize the risks of funding, limiting women entrepreneurs' access to formal finance. This could be a severe challenge for women in Palestine where resources and collateral are constrained and owned mainly by men (Althalathini *et al.*, 2020). Moreover, many women entrepreneurs follow their religious values and avoid applying for non-interest loans (Althalathini *et al.*, 2022). Despite a number of female-led SMEs, more than 60% of them lack or have limited access to finance and, hence, a majority are informal (ICF, 2016). Therefore, women entrepreneurs rely mainly on their personal savings for their start-ups (Owda *et al.*, 2019). While local and diaspora investors can play an essential role in contributing to their country's development through the transfer of knowledge, exchange of experience and financial support for investment, and rebuilding efforts, they are challenging to attract since they consider their homelands to be a risky investment environment (Gillespie *et al.*, 2001). For example, the Palestinians in the diaspora have a net worth of 120 billion (Bank of Palestine, 2016). However, they are still untapped resources for fostering economic development (Koch and Ragab, 2018).

Moreover, Israel has succeeded in turning the Palestinian economy into a dependent one, where the Palestinian market relies heavily on Israel as a trading partner. According to Palestine Monetary Authority (2021),

Israel is the primary source of goods consumed in the Palestinian market, accounting for 55% of total goods imports in 2020 while constituting around 82.5% of Palestinian imports. Israel controls the movement of goods to and from Palestine, which could increase the cost of production and impose difficulties for Palestinian products to compete in foreign markets (Ibid). Favorable market conditions are essential for encouraging investment and enhancing risk-taking behavior among women entrepreneurs. The small and fragmented domestic market and difficult economic conditions result in a limited domestic consumer market and lower the purchasing power of local customers. The Palestinian competition law, which has a negative effect on women's businesses' survival in competing with cheaper imported goods, is still under review. Informal entrepreneurship also means that women entrepreneurs have fewer professional networks, which limits their access to markets. Hence, women entrepreneurs rely on informal export, for example, via suitcases or logistics companies (Althalathini, 2020). However, the general perception and image of businesses in conflict contexts are still suspect, which means that products are of lower standards (Althalathini and Al-Dajani, 2021).

Furthermore, infrastructure is still underdeveloped, for example, power cuts of 16 hours per day are very common in the Gaza Strip, which negatively affects the productivity and profitability of women's businesses (Althalathini *et al.*, 2020). This is in addition to the challenges with the delay in logistics services and money transfers (Khoury and Prasad, 2016). The absence of an airport and limited use of the Gaza port inhibit access to external markets and increase transaction costs for women's businesses. Digital infrastructure is weak, and the coverage of internet services in Palestine is one of the lowest in the Middle East countries while being slow and costly (Palestine Monetary Authority, 2021). The third generation (3D) feature has only been available in the West Bank as of 2018, while the Gaza Strip is still limited to the second generation (2D) due to restrictions imposed by the Israeli occupation (MAS, 2019). E-commerce activity platforms such as PayPal and Amazon are not supported in Palestine (Bjørn and Boulus-Rødje, 2018). Palestinian customers also still lack trust in online banking services (Salem *et al.*, 2019). Indeed, deficiencies in infrastructure impose barriers to productive opportunities and increase costs of women's businesses.

A significant weakness of the entrepreneurial ecosystem is that the education system is geared to the needs of the public sector and does not enhance the entrepreneurial intention and critical thinking of graduates (Khatib *et al.*, 2013). Therefore, entrepreneurship is still not an attractive option for the young, educated people in Palestine, and advancement in education is found to negatively influence entrepreneurial entry (Morrar *et al.*, 2022). Nevertheless, significant efforts have been made to support the Palestinian entrepreneurial ecosystem, which provided training programs to promote entrepreneurship among female graduates. Entrepreneurship is a donor-driven activity in Palestine, where international organizations support the creation of business incubators and accelerators as a tool to change attitudes and leverage entrepreneurship activities, particularly in the information and communications technology (ICT) sector. There are different accelerators and incubators in the West Bank and Gaza Strip whose main aim is to create an entrepreneurial-friendly environment. They provide training, mentoring, and networking to motivate students and graduates, mainly women, to pursue entrepreneurial behavior (World Bank, 2018) and create start-ups that address the society's challenges and needs (Owda *et al.*, 2019). Indeed, these business incubators play a role in decreasing the high unemployment rate among the youth and female graduates. Despite the substantial amounts of grant financing, these incubators and accelerators, including mentors, are still maturing and lack the experience to support potential women entrepreneurs in establishing sustainable start-ups (World Bank, 2018). They are unable to provide quality services and network connections (Karaki, 2021). Moreover, they focus mainly on start-ups rather than creating and promoting an entrepreneurial mindset among the youth and women (Ahmed, 2021).

As a consequence of all these constraints, Palestine ranks 117 out of 190 countries in terms of ease of doing business (World Bank, 2020b). Unsurprisingly, and in contrast to the mainstream argument, Sabella *et al.* (2014) have found that entrepreneurship in Palestine has no significant impact on economic growth. Although the context of Palestine pushes women into entrepreneurship out of necessity, the tendency to engage in entrepreneurship among young Palestinians remains low (Morrar *et al.*, 2022). Women entrepreneurs still face several political, economic, and social challenges. However, numerous opportunities are available for women entrepreneurs, contributing to the emergence of social enterprises (Akella and Eid, 2018). The largely untapped source of young human resources needs further research and support to engage in entrepreneurship and contribute to the economy, mainly among women, who represent half of the population.

4. Women Entrepreneurs

The complex political and economic situation in Palestine has facilitated the fluidity of gender relations as both men and women have been forced to engage in a joint struggle for survival. The harshness of the crisis of men losing their sources of income, with no provision of welfare benefits for their unemployment, has changed the role of women as caregivers only, concentrated on domestic activities (Muhanna, 2013). Women have had better opportunities to participate in economic life to challenge the threats against their family's survival and security, particularly women with young children (Sabella and El-Far, 2019). Hence, while the conflict has strengthened conservative gender roles, it has also opened more opportunities for women entrepreneurs to break down some of the patriarchal social norms for the sake of the survival of their families (Shamieh and Althalathini, 2022). More women are engaging in entrepreneurial activities, whereas the Palestinian Central Bureau of Statistics (PCBS) (2021) data reveals that the rate of women entrepreneurs in Palestine in 2020 accounted for nearly 13.2% of women's employment, compared to 25.5% for men. Women own close to 62,000 micro, small, and medium enterprises (MSMEs), approximately a quarter of all enterprises in Palestine (ICF, 2016). Nevertheless, necessity entrepreneurship is prevalent among women (Althalathini *et al.*, 2020). The majority of women enterprises are microbusinesses (around 96%), employing less than 10 employees (Abddullah and Hattawy, 2014).

Around the first *Intifada,* women's committees set up economic cooperatives as a part of the popular front for mass mobilizing against the Occupation (Kuttab, 2014). Although the women focused on embroidery and local food production, these traditional activities empowered them economically and enhanced their political participation (Esim and Omeira, 2009). However, the post-Oslo period has shifted the women's

Exhibit 1. On the left, Bissan cuts flowers in her field, while in the right photo her sister, Elian, helps her prepare flowers for a customer, 2021.

Source: Yousef Amro.

movement to government and research institutions, professional NGOs, and women's centers, leading to marginalizing women cooperatives (Ibid). Nevertheless, the focus of international organizations on promoting women's empowerment through entrepreneurship has further enhanced women's economic participation. Although formal support such as training, small grants, and mentoring is available for women entrepreneurs, a lack of coordination between government agencies and NGOs where they compete for donors' funds results in redundancy of capacity-building training programs and general support for women entrepreneurs (Khoury *et al.*, 2018). Moreover, these programs do not take into consideration the patriarchal and politically unstable environment women entrepreneurs live in. Childcare and family responsibilities should be a priority for women according to gender norms. Therefore, women must work hard and be more resilient to start and survive their businesses (McNally and Khoury, 2022).

Constraints can be worsened for women entrepreneurs living in conflict contexts (Alsaba and Kapilashrami, 2016). These contexts are replete with regulative institutional voids, which might cause the asymmetry, where normative, patriarchal institutions compete or substitute the weak regulative institutions (Roomi *et al.*, 2018). Therefore, challenges such as restricted access to finance, gender-based violence, increased domestic burdens, and lack of security and skills are more common, which in turn hinder women's entrepreneurship (World Bank, 2014b). According to the

Palestine Economic Policy Research Institute (2013), women entrepreneurship in 2012 ranked 58th out of 67 studied countries in early-stage entrepreneurial activity and the second-lowest country for established-business female owners. The unsupportive formal and informal institutions might affect women more than men. Morrar *et al.* (2022) found that women in Palestine are less likely to become entrepreneurs than men due to structural inequalities that women face regarding new business creation. Although Al-Botmeh (2013) found that around 65% of Palestinian women expressed a willingness to engage in start-up businesses, women have a high fear of failure and low perceived self-efficacy, which are the main impediments to starting a business (Daoud *et al.*, 2020).

For women entrepreneurs living and running their businesses in conflict contexts, difficulties are part of their daily lives. Bullough and Renko (2017) found that family support has greater importance for women in Afghanistan than fear from external forces to pursue their entrepreneurial activities. Therefore, the support of men is very significant in patriarchal conflict contexts (Bullough *et al.*, 2017). In Palestine, strong family support acts as an enabler for women to overcome social norms and access finance and learning opportunities (McNally and Khoury, 2022). For example, Ahmed (2021) found that having a male co-founder from the family has enhanced the risk-taking behavior of women to engage in entrepreneurial activities and further improved their self-efficacy at the early stages of their entrepreneurial journey. Nevertheless, Palestinian women have to engage in an ongoing process of negotiation and legitimization of their entrepreneurship, similar to other women entrepreneurs in traditional Middle Eastern countries (Barragan *et al.*, 2018). Gendered practices and assumptions, such as prioritizing childcare and household responsibilities, can still be used as a guide for Palestinian women entrepreneurs to gain legitimacy (Althalathini *et al.*, 2020).

The growing research on gender and entrepreneurship has shifted the traditional view of entrepreneurship as a "positive economic activity" to "entrepreneurship as social change" (Calas *et al.*, 2009). Women have not just challenged gender-related issues but have also played a role in altering societal norms that perpetuate discrimination against them (Welter *et al.*, 2018). Despite their low participation rate in economic activities, Palestinian women entrepreneurs employed 5.6% of the total employed population

(Abdullah and Hattaway, 2014). Women entrepreneurs in Palestine have contributed to enhancing family income (Sabella and El-Far, 2019), creating jobs (Althalathini *et al.*, 2020), and defying and changing some of the patriarchal, gendered norms by working in male-dominated fields (Althalathini *et al.*, 2022). Palestinian women entrepreneurs can create economic and social value by challenging international perceptions of women in conflict contexts as victims and marginalized sections of society (Althalathini, 2022). Women's organizations and media reports can play a crucial role in supporting women's agenda in contexts affected by political instabilities (Metcalfe *et al.*, 2022). What has been found is that women's organizations in Palestine have contributed to promoting women's agency and enhanced their self-efficacy (Shamieh and Althalathini, 2022). Moreover, the media can raise awareness about gender issues and roles (Jayachandran, 2019), and give publicity to the experiences of women living in conflict contexts (Höijer, 2004). Therefore, the media has improved the visibility of women entrepreneurs in Palestine and their role in such contexts. It shows not only the negative side of the conflict but also their success and resilience stories where they strive and succeed in entrepreneurship and add economic and social value (Althalathini, 2022).

Regarding the types of businesses Palestinian women have, traditional activities such as embroidery, cooking, and soap making are very popular among women entrepreneurs. This is mainly due to a lack of resources

Exhibit 2. Women entrepreneurs work in male-dominated fields such as carpentry and fishing.

Source: Aaed Baker (left photo) and Hasan Aljadi (right photo).

Institutional challenges compel women to engage in traditional, feminine sectors that typically demand low capital and resources. This is further exacerbated by the widespread prevalence of traditional gender roles, where women are expected to fulfill the roles of full-time mothers and wives (Althalathini and Tlaiss, 2023). Women can pursue a business that is a "hobby", which hinders their growth potential. This could increase occupational segregation and confine women to traditional gender roles. Nevertheless, with the modernization of embroidery and food processing, such activities can promote women's entrepreneurship as a way to preserve the Palestinian heritage and identity (Althalathini, 2020). Moreover, women entrepreneurs are increasingly entering male-dominated fields such as carpentry, fishing, and technology where they have to demonstrate resilience in order to create social change (Althalathini, 2020).

In the context of the patriarchal Middle East, technology has played a significant role in enhancing women's political and economic participation. Technology has facilitated the growing involvement of women in political conversations and aided social change in this region (Howard *et al.*, 2011). With the enhancement in digital technology and the rise of social media, women in the Middle East have started engaging in entrepreneurship activities in the digital space. They run online home-based businesses to navigate entrepreneurial obstacles in their patriarchal contexts (McAdam *et al.* 2018). Hence, digital technologies have contributed

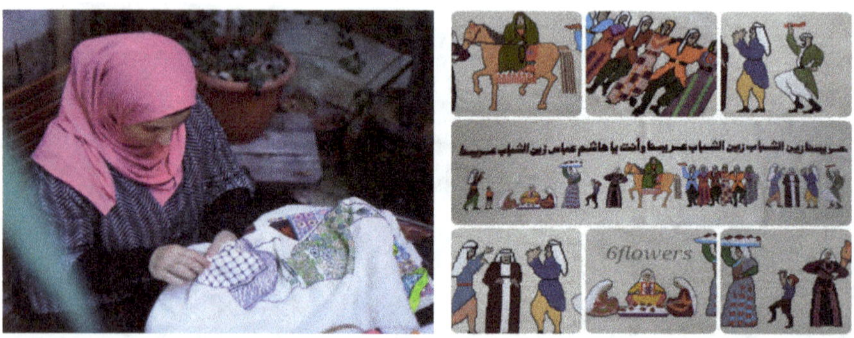

Exhibit 3. The photo on the left shows one of the six sisters is doing embroidery, while the photos on the right present samples of their products that preserve Palestinian heritage, 2022.

Source: Atia Hijazi.

to women's empowerment and emancipation (McAdam *et al.*, 2020). Similarly, digital technologies such as social media have enabled women in Palestine to pursue necessity entrepreneurship by overcoming the regulative and social challenges they face (Althalathini *et al.*, 2020). This was mainly facilitated where households have internet access. This was mainly facilitated in households where 80% have access to the internet (PCBS, 2020). Interestingly, the percentage of women who use social networks has reached 84% (88% of men) (PCBS, 2020). Therefore, with the popularity and affordability of social media platforms, Palestinian women entrepreneurs have begun using them for learning and marketing (Sultan and Sultan, 2020).

According to Bjørn and Boulus-Rødje (2018), these women are increasingly utilizing technology to mitigate the high level of unemployment and boost their economy. However, literacy in technology and the use of social media are crucial for success (Kamberidou, 2020), and the lack thereof might be one of the main obstacles for women entrepreneurs in conflict contexts, limiting the creative use of technologies (World Bank, 2014b). Nevertheless, the Palestinian tech ecosystem has been witnessing an increase in women's digital entrepreneurship in recent years due to the high percentage of women graduates from ICT-related fields (MAS, 2019), even though technology start-up founders in Palestine are predominantly male (World Bank, 2018). These highly educated women digital entrepreneurs are using the digital space to emancipate themselves

Exhibit 4. Tarneem is preparing Ramadan decorations, 2022.

Source: Nour Almadhoun.

Exhibit 5. Karama teaches Arabic to non-native speakers, 2022.
Source: Karama Fadel.

from their contextual challenges, including cultural, financial, and political ones (Ahmed, 2021). Despite the wide range of opportunities provided by the digital space for women entrepreneurs, the digital space is changing rapidly, and this requires women entrepreneurs to continue learning to grow their ventures. This is a major barrier for Palestinian women digital entrepreneurs, considering the significant political and social challenges they still encounter.

5. Toward the Future

Despite the remarkable progress Palestinian women have made over the past decades, the challenges they still face are considerable. This chapter's analysis of academic and non-academic literature has revealed the importance of contextualizing women's entrepreneurship research as political, economic, and social instabilities are part of the daily lives of Palestinian women entrepreneurs. The number of women entrepreneurs is still low, where they face barriers regarding access to financial resources, limited markets and social networks, lack of entrepreneurial education, and general social support. They still struggle with the underlying patriarchal structure of society. The high educational level of women and low labor market participation mean there is a significant loss of economic potential. Therefore, carrying out further research into the contextual embeddedness of women's experiences and realities enables us to understand and effectively promote their entrepreneurial behavior and activities (Yousafzai *et al.*, 2019). It is important to look holistically and take a multi-level approach to analyzing the entrepreneurial ecosystem where women entrepreneurs operate their businesses.

From a policy and practical perspective, strengthening the entrepreneurial ecosystem should be a priority by tackling the roots of the challenges women face. The continued occupation practices and measures would hinder any efforts to achieve economic and social development in Palestine. Lifting restrictions on the movement of people and goods and more advanced technology are key factors for women's entrepreneurial entry and success. Enacting laws and regulations that promote (women) entrepreneurship and provide incentives are important to developing the entrepreneurial ecosystem for the start-up and survival of SMEs. More importantly, the aim must be to strengthen the role of the PA instead of programs that created nongovernmental parallel systems that undermine the role of the PA. Moreover, finance is significant for any business, but banks in Palestine have a limited role in supporting women entrepreneurs. Hence, providing affordable and legitimate loans is also important.

Moreover, entrepreneurship education can be an effective tool to develop entrepreneurial intentions, mindsets and skills, and enhance the social legitimization of women's entrepreneurship. Education and more so higher education play a vital role in enabling women's entrepreneurship as education is considered a basic element in women's life in Palestine. The world is becoming increasingly technology-driven; therefore, providing education and training programs in digital literacy and social media is crucial. Palestine struggles with many challenges; nevertheless, these gaps can be opportunities for women to tackle them creatively. For example, the Gazan entrepreneur Majd Mashharawi contributed to addressing the power-cut crisis and restrictions on access to construction material due to the blockade in Gaza by developing affordable solar devices and creating environmentally friendly concrete blocks from ashes and rubble (*The Guardian*, 2019). The rise of women graduating from ICT fields means that they need tailored support to innovate and contribute to achieving the Sustainable Development Goals in Palestine. However, women entrepreneurs still lack managerial experience; therefore, training and mentoring would support these women to reduce their fear of failure and improve their skill perception. Capacity-building efforts and the professionalization of accelerators and incubators represent priorities in strengthening the ecosystem. Media is a key player in the entrepreneurial ecosystem to celebrate the success stories of these women, enhance their visibility, and change societal attitudes toward them. Exposure to local role models and sharing stories of women entrepreneurs who succeed in their entrepreneurial activities would encourage more women to start up businesses and enhance their self-efficacy.

Most importantly, women do not operate their businesses in isolation but rather in a collective and conservative society. Therefore, involving men in research and programs targeting women's entrepreneurship would help change some of the patriarchal gender norms (Althalathini and Al-Dajani, 2021). In particular, enhancing the participation of women in political and public decision-making will have a positive impact on women's participation in different aspects of society, including entrepreneurship. The lack of a clear vision on how to address women entrepreneurship resulted in random efforts and limited fruitful outcomes (Khoury *et al.*, 2018). Therefore, more joint cooperation among all key players such as government, policymakers, universities, and international and local NGOs would help to design effective interventions to further promote women's entrepreneurship in Palestine, thus enabling these critical drivers for growth and development.

References

Abddullah, S. & Hattawy, M. (2014). *Policies for Scaling Up Female Entrepreneurship in The State of Palestine*. Ramallah, Palestine: Palestine Economic Policy Research Institute (MAS).

Abdulhadi, R. (1998). "The Palestinian Women's Autonomous Movement: Emergence, Dynamics, and Challenges". *Gender and Society*, **12**(6), 649–673.

Ahmed, A. (2021). *The Digital Entrepreneurial Mindset Among Female Graduates in the Context of Siege and Conflict*. Master thesis, The Graduate Institute of Geneva.

Akella, D. & Eid, N. (2018). "Social Enterprises in Palestine: A Critical Analysis". *Journal of Enterprising Communities: People and Places in the Global Economy*, **12**(4), 510–544.

Al-Botmeh, S. (2013). *Barriers to Female Labour Market Participation and Entrepreneurship in the Occupied Palestinian Territory*. Birzeit University and Christian Aid.

Al-Dajani, H., Akbar, H., Carter, S., & Shaw, E. (2019). "Defying Contextual Embeddedness: Evidence from Displaced Women Entrepreneurs in Jordan". *Entrepreneurship & Regional Development*, **31**(3–4), 198–212.

Al-Dajani, H. & Marlow, S. (2010). "Impact of Women's Home-Based Enterprise on Family Dynamics: Evidence from Jordan". *International Small Business Journal,* **28**(5), 470–486.

Aljuwaiber, A. (2021). "Entrepreneurship Research in the Middle East and North Africa: Trends, Challenges, and Sustainability Issues". *Journal of Entrepreneurship in Emerging Economies*, **13**(3), 380–426.

Althalathini, D. (2020). *Resilience of Entrepreneurs in Conflict Zones: Evidence from Afghanistan, Iraq and Palestine*. Doctoral thesis, University of Plymouth.

Althalathini, D. (2022). "Value Creation in Conflict Zones: Evidence from Afghan and Palestinian Women Entrepreneurs". In Sh. Yousafzai, C. Henry, M. Boddington, Sh. Sheikh & Fayolle, A., (eds.), *Research Handbook of Women's Entrepreneurship and Value Creation*. Edward Elgar Publishing. ISBN: 978-1-789901368.

Althalathini, D. & Al-Dajani, H. (2021). "Policy Brief: Supporting Women Entrepreneurship in Conflict Ridden States". doi.org/10.24384/5CZK-QD44.

Althalathini, D., Al-Dajani, H., & Apostolopoulos, N. (2020). "Navigating Gaza's Conflict through Women's Entrepreneurship". *International Journal of Gender and Entrepreneurship,* **12**(4), 297–316.

Althalathini, D., Al-Dajani, H., & Apostolopoulos, N. (2022). "The Impact of Islamic Feminism in Empowering Women's Entrepreneurship in Conflict Zones: Evidence from Afghanistan, Iraq and Palestine". *Journal of Business Ethics*, 178, 39–55.

Althalathini, D. & Tlaiss, H. (2023). Of resistance to patriarchy and occupation through a virtual bazaar: An Institutional Theory Critique of the Emancipatory Potential of Palestinian Women's Digital Entrepreneurship. Entrepreneurship & Regional Development. http://dx.doi.org/10.1080/08985626.2023.2241412.

Amnesty International (2022). Israel's Apartheid Against Palestinians: Cruel System of Domination and Crime Against Humanity. Retrieved from: https://www.amnesty.org/en/documents/mde15/5141/2022/en/ (Accessed on 23 May 2022).

Arda, L. & Banerjee, S. (2021). "Governance in Areas of Limited Statehood: The NGOization of Palestine". *Business & Society,* **60**(7), 1675–1707.

Atyani, N. & Alhaj-Ali, S. (2009). *Problems of Micro, Small and Medium Enterprises in Palestine*. Ramallah, Palestine: Palestine Economic Policy Research Institute (MAS).

Bank of Palestine (2016). *Palestinian Diaspora — A Long Term Engagement Through Partnerships*. Retrieved from: https://thisweekinpalestine.com/wp-content/uploads/2016/09/Palestinian-Diaspora-a-long-term-engagement-through-partnerships.pdf (Accessed on 27 February 2022).

Barber, B. (2008). "Contrasting Portraits of War: Youths' Varied Experiences with Political Violence in Bosnia and Palestine. *International Journal of Behavioral Development*, **32**(4), 298–309.

Barragan, S., Erogul, M., & Essers, C. (2018). "Strategic Disobedience: Female Entrepreneurs Reflecting on and Acting Upon Patriarchal Practises". *Gender, Work and Organization*, **25**(5), 575–592.

Bashi, S. & Diamond, E. (2015). "Separating Land, Separating People: Legal Analysis of Access Restrictions between Gaza and the West Bank". Legal Center for Freedom of Movement, Gisha.

Bastian, B., Sidani, Y., & El-Amine, Y. (2018). "Women Entrepreneurship in the Middle East and North Africa: A Review of Knowledge Areas and Research Gaps". *Gender in Management: An International Journal*, **33**(1), 14–29.

Beinin, J. & Hajjar, L. (2014). *Palestine, Israel and the Arab-Israeli Conflict*. Washington: Middle East Research and Information Project.

Bjørn, P. & Boulus-Rødje, N. (2018). "Infrastructural Inaccessibility Tech Entrepreneurs in Occupied Palestine". *ACM Transactions on Computer–Human Interaction*, **25**(5), 26.

B'Tselem (2018). *Israel Destroying Gaza's Fishing Sector*. Retrieved from: https://www.btselem.org/gaza_strip/20170129_killing_the_fishing_sector (Accessed on 27 May 2022).

B'Tselem, (2021). *State Business: Israel's Misappropriation of Land in the West Bank Through Settler Violence*. Retrieved from: https://www.btselem.org/publications/202111_state_business (Accessed on 23 May 2023).

Bullough, A. & Renko, M. (2017). "A Different Frame of Reference: Entrepreneurship and Gender Differences in the Perception of Danger". *Academy of Management Discoveries*, **3**(1), 21–41.

Bullough, A., Renko, M., & Abdelzaher, D. (2017). "Women's Business Ownership: Operating Within the Context of Institutional and In-Group Collectivism". *Journal of Management*, **43**(7), 2037–2064.

Calas, M., Smircich, L., & Bourne, K. (2009). "Extending the Boundaries: Reframing "Entrepreneurship as Social Change" Through Feminist Perspectives". *The Academy of Management Review*, **34**(3), 552–569.

Daoud, Y., Sarsour, Sh., Shanti, R., & Kamal, S. (2020). "Risk Tolerance, Gender, and Entrepreneurship: The Palestinian Case". *Review of Development Economics*, **24**(3), 766–78.

Elnamrouty, Kh., Alhabil, A., & Althalathini, D. (2013). "Effect of Microgrants on Poverty Alleviation of Palestinian Families". *Journal of World Economic*, **2**(5), 82–88.

Esim S. & Omeira, M. (2009). *Rural Women Producers and Cooperatives in Conflicts Settings in the Arab States*. Lebanon: ILO, Regional Office for Arab States.

FAO (2011). *Palestinian Womens' Associations and Agricultural Value Chains*. Retrieved from: www.fao.org/3/al807e/al807e00.pdf (Accessed on 27 May 2022).

Farsakh, L. (2002). "Palestinian Labor Flows to the Israeli Economy: A Finished Story?" *Journal of Palestine Studies*, **32**(1), 13–27.

Gillespie, K., Sayre, E., & Riddle, L. (2001). "Palestinian Interest in Homeland Investment". *Middle East Journal*, **55**(2), 237–255.

Griffiths, M. & Repo, J. (2021). "Women and Checkpoints in Palestine". *Security Dialogue*, **52**(3), 249–265.

Hechavarría, D. & Ingram, A. (2019). "Entrepreneurial Ecosystem Conditions and Gendered National-Level Entrepreneurial Activity: A 14-Year Panel Study of GEM". *Small Business Economics*, **53**, 431–458.

Hiltermann, J. (1991). "The Women's Movement during the Uprising". *Journal of Palestine Studies*, **20**(3), 48–57.

Höijer, B. (2004). "The Discourse of Global Compassion: The Audience and Media Reporting of Human Suffering". *Media, Culture & Society*, **26**(4), 513–531.

Holt, M. (2003). "Palestinian Women, Violence, and the Peace Process". *Development in Practice*, **13**(2/3), 223–238.

Howard, Ph., Duffy, A., Freelon, D., Hussain, M., Mari, W., & Maziad, M. (2011). *Opening Closed Regimes: What Was the Role of Social Media During the Arab Spring*? Retrieved from: http://dx.doi.org/10.2139/ssrn.2595096 (Accessed on 17 January 2022).

Human Rights Watch (2021). *A Threshold Crossed: Israeli Authorities and the Crimes of Apartheid and Persecution*. Retrieved from: https://www.hrw.org/report/2021/04/27/threshold-crossed/israeli-authorities-and-crimes-apartheid-and-persecution (Accessed on 23 May 2022).

Human Rights Watch (2019). *World Report 2019: Events of 2018*. Retrieved from: https://www.hrw.org/world-report/2019/country-chapters/israel/palestine (Accessed on 12 March 2022).

ICF (2016). *IFC, Bank of Palestine Support Women Entrepreneurs in West Bank and Gaza*. Retrieved from: https://pressroom.ifc.org/all/pages/PressDetail.aspx?ID=16600 (Accessed on 12 March 2022).

International Labour Organization (2021). "The Situation of workers of the Occupied Arab Territories: Report of the Director-General". In *International Labour Conference 109th Session*.

International Monetary Fund (2018). *West Bank and Gaza Report to the Ad Hoc Liaison*. Retrieved from: https://www.imf.org/-/media/Files/Publications/CR/2018/wbg091718.ashx (Accessed on 13 February 2022).

Inter-Parliamentary Union (2019). *State of Palestine*. Retrieved from: https://www.idea.int/data-tools/data/gender-quotas/country-view/246/35 (Accessed on 29 January 2022).

James, M. (2013). "Women and the Intifadas: The Evolution of Palestinian Women's Organizations". *Strife Journal*, **1**, 18–22.

Júlia, P., Aas Rustad, S., Harpviken, K., & Methi, F. (2020). *Conflict Trends in the Middle East, 1989–2019*. PRIO Paper. Oslo: PRIO.

Kamberidou, I. (2020). "Distinguished Women Entrepreneurs in the Digital Economy and the Multitasking Whirlpool". *Journal of Innovation and Entrepreneurship*, **9**(3), 1–26.

Karaki, F. (2021). "Mapping Entrepreneurial Ecosystem (EE) of Palestine". *Journal of Entrepreneurship, Business and Economics*, **9**(2), 174–217.

Khatib, I., Tsipouri, L., Bassiakos, Y., & Haj-Daoud, A. (2013). Innovation in Palestinian Industries: A Necessity for Surviving the Abnormal". *Journal of the Knowledge Economy*, **4**(4), 492–510.

Khoury, G., Farraj, W., & Sultan, S. (2018). "Challenges to the Formalization of Palestinian Female-Owned Home-Based Businesses". In Sh. Yousafzai *et al.*, eds., *Women Entrepreneurs and the Myth of 'Underperformance'* (pp. 173–191). Cheltenham, UK and Northampton, USA. Edward Elgar Publishing.

Khoury, Th. & Prasad, A. (2016). "Entrepreneurship amid Concurrent Institutional Constraints in Less Developed Countries". *Business & Society*, **55**(7), 934–969.

Koch, K. & Ragab, N. (2018). *Mapping and Study of the Palestinian Diaspora in Germany*. Netherlands: Maastricht University.

Kostenko, V., Kuzmuchev, P., & Ponarin, E. (2016). "Attitudes Towards Gender Equality and Perception of Democracy in the Arab World". *Democratization*, **23**(5), 862–891.

Kuttab, E. (2014). "The Many Faces of Feminism: Palestinian Women's Movements Finding A Voice". In Nazneen, S., ed., *Voicing demands* (pp. 219–251). London, England: Zed Books.

Marktanner, M. & Merkel, A. (2019). "Conflict and Aid Dependency — An Explorative Study Motivated by the Case of Palestine". *Journal of Development Effectiveness*, **11**(3), 253–272.

MAS (2019). *Innovation and Digital Economy in Palestine: Challenges and Opportunities.* Ramallah: Palestine Economic Policy Research Institute.

McAdam, M., Crowley, C., & Harrison, H. (2018). "To Boldly Go Where No [Man] Has Gone Before: Institutional Voids and the Development of Women's Digital Entrepreneurship". *Technological Forecasting & Social Change*, **146**, 912–922.

McAdam, M., Crowley, C., & Harrison, R. (2020). "Digital Girl: Cyberfeminism and the Emancipatory Potential of Digital Entrepreneurship in Emerging Economies". *Small Business Economics,* **55**(2), 349–362.

McNally, B. & Khoury, G. (2022). "Accessing Human Capital Development and Learning Opportunities of Female Entrepreneurs in Palestine and Saudi Arabia: A Cross-country Comparison". In B. Metcalfe, B., Bastian, B., & H. Al-Dajani, (eds.), *Women, Entrepreneurship and Development in the Arab Middle East* (pp. 189–211). New York: Routledge.

Metcalfe, B., Bastian, B., & Al-Dajani, H. (2022). *Women and Entrepreneurship Development in the Middle East (WEDME).* London, UK. Routledge.

Morrar, R., Amara, M., & Syed Zwick, H. (2022). "The Determinants of Self-Employment Entry of Palestinian Youth". *Journal of Entrepreneurship in Emerging Economies*, **14**(1), 23–44.

Muhanna, A. (2013). *Agency and Gender in Gaza Masculinity, Femininity and Family During the Second Intifada.* London: Routledge.

Mundy, J. (2019). "The Middle East is Violence: On the Limits of Comparative Approaches to the Study of Armed Conflict". *Civil Wars*, **21**(4), 539–568.

Nziku, D. & Henry, C. (2021). "Policies for Supporting Women Entrepreneurs in Developing Countries: The Case of Tanzania". *Journal of Entrepreneurship and Public Policy*, **10**(1), 38–58.

OCHA (2019). *Gaza's Fisheries: Record Expansion of Fishing Limit And Relative Increase In Fish Catch; Shooting and Detention Incidents at Sea Continue*. Retrieved from: https://www.ochaopt.org/content/gaza-s-fisheries-record-expansion-fishing-limit-and-relative-increase-fish-catch-shooting (Accessed on 27 May 2022).

Owda, M., Owda, R., Abed, M., Abdalmenem, S., Abu-Naser, S., & Al Shobaki, M. (2019). "Entrepreneurs and Entrepreneurship in Gaza Strip between Reality and Ambition". *International Journal of Academic Management Science Research*, **3**(8), 27–38.

Palestine Economic Policy Research Institute (2013). *Palestine Country Report 2012 — The Global Entrepreneurship Monitor (GEM)*. Ramallah, Palestine.

Palestine Monetary Authority (2021). *Annual Report 2020*. Retrieved from: https://www.pma.ps/ (Accessed on 15 March 2022).

PCBS (2000). *Labour Market Survey: Third Quarter 2000*. Ramallah: The Palestinian Central Bureau of Statistics.

PCBS (2020). *The World Telecommunication and Information Society Day 17/05/2020*. Ramallah: The Palestinian Central Bureau of Statistics.

PCBS (2021a). *Percentage Distribution of Persons (15 Years and Over) by Educational Attainment, Region and Sex, 1995, 1997, 2000-2021*. Retrieved from: https://www.pcbs.gov.ps/Portals/_Rainbow/Documents/Education-1994-2021-10E.html (Accessed on 25 February 2022).

PCBS (2021b). *The Current Status of the Palestinian Labour Force in 2020*. Press Release, Retrieved from: https://www.pcbs.gov.ps/portals/_pcbs/PressRelease/Press_En_29-4-2021-workers-en.pdf (Accessed on 12 February 2022).

PCBS (2021c). *Palestine in Figures 2020*. Ramallah: The Palestinian Central Bureau of Statistics.

PCBS (2022). *The Status of Palestinian People at the End of 2021*. Ramallah: The Palestinian Central Bureau of Statistics.

Roomi, M., Rehman, S., & Henry, C. (2018). "Exploring the Normative Context for Women's Entrepreneurship in Pakistan: A Critical Analysis". *International Journal of Gender and Entrepreneurship*, **10**(2), 158–180.

Sabella, A. & El-Far, M. (2019). "Entrepreneuring as An Everyday Form of Resistance: An Exploration of the Experiences of Palestinian Women Street Vendors in the Occupied Old City of Jerusalem". *International Journal of Entrepreneurial Behavior & Research*, **25**(6), 1212–1235.

Sabella, A., Farraj, W., Burbar, M., & Qaimary, D. (2014). "Entrepreneurship and Economic Growth in West Bank, Palestine". *Journal of Developmental Entrepreneurship*, **19**(1), 1450003.

Sadeq, T., Hamed, M., & Glover, S. (2011). *Policies to Promote Female Entrepreneurship in the Palestinian Territory*. MAS, Ramallah: Palestine.

Sa'di, A. & Abu-Lughod, L. (2007). *Nakba: Palestine, 1948, and the Claims of Memory*. New York: Columbia University Press.

Sajjad, M., Kaleem, N., Chani, M. I., & Ahmed, M. (2020). "Worldwide role of women Entrepreneurs in Economic Development". *Asia Pacific Journal of Innovation and Entrepreneurship*, **14**(2), 151–160.

Salem, M., Baidoun, S., & Walsh, G. (2019). "Factors affecting Palestinian Customers' Use of Online Banking Services". *International Journal of Bank Marketing*, **37**(2), 426–451.

Samaroo, D. (2018). "The Political Participation of Palestinian Women in Official and Non-Official Organizations in Limited Horizon". *International Centre for the Study of Radicalisation*. London: King's College.

Sarsour, Sh. (2012). "Analyzing the Transmission Mechanisms of Monetary Policy in the Absence of a National Currency: The Palestinian Case". *Middle East Development Journal*, **4**(2), 1250012.

Sarsour, Sh., Naser, R., & Atallah, M. (2011). *The Economic and Social Effects of Foreign Aid in Palestine*. Palestine Monetary Authority, Ramallah.

Shamieh, S. & Althalathini, D. (2022). "Entrepreneurship in the Conflict Contexts of the Arab Middle East: A Contextual Gendered Lens on Empowerment and Resilience". In B. Metcalfe, B., Bastian, B., & H. Al-Dajani, (eds.), *Women, Entrepreneurship and Development in the Arab Middle East* (pp. 231–247). New York: Routledge.

Sharabati-Shahin, M. & Thiruchelvam, K. (2013). "The Role of Diaspora in University–Industry Relationships in Globalised Knowledge Economy: The Case of Palestine". *Higher Education*, **65**, 613–629.

Sultan, S. & Sultan, W. (2020). "Women MSMEs in Times of Crisis: Challenges and Opportunities". *Journal of Small Business and Enterprise Development*, **27**(7), 1069–1083.

Sultan, S., de Waal, A., & Goedegebuure, R. (2017). "Analyzing Organizational Performance of Family and Non-Family Businesses Using the HPO Framework". *Journal of Family Business Management*, **7**(3), 242–255.

The Guardian (2019). *The Palestinian Entrepreneur Bringing Power to Gaza*. Retrieved from: https://www.theguardian.com/global-development/2019/sep/27/the-palestinian-entrepreneur-bringing-power-to-gaza-majd-mash-harawi (Accessed on 30 March 2022).

Tlaiss, H. (2019). "Contextualizing the Career Success of Arab Women Entrepreneurs". *Entrepreneurship & Regional Development*, **31**(3–4), 226–241.

Tommaso, C., Chiara, K., & Menon, C. (2015). "Business as Unusual. An Explanation of the Increase of Private Economic Activity in High-Conflict Areas in Afghanistan". LSE Research Online Documents on Economics 65015, London School of Economics and Political Science.

UNCTAD (2015). *The Besieged Palestinian Agricultural Sector*. UNCTAD/GDS/APP/2015/1.

UNHCR (2021). *Middle East*. Retrieved from: https://reporting.unhcr.org/middleeast (Accessed on 25 January 2022).

United Nation (2022). *History of the Question of Palestine*. Retrieved from: https://www.un.org/unispal/history/ (Accessed on 25 May 2022).

UNRWA (2022). *Arab-Israeli War*. The United Nations Relief and Works Agency for Palestine Refugees in the Near East. Retrieved from: https://www.unrwa.org/content/arab-israeli-war (Accessed on 23 May 2022).

Welter, F., Baker, T., & Wirsching, K. (2018). "Three Waves and Counting: The Rising Tide of Contextualization in Entrepreneurship Research". *Small Business Economics*, **52**, 319–330.

World Bank (2003). *Twenty-Seven Months — Intifada, Closures and Palestinian Economic Crisis: An Assessment*. Palestine: Jerusalem.

World Bank (2004). *Four Years — Intifada, Closures, and Palestinian Economic Crisis: An Assessment*. Palestine: Jerusalem.

World Bank (2011). *Coping with Conflict? Poverty and Inclusion in the West Bank and Gaza*. Report No. 61293, Jerusalem.

World Bank (2014a). *West Bank and Gaza Investment Climate Assessment Fragmentation and Uncertainty*. Washington DC.

World Bank (2014b). *Striving for Business Success: Voices of Liberian Women Entrepreneurs*. Washington, DC: World Bank Institute, International Finance Corporation.

World Bank (2018). *Tech Startup Ecosystem in West Bank and Gaza Findings and Recommendations*. Retrieved from: http://www.worldbank.org/en/country/westbankandgaza/overview (Accessed on 24 February 2022).

World Bank (2020a). *World Bank Group Launches Initiatives Supporting Women Entrepreneurs*. Retrieved from: https://www.worldbank.org/en/news/press-release/2020/02/16/world-bank-group-launches-initiatives-supporting-women-entrepreneurs (Accessed on 25 February 2022).

World Bank (2020b). *Doing Business 2020*. Washington DC.

World Bank (2021a). *Gaza Rapid Damage and Needs Assessment June 2021*. Retrieved from: https://documents1.worldbank.org/curated/en/178021624889455367/pdf/Gaza-Rapid-Damage-and-Needs-Assessment.pdf (Accessed on 7 February 2022).

World Bank (2021b). *GDP Per Capita (current US$)*. Retrieved from: https://data.worldbank.org/indicator/NY.GDP.PCAP.CD (Accessed on 2 March 2022).

World Bank (2021c). *Literacy Rate, Adult Female*. Retrieved from: https://data.worldbank.org/indicator/SE.ADT.LITR.FE.ZS (Accessed on 15 March 2022).

Yousafzai, S., Fayolle, A., Saeed, S., & Henry, C. (2019). "The Contextual Embeddedness of Women's Entrepreneurship". *Entrepreneurship and Regional Development*, **31**(3–4), 167–177.

https://doi.org/10.1142/9789811283499_0012

Chapter 12

Women Entrepreneurs in the Kingdom of Saudi Arabia*

Wassim J. Aloulou[*,‡], Veland Ramadani[†,§], Mohammad Alarifi[*,¶], and Rasim Zuferi[†,||]

[*]*Imam Mohammad Ibn Saudi Islamic University, Kingdom of Saudi Arabia*
[†]*South-East European University, North Macedonia*
[‡]*wassim.aloulou@gmail.com*
[§]*v.ramadani@seeu.edu.mk*
[¶]*mohammed-alarifi@hotmail.com*
[||]*r.zuferi@seeu.edu.mk*

Abstract

This chapter aims to understand the development of women entrepreneurship in the Kingdom of Saudi Arabia (KSA). It provides a historical overview of the KSA and examines the entrepreneurial ecosystem and implications for women entrepreneurship in the country. The chapter highlights the deep transformation that the country has undertaken in all business sectors since the announcement of the 2030 vision of the Kingdom. The chapter concludes with a look toward the future of the KSA as it progresses to achieve its objectives for the next decade.

**Note*: This chapter is based on: Aloulou, W. J., & Alarifi, M. (2022). "The Context for Business in Saudi Arabia". In Dana *et al.*, eds., *Understanding Contexts of Business in Western Asia: Land of Bazaars and High-Tech Booms* (pp. 477–494). Singapore: World Scientific.

Keywords: Women entrepreneurs; entrepreneurial ecosystem; historical review; Saudi Vision 2030, the Kingdom of Saudi Arabia.

1. Introduction

The Kingdom of Saudi Arabia (KSA) is a country in the Middle East and located in the Southwest of Asia. It is extended from the Red Sea in the west to the Arabian Gulf in the east. Its borders are Jordan, Iraq, and Kuwait from the north, Yemen and Oman from the south, the Arabian Gulf and United Arab Emirates, Qatar, and Bahrain from the east, and the Red Sea in the west (Exhibit 1). The KSA covers around four-fifths of the Arab Peninsula, with a total area of around 2,000,000 km^2. It is the largest country in the Arabian Peninsula.[1] The capital city of the KSA is Riyadh with

Exhibit 1. Nations online map of the KSA (Nations Online Project, 2020).

Note: Everyone is free to use this map for educational purposes, referring to the Nations Online Project.

[1]General Authority of Statistics: https://www.stats.gov.sa/.

Exhibit 2. Flag of KSA.

over 7.5 million people and Jeddah is the second largest city, with 3,976,400 citizens (Khan and Khan, 2020).

The KSA is divided into 13 administrative regions (emirates). Each region has a certain number of governorates. Each emirate is ruled by a member of the royal family. This administrative division is shown, and the regions are mapped out as follows: (1) Riyadh, (2) Makkah Al-Mokarramah (Mecca), (3) Al-Madinah Al-Monawarah (Medina), (4) Al-Qassem, (5) Eastern Province, (6) Asser, (7) Tabouk, (8) Hail, (9) Northern Borders, (10) Jazan, (11) Najran, (12) Al-Baaha, and (13) Al-Jowf.[2]

The flag of the KSA (Exhibit 2) has the following meaning: First, the green color symbolizes richness and prosperity. Second, the sword represents strength and protection. Third, the Arabic words are the "Shahada", and they are meant to symbolize the Islamic origin of the state. As word of Tawheed, the Shahadah "There is no god but Allah, and Mohammed is his messenger" is the Islamic statement of faith. And by Saudi law, the flag of the KSA that carries the name of God and the Islamic testimony cannot be lowered.[3]

The KSA is a monarchy, with a constitution based on the Quran and Sharia (Islam) Law. It is a home to the two Holy mosques of Islam (located in Mecca and in Medina, see Exhibits 3 and 4), and Muslims from all over the world visit to perform their pilgrimage as that is the fifth pillar of Islam alongside Shahadah, Salat, Zakat, and Sawm. The King of

---

[2]General Authority for Statistics: https://www.stats.gov.sa/.

[3]According to Article 13 of the Saudi flag law: "It is not permissible to lower the Kingdom's flag or the King's flag that carries Al Shahada".

Exhibit 3. The Kaaba at the Holy Mosque of Mecca © Wassim J. Aloulou.

Exhibit 4. The Holy Mosque of Islam in Medina by night and by day © Wassim J. Aloulou.

Saudi Arabia is titled *The Servant of the Two Holy Mosques*. All these facts underscore how important the Islamic religion and rulings are in Saudi Arabia for the Saudi population. Faith has an undisputed influence on everyone's day-to-day activities in Saudi Arabia.

This chapter presents the historical context of Saudi Arabia and its impact on business in the country, the context for Saudi enterprises and the implications for doing business, and a look toward the future.

2. Historical Overview

2.1. *Historical context of KSA*

Islam is a religion that was started in Mecca, Saudi Arabia, at the beginning of the 7th century by the prophet Muhammad, peace be upon him (p.b.u.h), who was the last prophet. The word "Islam" means "submission to the will of God". People who believe in Islam are called Muslims. Masjids are places where Muslims go to perform prayers. There are three most famous Masjids, which are the Islamic holy places. The first one is Masjid Alharam, which is located in Mecca and has the Kaaba al-Musharrafah ("House of God 'Allah'") that is faced by Muslims, wherever they are in the world, when they perform prayers (Exhibit 3). The second is Al-Aqsa Masjid in Jerusalem, and the third is Prophet Muhammad's Masjid in Medina (Exhibit 4). The Quran al Kareem is the holiest book in, and the central religious text of, Islam (Exhibit 5). The start of the Islamic calendar was when prophet Muhammad, p.b.u.h., moved from Mecca to Medina with his supporters in 622 CE. This journey is known as the *Hijra*.

The start of Islam was around the year 610 CE when Prophet Muhammad, p.b.u.h., received a message from God (Allah) through the Angel Gabriel. In 622, Prophet Muhammad, p.b.u.h., moved to Yathrib, which is today called Medina. Few years later, some battles took place between the supporters of the Prophet Muhammad, p.b.u.h., and the pagans of Mecca. In 628, Medina was totally under the control of the Muslims, and the Prophet, p.b.u.h., had united the tribes so successfully that he and his supporters re-entered Mecca in a peaceful way without bloodshed.[4]

The next paragraphs describe the evolution of Saudi Arabia as the center of trade over time (Aloulou and Alarifi, 2022). For a long time, the country was considered as an ancient trade center and at the crossroads of

[4] See: https://www.saudiembassy.net.

Exhibit 5. The Noble Quran © Wassim J. Aloulou.

the ancient world with the development of caravan routes transporting different kinds of goods (agricultural, dates, aromatics, Spices, etc.). With the emergence of the Islamic empire, trade has flourished in the area of the two holy cities of Mecca and Medina during periods of *Hajj* (the annual five-day pilgrimage) and *Umrah* (minor pilgrimage). Additionally, the two cities remained the spiritual heart of the Islamic world and continued to attract pilgrims from many countries for many centuries. Trading activities during *Hajj* and *Umrah* bring to the KSA higher revenues each year originated from the pilgrims' spending.

With regards to women and entrepreneurship, Islam does not exclude women from business activities. The Almighty has given both genders equal abilities to accept responsibilities. In the Holy Qur'an, He says:

> "And do not wish for that by which Allah has made some of you exceed others. For men is a share of what they have earned, and for women is a share of what they have earned. And ask Allah of his bounty. Indeed, Allah is ever, of all things, Knowing." (Annisa: 32)

Exhibit 6. Women traditional attire in Saudi Arabia.

Source: Cloud Consciousness under the license of Wikimedia Commons.

If we recall the history, the wife of Prophet Muhammad p.b.u.h., Khadija r.a, was one of the most successful entrepreneurs of that period. Anggadwita *et al.* (2015) noted that according to Islam "gender is not an obstacle for women entrepreneurship. Gender equality in Islam covers all aspects, including the issue of rights and obligations. Women are allowed to work in various fields, as long as the work is done in an atmosphere of respectability and politeness, and they can maintain their religion. Besides, they must ensure to avoid negative impacts of the work on themselves and the environment" (p. 395). Exhibit 6 shows a women traditional attire in the KSA.

At the beginning of the 20th century, the Ottoman empire was partitioned and lost control of several parts of its territory. The empire was dissolved, and a United Arab State of Saudi Arabia emerged. The Unification of the Saudi-ruled Arabia was accomplished through many stages. The most remarkable stage was the battle of Riyadh. In 1902, King Abulaziz decided to retake Riyadh from the Al-Rashid family, who had taken over Riyadh earlier. King Abulaziz arranged to go to Riyadh with only 40 supporters to retake the city garrison, which was the Masmak Fortress. This occasion was the start of the modern Saudi state.[5]

After the success of capturing Riyadh as headquarters, in 1924–1925, King Abdulaziz united warring tribes into one nation through capturing all of the Hijaz, including Mecca and Medina. This led to the establishment of the KSA on September 23, 1932, an Islamic country that considers The Quran al Kareem as its constitution and uses Arabic as the main language.[6]

The stability in the KSA led to the discovery of oil in 1938. In 1933, a Concession Agreement was signed between Saudi Arabia and the Standard Oil Company of California (SOCAL), which was the start of the well-known company Saudi Aramco. To manage that agreement, a subsidiary company, called the California Arabian Standard Oil Company (CASOC) was established. After that, there was a surveying for the Saudi desert for oil. In 1935, the drilling started. After years of hard work, there was not much success, so in 1937 SOCAL executives decided to seek the advice of their chief geologist, Max Steineke. Based on Max Steineke's long experience in fieldwork, he recommended them to continue drilling. The success of Saudi Arabia and the Saudi Aramco company were clear when commercial quantities of oil were discovered at the aptly named "Prosperity Well" in Dammam in 1938.[7] The Saudi oil industry was established, and mass production of oil begun.

From the late 1940s, the company made rapid progress in oil production, and the country became very famous for its energy and natural resources by reaching milestones from one decade to another. The Saudi government showed its interest in Aramco by making huge investments on it. Throughout the 1990s, the company continued to extend its ties and partnerships across the world by making several international investments. The company is currently witnessing the advantages of technological and

[5]See: https://www.saudiembassy.net/history.

[6]See: https://www.saudiembassy.net/history.

[7]See: https://www.saudiaramco.com, The official website of the leading producer of the energy and chemicals in Saudi Arabia.

innovation advancements. And Saudi Arabia has become the world's largest exporter of petroleum and a leader in the Organization of the Petroleum Exporting Companies (OPEC). Oil exports account for more than 85% of government revenue. Further, Kalu *et al.* (2020) found "the growth of the Saudi economy as a positive function of renewable energy use and an insignificant function of fossil fuel consumption" (p. 29).

Saudi traditions are rooted in Islamic teaching and Arab customs and the country is characterized by a high degree of cultural homogeneity based on such Arab and Muslim heritages (Anishchenkova, 2020):

- *Muslim heritage*: The culture of Saudi Arabia is extensively influenced by the religion of Islam, which governs every aspect of a Muslim's life. This Islamic culture is based on ethics, respect, solidarity, and generosity since the religion of Islam is seen as a system of ethics. The Saudi culture follows Islam's guidance on the values of hardwork, dedication, moderation, discipline, equity, and excellence. The Islamic socio-economic system aims to guarantee individual liberty, freedom of choice, private property and enterprise, the profit motive, and possibilities of unlimited efforts and reward.
- *Arab heritage*: Saudi Arabian social and cultural norms are often associated with the social codes of Bedouin tribes. The Bedouin culture played and continues to play a very important role in the construction of the Saudi national identity. Such a culture is based on social interaction between tribal members and solidarity within the groups, prioritizing family over any other relationships throughout life. Saudi Arabia's culture is particularly collectivist since the most important social unit is the group, a close family, extended family, or extended relationships, to which loyalty and respect is due. Thus, Saudi people prefer doing business with those they know and trust.

2.2. *Important facts of KSA at a glance*

The population of Saudi Arabia in 2022 was 36,408,820 (nationals and non-nationals).[8] The median age is 31.8 years. More than 30% of the

[8] See: https://www.worldometers.info/.

Saudi population are expatriates (more than ten million) especially from Syria, India, Pakistan, Egypt, Yemen, Bangladesh, and Philippine. Most of them come for work. Saudi Arabia, along with other countries of the Gulf Cooperation Council (GCC), became the largest market for foreigner job seekers. The number of expatriates started to diminish a few years ago in private sectors after government measures toward Saudization in technical (engineering, accounting, IT-related) jobs and also in the industrial sectors. New Saudization labor initiatives have been launched to encourage Saudi entrepreneurship and startups.[9]

Saudi Arabia is the largest economy in the Middle East and the richest Arab country in the region. Its gross domestic product (GDP) was worth US$833.54 billion in 2021. Its growth rate was about 8.6% in Q3/2022, in the post COVID-19 pandemic global crisis.[10] In terms of Human Development Index, the KSA ranks second in the Arab world and 40th (with an index of 0.854) globally among countries with very high human development. It achieved the 10th place among the G20 countries (UNDP, 2020).

According to the World Bank Group's Doing Business 2020 report (World Bank, 2020), Saudi Arabia placed 62nd globally in ease of doing business rankings with an overall score of 71.6 out of 100. The government has implemented and carried out a record number of business reforms in the past year, earning the country a spot in this year's top 10 global business climate improvers. It made the greatest paces in the areas of starting a business (starting costs of about only 5.4% of income per capita with no required minimum capital); the protection of minority investors; and registering property by reducing the number of days and rendering the process entirely free. Additionally, new reforms in the area of getting electricity make it almost twice as fast for a business to obtain a permanent electricity connection in Saudi Arabia than it was a few years ago. In addition, the process can be accomplished in only two steps, making it one of only six economies around the world where it can be done in so few steps.

As per the Global Competitiveness Report 2020 published by the World Economic Forum (WEF), the KSA has been making good progress

[9] See "Saudization" rubric: http://www.arabnews.com/tags/saudization/.

[10] See: http://www/.stats.gov.sa/.

and is the only country from the Middle East region to jump in rank from the 39th place in 2018, to the 26th place in 2019, before climbing to the 24th place in 2020 (WEF, 2020).

According to the International Institute for Management Development (IMD) World Digital Competitiveness Index (2022), the KSA has been ranked among the top 10 countries in the world in digital/technological skills. The top three Digital Risers in the G20 are Saudi Arabia, USA, and Sweden. Governments around the world are now investing heavily in digital economy initiatives with the goal of enhancing value creation and national prosperity and reducing the impacts of the COVID-19 pandemic. The WEF attributed the KSA progress to four factors: adoption of information and communication technology (ICT), flexible work arrangements, the national digital skills, and the legal digital framework. The investments in King Abdullah Financial District represent a concrete example related to the aforementioned aspects.

Saudi Arabia's Economic Freedom score is 62.4, making its economy the 83rd freest in the 2020 Index. The country is ranked 9th among 14 countries in the Middle East and North Africa (MENA) region, and its overall score is nearly equal to the regional and world averages. Its overall score has increased by 1.7 points due to higher property rights and judicial effectiveness scores, given that the index of Economic Freedom is based on the rule of law, government size, regulatory efficiency, and open market dimensions. According to the Global Gender Gap Report (World Economic Forum, 2022), Saudi Arabia is ranked 127th out of 145 countries for gender parity with a score of 0.636. The country is among 2022's most improved countries in losing its gender gap. Table 1 shows the most important indicators and rankings of the KSA from the different perspectives of official reports and sources measuring its economic performance and considering it as an emergent high-income country in transition from a factor-driven to an efficiency-driven economy.

3. Entrepreneurial Ecosystem

3.1. *KSA and Vision 2030*

As a developing country, the KSA witnessed significant restructuration of its entire economy. A series of restructurations have been done up to now

Table 1. Landscape and main facts of the KSA.

Indicators	Facts and Rankings
Population (% Saudi) in 2022[b]	36,408,820 (more than 69%)
Population growth rate[f]	1.63%
GDP US$ (Growth rate in Q3 2022)[ac]	833.54 billion (8.6%)
Score in HDI index (and ranking)[d]	0.854 (40/189)
Ranking in "Ease of Doing Business" 2020[c]	62nd/190 (71.6/10)
WEF Global Competitiveness 2019[e]	36th/141 (70.0/100)
Ranking Digital competitiveness 2020 (score)[g]	35th/63 (73.87/100)
Unemployment rate[i]	7.36%
Global Innovation Index 2020[h]	51st/132 (33.4/100)
Economic Freedom Rank and Index[j]	118th–55.5/100
Global Gender Gap index 2022[e]	127th/145 (0.636/1)

Sources: [a]*Stats.gov.sa*; [b]Worldmeter.info, [c]World Bank (2020), [d]UNDP (2020), [e]World Economic Forum (2020), [f]World Factbook (2022), [g]IMD Digital World Competitiveness ranking 2022, [h]Dutta *et al.* (2022), [i]Statista (2021), and [j]Heritage Foundation (2022).

Exhibit 7. Logo of KSA Vision 2030.

Source: http://vision2030.gov.sa/.

under the Saudi Arabia Vision 2030 (Exhibit 7) as a National Reform Plan, including 12 programs such as the National Transformation Plan NTP (2020) among other programs that were developed to help fulfil the Saudi Vision (Saudi Council of Economic and Development Affairs, 2016).

Exhibit 8. Boulevard World in Riyadh with fireworks and city zones © Wassim J. Aloulou.

Three themes are the bases of the Saudi Vision 2030:

1. "A vibrant society with strong roots, fulfilling lives and strong foundations" to promote the Saudi cultural heritage, the religious tourism, provide healthy and balanced lifestyles, empower the society with the essentials of life, and build an effective healthcare system (see Exhibit 8).
2. "Thriving economy with rewarding opportunities and investment in the long term and open for business for leveraging the unique position of the KSA."
3. "Ambitious nation effectively governed" to increase the KSA's ranking in the Government Effectiveness Index from 80 to 20 and to raise the E-Government Survey Index ranking from 36 to among the top five nations; and responsibly enabled to raise household savings from 6% to 10%, to raise the nonprofit sector's contribution to the GDP from less than 1% to 5% and to rally 1 million volunteers per year.

The commitment of the KSA to the 2030 agenda for sustainable development and the achievement of the SDGs is reaffirmed and significant improvements in key aspects of human development have been recorded (Kingdom of Saudi Arabia, 2018). Accordingly, the Saudi

Arabia Vision 2030 aims to increase women's participation in the workforce from 22% to 30% and reduce the unemployment rate from 12.6% to 7%. It gives a significant emphasis to the Saudi woman and to her leading role as catalyst for change in both social and developmental areas and as a major growth driver for the country's diversification policy.

3.2. *Vision 2030, entrepreneurship and youth*

According to the 2019–2020 Global Entrepreneurship Monitor (Saudi National Report), the KSA ranks among the top 20 within the 54 economies on the overall National Entrepreneurial Context Index (3rd with regard to support and relevance of government policies, the 10th in the governmental taxes and bureaucracy, and the 13th in internal market dynamics). Regarding societal values about entrepreneurship, almost 70% of Saudi adults consider starting a business to be a good career choice, and about 79% believe that entrepreneurs are well regarded and enjoy high status within society.

These numbers along with the government vision of 2030 may indicate high expectations of increasing entrepreneurs in the country. In addition, a percentage of women entrepreneurs might be considerably incensed due to the recent policy in the country regarding women.

As a result, there might be an improvement in entrepreneurial activities in the country post the COVID-19 global pandemic. This may also help in developing the economy and decreasing the unemployment rate, which dropped to 5.77% in September 2022, through creating new jobs in the market and helping young citizens find jobs.[11]

3.3. *KSA: Land of traditional souqs, modern malls, and electronic markets*

The traditional shopping area in Saudi Arabia is generally located in the center of each city and is made up of small shops, situated along a street or clustered according to the type of merchandise handled (Anishchenkova, 2020; Leonidou, 1995). In the bazaar/*souq* economy, the competition is

[11]General Authority for Statistics: https://www.stats.gov.sa/.

Exhibit 9. From left to right, coffee broilers and traditional furniture store in the Al-Muqailia *Souq*, and a household utensils store in Ad Dirah *Souq* in Riyadh, © Mohammad Alarifi.

keen, and the prices are negotiated through a bargaining process between seller and buyer (Dana, 2000; Dana and Wright, 2015). In main regions of the KSA, especially Riyadh (center), Jeddah, Mecca and Medina (West), and Dammam (East), there are different kinds of traditional and popular markets or *souqs* for furniture, household utensils, and other goods (e.g., Al Owais *souq*, Ad Dirah's Gold *souq*, Al-Muqailia *souq* in Riyadh; and *souq* Al Zal, Qabel Trail, *souq* Al-Balad, *souq* Al-Bado, *souq* Al-Nada in Jeddah, etc.). Some of these *souqs* are shown in Exhibit 9. The old town of Jeddah has many khans (small shops) such as Khan Al-Honood (Indians), Khan Al-Qasaba, Khan Al-Dalaleen (auctioneers), and Khan Al-Attareen (Perfume makers/sellers).[12] These places still attract tourists from the several countries that visit the KSA.

With increasing urbanization in the KSA, which started in the 1970s, along with the traditional bazaar appear a new type of shopping experience inside modern, pleasantly decorated places regrouping stores, supermarkets, and boutiques (Anishchenkova, 2020; Leonidou, 1995). In addition to the shopping, malls perform the function of entertaining their visitors (especially women and children). In many cities of the KSA, the culture of malls is well spread. Different concepts are found for shopping high-end accessories, luxury brands, exquisite jewellery, trendy fashions,

[12] See: https://www.jeddah.gov.sa/english/jeddahcity/Markets/index.php.

electronics, and cheap souvenirs (dates, oud perfume, colourful dressing abaya for women, etc).

3.4. *The booming of e-commerce: E-malls and digital platforms*

Electronic commerce or e-commerce is flourishing in the KSA since 2016 with the announcement of the Saudi Vision 2030. Since then, the country has been supporting e-commerce as part of the transformation undertaken to transit to a new economy. According to Statista.com, revenue in the Saudi e-commerce market across all product categories was US$6.13 billion in 2017 and it is projected to reach US$7,051 million in 2021. It is expected to show an annual growth rate of 5.4% resulting in a projected market volume of US$8,697 million by 2025. Total revenue generated by the fashion market stood at US$1,628.3 million followed by electronic and media at US$1,580.1 million.[13]

The KSA is expected to be the top e-commerce market in the Middle East. Currently, the country ranks as the 30th largest market for e-commerce with a revenue of US$9.9 billion in 2021, placing it ahead of Denmark and behind Belgium. The Internet penetration is about 90% and user penetration is more than 95% and accounts for more than 25.6 million users of e-commerce in 2020.[14]

The cross-border trade within the regional context (with the GCC countries) is provided with known websites and digital platforms based in this context (noon.com, souq.com recently purchased by Amazon, Amazon Global, AliExpress, etc.). Such e-markets facilitate quick communication between buyers and sellers, information about the products, their options and promotions, and comparison of prices.

4. Women Entrepreneurs

Recently, women entrepreneurs have become a vital driving force of the KSA economy (Alshibani *et al.*, 2023; Dana *et al.*, 2022). According to

[13] See: https://www.statista.com/outlook/110/243/ecommerce/saudi-arabia.

[14] See: https://ecommercedb.com/markets/sa/all.

the Al-Eqtisadiah report, women entrepreneurs account for 39% of the total number of entrepreneurs in the KSA, up 35% over the past 10 years (Khan, 2020). The promotion of women entrepreneurship is at the heart of the Saudi Vision 2030, where the Dean of Prince Mohammed bin Salman College, Dr. Nabil Kushak, would say "The role of women in the business and financial environment is an integral part of what we aspire to through our vision, which is an important direction in our responsibility towards the country" (Khan, 2020, p. 13). Women entrepreneurship is considered a powerful tool of economic empowerment (Aloulou, 2018). New reforms enable Saudi women to establish their own businesses without any permission of a male guardian as the country pushes to expand a fast-growing private sector. Other institutional barriers are broken down to women's entrepreneurship, rendering Saudi Arabia a "new" gender-inclusive country (Al-Dajani and Alsahli, 2021). The Saudi institutions still have their impacts on female entrepreneurial activities (Aljarodi *et al.*, 2022).

Moreover, the *Saudi Gazette* (2022) claims that the rate of issuing commercial records for women entrepreneurs has increased by 112% during the past 6 years, with the Saudi Ministry of Commerce issuing 139,754 records in 2021 compared to 65,912 records in 2015. Further, according to the General Authority for Small and Medium Enterprises (SMEs) Report of 2022 (Monsha'at), around 45% of startups in the KSA are owned by women, a percentage that is doubled in comparison to 2017 due to the empowerment of women to deal with entrepreneurship, skills development programs, and incorporation of contemporary technologies in business (Siasat Daily, 2022). Saudi women are using their entrepreneurial space as a legitimate platform for change (Alkhaled, 2021; Alkhaled and Berglund, 2018). The socioeconomic power of women in the KSA was noted in several studies in the past (Almunajjed, 2006; Danish and Smith, 2012; Minkus-McKenna, 2009; Muhammad and Basheer, 2010), where, for example, Almunajjed (2006) noted that women possess 40% of private wealth in the KSA; 40% of real estate assets; 70% of the cash savings; 20% of investment funds and portfolios in banks; 18% of current accounts in banks; and 40% of ownership in family businesses, usually as silent partners.

As in other countries, women entrepreneurs in the KSA are driven by several motivational factors and face several barriers (Alsulami and

Abutaha, 2018; Latifi *et al.*, 2022). Alreshoodi *et al.* (2022) have found that passion, opportunity identification, dissatisfaction, and family support are considered as main motivational factors of Saudi women entrepreneurs, and work–life balance difficulties, lack of business networking, limited opportunities for obtaining financial resources, lack of business-related knowledge, deception fear, lack of trust, work-related travel, lack of experience, and non-willingness of male employees to work under women entrepreneurs are considered among the main barriers. Khan (2017), who studies women-owned startups in KSA, in the fashion, food, beauty, and spa sectors, found that planning difficulties, Saudi labor law knowledge, team building, and governmental policies are among the main challenges. Damanhouri (2017) found that lack of development and training is one of the most dominant challenges of women entrepreneurs in the KSA. In this regard, according to Welsh *et al.* (2014), women entrepreneurs in the KSA would like to have more training in purchasing (17%), marketing (15%), language (11%), finance (11%), and technology-based skills (5%). Further, they found that women entrepreneurs are supported by their family and friends, as follows: 75% of them claimed that parents are the biggest moral supporters, 60%–67% claimed spouses, siblings, relatives, and friends encouraged them, and 50% reported that their children have supported them in their business endeavors. Regarding the education level, Vijaya and Almasri (2016) found that most of the women entrepreneurs in the KSA are well-educated (Exhibit 10), with 49% having Bachelor's diplomas and 16% having Master's diplomas, while 35% of the respondents have completed high school. Further, 72.5% of Saudi women entrepreneurs are married and 27.5% are unmarried.

Alhothali (2020) has found that (a) 38.2% of women entrepreneurs in the KSA operate in the food industry, 35.3%, in handicrafts, art/paintings, and women accessories, and 26.5%, in the fashion and designing industry; (b) most of the women entrepreneurs, that is about 45.7%, are aged between 35 and 44 years, 28.6% are aged between 15 and 34 years, 11.4%, between 45 and 54 years, while the others are younger than 24 years old; (c) Around 49% of them do not have prior management experience, 20% have from 1 to 5 years' experience, 14.2% have 6–10 years' experience, 8.6%, more than 10 years, and 8.6%, less than one year; (d) 91.4% of women entrepreneurs have never owned a business before

Exhibit 10. Muna AbuSulayman, a well-educated and successful Saudi entrepreneur.
Note: Free to use under the Creative Commons Attribution-Share Alike 2.0 Generic license.
Source: Photo by Norbert Schiller, World Economic Forum.

and all of them entered in business through startup companies; (e) 74.3% of them employ from 1 to 5 employees, while 25.7% have no employees. Exhibit 11 shows some products (scarfs) produced by women.

Gangwani and Mohamed El-Sayed Shousha (2021) conducted a strengths, weaknesses, opportunities, and threats (SWOT) analysis of women entrepreneurs who operate in the culinary sector and came to the following findings (which can be related to the other sectors as well):

(a) *Strengths*: Supportive policies and programs for women entrepreneurs by the KSA government; financial assistance through loans for women entrepreneurs by the government; well-educated and financially powerful; usually supported by experienced and specialized persons; aspiring to be entrepreneurs; good communication and presentation skills; included to be supported within the Saudi Vision 2030.
(b) *Weaknesses*: Low entrepreneurial skills and business experience; unsuccessful management of risks and troublesome situations; lack of self-confidence in running a business; difficulties in balancing the

Exhibit 11. Scarfs produced by women handicraft entrepreneurs.
Source: Pixabay/no attribution required.

family and business requirements; lack of planning skills; mobility constraints; and social and cultural barriers.

(c) *Opportunities*: Universities provide adequate education on establishing and developing new companies; three pioneering bodies have been established for support; skills development programs have been made available; special entrepreneurial education courses for all; learning opportunities for new technologies and production methods; social media marketing training; and digital tools and resources.

(d) *Threats*: Obtaining support from banks and managing the working capital; severe competition from organized industries; delays of payments from clients; financial problems due to blockage of funds in raw materials, inventory, work-in-progress, finished goods; prejudice or sexual harassment; dependance on middlemen, which results in lesser sales and lesser profits; and gender bias.

Table 2. Top 10 Saudi women entrepreneurs.

No.	Women entrepreneur	Industry	Establishment	Headquarters
1	Razan Alazzouni	Fashion	2008	Saudi Arabia
2	Arwa Al Banawi	Fashion	2015	KSA and UAE
3	Honayda Serafi	Fashion	2016	Lebanon
4	Nora Al Shaikh	Fashion	2012	KSA
5	Dana Alalami	Jewellery	2015	KSA and UAE
6	Nourah Al Faisal	Jewellery	2014	France
7	Shahd AlShehail	Fashion	2017	KSA
8	Muneera Al Tamimi	Footwear	2013	UAE
9	Nour AlTamimi	Footwear	2017	UAE and UK
10	Fatima Batook	Fitness and Fashion	2012/2015	KSA

Source: Forbes (2020).

Forbes (2020), in its "Women Behind Middle Eastern Brands 2020" list, ranked the top 10 Saudi women entrepreneurs based on "the celebrities who believed in the brand, social media followers, revenues, growth rate, the number of countries the brand is present in, media coverage, years of experience, and editorial points". The list is led by Razan Alazzouni, a fashion entrepreneur, whose designs were worn by stars, such as Kendall Jenner, Emma Roberts, and Elizabeth Banks (Table 2).

The government of the KSA has identified the potential of women entrepreneurs for the socioeconomic development of the country and has therefore designed and established several supporting programs, agencies, and institutions, the most important of which are as follows (Algahtani, 2022; Hvidt, 2018):

(a) *National development plans* (NDPs), six so far, were focused on improving the education, health, and employment of Saudi people, of both genders. The fifth NDP program (2005–2009) provided full support for women entrepreneurs by facilitating the access to funds, regulations, and investment procedures. For example, this program enabled the removal of the restrictions related to business ownership by women, were the most popular was the requirement that women must have a male guardian to lead a business.

(b) *Entrepreneurship centers and foundations*: The aim of these centers is to create a better ecosystem for women entrepreneurs by providing different training and development programs so that they can overcome the growth barriers and other business challenges, especially those related to laws. The most important centers are the Al-Sayeda Khadija bint Khuwailid Businesswomen Centre, Al-Barakah Loan Center of King Abdul Aziz Women Charity, Alwaleed bin Talal Foundation, Abdul Latif Jameel Center, and Blossom Accelerator (focused on techno-women entrepreneurs).

Besides these programs, centers, and foundations, the Ministry of Commerce and Investment of the KSA plays a very important role in the development of women entrepreneurship by offering facilities in registering businesses and enhancing awareness about governmental policies and programs that are strictly related to women entrepreneurs.

5. Toward the Future

The KSA has witnessed incredible transformation in the span of a single generation (Saudi Arabian Ministry of Foreign Affairs, 2017). Since the adoption of the Vision 2030 as a road map for the KSA's future, a key focus in achieving this vision is to create an environment that unlocks business opportunities, extends the economic base, and creates jobs for all Saudis (men and women). This will include the following:

- Continuing the improvement of the business ecosystem and boosting women entrepreneurship and innovation (Aloulou and Al Othman, 2021; Aloulou, 2021b; Ashri, 2019; Dana *et al.*, 2021; Merani, 2019). Joint and concrete activities are required between the Saudi government, financial institutions, and social organizations to motivate and enable women to embrace entrepreneurship and successfully run their new businesses. In this way, they will make the women accept more challenging and rewarding career choices for themselves and create more opportunities for employment of other women (Gangwani and Mohamed El-Sayed Shousha, 2021).

- Taking the advantage of modern and emerging technologies to achieve the digital transformation, shape new digital entrepreneurial startups by women, and build the digital economy, society, and nation (Aloulou, 2019; 2021a; McAdam *et al.*, 2018; 2019).
- Including and motivating women entrepreneurs to participate in diversification and remodeling of the country's economy away from the dependence on traditional hydrocarbon-based industries (McKinsey and Company, 2015; Porter, 2012, Ramadani *et al.*, 2022).
- Motivating women entrepreneurs in the development of the tourism sector by investing in mega-projects and in Saudi heritage (such as the entertainment city near Riyadh at Qiddiya, northern megacity of NEOM, world-class exclusive wellness destination of Amaala, and UNESCO-listed cultural birth of the Kingdom in Diriyah).
- Helping the private sector to boost Saudization of jobs for male and female citizens, and economically empowering women, helping them to access employment, and enabling them to strengthen their future and contribute to the development of their family businesses, society, and economy (Aloulou, 2018; Aloulou and Alshaeel, 2023).
- Creating opportunities for women to transfer the technology and invest in technology: Tech investment is the way of the future in the KSA, and local companies are shaping the Saudi Arabia innovation ecosystem (Arabnet, 2017; Innovation Enabled, 2016; OC&C Strategy Consultants, 2018).
- Building the country's capacity for optimistic resilience in most challenging situations (such as the COVID-19 pandemic, high inflation, energy crises, etc.) from resilient sectors (education, healthcare, etc.) (Invest Saudia, 2020).

This chapter has illustrated how the KSA has started its deep transformation toward modernization and competitiveness, away from the historical aspect, and women's entrepreneurship since its unification in 1932. Last year, the KSA celebrated its 90th national day. It has also been noted throughout this chapter that the KSA is an emerging economy with diversified potentialities, especially with its growing young population, and with a challenging transformation plan, namely, the Saudi Vision 2030.

References

Al-Dajani, H. & Alsahli, M. (2021). "Can Women Entrepreneurs Thrive in Saudi Arabia?" *Entreprendre Innover*, **4950**(2), 100–109.

Algahtani, S. (2022). "Changing Society: Pioneering Women Entrepreneurs in Saudi Arabia". Robert Gordon University, PhD Thesis. Hosted on OpenAIR [online]. Retrieved from: https://doi.org/10.48526/rgu-wt-1677949 (Accessed on 23 December 2022).

Alhothali, G. T. (2020). "Challenges Facing Women Entrepreneurs Running Home-Based Business in Saudi Arabia". *Periodicals of Engineering and Natural Sciences*, **8**(3), 1386–1397.

Aljarodi, A., Thatchenkery, T., & Urbano, D. (2022). "Female Entrepreneurial Activity and Institutions: Empirical Evidence from Saudi Arabia". *Research in Globalization*, **5**(12), 100102.

Alkhaled, S. (2021). "Women's Entrepreneurship in Saudi Arabia: Feminist Solidarity and Political Activism in Disguise?". *Gender, Work & Organization*, **28**(3), 950–972.

Alkhaled, S. & Berglund, K. (2018). "'And Now I'm Free': Women's Empowerment and Emancipation Through Entrepreneurship in Saudi Arabia and Sweden". *Entrepreneurship & Regional Development*, 30(7–8), 877–900.

Almunajjed, M. (2006). *Saudi Women Speak: 24 Remarkable Women Tell Their Stories.* Beirut: Arab Institute for Research and Publishing.

Aloulou, W. J. & Alarifi, M. (2022). "The Context for Business in Saudi Arabia". In Dana, L-P., Salamzadeh, A., Ramadani, V. & Palalić, R., eds., *Understanding Contexts of Business in Western Asia: Land of Bazaars and High-Tech Booms* (pp. 477–494). Singapore: World Scientific Publishing.

Aloulou, W. J. & Alshaeel, R. (2023). "Family Business in Saudi Arabia". In *Family Business in Gulf Cooperation Council Countries* (pp. 91–119). Cham: Springer.

Aloulou, W. J. (2018). "Enhancing Women's Economic Empowerment Through Entrepreneurship in Saudi Arabia". In *Arab Women and Their Evolving Roles in the Global Business Landscape* (Chapter 6, pp. 120–151). IGI Global, Hershey PA.

Aloulou, W. J. (2019). "Entrepreneurship and Innovation in the Digitalization Era: Exploring Uncharted Territories". In Mezghani, K., Aloulou, W. J., eds., *Business Transformations in the Era of Digitalization* (Chapter 11, pp. 179–203). IGI Global, Hershey PA.

Aloulou, W. J. (2021a). "Instilling FinTech Culture in a Digitalized World: Defining, Issuing, and Opening Up". In Sghari, A., Mezghani, K., (eds.), *Influence of FinTech on Management Transformation*. IGI Global Publishing, Hershey PA.

Aloulou, W. J. (2021b). "Mapping Incubation Mechanisms in Saudi Arabia: State-of-the-Art and Challenges for the Future". In Mian, S., Klofsten, M., Lamine, W., (eds.), *International Handbook of Research on Business and Technology Incubation and Acceleration*. Edward Elgar Publishing, Cheltenham: UK.

Aloulou, W. J. & Al Othman, N. (2021). "Entrepreneurship in Saudi Arabia". In Dana, L-P., Palalic, R., & Ramadani, V., (eds.), *Entrepreneurship in the Gulf Cooperation Council Region. Evolution and Future Perspectives*. Singapore: World Scientific.

Alreshoodi, A. S., Ur Rehman, A., Alshammari, A. S., Khan, T. N., & Moid, S. (2022). "Women Entrepreneurs in Saudi Arabia: A Portrait of Progress in the Context of Their Drivers and Inhibitors". *Journal of Enterprising Culture*, **30**(3), 375–400.

Alshibani, M. S., Aloulou, J. W., & Ramadani, V. (2023). "New-Venture Gestation Processes Amid COVID-19 Pandemic: Antecedents of Saudi Female Nascent Entrepreneurs". *Business Process Management Journal*. doi:10.1108/BPMJ-11-2022-0555.

Alsulami H. & Abutaha, R. (2018). "Saudi Female Entrepreneurs, Situation and Challenges". In *2018 Portland International Conference on Management of Engineering and Technology (PICMET)* (pp. 1–6). Honolulu, HI, USA.

Anggadwita, G., Mulyaningsih, H. D., Ramadani, V., & Arwiyah, M. Y. (2015). "Women Entrepreneurship in Islamic Perspective: A Driver for Social Change". *International Journal of Business and Globalisation*, **15**(3), 389–404.

Anishchenkova, V. (2020). *Modern Saudi Arabia*. Understanding Modern Nations. ABC-CLIO.

Arabnet, (2017). *KSA Innovation Economy Tech Startups*. Report, in collaboration with the Saudi Ministry of Communication and Information Technology. Retrieved from: https://www.arabnet.me/ContentFiles/4195PDFFile1.pdf (Accessed on 23 December 2018).

Ashri, O. M. (2019). *On The Fast Track: Saudi Arabia's Entrepreneurship Ecosystem*. Retrieved from: https://www.entrepreneur.com/article/336766 (Accessed on 23 September 2019).

Damanhouri, A. M. (2017). "Women Entrepreneurship Behind the Veil: Strategies and Challenges in the Kingdom of Saudi Arabia". *Journal of Research in Business, Economics, and Management*, **9**(12), 1750–1762.

Dana, L-P. (2000). "Economic Sectors in Egypt and Their Managerial Implications". *Journal of African Business*, **1**(1), 65–81.

Dana, L-P. & Wright, R. W. (2015). "Bazaar Economies, Modern Networks and Entrepreneurship". *Wiley Encyclopedia of Management* (pp. 1–7). Cheltenham: Edward Elgar.

Dana, L-P., Palalic, R., & Ramadani, V. (2021). *Entrepreneurship in the Gulf Cooperation Council Region. Evolution and Future Perspectives.* Singapore: World Scientific.

Dana, L-P., Salamzadeh, A., Ramadani, V., & Palalić, R. (2022). *Understanding Contexts of Business in Western Asia: Land of Bazaars and High-Tech Booms*. World Scientific Publishing, Singapore.

Danish, A. Y. & Smith, H. L. (2012). "Female Entrepreneurship in Saudi Arabia: Opportunities and Challenges". *International Journal of Gender and Entrepreneurship*, **4**(3), 216–235.

Dutta, S., Lanvin, B., Rivera León, L., & Wunsch-Vincent, S. (2022). *Global Innovation Index 2022. What is the future of Innovation-Driven Growth?* 15th Edition. The World Intellectual Property Organization. Retrieved from: https://static.poder360.com.br/2022/09/Digital-Ranking-IMD-2022.pdf (Accessed on 29 December 2022).

Forbes (2020). *The 10 Most Successful Saudi Female Entrepreneurs Behind Homegrown Brands*. Retrieved from: https://www.forbesmiddleeast.com/leadership/women-leaders/the-10-most-successful-saudi-female-entrepreneurs-behind-homegrown-brands (Accessed on 10 January 2023).

Gangwani, S. & Mohamed El-Sayed Shousha, D. M. (2021). "Challenges of Saudi Women Entrepreneurs in Culinary Art Business". *Academy of Entrepreneurship Journal*, **27**(4), 1–13.

GEM (2020). *Kingdom of Saudi Arabia National Report 2019–2020*. Global Entrepreneurship Monitor. Retrieved from: https://www.gemconsortium.org/report/50534 (Accessed on 29 December 2022).

Heritage Foundation (2022). *2022 Index of Economic Freedom*. In Miller, T., Kim, A. B., & Roberts, J. M., (eds.), *The Heritage Foundation*. Retrieved from: https://www.heritage.org/index/pdf/2022/countries/2022_IndexofEconomicFreedom-Saudi-Arabia.pdf (Accessed on 31 December 2022).

Hvidt, M. (2018). *The New Role of Women in the New Saudi Arabian Economy*. Saudi Arabia: Center for Mellemoststudier.

IMD World Digital Competitiveness Center (2022). *Digital Competitiveness Index 2022: Report*. Retrieved from: https://static.poder360.com.br/2022/09/Digital-Ranking-IMD-2022.pdf (Accessed on 13 January 2023).

Innovation Enabled (2016). *Shaping the Saudi Arabia Innovation Ecosystem*. RTI International and RPD Innovations. Retrieved from: https://www.rti.org/sites/default/files/innovation_enabled_workshop_report_med.pdf (Accessed on 1 January 2023).

Invest Saudia (2020). *Investment Highlights*. Special Report, Opening Remarks at the Extraordinary G20 Leaders' Summit. Spring. Retrieved from: http://www.investsaudi.sa (Accessed on 20 June 2020).

Kalu, E. U., Nwafor, U. F., Arize, A. C., Dana, L-P., Malindretos, J., & Onwumere, J. U. (2020). "Green or Gas in OPEC Member Countries: A Linear and Asymmetric Investigation of Energy–Growth Nexus". *OPEC Energy Review*. doi.org/10.1111/opec.12190.

Khan, H. F. (2020). "Women Entrepreneurs in Saudi Arabia: Opportunities and Challenges". *International Journal of Commerce and Economics*, **2**(2), 13–16.

Khan, M. K., & Khan, M. B. (2020). *Research, Innovation and Entrepreneurship in Saudi Arabia: Vision 2030*. London: Routledge.

Khan, M. R. (2017). "Saudi Arabian Female Start-ups Status Quo". *International Journal of Entrepreneurship*, **21**(2), 1–27.

Kingdom of Saudi Arabia (2018). *Towards Saudi Arabia's Sustainable Tomorrow*. First Voluntary National Review 2018–1439. Retrieved from: https://sustainabledevelopment.un.org/content/documents/20230SDGs_English_Report972018_FINAL.pdf (Accessed on 15 May 2020).

Latifi, V., Ramadani, V., & Rexhepi, G. (2022). "Women Minority Entrepreneurs: Motivational Factors and Challenges". *Strategic Change: Briefings in Entrepreneurial Finance*, **31**(2), 219–225.

Leonidou, L. (1995). "The Saudi Distribution System: Structure, Operation and Behaviour". *Marketing Intelligence and Planning*, **13**(11), 27–35.

McAdam, M., Crowley, C., & Harrison, R. T. (2018). "The Emancipatory Potential of Female Digital Entrepreneurship: Institutional Voids in Saudi Arabia". In *Academy of Management Proceedings* (Vol. 2018, No. 1, p. 10255). Briarcliff Manor, NY: Academy of Management.

McAdam, M., Crowley, C., & Harrison, R. T. (2019). "To Boldly Go Where No [Man] Has Gone Before"-Institutional Voids and the Development of Women's Digital Entrepreneurship". *Technological Forecasting and Social Change*, **146**(3), 912–922.

McKinsey & Company (2015). *Saudi Arabia Beyond Oil: The Investment and Productivity Transformation, McKinsey Global Institute Report.* Retrieved from: http://www.mckinsey.com/ (Accessed on 20 December 2015).

Merani, M. (2019). *Driven by Growth: Saudi Arabia Sees a Rise in Support for Startups and Entrepreneurs.* Retrieved from: https://www.entrepreneur.com/article/339873 (Accessed on 30 September 2019).

Minkus-McKenna, D. (2009). "Women Entrepreneurs in Riyadh, Saudi Arabia". *Working Paper Series 2.* University of Maryland University College (UMUC).

Muhammad, A. S. & Basheer, M. A. G. (2010). "Doing Business with Impudence: A Focus on Women Entrepreneurship in Saudi Arabia". *African Journal of Business Management*, **4**(1), 1–11.

OC&C Strategy Consultants (2018). *Tech Entrepreneurship Ecosystem in Kingdom of Saudi Arabia.* Retrieved from: https://s3-eu-west-1.amazonaws.com/wamda-prod/resource-url/2018_KSA_Report_Digital_Version_OC%26C_Updated.pdf (Accessed on 10 December 2018).

Porter, M. (2012). *Entrepreneurship and Competitiveness: Implications for Saudi Arabia, Global Competitiveness Forum.* Saudi Arabia: Riyadh.

Ramadani, V., Agarwal, S., Caputo, A., Agrawal, V., & Dixit, J. K. (2022). "Sustainable Competencies of Social Entrepreneurship for Sustainable Development: Exploratory Analysis from a Developing Economy". *Business Strategy and the Environment*, **31**(7), 3437–3453.

Saudi Arabian Ministry of Foreign Affairs (2017). *Saudi Arabia and Political, Economic & Social Development 2017.* Retrieved from: https://www.saudiembassy.net/sites/default/files/WhitePaper_Development_May2017.pdf (Accessed on 10 December 2018).

Saudi Council of Economic and Development Affairs (SCEDA). (2016). *Saudi Vision 2030*, 24 April. Retrieved from: http://vision2030.gov.sa/download/file/fid/417 (Accessed on 2 June 2020).

Saudi Gazettes (2022). *Commercial Registrations by Saudi Women Jump 112% Over Six Years.* Retrieved from: https://saudigazette.com.sa/article/617211 (Accessed on 12 January 2023).

Siasat Daily (2022). *Women Own 45% of Start-Ups in Saudi Arabia: Report.* Retrieved from: https://www.siasat.com/women-own-45-of-startups-in-saudi-arabia-report-2401150/ (Accessed on 10 January 2023).

Statista (2020). *Global No. 1 Business Data Platform.* Retrieved from: https://www.statista.com/ (Accessed on 13 January 2021).

United Nations Conference on Trade and Development, UNCTAD (2019). *UNCTAD B2C E-Commerce Index 2019*. UNCTAD Technical Notes on ICT for Development No. 14. Retrieved from: https://unctad.org/system/files/official-document/tn_unctad_ict4d14_en.pdf (Accessed on 13 January 2021).

United Nations Development Programme (2020). *Human Development Report 2020. The next frontier. Human Development and the Anthropocene.* Retrieved from: http://hdr.undp.org/en/2020-report/download (Accessed on 12 January 2023).

Vijaya, G. S. & Almasri, R. (2016). "A Study of Women Entrepreneurship in Saudi Arabia". *International Journal of Advanced Engineering, Management and Science*, **2**(12), 1956–1959.

Welsh, D. H. B., Memili, E., Kaciak, E., & Al-Sadoon, A. (2014). "Saudi Women Entrepreneurs: A Growing Economic Segment". *Journal of Business Research*, **67**(5), 758–762.

World Bank (2020). *Doing Business 2020. Comparing Business Regulation in 190 Economies. Economy Profile Saudi Arabia. Country Report.* Retrieved from: https://www.doingbusiness.org/content/dam/doingBusiness/country/s/saudi-arabia/SAU.pdf (Accessed on 12 January 2023).

World Economic Forum (2020). *The Global Competitiveness Report. Special Edition. How Countries are Performing on the Road to Recovery.* Retrieved from: http://www3.weforum.org/docs/WEF_TheGlobalCompetitivenessReport2020.pdf (Accessed on 25 December 2020).

World Economic Forum (2022). *Global Gender Gap Report 2022. Insight Report*, July. Retrieved from: https://investinginwomen.asia/knowledge/global-gender-gap-report-2022/#:~:text=The%20suggests%20that%20the%20global,of%20136%20years%20to%20parity (Accessed on 12 January 2023).

World Factbook (2022). *Saudi Country Profile*. Retrieved from: https://www.cia.gov/the-world-factbook/countries/saudi-arabia/ (Accessed on 15 December 2022).

https://doi.org/10.1142/9789811283499_0013

Chapter 13

Women Entrepreneurs in Syria

Aidin Salamzadeh[*,§], Mirjana Radovic-Markovic[†,¶], and Slimane Ed-Dafali[‡,||]

[*]*Department of Business Management, Faculty of Management, University of Tehran, Tehran, Iran*
[†]*Belgrade Banking Academy, Belgarde, Serbia*
[‡]*Department of Management, National School of Commerce and Management, Chouaib Doukkali University, Morroco*
[§]*salamzadeh@ut.ac.ir*
[¶]*mirjana.radovic.markovic@bba.edu.rs*
[||]*slimane.eddafali@gmail.com*

Abstract

Women's entrepreneurship in Syria is highly affected by its historical facts and the wars that affected the business environment. This chapter tries to shed light on the history of entrepreneurship, especially women's entrepreneurship, in the country. Then, the authors add more details about the entrepreneurship ecosystem and relevant issues. Afterwards, the chapter explains the evolution of women's entrepreneurship and the challenges that can affect its trend. Finally, the authors mention some critical issues to improve women's entrepreneurship in Syria.

Keywords: Women entrepreneurship; female entrepreneurship; entrepreneurial ecosystem; challenges; Middle East; Syria.

1. Introduction

With the improvement of the situation of startup companies in the Middle East region in general and the increase in the presence of women as founders of businesses and employees, there must have been many challenges faced and overcome by young Syrian women, too, in establishing and running their businesses — some of which succeeded in Syria and other countries. In 2009, the participation of Syrian women in entrepreneurship was 4.4%, while this percentage increased to 22.4% in 2018, according to the Syrian National Report on Entrepreneurship. The numbers are low especially in light of the migration of young people due to the harsh conditions in which Syria lives (Zighan, 2021). This corresponds to a study on the development of entrepreneurship among women in the Middle East in 2016 (Mouselli and Khalifa, 2017). The percentage of women entrepreneurs in Morocco is 50%, and in Tunisia, it is 9%. In another study done in 2019, Jordan and Lebanon combined accounted for 34% of women entrepreneurs in the two countries (Al-Qahtani *et al.*, 2022).

More than a decade after the Arab Spring uprisings, most of the hopes and aspirations of change among the rebelling people are still pending (Coduras *et al.*, 2018; Ghazalian, 2022). After a quick look at the reality of the situation, the human rights activists, humanitarians, and political analysts were overwhelmed with the increase in violence in various forms, the domination of patriarchal authorities, and the increase in armaments and militarization. Amidst all this, women in the Middle East and North Africa (MENA) region continue their struggle against systemic discrimination and exclusion in all aspects of political, economic, cultural, and social life (Salamzadeh, 2018; Salamzadeh *et al.*, 2017, 2022) (Exhibit 1). In Syria, where women have always been excluded from the workforce, the circumstances of the wars have increased their burden and expelled them further, while most efforts at economic empowerment have been unsatisfactory (Al-Dajani, 2022). According to the UN Economic and Social Commission for Western Asia (ESCWA) report in 2019, social entrepreneurs have begun to take a creative approach to help Syrian refugees find work and project funding opportunities.

Based on the available evidence, it can be concluded that the entrepreneurship ecosystem of the country is heavily affected by wars. Therefore,

Exhibit 1. Syrian female protestor.

Source: https://pixabay.com/photos/golan-heights-demonstration-people-1899827.

compared to many ecosystems in the MENA region, the Syrian ecosystem is less developed (Dana *et al.*, 2022). The situation becomes more complicated when it comes to female entrepreneurs. Our main aim is to provide more insights into female entrepreneurship in Syria. The chapter is structured as follows. First, the historical aspects of women's entrepreneurship in Syria are reviewed. Then, the chapter adds some details about the entrepreneurship ecosystem of the country and women entrepreneurs. The chapter concludes with some remarks and directions for future research.

2. Historical Overview

Syrian women, like the majority of the Syrian people, have suffered, albeit doubly, from the systematic policies of marginalization and impoverishment pursued by the ruling regime, as it did not respect their political, social, economic, and legal rights. It even took more than five decades to distort the status of women, perpetuate their exclusion and poverty, and

Exhibit 2. Syrian women at a mosque.

Source: https://pixabay.com/photos/syria-damascus-omejaden-mosque-4033529.

create a weak stereotype of them (Leenders, 2012). This is due to customs and traditions, economic policies, and discriminatory laws (Exhibit 2). Looking at the official statistics, according to the Central Bureau of Statistics in Syria, one can see that the participation rate of women in the national labor force did not exceed 15%. However, the problem lies in the inaccuracy of these official statistics, as they do not include women working in the pastoral economy, doing domestic work, or providing social support, and therefore, do not consider the economic value of the work they do. Therefore, their economic participation is not included in the labor force (Bojica *et al.*, 2014; El Ali and Le Loarne-Lemaire, 2022). Specifically, it is difficult to estimate the number of Syrian female entrepreneurs in the country (Bayram, 2017).

Figure 1 summarizes working hours lost due to the COVID-19 crisis expressed as a number of full-time equivalent (FTE) jobs, for both genders in Syria as well as Arab countries and the countries of the Arab League. Gender differences could not be evaluated due to the lack of data in the case of Syria.

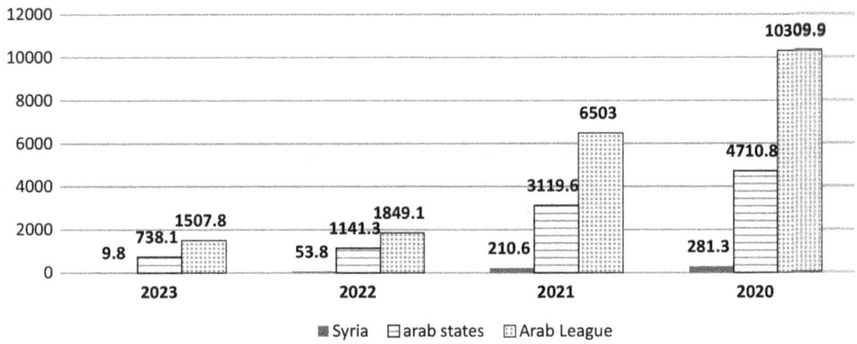

Figure 1. Working hours lost due to the COVID-19 crisis expressed as a number of FTE jobs, for both genders — International Labor Organization (ILO) modeled estimates (thousands).

Note: Full-time equivalence: based on 48 hours per week.
Source: ILO Stat database. Retrieved from: https://www.ilo.org/shinyapps/bulkexplorer8/ (Accessed on 13 February 2023).

With the outbreak of the Syrian revolution in March 2011, women found the opportunity to claim their rights, so they took their turn and participated in demonstrations and humanitarian, human rights, media, political, and community work. However, transforming the popular movement in Syria into an armed conflict made women pay a higher price, as a result of the various forms of violence against them, especially sexual violence (Lasic, 2018). Today, the situation is worse, as they are threatened with starvation, oppression, and exploitation. Despite this, Syrian women persisted in their struggle to confront a patriarchal society and other regimes of oppression and marginalization that denied women their rights and freedoms, their education, and access to resources, which increased their economic vulnerability and reinforced their exclusion (Ng *et al.*, 2022).

Figure 2 summarizes the ratio of total weekly hours worked to the population aged 15–64, by sex — ILO modeled estimates, for both genders in Syria and Arab countries. Gender differences could not be evaluated due to the lack of data in the case of Syria.

The circumstances of the war have also added a new direction to the struggle of Syrian women, which is represented in assuming complex economic responsibilities, with the absence of the traditional breadwinners and

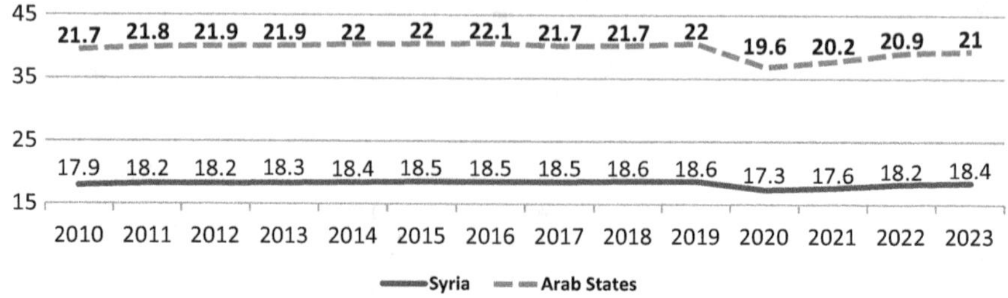

Figure 2. The ratio of total weekly hours worked to population aged 15–64, by sex.

Note: ILO modeled estimates.

Source: ILO Stat database. Retrieved from: https://www.ilo.org/shinyapps/bulkexplorer8/ (Accessed on 13 February 2023).

considering their physical disabilities, especially in the northwestern regions outside the control of the regime. The poor economic conditions forced women to work in a way that traditional Syrian society was not familiar with, to secure the necessities of life under extremely harsh conditions (Exhibit 3). This included attempts by civil society organizations in those areas to fill the void as a result of the absence of state institutions, providing services and job opportunities to a lesser degree.

3. Entrepreneurial Ecosystem

A 2019 report on the entrepreneurship environment in the Arab region included statistics on the spread of entrepreneurship and startups in various Arab countries. Based on this report, the number of startups in the Arab countries was estimated to be about 10,000 firms, with a financing volume of more than $2 billion (Aminova *et al.*, 2020). About a third of these firms (35%) are in the UAE, followed by Egypt, which contains (19%) of these firms, and the volume of investment deals in 2018 amounted to about $900 million (Slaoui 2022). Most Arab startups work in the field of Fintech (12%), e-commerce (11%), transportation and delivery (8%), and information technologies (IT) (8%) (Dana *et al.*, 2022). In the absence of local statistics, the report indicates that the number of startups in Syria has reached (1%) of the total number of these firms in the Arab region (Aminova *et al.*, 2020). The number of these firms in Lebanon is

Exhibit 3. Bedouin woman.
Source: https://pixabay.com/photos/bedouin-woman-nomad-jerusalem-62845.

about (7%) of the total number in the region (Aminova *et al.*, 2021; Franzke *et al.*, 2022). In light of the bad economic conditions and the absence of support and financing mechanisms for the growth of these companies in Syria, a large number of Syrian companies tend to transfer their firms from Syria to other countries, especially the UAE, which is characterized by the openness of its market and the presence of an environment that supports the growth of these firms (Jürgens *et al.*, 2022). Table 1 shows the country's rank, in terms of doing business in 2020.

According to a survey by Bayram (2017), the concentration of start-ups is highest in Damascus at 72.9%, followed by Homs and Hama at 5.9%, Aleppo and Tartous at 4.7%, Latakia at 3.5%, and rural Damascus

Table 1. Doing business indicators in Syria (2020).

Indicator	Rank
Starting a business	143
Dealing with construction permits	186
Getting electricity	160
Registering property	162
Getting credit	176
Protecting minority investors	97
Paying taxes	91
Trading across borders	178
Enforcing contracts	160
Resolving insolvency	158

and As-Suwayda at 2%. It should be emphasized that 73% of these firms are still in the idea stage, while only 2% have moved on to the growth stage.

Very few so-called innovation mechanisms (incubators and accelerators) have been established in Syria (Salamzadeh and Ramadani, 2021). Among these institutions, we mention three business incubators of the Syrian Scientific Society for Informatics in Damascus, Latakia, and Homs, an incubator in the Damascus Chamber of Commerce, as well as a private accelerator — the only one in Damascus. Several international bodies and organizations also launched competitions for entrepreneurship to spread this culture among young people and support their projects. This is not the case in Syria in which no government agency is mainly concerned with entrepreneurship, except for the Small and Medium Enterprises Development Corporation, whose activities are predominantly training professionals and not entrepreneurs. The Syrian government and its ministries do not have any strategy to develop a stimulating environment for entrepreneurial projects, especially in light of the high unemployment rates among youth (Daher, 2020).

Figure 3 plots the evolution of the unemployment rate for young adults by sex in the Syrian Arab Republic. It is critical to consider the

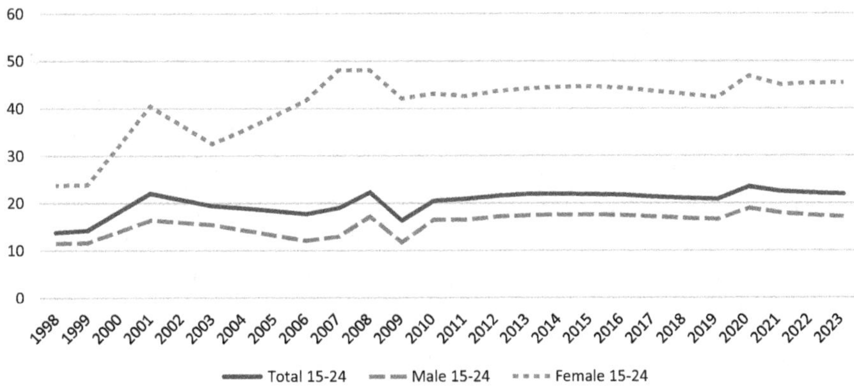

Figure 3. Unemployment rate by sex — ILO modeled estimates, November 2022 (%) for young adults (1998–2023).

Source: ILO Stat database. Retrieved from: https://www.ilo.org/shinyapps/bulkexplorer8/ (Accessed on 13 February 2023).

youth (15–24) as a target audience for programs aimed at increasing women's entrepreneurial potential (ESCWA, 2019), as in the Syrian Arab Republic there are still gender variations in youth unemployment. The figure highlights the weaknesses of the Syrian Arab Republic in entrepreneurial initiatives designed to address the gender participation gap in the workforce.

The Syrian government steps aside and does not play a clear role in this field. Thus, one could rarely find inclusive support packages for newly established ventures. Besides, young entrepreneurs lack managerial skills, economic knowledge, and exposure to neighboring and global markets (Radović-Marković *et al.*, 2012, 2013). Most projects are similar, aiming to establish new websites or address some of the previously identified needs. The absence of institutions and mechanisms supporting start-ups in their early stages of establishment and growth has led to the failure of these firms and there will be no guarantee of achieving a return on investment (Street *et al.*, 2022).

Entrepreneurial firms are characterized by offering their products under conditions of high risk, which requires them to obtain great support and financing, especially in their early stages, and venture capital is one of the most important means of financing for these firms, along with other traditional financing methods (Boufeldja, 2014). Besides, awareness is growing today about the importance of women's economic empowerment and bridging the gap between women and men to achieve gender equality. Thus, women's entrepreneurship is an important strategy for advancing women's economic empowerment while reducing gender inequality. In the Arab region, the promotion of women's entrepreneurship has gained momentum over the last decade and is seen as a valuable approach to job creation in an environment that generally discriminates between women and men (Bouguerra, 2015; Ng *et al.*, 2022).

Today, information and communication technologies, especially mobile phones, the Internet, and computers, play an important role in accelerating business growth. At a time when information and communication technology (ICT) is increasingly being integrated into business practices, digital skills are essential to creating business models, developing business plans, raising capital, interacting with stakeholders and clients, and building networks and social-professional relationships (Bouzari *et al.*, 2021; Steel, 2021). While the COVID-19 pandemic and the resulting lockdown measures have underlined the importance of ICT as a tool to support the resilience and competitiveness of SMEs (Salamzadeh and Dana, 2021, 2022), at the same time they have weakened many small businesses that are not digitally ready (Dheer and Salamzadeh, 2021; Pereira *et al.*, 2021; Abuhussein *et al.*, 2022).

4. Women Entrepreneurs

As the battles settled at the end of 2018, organizations began to pay attention to capacity-building programs and supported livelihoods by providing grants to establish individual projects such as vocational training and cash-for-work projects (for example, work in harvesting crops or knitting for cash for women). The organizations that sponsor these programs consider that this type of project has a role in raising the standard of living, and reducing poverty and unemployment rates, as women's products are distributed to the most vulnerable groups, such as children, for example. Although these efforts do not specifically target women, they do make an effort to include them, as selection criteria are often designed in such a way as to provide greater opportunities for women (Caputo *et al.*, 2017; Franzke *et al.*, 2022).

However, based on previous studies, it has become clear that these programs did not lead to the economic empowerment of women as a whole, but were limited to empowering a specific group of them — women who were breadwinners for their families. The selection mechanism for female beneficiaries of these projects relied on the criteria of "weakness and vulnerability" of the breadwinners of families if they were without a male breadwinner, or if the male breadwinner was in a state of disability. Among the groups targeted by these programs are also divorced women and widows, if they have children. These programs included the integration of such poor, non-working women, who had lost the breadwinner of the family, in micro or small projects to ensure a monthly income that is commensurate with the social context and professional capabilities of the women, especially those with a low level of education and skills (Senthanar *et al.*, 2021; El Ali and Le Loarne-Lemaire, 2022). While the criteria focused on supporting the family and not supporting women's rights to empowerment, access to the labor market, participation in the production process, and their right to have their various roles observed in the formal economy were lacking. Thus, these programs reclassified traditional gender roles, starting with their approach from a narrow masculine perspective that still views women as extensions of families and not as independent citizens with rights and entitlements that must be achieved and preserved within and outside these family systems (Rahman *et al.*, 2022; Ramadani *et al.*, 2022).

These approaches were also limited to increasing the productive role of some groups of women, without looking structurally at the economic value of their pastoral, domestic, or community work, as the saying that "women do not work" is just a heresy, for women play several complex roles, whether pastoral, domestic, or societal (Karlowska, 2019) and in terms of community activities or healthcare. Accordingly, the real problem, on the one hand, lies in the failure to value these works and roles and the societal view of them as inferior, so that they remain outside the indicators of economic growth. On the other hand, these projects did not notice the hard roles and the increasing burdens that fell on women's shoulders, as they did not look structurally to change the existing economic structures, but to involve women in the labor market without looking at their conditions, positions, and the challenges they face. Moreover, the nature of these interventions does not take into account the economic well-being of women but is sufficient to support the family, not the women, and provide access to the basic and minimum needs, which prevents women from achieving their well-being, even partially (Aymé, 2022).

Syrian women, in general, still practice traditional jobs that perpetuate the stereotypical roles imposed by patriarchal authority, customs, and traditions, such as working in office jobs or those imposed by the need for women to deal with women. And if some women can take a step toward owning a business, by obtaining grants to establish their project, a good number remain within the framework of home projects and traditional professions such as sewing, providing beauty salon services, wool weaving, domestic dairy farming and cheese production, and making handicrafts. This is in compliance with the customs of the society that enshrine the place of women in the private space and the home, or because these opportunities are limited to projects that can only be implemented from within the home — the private space (El Ali *et al.*, 2022). The study of Bayram (2017) also reveals a significant improvement in the contributions made by women entrepreneurs, who now account for 22.4% of all business owners. This is a result of many women taking on the new role of the family's primary breadwinner, while many men have been forced to leave their homes or join the armed struggle. This study also identified 10 Challenges of Syria's Startups when building and running startups: insecurity and political instability, scarcity of financial support, access to market limitation, collapsing infrastructure, sanctions and payment restrictions, increasing economic burdens, dwindling human skills, diminishing market size, unfriendly regulatory environment, and dysfunctional entrepreneurship education.

Thus, the percentage of female participants in grant programs is still low, due to the fear of some of them of assuming this responsibility, and the lack of building their financial knowledge and awareness of the importance of productive work and the feasibility of these projects and their impact on their lives and futures. The new women in the labor market, in addition to their limited professional experience, and the difficulty of separating them from the social and cultural conditions that govern their lives, have other issues such as taking the burden of the negative image of a mother, one who sacrifices herself to preserve the marriage, or the illusion of protecting the family in exchange for their safety and happiness, which impacts their performance (Aljaouni *et al.*, 2020).

Many Syrian businesswomen and businessmen have fled the country in order to start or expand their companies in more stable foreign nations, rebuild their lives, or benefit from more favorable business environments abroad. Syrian entrepreneurs are forced by the current political climate to establish civil initiatives outside of their country of origin. This is in contrast to entrepreneurs in other arid nations that are characterized by economic and political stability who choose to create nongovernmental organizations (NGOs) and joint initiatives in order to develop their national entrepreneurial ecosystem. As an illustration, consider the Syrian International Business Association, which was founded to help the economic and social integration of Syrian refugees and immigrants and to further the participation of women in particular. The foreign-born individuals conducting such immigrant entrepreneurship are also called Born global entrepreneurs. For an instant, Alexandre *et al.* (2019) found that 71% of Syrian refugees appear to be willing to establish a new business in Lebanon, although some Syrian immigrant entrepreneurs expressed an intention to return to their origin country (Ozmen *et al.*, 2021), Recent evidence has revealed that 72% of Syrian entrepreneurs do not want to return to Syria even if the crisis is over (Kadkoy, 2020). On the other hand, Syrian refugees who receive assistance from family and friends are not always more likely to have ambitions to open their own businesses in Turkey (Almohammad *et al.*, 2021), for example.

5. Toward the Future

Despite all of the above challenges, women in Syria are strongly investing in the changes imposed by the war. Women began to notice their marginalization, exploitation, and the violence against them, especially economic violence. Accordingly, their self-awareness and understanding of their rights and what is going on around them began to expand, and they began to think about this by searching for real opportunities and feeling their human values (Steel, 2021). Therefore, they discovered their skills and determined what they could do and even what they wanted to achieve because they saw the development of their status and the experiences they gained. This is because women always compare their current situations to the past and other women in the family and the surroundings, so they feel the value of their progress and consider it a step in their struggle to obtain their rights and end discrimination against themselves.

Women also seek to preserve these entitlements and gains in the coming periods, as after the end of wars or conflicts, women are often expected to return to practicing their traditional roles, and to bargain over any gains they achieved during conflicts and wars (Althalathini *et al.*, 2021). These observations stem from the fact that the change that occurred in the roles of women came as a result of necessity and not as a result of a comprehensive structural change, which makes compromising it and losing it more likely (Dijkhuizen, 2019). Women in Syria continue their revolution against their reality, even with simple tools. They strive hard to preserve their gains and their new roles and build on them so that what they have achieved is a first but firm step in confronting economic violence toward achieving gender justice in economic participation.

Besides, in order to economically empower Syrian women, grant programs must be accompanied by policies that challenge discriminatory structures such as patriarchal norms at the societal, economic, and domestic levels. Women still take the burden of domestic work with the absence of the concept of participation, because they have not made the required structural change, neither in the community nor in the family. Women cannot achieve their freedom and independence without a major change in the mindset of the activists and the supporters of the entrepreneurship ecosystem. Despite the slight change in men's views of women's work, they are the ones who decide what women do, how, and when, and they are the ones who set the conditions. Therefore, the majority of women feel insecure and do everything possible to defend their achievements. That is why the authors find that the reality of women in Syria is still far from the real goal of empowerment, in terms of supporting their access to and control over economic resources, the ability to manage and make economic decisions to achieve economic independence, and increasing participation in development and work in public affairs (Vorobeva, 2022).

References

Abuhussein, T. (2022). "The Impact of COVID-19 on Refugee Women's Entrepreneurship in Jordan". *Journal of Enterprising Communities: People and Places in the Global Economy* (Ahead-of-print).

Al-Dajani, H. (2022). "Refugee Women's Entrepreneurship: Where from and Where to Next?". *International Journal of Gender and Entrepreneurship* (Ahead-of-print).

Alexandre, L., Salloum, C., & Alalam, A. (2019). "An Investigation of Migrant Entrepreneurs: The Case of Syrian Refugees in Lebanon". *International Journal of Entrepreneurial Behavior & Research*, **25**(5), 1147–1164.

Aljaouni, N. W., Alserhan, B., Gleason, K., & Zeqiri, J. (2020). "Financial Literacy Programs and Youth Entrepreneurial Attitudes: Some Insights from the Jordanian Community". *Journal of Enterprising Communities: People and Places in the Global Economy*, **14**(5), 787–810.

Almohammad, D., Durrah, O., Alkhalaf, T., & Rashid, M. (2021). "Entrepreneurship in Crisis: The Determinants of Syrian Refugees' Entrepreneurial Intentions in Turkey". *Sustainability*, **13**(15), 8602.

Al-Qahtani, M., Fekih Zguir, M., Al-Fagih, L., & Koç, M. (2022). "Women Entrepreneurship for Sustainability: Investigations on Status, Challenges, Drivers, and Potentials in Qatar". *Sustainability*, **14**(7), 4091.

Althalathini, D., Al-Dajani, H., & Apostolopoulos, N. (2021). "The Impact of Islamic Feminism in Empowering Women's Entrepreneurship in Conflict Zones: Evidence from Afghanistan, Iraq and Palestine". *Journal of Business Ethics*, **178**, 39–55.

Aminova, M., Mareef, S., & Machado, C. (2020). "Entrepreneurship Ecosystem in Arab World: The Status Quo, Impediments and The Ways Forward". *International Journal of Business Ethics and Governance*, **3**(3), 1–13.

Bayram, A. S. (2017). "Entrepreneurship In Conflict Zones: Insights on The Startup In Syria". Ahmad Sufian Bayram. Retrieved from: https://ahmadsb.com/books/entre-in-conflict-zone/ENTREPRENEURSHIP-IN-CONFLICT-ZONES.pdf (Accessed on 14 February 2023).

Bojica, A. M., Istanbouli, A., & Fuentes-Fuentes, M. D. M. (2014). "Bricolage and Growth Strategies: Effects on the Performance of Palestinian Women-Led Firms". *Journal of Developmental Entrepreneurship*, **19**(04), 1450023.

Boufeldja, G. (2014). "Social Change and Women Entrepreneurship in Algeria". *Journal of Women's Entrepreneurship and Education*, **1**(2), 119–131.

Bouguerra, N. (2015). "An Investigation of Women Entrepreneurship: Motives and Barriers to Business Start Up in the Arab World". *Journal of Women's Entrepreneurship and Education*, **7**(1–2), 86–104.

Bouzari, P., Salamzadeh, A., Soleimani, M., & Ebrahimi, P. (2021). "Online Social Networks and Women's Entrepreneurship: A Comparative Study between Iran and Hungary". *Journal of Women's Entrepreneurship and Education*, (3–4), 61–75.

Caputo, A., De Vita, L., Mari, M., & Poggesi, S. (2017). "Female Entrepreneurship in Developing Contexts: Characteristics, Challenges, and Dynamics". In *Women Entrepreneurship in the Family Business* (pp. 183–207). London, UK: Routledge.

Coduras, A., de la Vega, I., & Salman, M. B. (2018). "Entrepreneurial Ecosystems in Arabic Countries: A Recent Overview". *Entrepreneurship Ecosystem in the Middle East and North Africa (MENA) Dynamics in Trends, Policy and Business Environment* (pp. 283–302).

Daher, J. (2020). *The Syrian Chambers of Commerce in 2020: The Rise of a New Business Elite*. European University Institute. San Domenico di Fiesole, Italy

Dana, L. P., Salamzadeh, A., Mortazavi, S., & Hadizadeh, M. (2022). Investigating the impact of international markets and new digital technologies on business innovation in emerging markets. *Sustainability*, **14**(2), 983.

Dheer, R. J. & Salamzadeh, A. (2022). "Pandemic Threats: How Smes Can Respond to the Challenges from Global Crises". *International Journal of Globalisation and Small Business*, **13**(1), 1–17.

Dijkhuizen, J. (2019). "Exploring Degrees of the Wellbeing of Women Entrepreneurs In Refugee Settlements in the Middle East: A Personal Account". In *The Wellbeing of Women in Entrepreneurship* (pp. 345–356). London, UK: Routledge.

El Ali, R. & Le Loarne-Lemaire, S. (2022). "The Role of Spousal Support In The Emancipation of Refugee Women Entrepreneurs In Practice: The Case of Syrian Women Entrepreneurship in Lebanon". In *Women, Family and Family Businesses Across Entrepreneurial Contexts* (pp. 77–113). Cheltenham, UK: Edward Elgar Publishing.

ESCWA (2019). Innovation and Entrepreneurship: Opportunities and Challenges for Arab Youth and Women. Economic and Social Commission for Western Asia (ESCWA), United Nations. Retrieved from: https://archive.unescwa.org/sites/www.unescwa.org/files/publications/files/innovation-entrepreneurship-opportunities-challenges-arab-youth-women-english.pdf.

Franzke, S., Wu, J., Froese, F. J., & Chan, Z. X. (2022). "Female Entrepreneurship in Asia: A Critical Review and Future Directions". *Asian Business & Management*, **21**(3), 343–372.

Ghazalian, P. L. (2022). "The Effects of the Arab Spring on Female Labour Force Participation in the MENA Region". *Economics of Transition and Institutional Change*, **30**(4), 869–900.

Jürgens, C., Ramalingam, A., Zarembski, R., Harima, A., & Yeshi, T. (2022). "Relational Dynamics within Refugee Business Incubators: Bridging Refugee Entrepreneurs to the Host-Country Entrepreneurial Ecosystem". In *Disadvantaged Entrepreneurship and the Entrepreneurial Ecosystem* (Vol. 14, pp. 147–169). Bingley, UK: Emerald Publishing Limited.

Kadkoy, O. (2020). "Syrian entrepreneurs in Turkey: Emerging Economic Actors and Agents of Social Cohesion". *Turkey's Political Economy in the 21st Century* (pp. 115–129).

Karlowska, K. H. (2019). *Women's Security and Empowerment in the Context of Forced Displacement: A Case Study of Humanitarian Policies for Syrian Refugee Women in Turkey.* Doctoral dissertation. University of Massachusetts Boston.

Lasic, L. (2018). *Digital Social Entrepreneurship and the Path to Ending Intimate Partner Violence in the Syrian Refugee Population.* Doctoral dissertation. Boston College, College of Arts and Sciences.

Leenders, R. (2012). "Collective Action and Mobilization in Dar'a: An Anatomy of the Onset of Syria's Popular Uprising". *Mobilization: An International Quarterly*, **17**(4), 419–434.

Mouselli, S. & Khalifa, B. (2017). "Entrepreneurship in Crisis: The Determinants of Syrian Students' Entrepreneurial Intentions". *Business, Management and Economics Engineering*, **15**(2), 159–173.

Ng, P. Y., Wood, B. P., & Bastian, B. L. (2022). "Reformulating the Empowerment Process Through Women Entrepreneurship in a Collective Context". *International Journal of Entrepreneurial Behavior & Research*, **28**(9), 154–176.

Ozmen, O., Grosu, R. M., & Dragusin, M. (2021). "Immigrant Entrepreneurship in Romania: Drawing Best Practices from Middle Eastern Immigrant Entrepreneurs' experiences". *Amfiteatru Economic*, **23**(56), 260–275.

Pereira, J., Braga, V., Correia, A., & Salamzadeh, A. (2021). "Unboxing Organisational Complexity: How Does it Affect Business Performance During the COVID-19 Pandemic?" *Journal of Entrepreneurship and Public Policy*, **10**(3), 424–444.

Radović-Marković, M., Lindgren, C. E., Grozdanić, R., Marković, D., & Salamzadeh, A. (2012). "Freedom, Individuality and Women Entrepreneurship Education". *Ecologica: nauka, privreda, iskustva*. Kiten, Bulgaria.

Radović-Marković, M., Salamzadeh, A., & Razavi, M. (2013). "Women in Business and Leadership: Critiques and Discussions". In *The Second International Scientific Conference on Employment, Education and Entrepreneurship, Belgrade, Serbia* (pp. 19–31).

Rahman, M. M., Salamzadeh, A., & Tabash, M. I. (2022). "Antecedents of Entrepreneurial Intentions of Female Undergraduate Students in Bangladesh: A Covariance-Based Structural Equation Modelling Approach. *Journal of Women's Entrepreneurship and Education*, (1–2), 137–153.

Ramadani, V., Rahman, M. M., Salamzadeh, A., Rahaman, M. S., & Abazi-Alili, H. (2022). "Entrepreneurship Education and Graduates' Entrepreneurial Intentions: Does Gender Matter? A Multi-Group Analysis Using AMOS". *Technological Forecasting and Social Change*, **180**, 121693.

Salamzadeh, A., Arasti, Z., & Elyasi, G. M. (2017). "Creation of ICT-Based Social Start-Ups in Iran: A Multiple Case Study". *Journal of Enterprising Culture*, **25**(01), 97–122.

Salamzadeh, A. (2018). *Start-Up Boom in an Emerging Market: A Niche Market Approach* (pp. 233–243). Cham, Switzerland: Springer International Publishing.

Salamzadeh, A. & Dana, L. P. (2021). "The Coronavirus (COVID-19) Pandemic: Challenges Among Iranian Startups". *Journal of Small Business & Entrepreneurship*, **33**(5), 489–512.

Salamzadeh, A. & Dana, L. P. (2022). "A systematic Literature Review of Crisis Management in and by Small and Medium-Sized Enterprises". *Small and Medium Sized Enterprises and the COVID-19 Response* (pp. 38–61).

Salamzadeh, A. & Ramadani, V. (2021). "Entrepreneurial Ecosystem and Female Digital Entrepreneurship–Lessons to Learn from An Iranian Case Study". In *The Emerald Handbook of Women and Entrepreneurship in Developing Economies* (pp. 317–334). Emerald Publishing Limited.

Salamzadeh, A., Radović-Marković, M., & Ghiat, B. (2022). "Women Entrepreneurs in Algeria". In *Women Entrepreneurs in North Africa: Historical Frameworks, Ecosystems and New Perspectives for the Region* Singapore: World Scientific Publishing (pp. 87–102).

Senthanar, S., MacEachen, E., Premji, S., & Bigelow, P. (2021). "Entrepreneurial Experiences of Syrian Refugee Women in Canada: A Feminist Grounded Qualitative Study". *Small Business Economics*, **57**, 835–847.

Slaoui, C. B. (2022). The entrepreneurial ecosystem in MENA countries: A temporal and spatial comparison. *Journal of Social Science and Organization Management*, **3**(2), 253–268.

Steel, G. (2021). "Going Global–Going Digital. Diaspora Networks and Female Online Entrepreneurship in Khartoum, Sudan". *Geoforum*, **120**, 22–29.

Street, C. P., Ng, P. Y., & Al-Dajani, H. (2022). "Refugee women Business Mentors: New Evidence for Women's Empowerment". *Sustainability*, **14**(15), 9154.

Vorobeva, E. (2022). "The Context for Business in Syria". In *Understanding Contexts of Business in Western Asia: Land of Bazaars and High-Tech Booms* Singapore: World Scientific Publishing (pp. 369–382).

Zighan, S. (2021). "Challenges Faced by Necessity Entrepreneurship, the Case of Syrian Refugees in Jordan". *Journal of Enterprising Communities: People and Places in the Global Economy*, **15**(4), 531–547.

https://doi.org/10.1142/9789811283499_0014

Chapter 14

Women Entrepreneurs in the United Arab Emirates

Sayed Abdul Majid Gilani[*,§], **Naveed Yasin**[†,¶], **and Abdullah Alshammaa**[‡,||]

[*]*Assistant Professor of Small Business, Department of Creative Industries and Entrepreneurship; Faculty of Communication, Arts and Sciences; Canadian University Dubai*
[†]*Professor of Entrepreneurship, Head of the Department of Creative Industries and Entrepreneurship; Faculty of Communication, Arts and Sciences; Canadian University Dubai*
[‡]*Department of Management, Canadian University Dubai*
[§]*sayed.gilani@cud.ac.ae*
[¶]*naveed.yasin@cud.ac.ae*
[||]*20170005538@students.cud.ac.ae*

Abstract

This chapter provides an exploration of female entrepreneurs in the United Arab Emirates (UAE) with a particular focus on the UAE's entrepreneurship ecosystem. Based on a comprehensive review of published literature sources in December 2021, the findings highlight numerous opportunities and supporting mechanisms that have been instrumental in successfully accelerating the quantity and quality of startup enterprises across the Emirates. This chapter also highlights the success stories of UAE-based female entrepreneurs. The implications of this chapter are for academics, policymakers, business support agencies, and entrepreneurship practitioners.

Keywords: Female; entrepreneurs; ecosystems; Arab; UAE.

1. Introduction

The role of entrepreneurship is crucial in job creation, economic growth, and innovation. This has attracted the attention of academics and policymakers, particularly in understanding how entrepreneurship can empower and increase social inclusivity and mobility among underrepresented communities such as women, ethnic minorities, and people with determination. Although there is no universal definition of an entrepreneur, it is widely accepted that entrepreneurs create new forms of organization (Jones *et al.*, 2018; Gartner, 1988). Entrepreneurship and small businesses are the backbones of most advanced economies and therefore promoting entrepreneurship through a robust entrepreneurial ecosystem can foster an entrepreneurial culture that results in the development of new products and services.

Jones *et al.* (2018) identified that entrepreneurship leads to entrepreneurs enjoying benefits like a flexible working life, a sense of personal achievement, better self-esteem, the opportunity to learn new skills, create wealth for themselves and other businesses, improve living standards, create jobs, improve local and national economies, and create a positive social impact. It can be argued that benefits like flexible working life as a result of entrepreneurship can act as an opportunity for women to manage the duality of family life and work life through entrepreneurship. Therefore, understanding the role of gender in entrepreneurial activities among women may have underlying benefits for the wider population.

As a result of the scholarly attention and focus on the intersection of gender and entrepreneurship, there has been an increase in the development of dedicated and contextualized models in the entrepreneurship literature that explains the entrepreneurial process, challenges, and opportunities for female entrepreneurs. Albeit, these models are largely "Western-centric" and have been developed in a Western paradigm that is informed by its institutional, historical, and social contextualization, respectively. As a result, there is relatively little known about the entrepreneurial ecosystem of the UAE that actively promotes entrepreneurial endeavors among female entrepreneurs in a dynamic and fast-growing knowledge-based economy.

2. Benefits of Female Entrepreneurship

In a study McGowan *et al.* (2011) highlighted that female entrepreneurship can lead to benefits for the wider population, which may include improved networking opportunities with other companies, therefore, leading to more opportunities for different stakeholders (e.g., job creation, increased income, increased awareness, and better promotion of services between companies). McGowan *et al.* (2011) also identified that female entrepreneurs may have better intuition in comparison to their male counterparts while making crucial decisions (e.g., male entrepreneurs may be hastier in decision-making than their female equivalents). Furthermore, it is believed by McGowan *et al.* (2011) that female entrepreneurs can play an important role toward improving overall economic growth as well as stability and opportunity for job creation within a region. Further emphasizing the benefits of female entrepreneurship, Griffin and Alajaji (2017) stated that female entrepreneurs may have the ability to inspire other females to take a risk by starting a business. This would, therefore, lead to an increase in job creation for women, which will eventually lead to a reduction in the gender gap across a nation's workforce.

It should be noted that governments around the world have developed proactive policies and strategic initiatives to support women's employability, which also includes female entrepreneurship (McGowan *et al.*, 2011; Omeihe *et al.*, 2019). Governments have proposed funding and policies to support women during pregnancy and during their transition into employment in addition to training or academic courses that equip women across a range of sectors, including entrepreneurship and self-employment (McGowan *et al.*, 2011; Omeihe *et al.*, 2019). For example, the Women in Innovation Awards, "Back Her Business", Global Fund for Women, and Cartier Women's Initiative are some examples of private or government-funded initiatives within the UK to support female entrepreneurship (Omeihe *et al.*, 2019).

Omeihe *et al.* (2019) support the works of McGowan *et al.* (2011) by identifying the skill of multitasking to be a common strength highlighted among female entrepreneurs, which is even more so prominent in comparison to male entrepreneurs. Omeihe *et al.* (2019) also highlighted that women entrepreneurs appear to be better communicators and listeners in comparison to men. Therefore, the natural strengths of communication, networking, intuition, and multitasking highlight some clear benefits of female entrepreneurship, which may have positive implications for the wider population.

The next section of this chapter presents a historical overview of the UAE.

3. Historical Overview

The UAE is situated in the Arabian Peninsula, bordering the Kingdom of Saudi Arabia and the Sultanate of Oman. The UAE comprises seven emirates, which include Abu Dhabi, Dubai, Sharjah, Ajman, Umm Al Quwain, Ras Al Khaimah, and Fujairah. According to the World Bank (2020), the UAE has a population of approximately 9.89 million with a reported population growth rate of 1.2%. The official language of the UAE is Arabic, and most of the population subscribes to the Islamic faith. However, the Emirate of Dubai is best described as a *melting pot* owing to its super-diverse ethnic diversity that is reflected across all its sectors. Although recognized as an oil-rich nation, the Emirate of Dubai has actively diversified its economy toward luxury tourism and international commerce, and continues to reduce its reliance on its natural oil resources as it strives to become a tourism, financial, and knowledge-based epicenter.

In 2019, the World Economic Forum praised Dubai's remarkable transformation, describing its rapid progression from being a "fishing village to [a] futuristic metropolis". This captured the attention of academics, international policymakers, and private sector foreign investors, attracting global talents of employees and transnational entrepreneurs. Over the last few decades, the UAE government exhibited remarkable support for advancing entrepreneurial culture through knowledge-transferring and knowledge-sharing training programs, financial and legal assistance, and access to required social capital. The impressive economic revolution since 1971 transformed this desert to having the largest share in hosting startups in the Middle East and North Africa (MENA) region — accommodating 35% of all startups in MENA countries.

The UAE's indigenous population of citizens comprise 11.5%, whereas the remaining residents comprise expatriate workers from South Asian countries (59.4%), Egyptians (10.2%), Filipinos (6.1%), and others (12.8%). There is a larger male population in the UAE (approximately 6.3 million), whereas females comprise only a total population of 3.1 million (Statista, 2022). According to the UAE's official statistics (The World Bank, 2020), there were 151,875 Small and Medium-sized Enterprises (SMEs) registered. Boosted by several supportive policies for the development of the SME landscape such as the Mohammed Bin Rashid Establishment for SME Development and the Khalifa Fund, the Ministry of Economy (UAE, 2021) highlights the significance of the SME sector of Dubai as it reported that it contributes 95% of all companies and employs 42% of the workforce while also contributing 40% of Dubai's gross domestic product (GDP).

Women employees account for approximately 70% of the university graduates in the UAE and over 44% of the total UAE workforce (Sharjah Media City, 2022; UAE Gender Balance Council, 2020). These findings highlight the importance of female entrepreneurship for the growth of the UAE economy (Sharjah Media City, 2022). Griffin and Alajaji (2017) identify that there has never been a better entrepreneurial climate for women in the UAE attributing to an increase in women entrepreneurship-related support groups along with increased funding for new businesses offered in the UAE.

There has been substantial growth in female entrepreneurial activity in the UAE with a rising number of SME owners that has increased by a factor of 14 during the period of 2006–2013 (Women at Work, UAE). A report presented by Deloitte and the Business and Industry Advisory Committee to the Organization for Economic Cooperation and Development (OECD) demonstrates that for female entrepreneurs to make a greater impact across economies in different regions, further attention is needed on policies including but not restricted to education, and non-discrimination, in areas such as access to property rights and finance. The survival and growth of female entrepreneurs are crucial to the growth of economies around the world as such individuals attribute to widespread benefits such as job creation and positive economic output.

4. Entrepreneurship Ecosystem

Griffin and Alajaji (2017) highlight that the business environment in the UAE is committed to driving equality in the business world. The UAE acknowledges that a greater level of gender equality than other nations within the MENA region is a key priority (Embassy of the United Arab Emirates, 2021; Hamade, 2016). It should be noted that the UAE government has proactively implemented policies and initiatives to promote gender equality within the workforce in the region (Hamade, 2016; Sharjah Media City, 2022). For example, the UAE government pledged $50 million toward the Women Entrepreneurs Finance Initiative fund in 2017, which led to a 64% decrease in the overall UAE workforce gender gap in terms of employment numbers (Hamade, 2016; UAE Gender Balance Council, 2020). Additionally, gender equality is one of the UAE government's most prominent outlined sustainable development goals (SDGs) in order for it to achieve its long-term goal of becoming one of the top 25 nations in the world recognized for gender equality (Sharjah Media City, 2022; UAE Gender Balance Council, 2020).

Assi and Marcati (2020) highlight that many opportunities are currently available to women entrepreneurs in the UAE, regardless of ethnic origin or original place of birth. Several initiatives have been authorized and executed by the UAE government to aid women entrepreneurs in becoming successful. One of the widely known initiatives is the Dubai Businesswomen Council (DBWC), which is a nonprofit organization that offers education, funding as well as training opportunities to aid and support the entrepreneurial aspirations of businesswomen based in the UAE (Embassy of the UAE, 2021; UAE Gender Balance Council, 2020).

The integrated and innovative business incubator for UAE-based women offered by the Abu Dhabi Businesswomen Council (ADBWC) supports new business ideas. This is another example of an initiative implemented by the UAE government to support the growth of women entrepreneurs in the region (Embassy of the UAE, 2021; UAE Gender Balance Council, 2020). Additionally, this incubator aids women in identifying their latent creative potential, which may lead to translating ideas into productive projects (Sharjah Media City, 2022; UAE Gender Balance Council, 2020). It should be noted that this initiative also offers technical support, advice, and guidance, as well as funding opportunities for aspiring women entrepreneurs (Hamade, 2016; UAE Gender Balance Council, 2020).

The Dubai Women Establishment (DWE) is a long-term initiative that hosts an annual Women Leadership Exchange Program to provide guidance and support on sustainable leadership practices as well as offer networking opportunities for aspiring women entrepreneurs in the UAE, regardless of ethnic or social background (Sharjah Media City, 2022; UAE Gender Balance Council, 2020). Another option to support the growth and development of women entrepreneurs in the UAE is partnerships between private and government institutions based in the UAE that offer the opportunity for in-depth training as well as increased capital to women entrepreneurs (Embassy of the United Arab Emirates, 2021; Hamade, 2016).

The Women Entrepreneurship Summit of MENA is a platform strategically aimed at supporting women entrepreneurs from regions within the Middle East and North Africa (Griffin and Alajaji, 2017; Sharjah Media City, 2022). Furthermore, another avenue that has supported the growth of female entrepreneurs in the UAE is the media company of 'Womena', which produces content focused on female founders and functions as a networking platform for women entrepreneurs (Assi and Marcati, 2020; UAE Gender Balance Council, 2020). Additionally, the Cherie Blair Foundation for Women, in partnership with the JPMorgan Chase Foundation, offers business training to aspiring UAE-based women entrepreneurs (Embassy of the UAE, 2021; Griffin and Alajaji, 2017). Facebook, with support from the Emirates Foundation and Sheera Sharjah, has launched the 'She Means Business' (SMBs) initiative that was designed to train and facilitate UAE-based women entrepreneurs in establishing their businesses online (Assi and Marcati, 2020; Embassy of the United Arab Emirates, 2021).

Additionally, the Khalifa Fund is handled by the UAE government — it aims to support UAE-based women entrepreneurs by securing funds along with providing legal support and other procedural assistance where women have the option of applying for funds for different programs catering to different financing needs (Assi and Marcati, 2020; Sharjah Media City, 2022). The Khalifa Fund was established in 2007 by the UAE government's socioeconomic development agency division as a nonprofit institution with the sole purpose of supporting the survival and growth of SMEs in the UAE (Devex, 2022; UAE Ministry of Economy, 2022). This initiative aims to instil as well as enrich a culture of investment among UAE national-owned businesses, as well as support and develop small to medium-sized investments in the Emirates (Devex, 2022; UAE Ministry of Economy, 2022). The Khalifa Fund was initiated with a capital of 300 million AED (Arab Emirati Dirham) solely focusing on Abu Dhabi; however, this was eventually increased to 2 billion AED (Devex, 2022; UAE Ministry of Economy, 2022). In 2007, the Khalifa Fund initiative started with branches in Abu Dhabi, Al Ain, and the Western Region of the UAE, however, the Khalifa Fund was expanded out to the Northern Emirates from 2011 onwards (Devex, 2022; UAE Ministry of Economy, 2022). This led to more branches in areas like Ajman, Ras Al Khaimah, and Fujairah (Devex, 2022; UAE Ministry of Economy, 2022).

Hamade (2016) identifies that free zones are developed by the UAE government as a convenient location for entrepreneurs to start their businesses, as such locations offer business owners a more streamlined setup process. This is due to such locations giving business owners the ability to set up customizable as well as flexible offices/workstations, and these locations may act as one-stop resource hubs for government services. Free zones are free-to-trade zones within the Emirate of Dubai where organizations operate for tax exemptions from Value Added Tax (VAT), Income Tax, Corporate Tax, and Customs, etc. (Bayut, 2021; Hamade, 2016). Additionally, the business owners within free zone areas in Dubai have 100% ownership of their businesseses (Bayut, 2021; Hamade, 2016).

Businesses within the UAE are developing technology-based solutions to make the return-to-work process seamless for women returning to work after childbirth (Assi and Marcati, 2020; Sharjah Media City, 2022). For example, the recruitment company Hopscotch (Dubai based) offers an online platform through which female employees can undergo training and skills sessions (Sharjah Media City, 2022). Additionally, Hopscotch provides opportunities to women at all stages of their respective careers through its networks and initiatives (Embassy of the UAE, 2021; Sharjah Media City, 2022). Hence, creating an inclusive work environment that accommodates the whole population, regardless of individual commitments, has supported the growth of the UAE economy and encouraged the emergence of more women business owners (Assi and Marcati, 2020; Sharjah Media City, 2022). Therefore, a greater number of women across different industries are targeting the UAE to set up businesses due to eased access to financing options, business networks, and coaching opportunities (Griffin and Alajaji, 2017; Sharjah Media City, 2022). Additionally, the Sharjah Media City (Shams) free zone offers a wide range of options and extensive support for Emirati citizens as well as expatriate women entrepreneurs, which is why Sharjah Media City (Shams) has gained significant popularity in comparison to other free zones for business creation (Sharjah Media City, 2022).

5. Female Entrepreneurs: Success Stories

This section focuses on featuring some of the key successes of female entrepreneurs in the UAE as detailed in Table 1.

Her Excellency (HE) Laila Rahhal El Atfani is the founder and President of Business Gate in addition to being the Global President for CECUK (HAFA Exhibitions, 2022). Business Gate is one of the most respected and high-profile organizations that focuses and specializes in the areas of business studies, financial analysis, evaluation of new/existing projects, and measuring the feasibility of business projects within the

Table 1. Description of female entrepreneurs in the UAE.

Name of Female Entrepreneur	Name of Enterprise
Her Excellency (HE) Laila Rahhal El Atfani	Business Gate
Nayla Al Khaja	Nayla Al Khaja Films
Hudda Kattan	Huda Beauty
Alanoud Badr	Fozaza
Sara Jappanwalla	Fashion Illustrator
Tarsila Schubert	Blue Cave Art
Jumana Abu-Hannoud	SOS Children's Villages International
Shabana Karim	The Nail Spa & Marquee Salon
Nabaa Kamal	Nabi Café

Middle East (HAFA Exhibitions, 2022). Additionally, HE Laila Rahhal has been awarded the title of Goodwill Ambassador of "FAAVM" Women Empowerment and the President of International Affairs Anouar, and she also holds the designation of Vice President of *Voice Magazine* besides being engaged with various nonprofit institutions around the world (HAFA Exhibitions, 2022).

Nayla Al Khaja is a widely known and celebrated female entrepreneur in the UAE. She is one of the first female movie directors who paved the way for other Arab female artists in the entertainment industry (Nayla Al Khaja Films, 2021). Khaja's biggest achievements are being known as one of the top 50 most powerful personalities in Arab Cinema by *Variety*, being recognized as one of the top 100 most powerful Arabs under 40 by the Arabian Business media, and receiving the Visionary of the Year Award at the Arabian Business Awards (Nayla Al Khaja Films, 2021). In 2017, Nayla was recognized as the Entrepreneur of the Year at the Gulf Business Awards. In 2019, she was awarded the Black Swan Award for Women Empowerment by AsiaOne and was listed among the top four Emirati women by *Forbes* (Nayla Al Khaja Films, 2021). Recently, she was recognized as the Businesswoman of the Year by the Gulf Business Awards in 2020 (Nayla Al Khaja Films, 2021).

Huda Kattan is identified as the owner of Huda Beauty, which was established in 2013. Huda's business was estimated to be worth around $1.2 billion in 2017 (*Forbes*, 2022). Huda is known to be one of the first major online influencers on social media platforms and she has used this status to promote all her products (Forbes, 2022). She has widely admitted to having never spent any money on advertising due to the nature of her online social media profile with over 50 million followers (Forbes, 2022). Huda is currently a resident of Dubai UAE (*Forbes*, 2022).

Alanoud Badr also known as Fozaza is a Saudi-Lebanese-origin influencer resident in Dubai, UAE (Emirates Woman, 2022). She is the founder and fashion designer behind the brand "Lady Fozaza" (Emirates Woman, 2022). Alanoud has established herself as one of the most sought-after designers and online social media influencers in the Middle East region (Emirates Woman, 2022). Her popularity has especially increased during the COVID-19 pandemic era when consumers have become more inclined toward online shopping (Emirates Woman, 2022).

Sara Japanwalla is a renowned fashion illustrator based in Dubai where she has only been in the industry since 2012 (Emirates Woman, 2022). She has worked with major brands like Bloomingdale's, Ralph Lauren, Harvey Nichols, and Maserati (Emirates Woman, 2022). She has acknowledged working at Maserati as her career highlight as she was selected as one of the top 100 creative minds from around the world to contribute to a limited coffee table book edition (Emirates Woman, 2022). Sara aims to develop her name as a brand and a business that will be synonymous with prominent artistic works around the world (Emirates Woman, 2022).

Tarsila Schubert is originally a street artist who is now the owner of Blue Cave Art Factory in Downtown Dubai (Emirates Woman, 2022). She began her career as an artist in the late 2000s and since her entry into the industry she has worked with major brands like Hermès, Pepsi, and Sephora (Emirates Woman, 2022). Tarsila is widely known as the first woman to paint a mural in Jordan to honour the International Association Football Federation (FIFA) Women's World Cup (Emirates Woman, 2022).

Jumana Abu-Hannoud is the Managing Director of SOS Children's Villages International where her aim is to expand her network of partners toward a sustainable future through the development of strategies while mobilizing resources as well as spreading awareness of children's rights and healthcare issues (Emirates Woman, 2022). Jumana has worked under Her Royal Highness (HRH) Princess Haya for over five years, where she aided in implementing national, regional, and international strategies focusing on improving education, peace, and health in the Middle East region (Emirates Woman, 2022). Additionally, while serving HRH Princess Haya, she served as a Public Relations Officer for the United Nations High Commissioner for Refugees (Emirates Woman, 2022).

Shabana Karim is the Chief Executive Officer (CEO) and founder of The Nail Spa & Marquee Salon based in Dubai UAE (Emirates Woman, 2022). Shabana established her business in 2002, however, the creation of the business was preceded by intense market research by her into the industry (Emirates Woman, 2022). This market research involved Shabana traveling around the world quite extensively to study and learn about the beauty industry to better inform her in how to run her business on an

Figure 1. Nabaa Kamal, CEO and Founder of Nabi Café.

optimal level (Emirates Woman, 2022). Currently, her business has over 16 branches around the UAE (Emirates Woman, 2022).

Nabaa Kamal is a successful UAE-based female entrepreneur and founder of Nabi Café that is established in the Business Bay district of Dubai (see Figure 1). Miss Kamal was born and raised in the UAE, but belongs to Iraqi ethnic origins. She previously worked in the construction and property management business before establishing a vibrant café at a highly sought location in downtown Dubai. Nabi café remains popular among the youth of Dubai, but it also successfully attracts tourists, locals, young couples, and business professionals.

6. Toward the Future

Based on the review of the published literature, it is evident that female entrepreneurship is thriving in the UAE based on a highly conducive and supportive entrepreneurship ecosystem that has largely been encouraged by the government of the UAE. This has led to the UAE establishing new forms of businesses with notable outcomes that are benefiting both local and expatriate communities. The support mechanisms available to female entrepreneurs demonstrate the proactiveness of the UAE government in developing a diverse, inclusive, and engaged society that is underpinned by a strong culture and ethos for entrepreneurship. Working toward the future, the worldclass entrepreneurship ecosystem provided by the UAE will certainly continue to attract female entrepreneurs from the local talent pool as well as foreign expatriates to capitalize on opportunities both locally and regionally. This chapter emphasized the importance of female entrepreneurship and its multiple benefits for economic and social growth of the economy, while also highlighting key notable female entrepreneurial figures that may act as role models for aspiring and budding entrepreneurs.

References

Assi, R. & Marcati, C. (2020). *Women at Work*. Retrieved from: https://www.mckinsey.com/~/media/mckinsey/featured%20insights/middle%20east%20and%20africa/women%20at%20work%20in%20the%20middle%20east/women-at-work-in-the-middle-east.pdf (Accessed on 3rd January 2022.

Bayut (2021). *A Complete Guide to Free Zones in Dubai*. Retrieved from: https://www.bayut.com/mybayut/guide-free-zones-dubai/ (Accessed on 5 January 2022).

Devex (2022). *Khalifa Fund for Enterprise Development (Khalifa Fund)*. Retrieved from: https://www.devex.com/organizations/khalifa-fund-for-enterprise-development-khalifa-fund-120775 (Accessed on 5 January 2022).

Embassy of the United Arab Emirates (2021). *Women in the UAE*. Retrieved from: https://www.uae-embassy.org/about-uae/women-uae (Accessed on 3 January 2022).

Emirates Woman (2022). *Alanoud Badr: Founder and Designer of Lady Fozaza*. Retrieved from: https://emirateswoman.com/awards-2017/achievers/alanoud-badr/ (Accessed on 4 January 2022).

Forbes (2022). *#65 Huda Kattan*. Retrieved from: https://www.forbes.com/profile/huda-kattan/?sh=738c2b8b3cec (Accessed on 4 January 2022).

Gartner, W. (1988). "Who is an Entrepreneur? Is the Wrong Question?". *American Journal of Small Business*, **12**(4), 11–32.

Griffin, C. & Alajaji, N. (2017). *Powering the UAE digital economy Developing the UAE's computer science talent*. Retrieved from: https://impact.economist.com/perspectives/sites/default/files/powering_the_uae_digital_economy_-_google.pdf (Accessed on 3 January 2022).

HAFA Exhibitions (2022). *Her Excellency (HE) Laila Rahhal El Atfani*. Retrieved from: https://ime-europe.eu/speakers/h-e-laila-rahhal-el-atfani/ (Accessed on 5 January 2022).

Hamade, M. (2016). *Women and Emiratisation in the UAE Workforce*. Retrieved from: https://www.repository.cam.ac.uk/bitstream/handle/1810/288678/thesis%20(36)_copyright.pdf?sequence=1 (Accessed on 3 January 2022).

Jones, C., Penaluna, K., Penaluna, A., & Matlay, H. (2018). *The Changing Nature of the Enterprise: Addressing the Challenge of Vesper and Gartner*. Retrieved from: https://journals.sagepub.com/doi/full/10.1177/0950422218804075 (Accessed on 4 January 2022).

McGowan, P., Redeker, C., Cooper, S., & Greenan, K. (2012). "Female Entrepreneurship and the Management of a Business and Domestic Roles: Motivations, Expectations, and Realities". *Entrepreneurship & Regional Development*, **24**(1–2), 53–72.

Nayla Al Khaja Films (2021). *Nayla Al Khaja is the First Female Film Director in the United Arab Emirates*". Retrieved from: https://www.naylaalkhaja.com/about-nayla (Accessed on 4 January 2022).

Omeihe, K., Dakhan, S., Khan, M., Gustafsson, V., Amoako, I. (2019). *Riding the Wave: Understanding the Context of Female Entrepreneurship in Pakistan*. Retrieved from: https://www.igi-global.com/chapter/riding-the-wave/220022 (Accessed on 4 January 2022).

Sharjah Media City (Shams) (2021). *Why Should Women Entrepreneurs Consider the UAE To Start a Business?* Retrieved from: https://www.shams.ae/community/blog/81/why-should-women-entrepreneurs-consider-the-uae-to-start-a-business (Accessed on 1 January 2022).

Statista (2022). *United Arab Emirates*. Retrieved from: https://www.statista.com/markets/422/topic/1037/united-arab-emirates/ (Accessed on 5 January 2022).

The World Bank (2020). *United Arab Emirates*. Retrieved from: https://data.worldbank.org/country/AE (Accessed on 5 January 2022).

UAE Gender Balance Council (2020). *UAE Women FAQs*. Retrieved from: https://www.gbc.gov.ae/facts.html (Accessed on 2 January 2022).

United Arab Emirates Ministry of Economy (2022). *Creating Opportunities to Boost the UAE's Entrepreneurial Ecosystem*. Retrieved from: https://www.moec.gov.ae/en/khalifa-fund-for-enterprise-development (Accessed on 5 January 2022).

https://doi.org/10.1142/9789811283499_0015

Chapter 15

Toward the Future

Dina Modestus Nziku

School of Business and Creative Industries,
University of the West of Scotland, Glasgow, Scotland
Dina.Nziku@uws.ac.uk

Abstract

This chapter provides condensed details on the expected future of women entrepreneurs and their entrepreneurial ventures from all 11 countries of the Middle East discussed in this book. The assessments of the future of women entrepreneurs are all based on the discussions provided by authors who made contributions to this with reach and potential insights about the topic from some of the countries of discussion within the region. The authors have raised some thought-provoking points with some encouragement for some patriarchal societies in the region having a positive outlook on women's entrepreneurial activities.

Keywords: Women entrepreneurs; entrepreneurship policy; future perspectives; potential insights; the Middle East.

1. Introduction

The Middle East has long been a crossroads of trade and hence an important centre for entrepreneurship. Across Western Asia, cultural, linguistic, and religious factors are still profoundly dominant, affecting business context. A reminder of Islam's early days is the privileged social status accorded to self-employed merchants and artisans. Prophet Muhammad was personally impressed by the camel caravan voyages of traders, and on several occasions he traveled with them in his youth. He spent over a decade in caravan trading, covering a wide territory from the Mediterranean to the Indian Ocean. His first wife, Khadija, was a successful merchant whom he worked for and later worked with (Dana, 2022). This book is for and about the women entrepreneurs of this region. Using a gender lens, this research-based book has provided a mixture of both theoretical and empirical analysis from the Middle East while adding to the knowledge of a wide range of both entrepreneurial opportunities and challenges faced by women entrepreneurs along with the roles of institutions and entrepreneurship policies.

2. Structure of the Book

This edition of *Women's Entrepreneurship in the Middle East* consists of 15 chapters.

Chapter 1 is an introduction to the Middle East, this chapter introduces the reader to the structure and flow of this book. This chapter has been written by editors to guide readers on the contents and flow of the book as well as its development and authorship of each chapter.

Chapter 2 an entrepreneurial ecosystem in the middle east has been authored by Balslev Clausen and Dana depicts the entire *entrepreneurial ecosystem of the middle east.* The chapter presents a discussion on how various governments in the Middle East seek to strengthen the relationship with academia and industries in order to create a triple helix that will provide frameworks for an entrepreneurial ecosystem apart from a lack of clear understanding of other sectors that might still hinder such collaboration. Yet, the authors acknowledge the emergent economic nature of various countries within the region as well as other countries that remains in a struggle of poverty, social exclusion as well as gender inequality.

Chapter 3 of the book contains a general discussion of *women entrepreneurs in the Middle East.* Here Nziku, Mugione and Salamzadeh have presented the overall introduction of the book in the context of the middle east. Authors in this chapter have stressed the importance of developing strategies for achieving women's economic empowerment as a critical aspect of achieving sustainable development goals and fostering high-quality entrepreneurial activities in the region. Nevertheless, an overview of women entrepreneurship in the Middle East and Africa (MEA), (FinTech Times, 2021) implies that the region is home to the World's highest and lowest rates of female entrepreneurship.

Apart from the World Economic Forum (WEF, 2021) reporting that the Middle East and North Africa region need almost 143 years to close the gender gap at the most current rate. Yet, the authors in this chapter have noted that the number of women entrepreneurs in the Middle East has steadily risen in some economies like Israel, the United Arab Emirates (UAE) and Jordan. Women entrepreneurs are currently having engagement in establishing foundations in arts, education, and health, sectors to create role models for these entrepreneurial activities hence contributing towards closing the gender gap (Gadi, 2022; and Nziku, 2016; 2014).

Chapter 4 is about women entrepreneurs in *Bahrain* where Salamzadeh and Dana have discussed the diverse nature of the people of this nation caused by the different walks of life and religions. Historically authors depict that women in this country have been dealing with business activities earlier even before being forced to convert to Islam, yet the nation has a sheer amount of evidence that confirms the Islamic and male-dominant culture like most of the Arab countries in the region causing threat on the potential of women entrepreneurship. Despite the country being multireligious, cultural deference remains to be an ongoing barrier in some developmental activities. This led to significant changes in the business environment in the past two decades with some social ties improving the ease of doing business. The situation seems to have been highly contributed by entrepreneurial ecosystem players who promote entrepreneurial lifestyles amongst Bahraini women entrepreneurs.

Chapter 5 cover women entrepreneurs in *Egypt* with a very interesting history from the Ptolemaic and Roman period of the country with the involvement and significant role played by women in entrepreneurial activities and contribution to the general economy of the country.

Vorobeva in this chapter has discussed the considerable progress made by the government towards gender equality and empowerment of women in the country. apart from the International Labour Organisation (ILO, 2016) describing the number of women entrepreneurs in Egypt as being the lowest in the MENA region and sub-Saharan Africa.

Hassan and Zaharia (2021) argue on the roles of Egyptian women in society being reduced to simply those of mothers and housewives with the professional capabilities being so often called into question. Following, the Doing Business 2020, report of the World Bank ranked Egypt 114 out of 190 world economies on the ease of starting and running an enterprise in the country (World Bank, 2020). The analysis presented in this chapter shows that Egypt has improved its position in the ranking during the last few years. In 2016, Egypt Vision 2030 was just introduced by His Excellency President el-Sisi, and the country occupied 131 places among the other 190 states globally (World Bank, 2016).

Chapter 6 of this book is on women entrepreneurs in *Iran*. In this chapter, Salamzadeh and Dana have presented the reality of women entrepreneurs in the country following the women's employment index of war-torn countries like Syria, Iraq, Afghanistan, Yemen, and Palestine. The index shows a slow increase in women's employment back in the 1970s which then broke mid-1980 with unsuccessful efforts of restoring. Apart from the scarcity of national research on women's entrepreneurship in the country; women's employment in Iran has always faced problems, with women's entrepreneurship continuing to face increasing problems (Bahramitash and Esfahani, 2014).

Sarfaraz and Faghih (2011) indicate that there has not been any improvement in the Iranian women's employment ratio for almost 20 years besides the ratio of employment amongst men becoming 5 times that of women with the number of female students being higher than that of male students within the country. Against the odds, the analysis indicates that besides the annual growth rates of the ratio of employment to the female population in the last 30 years show that Iran is in an optimistic situation and if it maintains a continuous growth trend and uses the existing capacities, it can add an average of 1% to its female employment ratio annually (Sarfaraz, 2017). According to (WEF, 2021) Iran needs almost 28 years to cover this distance from 12% to 40%.

Chapter 7 women entrepreneurs in *Israel*, Okirav, Dana, Degen, Galperin, and Medzini have indicated how education, science and industry have made important elements of Israel's culture before the birth of Israel nation with explosive growth in the past two decades. According to Yin (2017), foreign investors seem to be attracted to Israel and motivated by their workforce and industrial parks that are highly concentrated on technology. This chapter indicates how Israel's law provides strong protections for trade patents, copyrights, and trademarks.

The chapter insists on the subsequent change in the role of women within Israel and other neighboring countries. This is not only because of the Kibbutz movements but also the equal participation of both men and women on a rotational basis in various jobs. Telles (2020) indicates how the Israelites' law contemplates numerous scenarios for distressed companies together with voluntary liquidations and court-supervised voluntary liquidations and reorganizations of business ventures.

Chapter 8 women entrepreneurs in *Jordan*, Al-Dajani starts by presenting the state of women's entrepreneurship research in the Kingdom of Jordan, challenges, and opportunities. While citing Metcalfe *et al.* (2022) the state of policy and practices that supports and advance women's entrepreneurship in the Arab world over the last 5 years is on the sharp rise with no exception to Jordan. According to the Global Entrepreneurship Monitor (GEM), the ratio of women's to men's total entrepreneurial activity increased from 0.26 in 2016 to 0.59 in 2019, an improvement of around 127% in 3 years (GEM, 2020). Such an achievement is aided by the Kingdom's young and evolving entrepreneurship ecosystem (El Kharouf *et al.*, 2022), and the legal gender equality regulations and policies for women's and men's engagement in entrepreneurship (World Bank Group, 2022). Nevertheless, the rate of women's labor force participation remains amongst the lowest in the world at 14% (Robbin, 2022), and lower than neighboring Lebanon (23%), Saudi Arabia (22%), and Palestine (18%) (ILO, 2022).

The analysis of women entrepreneurs in Jordan within this chapter indicates that; Jordan is not immune to the economic and social repercussions of the measures put in place locally, regionally, and internationally, to combat the COVID-19 pandemic, nor to the regional political and economic affairs. Following the World Bank Group, (2022) the Kingdom's economic rebound during the first nine months of 2021 was steady but was below expectation at 2.1% growth. Chapter analysis on the future of the kingdom indicates that organizational performance within Jordan's entrepreneurial ecosystem might be affected since projections show that economic growth might remain modest for the foreseeable future, coupled with stubbornly high rates of unemployment, and low rates of labor force participation, especially amongst women. Given the growth and developments in women's entrepreneurship in Egypt, Saudi Arabia, and the United Arab Emirates (UAE), Jordan cannot afford to stagnate as it will fall behind in the region. This is important for Jordan's economy as the trend of employment in the GCC is diminishing given that those nations are now prioritizing their own citizens who have become equally qualified.

Chapter 9 of this edition, authored by Shamieh and Gerges on women entrepreneurs in Lebanon, provides practical recommendations for supporting and enhancing the role of women in Lebanon's entrepreneurial ecosystem. It emphasizes the need for targeted policies, greater access to funding, and societal support systems to overcome cultural and economic barriers. The chapter also underlines the importance of fostering an inclusive environment that recognizes and leverages the unique strengths and contributions of women entrepreneurs in driving economic growth and innovation in Lebanon.

Chapter 10 women entrepreneurs in *Oman*, presents women as the fastest-growing segment in the realm of entrepreneurship. Authors of this chapter, Razzak and Jassem, reveal the state of women's entrepreneurship growth in Oman following the case study conducted in the country by Mustafa *et al.* (2021) with an indication revealed that women business owners had tremendous resilience on general adversities which comes to be of great potential in the entrepreneurial process. Although, the overall percentage of women who embark on the entrepreneurial journey is significantly lower than that of men (PwC, 2017), and this difference is greater depending on the cultural context (GEM Report, 2019–2021).

Nonetheless, culture plays a significant role in determining the likelihood of women embarking on the entrepreneurial journey. Authors in this chapter have used examples of East Asians in discussing the significance and high involvement of women in entrepreneurship when compared to the Middle East and North Africa (MENA). The situation seems very distinct in the most conservative societies that dominate the Gulf Cooperation Council (GCC), which includes Bahrain, Oman, Saudi Arabia, Kuwait, Qatar, and the United Arab Emirates (UAE).

Furthermore, the authors in this chapter provide a general analysis of Oman Vision 2040, which seems to underly the overall theme of Omanization as the program for not only replacing foreign workers with Omani citizens but also emphasizes the growth of business ownership to women who are the most under-represented in the society. Therefore, Tanfeedh has been created in Oman for the purpose and the priority of developing the general entrepreneurship agenda (Al Sinani *et al.*, 2021). This has been together with an improvement in women's participation in business and other economic activities in their society. Andriamahery and Qumruzzaman, (2022) present a significant change in most of the Formal Financial Institutions (FFI) which formally had a poor record of gender diversity in their loan portfolio but now they seem to have gained confidence and are comfortable with providing finance to some women entrepreneurs.

Following the analysis of the past and current state of women entrepreneurs in Omani, their future seems to show some hope, though it might take a little longer for the gender gap within the region to close. Omani women are now receiving significant support from their families with encouragement for young Omani women deciding to pursue the entrepreneurial path is likely to be much easier considering the low barrier to entry into the business through Internet platforms. In fact, the authors of this chapter reveal that many women can start their businesses in parallel with their household responsibilities and their regular jobs. Family restrictions for younger Omani women to start their own businesses could be considerably less of a factor in the age of digitalization.

Chapter 11 women Entrepreneurs in *Palestine*, Althalathini has presented with clarity on the reality of women entrepreneurs in the country by analysing the historical background of women entrepreneurs, their framework, and ecosystem and with analysis of the government policies and strategies for supporting women's entrepreneurial activities, recommendations toward the future have been presented. This is a country with great potential despite the significant progress made by Palestinian women entrepreneurs over the past decade author of this chapter insists on the importance of contextualized research on women's entrepreneurship policy. This is together with enhancing entrepreneurship education as an effective tool for developing entrepreneurial intentions, mindsets, and skills.

Chapter 12 women entrepreneurs in the Kingdom of Saudi Arabia (KSA), in this chapter Aloulou, Ramadani, Alarifi and Zuferi have discussed the reality of women entrepreneurship in the country and the entrepreneurial ecosystem. GEM's 2020/2021 National Expert Survey ranked Saudi Arabia first among 44 economies surveyed in terms of COVID-19 *entrepreneurial response rank* and *government response rank.* The ranking reflects confidence in the Government's ability to maintain strong entrepreneurial conditions despite the turmoil arising from the pandemic.

Women in the Kingdom of Saudi Arabia are free to start their own businesses without the permission of a husband or any male guardian. The participation of Saudi women in the labour market is currently a top priority of the KSA national development plan amongst other priorities and initiatives. Therefore, based on the authors' analysis the KSA seems to have already started an intensive transformation towards modernization and competitiveness from a historical aspect and women entrepreneurship since its unification back in 1932.

Chapter 13 presents the discussion of women entrepreneurs in *Syria* as authored by Salamzadeh, Markovic, and Ed-dafali. The authors of this chapter portray most of the challenges facing women entrepreneurs in the country together with the significant changes imposed by the ongoing war. This should not go without noting women's realization and recognition of the level of marginalization, exploitation as well as economic violence against women in the country. Steel (2021) argues that women entrepreneurs' awareness and understanding of their rights are among the positive factors towards opportunity identification and recognition of their human values.

Therefore, the authors recommend that any economic empowerment of women entrepreneurs by the Syrian government must ensure that any grants programmes and schemes are accompanied by specific policies that can challenge any possible discrimination caused by structures like patriarchal norms in the society, economic as well as at the domestic levels. To achieve women's freedom and independence in the country, a major change in the mindset of supporters and activists of the entrepreneurial ecosystem.

Chapter 14 women entrepreneurs in the *United Arab Emirates (UAE).* Gilan, Yasin, and Alshammaa contributing authors of chapter fourteen have indicated that UAE women entrepreneurs are thriving due to the most conducive and supportive entrepreneurial ecosystem highly encouraged by the country's government. This is vivat the country has already built some entrepreneurial ecosystem and continues to make some policies and strategies that suggest towards the future of women entrepreneurs in the UAE the direction of higher success as long as other factors of the economy in the country remain to be under good control.

Chapter 15 of this book offers the conclusion of the analysis and discussion of women entrepreneurs in the Middle East, their history, frameworks, and ecosystem discussion of women. In this chapter, the author provides recommendations based on the analysis of the current government policies and strategies and what can be anticipated *toward the future* of women entrepreneurs in the Middle East region based on the analysis of the countries discussed in the book.

3. Conclusions and Toward the Future

Concluding this discussion of women entrepreneurs in the Middle East, specifically 11 countries; both editors of this book and the authors of the contributing chapters have demonstrated that the potential of women's entrepreneurship is manifold (Simba and Nziku, 2022). The editors of this book would like to recommend an empirical study to be conducted within the region in the context of women entrepreneurs. Any empirical analysis will enable and play a significant role toward equipping policymakers toward the proper formulation of policies for enhancing entrepreneurial ecosystems across different countries in the region where the current analysis indicates the need for more strategies on the topic.

References

Andriamahery, A. & Qamruzzaman, M. (2022). "Do Access to Finance, Technical Know-How, and Financial Literacy Offer Women Empowerment Through Women's Entrepreneurial Development?". *Frontiers in Psychology*, **12**, 776–798.

Bahramitash, R. & Esfahani, H. S. (2014). "Gender and Entrepreneurship in Iran". *Middle East Critique*, **23**(3), 293–312.

Dana, L. P. (2022), "Preface". In Léo-Paul Dana, Aidin Salamzadeh, Veland Ramadani, & Ramo Palalic, (eds.), *Understanding Contexts of Business in Western Asia: Land of Bazaars and High-Tech Booms.* Singapore: World Scientific.

El Kharouf, A., Abualbasal, A., Abbadi, H., & Weir, D. B. (2022). "The Entrepreneurship Ecosystem for Enhancing Women's Entrepreneurship in Jordan". In Metcalfe, B., Bastian, B., Al-Dajani, H., (eds.), *Women, Entrepreneurship, and Development in the Middle East* (pp. 133–151). Routledge, London.

Gadi, N. (2022). "Increasing Women's Employment Opportunities in Digitalizing Saudi Arabia's Economy". *Open Journal of Business and Management*, **10**, 2869–2902. doi:10.4236/ojbm.2022.105142.

Global Entrepreneurship Monitor (GEM, 2021). "Sultanate of Oman: *National Report*. Global Entrepreneurship Monitor". Retrieved from: https://www.unizwa.edu.om/Final%20Oman%20GEM%20National%20report 2019_2020_Oct%2020.pdf.

Global Entrepreneurship Monitor (GEM, 2020). *Jordan National Report 2019–2020*. Amman, Jordan: Global Entrepreneurship Monitor.

International Labour Organisation (ILO, 2022). "STAT Database". Retrieved from: https://data.worldbank.org/indicator/SL.TLF.CACT.FE.ZS?locations=ZQ&most_recent_value_desc=false (Accessed on 16 March 2022).

Metcalfe, B., Bastian, B., & Al-Dajani, H. (2022). "The Mosque and the Satellite: Exploring the Multi-Level and Multi-Agency Dynamics of Women's Entrepreneurship Development in the Middle East". In Metcalfe, B., Bastian, B., Al-Dajani, H., (eds.), *Women, Entrepreneurship, and Development in the Middle East* (pp. 3–32). Routledge, London.

Mustafa, F., Khursheed, A., Fatima, M., & Rao, M. (2021). "Exploring the Impact of the COVID-19 Pandemic on Women Entrepreneurs in Pakistan". *International Journal of Gender and Entrepreneurship*, **13**(2), 56–72.

Nziku, D. M. (2016). "Strategies and policies influencing entrepreneurship start-up decisions: evidence from Tanzania". In Diaz-Garcia, C., Brush, C.G., Gatewood, E. J., & Welter, F., (eds.), *Women's Entrepreneurship in Global and Local Contexts*. Cheltenham, UK: Edward Elgar.

Nziku, D. M. (2014). *Tanzania Female Entrepreneurship: Strategies for Sustainability and Growth*. Doctoral Thesis. United Kingdom: Southampton Solent University.

PricewaterhouseCoopers (PwC) Report (2017). *Women Unbound: Unleashing Female Entrepreneurial Potential*. Retrieved from: https://www.pwc.com/gx/en/diversity-inclusion/assets/women-unbound.pdf.

Robbin, Z. H. (2022). *Women's Labor Force Participation and COVID-19 in Jordan*. Washington D.C.: Middle East Institute.

Sarfaraz, L. (2017). *Women's Entrepreneurship in Iran*. Switzerland: Springer.

Sarfaraz, L. & Faghih, N. (2011). "Women's Entrepreneurship in Iran: A GEM based-Data Evidence". *Journal of Global Entrepreneurship Research*, **1**(1), 45–57.

Simba, A., & Nziku, D. M. (2022). "Women Entrepreneurs in Zimbabwe". In Dabic, M., Dana, L. P. D., Nziku, M., & Ramadan, V., (eds.), *Women Entrepreneurship in Sub-Saharan Africa: Historical Framework, Ecosystem and Future Perspectives for the Region*. Springer.

Steel, G. (2021). "Going Global–Going Digital. Diaspora Networks and Female Online Entrepreneurship in Khartoum, Sudan". *Geoforum*, **120**, 22–29.

The FinTech Times (2021). "Why the Right of Partnership a Win for Fintech, Banks and Consumers?" Retrieved from: https://thefintechtimes.com/an-overview-of-women-entrepreneurship-in-the-middle-east-and-africa/ (Accessed on 15 January 2022).

The World Economic Forum (WEF, 2021). "The World Economic Forum Gender Gap Report".

World Bank (2022). "The World Bank in Jordan". Retrieved from: https://www.worldbank.org/en/country/jordan/overview#1 (Accessed on 16 March 2022).

Yin, D. (2017). "What Makes Israel's Innovation Ecosystem So Successful," *Forbes Asia*. Retrieved from: https://www.forbes.com/sites/davidyin/2017/01/09/what-makes-israels-innovation-ecosystem-so-successful/?sh=595e9ab270e4 (Accessed on 25 November 2022).

https://doi.org/10.1142/9789811283499_bmatter

Index

A
Abu Dhabi, 129
accelerators, 183
access to networks, 30, 48
Achaemenid Empire, 88–89
Achaemenid period, 89
Africa, 127
agricultural productivity, 46
agricultural-based economies, 26
Alzheimer patients, 127
Arab region, 288
Arab Spring, 284
Arab women in entrepreneurship, 203
Arameans, 55
Assyrians, 55
Austro-Hungarian empire, 116

B
Babylon, 89
Babylonians, 55
Bahai, 108
Bahrain, 53, 129
barriers, 67, 70, 73, 79
  cultural, 98
  economic and business, 100
  individual, 99
  information, 100
  legal, 99
  social, 99
bazaar, 58, 71, 78, 130
bazaar/*souq*, 266
Bedouin, 114, 119, 134
Born global entrepreneurs, 295
British, 119
burden of balancing family responsibilities, 194
business conglomerates, 44
business context, 317
business creation, 311
business environment, 48, 283, 319
business knowledge, 47
business networks, 48
business ventures, 321
Byzantine Empire, 112

C
capital, 183
Cartier Women's Initiative, 305
challenges and opportunities for women entrepreneurs in Oman, 205
Christians, 108
Circular 331 (C331), 174–175, 187

commercial activities, 69, 71
commercial entities, 32
commercial lenders, 47
comprised, 114
computer chips, 128
conflict contexts, 222, 232, 235–237, 239
constraints, 79–80, 178
context, 18
contextualization, 304
contextualized models, 304
contextualized research, 324
convenient location, 310
copyrights, 6
Corruption Perceptions Index, 172
corruption, 27
cosmetics, 109
cotton, 55
COVID-19 crisis, 286
COVID-19 pandemic, 41, 90, 172, 322
crisis, 172
crude oil, 54
Crusaders, 112
cultural systems, 47
culture, 2, 5, 8
customs formalities, 29
Cyrus the Great, 88

D

developing strategies, 319
diaspora women, 29
digital platforms, 44, 268
Digital Risers, 263
digitalization, 215
disabled people, 108
discrimination, 179, 296
diversification strategies, 45
doing business, 289
domestic policies, 49
donor-driven, 34
Druze, 108

E

earthquake victims, 128
ease of doing business, 173
e-commerce, 31
economic activities, 68–69, 71–72
economic agents, 25
economic development, 27, 31
economic empowerment, 30, 46, 269, 284, 292
economic engagement, 25, 38
economic growth, 26, 322
economic inclusion, 41
economic independence, 25
economic potential, 67–68, 71
economic reforms, 26
economic revolution, 306
economic rights, 82
economic shock, 40
ecosystem, 15, 53–54, 59–60, 93, 175, 274
educated female workforce, 42
educational opportunities, 87
eGovernment effort, 28
Egypt, 89
Elamite culture, 88
empirical analysis, 326
employability, 305
employment index, 320
employment, 2, 5
empowerment of women, 67, 77–78
empowerment, 180–181, 183, 186, 296
encouraging entrepreneurship, 202
endoscopy, 130
engineers, 136

entrepreneurial accelerators, 38, 175
entrepreneurial activities, 35, 319, 324
entrepreneurial conditions, 324
entrepreneurial culture, 304, 306
entrepreneurial ecosystem, 1–4, 7, 9–11, 28, 30, 32, 40, 141–142, 145–149, 155–158, 161–165, 263–268, 318, 325
entrepreneurial environment, 28
entrepreneurial firms, 291
entrepreneurial initiatives, 3
entrepreneurial intentions of Omani women, 205
entrepreneurial intentions, mindsets, and skills, 324
entrepreneurial landscape, 174
entrepreneurial lifestyles, 319
entrepreneurial path, 195, 323
entrepreneurial risk, 31
entrepreneurship agenda, 39, 323
entrepreneurship and empowerment, 33
entrepreneurship development, 47, 197
entrepreneurship ecosystem, 314–315
entrepreneurship environment, 288
entrepreneurship policy, 318, 324
entrepreneurship skills, 48
environment for women, 11
environment for women's empowerment, 33
environmental challenges, 48
environmentally friendly, 47
environmentally sustainable, 38
equal opportunities, 2
equal participation, 321
equal pay, 25
equal rights, 46
e-services, 47
ethnic minorities, 304
exclusive training for women entrepreneurs, 216
existing condition of women entrepreneurs in Oman, 194
expanding trade, 69
extreme context, 172

F

family support and encouragement, 206
family traditions, 208
Farsi, 54
female entrepreneur, 304, 312
female entrepreneurship development, 212
female entrepreneurship, 285, 314
female representation, 45
female role models, 206
female students, 96
financial analysis, 311
financial institutions, 47
first factories, 71
Forbes, 185
foreign expatriates, 315
foreign investments, 71
foreign investors, 321
formal financial, 181
formalizing, 27
free economy, 172
funding opportunities, 309

G

gender balance, 37, 308
gender diversity, 39
gender equality, 24, 180, 182, 292, 308, 320–321
Gender Gap Report, 24

gender gap, 4, 8, 44, 305, 319
gender inequality, 20, 318
gender justice, 296
gender lens, 318
gender parity, 46
German Colony, 114
global economy, 26
Global Entrepreneurship Monitor (GEM), 17
globalization, 95
Golan Heights, 124
government institutions, 309
government mandates, 36
governmental assistance, 74, 82
gross domestic product (GDP), 172–173, 177
Gulf Cooperation Council (GCC), 211

H

herpes, 128
high priority innovation-driven, 200
high unemployment, 71, 73, 76
Hindi, 54
Holy mosques, 255
household responsibilities, 324
human capital, 4
Human Resources Development Fund, 32
human values, 325

I

immediate environment, 45
impediment, 67–69, 74, 79–80
inclusive entrepreneurial, 40
increasing volunteerism, 41
incubation, 75
incubators, 36, 74–75, 81, 175, 183
industrialist, 109
inequality, 76
influx of young women, 204
Information and Communication Technology (ICT), 185
infrastructure deficiencies, 34
Initiative fund, 308
innovation, 17, 109
institutional quality, 27
institutions, 224, 230–231, 235–236
intensive transformation, 324
international cooperation, 49
international networks, 36
intersection, 76
intersectionality, 82
invasion by Muslim Arabs, 89
invention, 111
involvement of women, 323
Iran, 85, 89
Irdabama, 89
Islam, 255

J

Jews, 55
job creation, 304
Jordan, 141–150, 154–155–158, 160–163, 165

K

Kingdom of Saudi Arabia (KSA), 254
knowledge-based economy, 304
knowledge-based, 29

L

labor force participation, 322
labor force, 321
Labor Party, 110
land ownership, 43
Lebanese Civil War, 57

Lebanese diaspora, 38
Lebanese, 177
Lebanon, 171–172, 178, 182
legal framework, 43
less access to external finance, 206
level of marginalization, 325
liberal economy, 172
liberalization, 111
lower wages, 43
lowest rates, 319
Lutheranism, 114

M

male-dominant culture, 319
male-dominated, 184, 186
Mandatory Palestine, 118
marginalization, 39, 178–179
market-oriented economy, 68, 72
maternity leave, 2
m-commerce, 110
Median Empire, 88
Mediterranean Sea, 114, 117
mentorship, 35
Mesopotamia, 89
microfinance, 181
Microsoft, 133
Middle East and Africa (MEA), 24
Middle East and North Africa (MENA), 2, 284, 306
Middle East, 2, 284
more and more younger women, 209
Morocco, 130
multilateral frameworks, 26
multiple initiatives, 45
multiple sclerosis, 128
Muslim conquest, 112
Muslim states, 70
Muslims, 108
Muslims' conquest, 55

N

national-owned businesses, 310
natural resources, 32
networking opportunities, 305
non-government organizations (NGOs), 181
non-oil, 28
nonprofit organization, 308
norms, 178
number of female participations, 204
number of girls applying for admissions, 199
nurturing women, 46

O

occupation, 223, 225–227, 232, 234, 241
officially unregistered, 25
oil, 54
Oman the majority of population are Omani citizens, 197
Oman Vision 2040, 197, 218
Oman, 55, 129
Omani women business owners, 210
Omani women toward pursuing entrepreneurship, 196
Omani women, 208, 215–216, 218
Omanization, 39, 198
one-stop resource, 310
online influencers, 312
opportunity identification, 325
Ottomans, 112

P

Palestine Liberation Organization (PLO), 126
Palestine, 221–223, 225–227, 229–234, 236–237, 239, 241–242
Parthians, 88

patriarchal society, 178–179
pearl fisheries, 56
pearl, 55
pediatric heart surgery technique, 128
Persepolis, 89
Persian Empire, 54
Persian Gulf, 53
Persians, 55
petroleum, 56
policies, 173
political instability, 27, 45
political participation, 61
Portuguese Empire, 55
possible discrimination, 325
poverty, 172
private equity funds, 175
professional capabilities, 320
promoting entrepreneurship, 304
property management, 314
Public Authority of SME Development (PASMED), 202

Q

Qatari Businesswomen Association (QBWA), 30
quite extensively, 313
Quran, 255

R

reduce informality, 49
refugee entrepreneurs, 29
refugee entrepreneurs, 45
refugees, 171
regulatory framework, 28
religion, 26
religious conflicts, 4
resilience, 292
resource dependency, 26
right to vote, 2, 132
Robust Economy, 74
role models to start a business, 216
role of gender, 304
Romans, 111
Roy Clapham, 15–16
rural areas, 68, 71, 80, 82
rural development, 46
rural entrepreneurship, 181

S

Samaritans, 108
Sassanid Empire, 89
Saudization, 262
self-employed, 317
self-employment, 305
services community, 39
Shi'a Islam, 55
Shi'a, 57
Silicon Valley, 128
Sinai, 124
small-scale enterprises, 62
social barriers, 42
social capital, 306
social culture, 36
social enterprise, 186
social entrepreneurs, 41
social exclusion, 20
social exclusion, 318
social inclusion, 186
social innovation parks, 48
social media, 44
social networks, 24
social status, 61
social, cultural, and geographical contexts, 211
sociocultural norms, 68, 80
stability and opportunity, 305
stable businesses, 206
startup ecosystem, 74–76

startups, 294
State of Bahrain, 57
Stockholm-Kista, 128
structural reforms, 38
struggles related to business survival, 194
sub-Saharan Africa, 320
success stories, 175
success stories, 185–186
Sudan, 130
Suez Canal, 121
sufficient access to market information, 217
Sultan Qaboos University, 204
Sunni, 57
support programs, 182
support women, 305
supporting women entrepreneurs, 46
supportive policies, 307
sustainable development goals, 319
sustainable development, 24, 67–68, 78, 82
Syria, 89, 283
Syrian revolution, 287

T

Tagalog, 54
tailored support, 48
technical training and mentorship for building business management skills, 207
technology startups, 75
technology, 110
technology-driven ventures, 218
television, 109
the Netherlands, 108
total entrepreneurial activity (TEA), 169
total entrepreneurial activity (TEA), 2
tourism, 54
tourists, 54
trademarks, 6
tradition, 2, 10
traditional industries, 44
training institutions, 31
transformation, 39
transformational challenges, 49
transnational entrepreneurs, 306
Treaty of Versailles, 117
tremendous resilience, 323
Trump, Donald, 129

U

unemployment rate, 2, 25, 86
unemployment, 172–173
United Nations, 181
university, 110
Urdu, 54
USB stick, 111

V

valuable skills, 42
venture capital, 35, 47, 110, 175
violence, 61
Virgin Mary, 107
vocational training, 47
voluntary liquidations, 321
vulnerable position, 76

W

widespread languages
  Amharic, 110
  Arabic, 110
  English, 110
  French, 110
  Hebrew, 110
  Russian, 110
  Spanish, 110

women as entrepreneurs, 194
women business owners, 311
Women Empowerment, 312
women entrepreneurs in Oman, 209
women entrepreneurs, 2–4, 6, 8, 37, 40, 42, 46, 48, 141–142, 147, 149–150, 156–159, 161–164, 213, 308, 311, 318, 324–325
women entrepreneurship, 41, 307, 319, 324
women in Oman, 213
women inheriting, 44
Women Leadership, 37
women, 177–178
women's businesses, 43
women's employment, 320
women's entrepreneurship, 5–7, 39, 221, 223, 235, 238, 240–242, 283, 320
women's participation, 31
women-led businesses, 43
workforce protection, 33

Y

young entrepreneurs, 291
young women venturing, 204
YouTube, 209

Z

Zionism's goal, 116
Zoroastrians, 55

www.ingramcontent.com/pod-product-compliance
Lightning Source LLC
LaVergne TN
LVHW010330220926
848484LV00004BB/872